Shakespeare's Italy

D1334163

Italy loomed large on the English Renaissance stage. The works of Shakespeare, Dekker, Jonson, Webster and Middleton are full of Italian references and settings. But what did Italy signify to these playwrights and their audiences? How did the mythological construct of Italy affect a play's dramatic world?

Renaissance scholars from around the world each contribute a different perspective to these central issues. This collection of essays covers four main topics: 'Images and culture', 'Themes and tradition', 'Venice: spectacle and polis' and 'Language and ideology'. Among the distinguished line-up of contributors are Harry Levin, J. R. Mulryne, Giorgio Melchiori, Agostino Lombardo, Leo Salingar, Avraham Oz and Manfred Pfister.

By challenging traditional readings of the subject, this collection helps students of Renaissance drama to view the exploitation of the Italian setting as a structural constituent in English Renaissance theatres, contributing to dramatic effect, moral and political implications and audience response.

Michele Marrapodi is Associate Professor and Marcello Cappuzzo is Full Professor of English Language and Literature at the University of Palermo; A. J. Hoenselaars is Associate Professor of English at the University of Utrecht; L. Falzon Santucci was Full Professor of English at the University of Messina.

Shakespeare's Italy

Functions of Italian locations
in Renaissance drama

Revised edition

*edited by Michele Marrapodi, A. J. Hoenselaars,
Marcello Cappuzzo and L. Falzon Santucci*

Manchester University Press
Manchester and New York

distributed exclusively in the USA by St. Martin's Press

Published by Manchester University Press
Oxford Road, Manchester M13 9NR, UK
and Room 400, 175 Fifth Avenue,
New York, NY 10010, USA

Distributed exclusively in the USA by
St. Martin's Press, Inc.,
175 Fifth Avenue, New York, NY 10010, USA

Distributed exclusively in Canada by
UBC Press, University of British Columbia, 6344 Memorial Road,
Vancouver, BC, Canada V6T 1Z2

British Library cataloguing-in-publication data
A catalogue record for this book is available from the British Library.

Library of Congresss cataloging-in-publication data
Shakespeare's Italy : functions of Italian locations in Renaissance
 drama / edited by Michele Marrapodi ... [et al.]
     p.   c.m.
   Includes bibliographical references and index.
   ISBN 0-7190-5220-3 (pbk.) — ISBN 0-7190-4089-2 (cloth)
   1. Shakespeare, William, 1564–1616—Knowledge—Italy.
 2. English drama—Italian influences. 3. Renaissance—England.
 4. Italy—In literature. I. Marrapodi, Michele
 PR3069.I8S53   1997
 822.3'3—dc21   97-16566

ISBN 0 7190 5220-3 *paperback*

Revised paperback edition published 1997

Typeset in Monotype Bell
by Koinonia Ltd, Manchester
Printed in Great Britain,
by Bookcraft Ltd, Midsomer Norton

Contents

Preface to paperback edition

As its title indicates, the present collection of essays focuses on the dramatic use of stage topography, i.e. its role and function in the construction and general design of early modern English drama. More specifically, it deals with the theatrical representation of Italy and Italian localities operating in the linguistic, thematic and ideological structure of the plays. The basic idea of the project is that the question of the Italianate setting was in itself semantically over-determined for the Elizabethans: it implied a variety of dramatic issues and responses, for both playwrights and audience, affecting imagination and culture, social customs and traditions, theatricality and characterisation, language and ideology, as the four parts of the volume aim to suggest.

The original plan of the project greatly profited from the encouragement received and the interest aroused in a number of discussions, academic and otherwise, with colleagues and friends, some of whom subsequently became co-editors or contributors. And I like to recall that the decision to give the project a book-length form, involving a group of experts in the field, was taken on the occasion of the Twenty-Fourth International Shakespeare Conference at Stratford-upon-Avon in August 1990, during a friendly talk with Ton Hoenselaars in the bar of the Shakespeare Hotel: certainly an appropriate site for a volume concentrating on Shakespeare's exploitation of locality! The outline of the project was rapidly sketched out in a score of minutes, although the final work had to wait three more years among various difficulties, organisational and editorial, before its actual publication.

Since the volume appeared in November 1993 it has been graced by reviewers with largely favourable responses, and only a few critical works have been published in the same or ancillary areas to testify to its as yet untrodden territory. American new historicism and British cultural materialism have not yet really embarked on a rethinking of the subject, as Manfred Pfister rightly hoped or foresaw in the Afterword, and if they have given signals of interest in the Italianate affair, the cultural poetics of their theoretical premises has been questioned, as is partially the case of the other powerful trend of criticism of this last decade: that of feminism.[1] After a period of provocative critical revolution it seems that we are now moving towards a recovery of the past, although totally recast by experience. And the book's deliberate strategy of offering a spectrum of different methodological perspectives, instead of singling out a monistic overall interpretation, has proved both appropriate and rewarding.

I will not mention the extent of agreement (or disagreement) with the four parts of the volume, nor the forms of attention drawn by their individual chapters. As this is a paperback edition which by its very nature aims to gain the readership of young scholars and university students (ultimately the natural goal of any critical achievement), I would leave to them the evaluation of the book's utility. The students of my university courses, who have read, studied and debated the book's contents and, in many cases, enthusiastically chosen the same topic for their dissertations, have represented the most difficult test the collection as a whole has had to face since its appearance.

I have limited the editorial revision to minor questions of spelling and misprints while I thought it useful to supplement and update the bibliography with recent relevant material. Finally, in sending the Press this new edition I should like to commemorate two eminent scholars who, in their different roles, contributed to the success of the volume: Lino Falzon Santucci as one of the co-editors and Harry Levin as a contributor. To their memory as leading Shakespeareans and upright Humanists this paperback edition is gratefully dedicated.

Michele Marrapodi

Note

1. See respectively, among others, Graham Bradshaw, *Misrepresentations: Shakespeare and the Materialists*, Ithaca and London, 1993, and Richard Levin, 'Feminist thematics and Shakespearean tragedy', *PMLA*, 103 (1988), pp. 125-38. Levin's critique and the feminist controversy prompted a collective response in the anthology *Shakespeare Left and Right*, ed. Ivo Kamps, London, 1991.

Acknowledgements

A few chapters of this volume have been published elsewhere in the same or in a somewhat different form: 'Shakespeare's Italians' by Harry Levin first appeared in *Harvard Library Bulletin*, n.s., 1, 4, 1990–91; J. R. Mulryne's 'History and myth in *The Merchant of Venice*' is a revised version of an article included in *Mélanges offerts à Marie-Thérèse Jones-Davies: L'Europe de la Renaissance – Cultures et Civilisations*, eds Jean-Claude Margolin and Marie-Madeleine Martinet, Paris, Touzot, 1988; Agostino Lombardo's 'The Veneto, metatheatre and Shakespeare' was previously read in Italian at the 1986 International Conference in Verona and published in the seminar proceedings *Shakespeare a Verona e nel Veneto*, ed. A. Lombardo, Verona, 1987; Leo Salingar's 'The idea of Venice in Shakespeare and Ben Jonson' was read with a different title in Paris at an international meeting on *L'Image de l'Europe des nations sur scène*, and it is to appear in the confererence proceedings edited by the French CNRS; finally, an earlier draft of Michele Marrapodi's '"Of that fatal country": Sicily and the rhetoric of topography in *The Winter's Tale*' was presented in 1990 at the seminar on 'Language' during the Twenty-Fourth International Shakespeare Conference at Stratford-upon-Avon and later published in *Nuovi Annali della Facoltà di Magistero dell'Università di Messina*, 8–10, 1990–92. We wish to thank all the editors and publishers of the aforementioned publications for permission to reprint or revise copyright materials.

Editing a collection of essays is a long and exhausting job. During these past two years we have profited from the encouragement and criticism of a number of colleagues and friends whose help we want to acknowledge here. We are particularly indebted to J. R. Mulryne, Robert S. Miola, Giorgio Melchiori, Agostino Lombardo,

William Dodd, Keir Elam, Roberta Mullini, Peter Dawson and Martin Michael Driessen. We are also grateful to Anita Roy of Manchester University Press for having enthusiastically trusted in the idea of the project from the outset. Special thanks are due to the Italian Consiglio Nazionale delle Ricerche (CNR) and to the Rector of the University of Messina, Guglielmo Stagno d'Alcontres, for providing generous financial assistance at various stages.

The editors

Introduction

Michele Marrapodi

When Ben Jonson criticised the improbability of the setting and the lack of geographical exactitude in Shakespeare's *The Winter's Tale*, he aimed to draw his contemporaries' attention to the necessity of greater accuracy in the stage topography of drama.[1] In his attempt to gratify his own ego by singling out some flaws in the works of the presiding genius of the age, Jonson may not have been aware that he was posing a problem concerning one of the elements specific to the world of the theatre, of which he himself claimed to be a master: the close relationship between locale and dramatic structure. Shakespeare's treatment of locality was in most cases too different from conventional practice to please Jonson's sense of verisimilitude, as well as his general observance of classical rules. As the dramatist who changed the initial Italianate version of *Every Man in His Humour* into a London play, Jonson gives evidence of privileging, for satiric purposes, matters domestic – as he asserts in *The Alchemist*[2] – as against Shakespeare's various international settings and greater universal concerns.[3] Yet the lore of Italy in the two dramatists' imagination, as well as in that of other Renaissance playwrights, produces revealing examples of location usages which can throw light on the dramatic functions of Italian settings in Tudor and Stuart drama alike. The primary aim of this collection of essays is precisely to attempt to study the use and importance of Italy and of Italian locations as a structural constituent in English Renaissance theatre. It should be emphasised from the outset, however, that imposing a unitary frame upon the chapters has never ranked high among the editors' intentions. Rather, the papers collected here seek to provide a wide-ranging treatment of a multifaceted topic, adopting diverse methodologies and critical viewpoints, in order to supply a fresh approach to a much discussed subject by the

1

coherence deriving from a *concord in discord* strategy. So as to avoid repetitious overlapping, the present introduction will only make some general observations on the use of Italy in Renaissance drama, while the essays which follow will explore, from different perspectives, specific questions at issue in a number of individual plays.

1

Italianate drama of the English Renaissance may be regarded as the most significant case of appropriation of an alien culture, relying upon a protean myth which could easily be moulded to the dramatic needs of every playwright. The reasons for this pliability depended on the wide variety of historical, literary and fictional sources which nurtured the Elizabethans' fascination for the Mediterranean nation. Apart from direct knowledge of contemporary political and social events, and the influence of the classical and the humanistic tradition, as well as the great bulk of English translations of Italian *novelle*, poetry and drama, what played a fundamental role in the formation of the notoriously ambiguous view of Italy was the great number of treatises, travel books and travellers' reports which gave a vivid, if often imaginary, picture of Italy and of its inhabitants.[4] The alluring ambivalence of Italy was often encountered even in the narrative of one and the same author. From William Thomas's *History of Italy* (1549) to the diaries of the most famous Elizabethan travellers, such as George Sandys, Thomas Hoby and William Lithgow, we find frequent accounts of Italy's ambivalent reputation. Coryat's influential *Crudities*, as proved by Jonson's prefatory lines, was one of the most widely known travel books of the age. Here, as in many other written records, northern Italy is referred to both as a pleasant and fruitful land and as a country which tolerates any kind of vice:

> For as Italy is the garden of the world, so is Lombardy the garden of Italy, and Venice the garden of Lombardy. It is wholly plaine, and beautified with such abundance of goodly rivers, pleasant meadowes, fruitfull vineyardes, fat pastures, delectable gardens, orchards, woodes.[5]

In *The Taming of the Shrew*, Lucentio's informative lines 'I am arriv'd for fruitful Lombardy, / The pleasant garden of great Italy'[6] both locate the play's action and single out this aspect of the myth. Coryat's ludicrous descriptions of Venetian women's dressing habits, however, and his comments on their use of forks at meals, as well as his sympathetic treatment of the Venetian courtesans – 'these kinde of Laides and Thaides [...] these amorous Calypsoes'[7] – must have confirmed Jonson's comic handling of his female characters in *Volpone*, as has recently been pointed out.[8] Without necessarily relying on any precise knowledge of Italian history or geography, this iconology of Italy was mostly derived from the works of Renaissance historians and humanists such as Machiavelli, Guicciardini, Castiglione, Ariosto, Tasso, and from the influence of *novelle* and of Cinquecento Italian theatre – Bandello, Aretino, Cinthio, Guarini – whose sometimes lurid stories of deceit, intrigue, jealousy and passion provided a perfect setting for both comedy and tragedy.[9]

Protestant England's aversion to Papistry was greatly influential in inspiring the evil side of the Italian picture. In Fynes Moryson's description of 'the Popes territory' we are informed that 'these inhabiters of Marca [*sic*] are accounted a wicked generation, the greatest part of the cut-throtes and murtherers dispersed through Italy, being borne in this Country'.[10] Moryson is very good at collecting proverbs throughout Europe. Of Italian women he reports: 'They are Magpyes at the doore, Saints in the Church, Goates in the garden, Divels in the house, Angels in the street, and Syrens at the window'[11] – a record of prejudice which was very widespread at the time and which can be found in many other sources. A ludic passage from Peter Heylyn's *Microcosmus* ironically gathers together the commonest stereotypes about Italians:

> The people are for the most part graue, respectiue, and ingenious; excellent men [...] but for three things; 1 in their lusts they are vnnatural, 2 in their malice vnappeasable: 3 in their actions deceitfull. To which might bee added, they will blaspheame sooner then sweare, & murther a man rather then slander him. They are exceeding iealous ouer their wiues, insomuch that they shut them vp from the common view, and permit them to discourse with few or none. The locke which a Gentleman of *Venice* used to keepe his wife true in his absence, is so common, it needeth no relation.[12]

In *Women Beware Women*, Leantio's ironic allusion to the precaution Heylyn refers to is surely appropriate, since it did not prevent his wife from wantonness;[13] and in *The Malcontent*, the character of Mendoza is given the double task of uttering, in two consecutive scenes, both excessive praise of and extreme bias against Italian women.[14]

The Italian court as synonym of mischief, poison and corruption is another fundamental issue in all Italianate Stuart drama. In Middleton's tragedy cited above, the Duke of Florence's residence is the place where 'there is / As much redemption of a soul from hell / As a fair woman's body from his palace' (III.ii.330–2). Marston's Malevole expresses this same concept even more directly: 'I would sooner leave my lady singled in a bordello than in the Genoa Palace' (III.ii.26–7). Retaliation in its most violent forms takes place also in the dramas set in Italy, especially when it is carried out as retribution for political intrigue and social corruption.[15] *The Revenger's Tragedy* is the most eloquent case in point. Here, the representation of court corruption is shown as closely related to excessive sexuality; the court itself becomes 'this unsunned lodge / Wherein 'tis night at noon, [...] this luxurious circle',[16] a locale for illicit relations, where Machiavellian plotting and counterplotting as well as all transgressive forms of lust such as adultery, rape and incest are depicted as inherent aspects of the same process, which 'involves an incessant drive for self-fulfilment through domination of others', culminating in dissolution and death.[17] In *'Tis Pity She's a Whore*, Vasques's 'Now you begin to turn Italian' is meant to approve Soranzo's decision to seek vengeance, and Vasques himself triumphantly acknowledges his Italianate attitude at the conclusion: 'I rejoice that a Spaniard outwent an Italian in revenge.'[18] To Webster, as well as to other Jacobean and Caroline dramatists, Italianate courts often offer the cover for writing tragical satires exposing contemporary abuses at home. J. W. Lever has suggested that the court of *The Duchess of Malfi* 'presents in miniature the court of Whitehall, with its adventurers, its feverish pulling of strings for office and promotion, its heedless and heartless pursuit of privilege'.[19] And Martin Butler has also numbered Italian-located Caroline drama amongst the commonest devices used by a certain type of court theatre which, 'without openly bringing political events and issues on stage, alluded to them obliquely'.[20]

The proverbial inconstancy and promiscuity of Italian women are emphasised also in Heylyn's diary, in almost the same words as Moryson's:

> The women are generally witty in speech, modest in outward carriage, and bountifull where they beare affection: and it is proverbially said, that they are *Magpies at the doors, Saints in the Church, Goates in the Garden, Diuells in the house, Angells in the streets, and Syrens in the windowes.*[21]

Iago's misogynist speech to Emilia and his obsessive mistrust of Venetian women are rooted in the biased opinion of this social context: 'you are pictures out o' doors; / Bells in your parlours; wild-cats in your kitchens; / Saints in your injuries; devils being offended; / Players in your housewifery; and housewives in your beds.'[22] The construction of Iago's character may be considered the most instructive of all in terms of appropriation of the Italian myth. In his complex characterisation a concentration of elements in fact coheres which makes Iago's case paradigmatic of the use of Italy in Renaissance drama as a whole. Starting from Cinthio's *novella* which he moulds to his dramatic ends, Shakespeare plays with national stereotyping and with a cluster of 'exotic' commonplaces about Italians firmly embedded in the Elizabethans' imagination: the rise of jealousy and desire for revenge, the joy for mischief and plotting, Machiavellian astuteness and dissimulation, racist hatred for strangers, Senecan theatricalism and so forth. This spicy local colour and the many references to Italian places and names in the stage topography of drama enhance the sense of locality as a structural factor, producing the effect of accentuating the Italianate colouring of the play. In answering Roderigo's warning against robbery, Brabantio's 'this is Venice, / My house is not a grange' (I.i.105-6) depicts a background of safety and social rigour in line with contemporary accounts of a town administered by strict justice. The feverish mercantile activity of the city, though, the centre of intense trade and banking operations, is embodied as Italian vices in Iago's character. His greed for money and his Machiavellian dissimulation operate, from the outset, as a subversive impact on that moral and social order. Iago's simile of 'the fire [...] spied in populous cities' (I.i.76-7), his obscene visual images of 'the black ram' and the 'white ewe' (I.i.88-9), of 'the beast with two backs' (I.i.116-17), and the recurrent use of economic terms are part of a coherent metaphoric imagery ironically put into contrast with Brabantio's ideal social picture. That the evil side of Venice is an inherent aspect of the same society is evident in the abrupt wave of racism and patriarchal authority breaking out against Desdemona's 'gross revolt' (I.i.134). As I have written elsewhere, despite the traditional view of a passive heroine, her role unmasks the contradictions of the apparent stable world and is opposed to that of Iago on both symbolic and linguistic levels.[23] Of course certain dramatic features of Italian-based theatre draw upon a number of theatrical conventions which are also rooted in the medieval heritage of English drama. Iago as a typically Elizabethan villain shares his Italianate origin with the Englishness of medieval vice.[24] But does the preference for Italian-located plays entirely obey a mere dramatic convention, or does it reveal a precise ideological choice on the part of the dramatist? And to what extent does the mythological construct of Italy affect the play's dramatic world?

2

Clifford Leech maintained, more than twenty years ago, that what he considered 'an important part' of sixteenth- and seventeenth-century dramaturgy needed further study: 'how the idea of a locality contributed to the play's structure and effect'.[25] Leech's assertion, and his essay, presuppose, among other things, that the playwright's choice and treatment of location form part of his strategy for guiding audience response. In order to verify this statement, we need to turn more closely to the function of topography in the theatre.

Broadly speaking, three kinds of location usage are most frequently recognisable in English Renaissance drama: the concentration on a single locality, the contrast between two localities, and the multiple use of different localities. A fourth type could be added, namely the case when location is deliberately undetermined, and therefore almost completely bereft of clues or allusions to the thematic structure of the play. This form of setting can be fantastic, no distinguishable sign being given to suggest topography of any kind, and its theatrical function being to evoke an imaginary no man's land particularly appropriate to the ludic climate of light comedy or romance, as in *Endymion* or *The Old Wives Tale*. This use of locality is evident when place is indicated by such generic names as 'a plain', or 'a forest', a strategy which tends to stress improbability and emphasise unreality. In these dramas the centre of the action is often located in a wood and the comedic world contains much of the magical, of the fabulous, of the mysterious.

On the other hand, when topography is clearly referred to (whether single, double or multiple localities are employed), it is often loaded with a series of theatrical pointers which aim at indicating an ambience and therefore a social and political climate strictly related to the message of the play. This precise sense of location, often signalled by means of deft verbal scenography and coherent metaphoric imagery, reveals the dramatist's awareness of ideological implications and of audience reaction through reference to or association with old beliefs, commonplaces and cultural constructs thematically tied to the concerns of the play. The preference for this kind of setting is, in fact, never accidental; even if it is prompted by a written source, the dramatist transforms the location he inherits into a structural element of his text, affecting the dramatic texture of the play at a multiplicity of levels – the thematic, the rhetorical, the ideological, the linguistic-stylistic, as well as using it as a means of individual characterisation. The ways in which Elizabethan playwrights construct their audiences' response by using appropriate locations produce multiple strategies in relation to the threefold typology mentioned above. Affinities and contrasts between different stage-worlds are among the main rhetorical devices found in all Renaissance drama.

Topoanalysis offers, to various degrees, the possibility of exploring dramaturgical space in order to identify diverse ideological procedures of representation of the fictional world of drama. This implies that the use of place and locale is not 'neutral', but semantically over-determined: it acts on the playtext, determining the local climate, and colouring the dramatic interactions which take place within its boundaries.[26]

Although Italy was an ambivalent country for the Elizabethans (the cradle of European civilisation, of poetry and art, as well as the 'Academie' – in Nashe's words – of political intrigue, poisoners and sinners), it is generally overlooked that this same ambivalence forms part of the playwrights' exploitation of theatrical effects so as to influence audience response and, in some cases, provide cover for political opposition. All this shows the possibility of using Italian historical context (real or imaginary) as an important dramaturgical expedient for acting upon the audience's moral attitudes and contributing to the play's ideology. It is true that the ideological significance given to Italian settings in English Renaissance theatre reveals different levels of awareness in different dramatists and expresses differing ethical and political views. Most of the Italianate drama of the age also follows contemporary theatrical conventions and plays on the Elizabethans' fascination with exoticism and foreignness. Yet in all Italianate drama it is possible to discern a direct functional link between the social environment represented and the play's dramatic world.

Controversy over the kind of influence that Italian settings exerted on Shakespearean and seventeenth-century dramaturgy starts with Praz's and Draper's various treatments of the subject[27] and leads, through varying degrees of analysis, to Leech's pioneering discussion of the general problems involved and to Andrew Gurr's idea of the fictional use of locality in Shakespeare;[28] it ranges from Levith's traditional view of Italy as a metaphor for England[29] to Lever's and Butler's interpretations of the politics of Italianate Jacobean and Caroline theatre.[30] As Agostino Lombardo's article makes clear in Part III, the reasons for this multiplicity of interpretations depend on the pliability of the Italian myth itself:

> Shakespeare's Italy is a country in which the 'real' features – social, historical, geographical, political, cultural – are inextricably intertwined with the imaginary. His Italy is the product of the written and oral traditions, and of the imagination, and is itself a mask behind which are hidden the features and problems of London and England. Italy is an Elizabethan myth fed by a thousand sources, not least by the travellers who 'narrate' it. Italy is the Papal State, the courts of the Renaissance, Machiavelli; it is desire, nostalgia, utopia; it is the stage on which anything can happen – loves, murders, political intrigue, tragedies, comedies.[31]

One further consideration can be added to these rather scattered observations on Italianate drama. If the manifold exploitation of Italy in Elizabethan theatre determines, in different degrees, the plays' ideology, colours their stage-world and affects their social and political implications – owing to a cultural process of appropriation of a mythological construct – this same alluring quality is in its turn fed by the dramatic characteristics of single Italian-located plays, which renovate the powerful suggestions of the Italian myth by adding their own thematic concerns. In this circularity lies, perhaps, the real 'take' of the myth, its appeal and theatrical efficacy for generations of dramatists.

3

The editors of the present volume have taken up Leech's suggestions, and have asked for contributions that analyse the issue of Italian locations as an essential aspect of the dramatic construction of English Renaissance drama. Obviously this collection of papers does not claim to be either exhaustive or definitive; most of Leech's points are still open to debate and some of his proposals remain to be carried out, including a systematic tabulation of the diverse locations used in the plays. But the editors believe that most of the chapters of this book add a new dimension to the field considered, venturing beyond traditional studies of the Italian influence on Elizabethan theatre. We have tried to contain the breadth of the issues at stake by subdividing the subject-matter into four parts which deal with the main aspects of the topic: 'Images and culture', 'Themes and tradition', 'Venice: spectacle and polis', and 'Language and ideology'. In each section, individual papers aim to provide a diversity of opinions and procedures. These views on the subject are rounded off with an Afterword on further methods and prospects and with a Bibliography. We have invited contributions from a range of scholars from different countries, in the hope of representing various approaches to the problem of the Italian setting in Renaissance theatre, and stimulating a renewed interest in the dramatic impact of the exploitation of intercultural references in English Renaissance plays.

Harry Levin's opening paper to Part I is mostly concerned with the ways in which stage Italians are represented in Shakespeare's plays and provides a wide-ranging view of Italian themes appropriately exploited for their comedic and tragic outputs throughout the canon. A. J. Hoenselaars proposes a reassessment of Italianate drama, arguing from textual evidence that a dramatically coherent social, if not geographical, accuracy reveals the stage Italy of the English Renaissance 'as an independent nation with its own identity–alterity construct'. A useful method for detecting this is to look at the many references to England in the Italian-located plays, so that the ideological construct of Italy comes out as the result of a two-way confrontation. Questions of cross-cultural exchanges, of gender, of Italian vices seen in the construction of the Italian myth in the eyes of Elizabethan dramatists constitute the main concerns of Andreas Mahler's contribution. Angela Locatelli discusses the Italian setting of *Romeo and Juliet* as a thoroughly fictional world, adopting Lotman's semiotic theory of culture for an investigation into the issue of cultural space as an intercultural construct. The ideological construction of the foreign setting emerges from a cultural process of renaming, mythmaking and stereotypic labelling under which are hidden the social features of London.

In Part II, J. R. Mulryne scrutinises the historical and mythical background of *The Merchant of Venice*, producing fresh insights into the strategy of alternative settings and of their moral counterparts which characterises the world of the play. For Mulryne the balanced opposition of Venice and Belmont in moral as well as architectural terms reflects new developments in the cultural, literary and architectural history of sixteenth-century Venice. Giorgio Melchiori's contribution makes a case that Anthony Munday's adaptation of *The Two Italian Gentlemen* from *Il Fedele* by Pasqualigo has transformed the traditional *miles gloriosus* into the English prototype of the Falstaff we find in *The Merry Wives of Windsor*, inadvertently inventing a new genre – English romantic comedy – from the conflation of English humour and Italian *commedia erudita*. Sergio Rossi discusses the Italian art of duelling in *Romeo and Juliet* and considers the importance of the Elizabethan translations of swordfighting manuals from Italian. Italian treatises on duelling provide material for a fresh treatment of the Italian character of this tragedy. Viviana Comensoli argues from textual evidence the influence of *commedia dell'arte* on Dekker's *Honest Whore* plays, demonstrating how several stock characters, particularly Candido, are modelled on the Italian popular *maschera* of Pantalone.

Part III begins with Agostino Lombardo's presentation from a metatheatrical perspective of Shakespeare's Veneto-located plays. He views the world of these dramas as a great stage on which the art of the dramatist expresses and reflects itself in terms of metadrama. On the other hand, the theatricality of Venice as a 'spectacular' town is seen by Roberta Mullini in the public and private ceremonies, in the numerous pageants and processions, and in the architecture itself which contributed to the city's whole scenographic display. Shakespeare and Jonson use city locations as stages in a deeply dramatised society where the sense of spectacle is inherent in the town's multifarious people, in its background, in its architecture and institutions. Leo Salingar reconstructs the unique image of Venice in Elizabethan eyes in its manifold aspects of a great commercial capital characterised by strict justice, cosmopolitanism and material splendour. He demonstrates how all these aspects coalesce in a dramatically significant idea of Venice as a constructive factor for both Shakespeare and Jonson. Venice as an ideological construct in which racist hatred and religious strife take place, shifting the characters' identities and alterities, is the subject of Avraham Oz's paper.

Michele Marrapodi opens the book's last section on language and ideology with a discussion of the topographical tropes of *The Winter's Tale*. Shakespeare's shift from his narrative source is part of a general strategy of ironical anticipations, echoes, parallels and contrasts, affecting, in varying degrees, the entire play's verbal and rhetorical structure. An essay by Mariangela Tempera explores how Webster goes beyond the conventional introduction of poison as a device to ensure spectacular plot twists. The Websterian stage-world makes full use, at a linguistic level, of the split between *seeming* and *being* that his method of bringing about death conveys. Zara Bruzzi and A. A. Bromham discuss the use of an Italian setting in Middleton's *Women Beware Women* in the light of the tragedy's concern with contemporary political issues. Their argument re-proposes the study of Italianate drama as a criticism of court corruption in Jacobean society. A. J. Hoenselaars sees in the use of foreign languages in the Italian-based drama of Shakespeare and his contemporaries a rhetorical strategy which enhances the Italian setting as the main locus to grant the English language its much desired international status. The Afterword by Manfred Pfister gives evidence of the difficulty that the 'local colour' critics encounter in providing fresh insights into the issue of Shakespeare's Italy and Italianate drama because of their excessively generalising methods of inquiry. New Historicism and factual analyses of the textuality of the individual plays might break new ground in the specific construction of this 'important part' of sixteenth- and seventeenth-century English dramaturgy.

Notes

1 'Shakespear in a play brought in a number of men saying they had suffered Shipwrack in Bohemia, wher ther is no Sea neer by some 100 Miles' in C. H. Herford and P. Simpson, *Ben Jonson*, 10 vols, Oxford, 1925–52, 'Conversations with William Drummond of Hawthornden', 1, p. 138. On Jonson's criticism on Shakespeare, see E. A. J. Honigmann, *Shakespeare's Impact on his Contemporaries*, London, 1982, pp. 40–5 and pp. 91–103. For an interesting attempt to bridge the separation between the two playwrights' work, see Russ McDonald, *Shakespeare and Jonson/Jonson and Shakespeare*, Brighton, 1988, especially Chap. 2, pp. 31–55.

2 Ben Jonson, *The Alchemist*, ed. Douglas Brown, London, 1966, *Prologue*, ll. 5–6: 'Our scene is London, 'cause we would make known, / No country's mirth is better than our own.'

3 On the topographical and structural differences between the 1601 Quarto and the 1616 Folio edition of the play, see J. A. Bryant Jr, 'Jonson's revision of *Every Man in His Humour*', *Studies in Philology*, 59, 1962, pp. 641–50; Anne Barton, *Ben Jonson, Dramatist*, Cambridge, 1984, pp. 29–57.

4 Cf. John W. Stoye, *English Travellers Abroad, 1604–1667: their Influence in English Society and Politics* , revised edition, New Haven and London, 1989, pp. 71–116.

5 Thomas Coryat, *Coryat's Crudities* (1611), 1, Glasgow, 1905, p. 238.

6 *The Taming of the Shrew*, ed. Brian Morris, London, 1981, I.i.3–4.

7 Coryat, p. 403. It is worth mentioning that for Coryat Venetian brothels may be considered 'The Paradise of Venus'.

8 Cf. David C. McPherson, *Shakespeare, Jonson, and the Myth of Venice*, Newark, 1990, pp. 43ff. Although Coryat's *Crudities* was written too late to influence the play, Jonson may well have acquired his Venetian information from other diaries (such as Moryson's) which circulated in manuscript and, above all, from his Italian friend John Florio. Cf. Frances A. Yates, *John Florio: the Life of an Italian in Shakespeare's England*, Cambridge, 1934, pp. 281ff.; Brian Parker, 'An English view of Venice: Ben Jonson's *Volpone*', in *Italy and the English Renaissance*, eds Sergio Rossi and Dianella Savoia, Milan, 1989, pp. 187–201; and, by the same, 'Jonson's Venice', in *Theatre of the English and Italian Renaissance*, eds J. R. Mulryne and Margaret Shewring, London, 1991, pp. 95–112.

9 Cf. Lewis Einstein, *The Italian Renaissance in England*, New York, 1903, pp. 316–72; Mario Praz, *The Flaming Heart: Essays on Crashaw, Machiavelli, and Other Studies in the Relations between Italian and English Literature from Chaucer to T. S. Eliot*, Gloucester, Mass., 1966, pp. 90–167; John Lievsay, *The Elizabethan Image of Italy*, Folger Shakespeare Library Publications, Ithaca, N.Y., 1964, pp. 1–30; R. C. Jones, 'Italian settings and the "world" of Elizabethan tragedy', *Studies in English Literature*, 10, 1970, pp. 251–68; Louise George Clubb, *Italian Drama in Shakespeare's Time*, New Haven and London, 1989, especially chaps. 1–3, pp. 29–92.

10 Fynes Moryson, *An Itinerary* (1617), 1, Glasgow, 1907, p. 210.

11 Moryson, p. 459.

12 Peter Heylyn, *Microcosmus: a Little Description of the Great World*, Oxford, 1625 (first ed. 1621), p. 152.

13 Thomas Middleton, *Women Beware Women*, ed. J. R. Mulryne, London, 1975, III.ii.131–2: 'Kept close! not all the locks in Italy / Can keep you women so.'

14 John Marston, *The Malcontent*, ed. Bernard Harris, London, 1967. Cf. the Hamlet-like tirade of I.v.40–50 and the rather opposite view on women in I.vi.78–93.

15 See G. K. Hunter, 'English Folly and Italian vice: the moral landscape of John Marston,' in *Jacobean Theatre*, eds J. R. Brown and Bernard Harris, Stratford-upon-Avon Studies 1, London, 1960, p. 103: 'As a mere location for sin other places were as effective as Italy, and went on being used; but for the background for political plotting and counterplotting Italy remained, from the time of Marston, the favourite location.'

16 Cyril Tourneur, *The Revenger's Tragedy*, ed. Brian Gibbons, London, 1967; III.v.18–22.

17 Jonathan Dollimore, *Radical Tragedy: Religion, Ideology and Power in the Drama of Shakespeare and his Contemporaries*, New York and London, 1989, p. 146.

18 John Ford, *'Tis Pity She's a Whore*, ed. Brian Morris, London, 1968; V.iv.28 and V.vi.146–7.

19 James W. Lever, *The Tragedy of State: a Study of Jacobean Drama*, London

and New York, 1971, p. 87.

20 Martin Butler, *Theatre and Crisis, 1632–1642*, Cambridge, 1984, p. 6. See, for instance, Butler's discussion of Brome's *The Queen and Concubine* set in Sicily, pp. 35–42. On the dramatic exploitation of Sicily in Jacobean and Caroline theatre, see Michele Marrapodi, *La Sicilia nella drammaturgia giacomiana e carolina*, Rome, 1989. On the theme of opposition drama, see also Margot Heinemann, *Puritanism and Theatre: Thomas Middleton and Opposition Drama Under the Early Stuarts*, Cambridge, 1980.

21 Heylyn, pp. 152–3.

22 *Othello*, ed. M. R. Ridley, London, 1958, II.i.109–12.

23 The two antagonists' rhetoric, albeit similar in structure – e.g. 'as I am a Christian' (IV.ii.84) versus 'as I am an honest man' (II.iii.258) – differs in its ends and intentions. Desdemona's language is univocal, exclamatory, paraphrastic, aiming at the *affirmation* of human or divine virtues; it adheres to the planes of reality and existence, and symbolises the world of truth and being. Iago's is ambiguous, contrastive, reticent; it relies on *negation* and expresses a will for simulation and dissimulation which contributes to deceit and persuasion; it utilises sophisticated rhetorical techniques for suggestion and the suspension of thought, counterfeiting in tautology and *amplificatio* a mask of seeming virtue. For a detailed confrontation of the two characters' rhetoric, see Michele Marrapodi's 'Let her witness it', *Nuovi Annali della Facoltà di Magistero dell'Università di Messina*, 2, 1984, pp. 403–30. Cf. also Giorgio Melchiori, 'The rhetoric of character construction: *Othello*', *Shakespeare Survey*, 34, 1981, pp. 61–71.

24 Cf. G. K. Hunter, 'English folly and Italian vice', p. 103. See also, on this same subject, the classic study of Bernard Spivack, *Shakespeare and the Allegory of Evil*, New York, 1958.

25 Clifford Leech, 'The function of locality in the plays of Shakespeare and his contemporaries', in *The Elizabethan Theatre: Papers Given at the International Conference on Elizabethan Theatre held at the University of Waterloo, Ontario in July 1968*, ed. and with an Intro. by David Galloway, London, 1969, p. 105.

26 Cf. Darko Suvin, 'Verso una topoanalisi ed una paradigmatica dello spazio drammaturgico', *Intersezioni*, 6, 3, 1986, pp. 503–27. See also on the subject: Alan C. Dessen, 'The logic of "place" and locale', in *Elizabethan Stage Conventions and Modern Interpreters*, Cambridge, 1984, pp. 84–104; Keir Elam, *The Semiotics of Theatre and Drama*, London and New York, 1980, pp. 44–5 and 56–69.

27 See Bibliography, pp. 313–14; 308.

28 Andrew Gurr, 'Shakespeare's localities', in *Shakespeare a Verona e nel Veneto*, ed. A. Lombardo, Verona, 1987, pp. 55–66.

29 Murray J. Levith, *Shakespeare's Italian Settings and Plays*, London, 1989.

30 Lever, *The Tragedy of State*; Butler, *Theatre and Crisis*.

31 Agostino Lombardo, 'The Veneto, metatheatre, and Shakespeare', pp. 144–5.

PART I

Images and culture

Shakespeare's Italians*

Harry Levin

A question that addresses our subject was posed – in strikingly melo-
dramatic *chiaroscuro* – by an Englishwoman living in Florence, Violet
Paget, who wrote a cultivated, opinionated and prolific series of articles
and books under the pseudonym Vernon Lee. Her essay, 'The Italy of
the Elizabethan dramatists', appears in a volume dedicated to her
aesthetic mentor, Walter Pater, under the Faustian title, *Euphorion*.
There, while duly acknowledging Italian arts and culture as the source
of so much that went on to develop in England and the rest of Europe,
she dwelt more heavily and obsessively upon 'the monstrous immorality of the Italian Renaissance'. She expressed surprise that the
infamous careers of Sigismondo Malatesta, Lodovico Sforza and Cesare
Borgia had prompted no echo among the pastorals and classical exercises
of Italian Renaissance drama. On the other hand, she argued, the
impact of those villainies had been incisively registered in the plays of
John Webster, John Marston, Cyril Tourneur, Thomas Middleton and
John Ford. Incidentally, these were Jacobean playwrights (the last one
Caroline), and Stuart England had scandals enough of its own. Nor –
to cite a single Tudor figure – could Henry VIII be held up as a model
of domestic or political innocence. Moreover, it would not be difficult
to note some resemblances between the biography of Mary, Queen of
Scots, and the scenario of *The Duchess of Malfi*.

Yet Vernon Lee could persist with her paradox: 'And the nation
which was chaste and true wrote tales of incest and treachery, while
the nation which was foul and false wrote poetry of shepherds and

---

*This essay is based on a lecture presented at the Villa I Tatti (the Harvard University
Center for Italian Renaissance Studies) in Florence on 7 December 1989. Textual references
are to *The Riverside Shakespeare*, ed. G. B. Evans *et al.*, Boston, 1974. The reference to Ben
Jonson is from The Revels Plays edition of *Volpone* by R. B. Parker, Manchester, 1983.

knights-errant.' Leaving aside this somewhat Podsnappian view of the British so steeped in virtue that they had to import their vice at second hand, there is more to be said on the Italian side of the paradox. Indeed it had already been said by the Jacobean voyager, Fynes Moryson: 'their plays were of Amorous matters, Neuer of historyes, much less of tragedies, which the Italyans nature too much affects to imitate and surpasse.' When nature surpasses art, what need of imitation? The observation seems to have some grounding in cultural history, despite its undertone of blimpish suspicion toward foreigners. After all, the Elizabethans reserved their deepest scorn for their own compatriots who had been corrupted by travel abroad, and this attitude could best be summed up in their Italianized proverb: *'Inglese italianato è un diavolo incarnato'*. The demoralisation of Shakespeare's Richard II, in the opinion of his ducal uncles, had been adversely influenced by

> Report of fashions in proud Italy,
> Whose manners still our tardy, apish nation
> Limps after in base imitation. (II.i.21–3)

Yet, with the widespread vogue of Italian literature among Shakespeare's contemporaries, few works were esteemed so highly or taken so seriously – whether in the original or in Sir Thomas Hoby's translation – as Castiglione's guide to good behaviour, *Il cortegiano*. The object lesson of the incarnate devil might well be offset, in the long run, by the idealized model of the perfect courtier.

When Ben Jonson's Volpone is visited by an English bluestocking, Lady Would-Be, he tries to fend her off by quoting some poet or other on feminine modesty. Her response is instantaneous and overwhelming:

> Which o' your poets? Petrarch? or Tasso? or Dante?
> Guarini? Ariosto? Aretine?
> Cieco di Hadria? I have read them all. (III.iv.79–81)

It will be recalled that Gonzago's murder, the story of Hamlet's play-within-the-play, was originally 'written in very choice Italian' (III. ii. 263). Academic drama had furnished some helpful precedents and patterns, filtered from the Italian courts through the English Inns of Court, those legal societies which engaged in dramatics: particularly those criteria which distinguished tragedy from comedy, and – most important – *versi sciolti*, which inspired blank verse. But the sensibilities of the Cinquecento, as Francesco De Sanctis would confirm, tended toward the idyllic and the romantic. Actually a foreign importer of intrigue would not have needed to depend on Italy for his plots. We could think of Marlowe's *Massacre at Paris* or Chapman's French tragedies, of that perennial favourite, Kyd's *Spanish Tragedy*, or of Middleton's major tragedy, *The Changeling*, set at Alicante, not far from Gibraltar. Xenophobia could be focused upon the national enemy, Spain, through such Shakespearean characters as the fantastical Don Armado – the very name does battle in *Love's Labour's Lost* – or the bastard Don John, so ineffectual a malcontent in *Much Ado about Nothing*. Nor were indigenous crimes to be neglected: witness *Arden of Feversham*, *The Yorkshire Tragedy*, and a long line of gory domestic dramas.

Vernon Lee's simplistic views would be questioned – notably by Mario Praz, whose critical eye was especially sensitive to literary manifestations of the sensual, the sinister and the macabre. Perhaps it is worth noting that, when he uncovered such elements even in the Victorian period, the arresting title of his book, *La carne, la morte e il diavolo nella letteratura romantica*, was neutralised by its English translator into *The Romantic Agony*. Now it should be acknowledged, in all fairness, that Shakespeare had been exempted from Vernon Lee's generalisations. Thus all too often he has been placed in a class by himself, and thereby rendered unapproachable, while 'others abide our question'. He was not less but more responsive than others to the currents of his age; and if his achievements turned out to be uniquely humane, he had achieved them by using the same materials and techniques that they did, and can be most fully understood in the light of conditions they shared. He himself recognised that he had been drawing upon the standard traditions of comedy when his stage directions referred to certain stock characters not by name but as Pantaloon, Pedant and Braggart – types, if not stereotypes, that had scarcely been novel with Aristophanes and were currently animating the *commedia dell'arte*.

Admittedly, as we are told in *The Taming of the Shrew*, it is hard to outdo 'an old Italian fox' in craftiness (I. i. 403). In his book *The Lion and the Fox* Wyndham-Lewis went so far as to trace a Machiavellian pattern throughout Shakespeare's works. This was going too far – a frequent procedure for Lewis. Yet it was an English Shakespearean monarch, Richard III, who – while Duke of Gloucester in *3 Henry VI* – had vowed to 'set the murtherous Machevil to school', to give a few lessons in villainy to Machiavelli himself (III. ii. 193). It should be conceded that *Cymbeline* – Shakespeare's belated, long-drawn-out and overly conventionalised romance – does indeed present a stereotypic contrast between the ingenuous natives of Roman Britain, with side-trips to an even more primitive Wales, and 'that drug-damn'd Italy', damned not for opium or crack but for its aura of potions and poisons (III. iv. 15); and it is thence that the villain must be recruited, 'some jay of Italy' (III. iv. 49). He is the Duke of Siena's brother, Jachimo, who, in fulfilment of a cosmopolitan wager invidiously comparing English-women with 'the shes of Italy', seeks to seduce the Britannic heroine, Imogen (I. iii. 29). When he fails and fakes the evidence, he is caught and denounced as 'Italian fiend' by her husband, Posthumus, and as 'slight thing of Italy' by a masque of ancestral ghosts (V. v. 210; V. iv. 54). Handily he confesses his guilt, but with an innuendo touching British intelligence: 'mine Italian brain / Gan in your duller Britain operate / Most vilely' (V. v. 196–8). Even while admitting the moral impeachment, he still takes for granted an intellectual superiority.

Speaking in *Othello* from pretty much the same viewpoint, Iago says: 'I know our country disposition well' (III. iii. 201). Iago too has been in England, where he seems to have picked up his drinking songs; it was the right place, since its country disposition is more 'potent in potting' than that of the Danes, the Germans, the Hollanders, or other hard-drinking nationalities (II. iii. 77). Shakespeare did not spare the satire in dealing with his fellow countrymen. When Portia jests about her international bevy of suitors, putting each of them down with an ethnic remark, the English baron is dumb, since he has no languages; nor has he any style, since he mixes up his garments as well as his manners. But, although Shakespeare could easily spin off such carica-tures, his fundamental concern was with human beings. As consum-mate master of the English language, he was much interested in other languages. He even invented one, to bedazzle his cast of characters in *All's Well that Ends Well*: '*Oscorbidulchos volivorco*' (IV. i. 79). Though that is not intended to have any meaning, it sounds impressive. He knew French well enough to have some fun with it, even to risk some ribald puns in *Henry V*, where he goes on to differentiate between Anglo-Welsh, Anglo-Scottish, and Anglo-Irish dialects. He cannot have known much Italian, but he seems to have made use of a few untranslated sources: specifically, the old play *Gl'Ingannati* for *Twelfth Night* and a *novella* by Giraldi Cinthio for *Othello* – which also confirmed him in using modern rather than mythological subject-matter.

The dialogue of *The Taming of the Shrew*, in particular, is sprinkled here and there with Italian words and phrases, polite clichés which might well have been acquired from John Florio's conversational handbook: *ben trovato, mi perdonato, basta*. It would be hard to say whether the braggart ensign Pistol is speaking Italian or Spanish in *2 Henry IV* – or is he looking forward to Esperanto? – when he consoles himself with the maxim: *'Si fortune me tormente, sperato me contento'* (II. iv. 181ff.). In any case, the meaning is all too obvious. Choice of names is usually more or less appropriate, and sometimes quite meaningful. Benvolio is clearly a man of good will, just as Malvolio is a man of ill will. Servants tend to be indelibly anglicised; even in the homeland of Brighella and Arlecchino, they are named Potpan and Sugarsop, Hugh Oatcake and Susan Grindstone. Prince Escalus, the Latinised representative of the Scala family presiding over Verona, dwells in Freetown, an anglophone version of Villafranca. When Jonson made his first theatrical hit with *Every Man in His Humour*, its scene was set in Florence and its cast was Italian. Revising the play for his Folio, he transposed the setting to London and rebaptised the *dramatis personae* with English names. Shakespeare never undertook such vernacularisation; his single comedy in native dress, *The Merry Wives of Windsor*, is essentially an appendage to the history plays.

Charles Lamb once remarked: 'I am sometimes jealous that Shakespeare laid so few of his scenes at home.' Lamb may have temporarily forgotten that Italy, so near and yet so far, had established itself as the ideal playground for comedy: a federation of comic-opera principalities – or so it must seem at this aesthetic distance – and of comparably operatic personalities, attractive, sophisticated and slightly larger than life. It could represent what Jonson termed a 'fustian country', a histrionic perspective, a terrain for make-believe. Nine of Shakespeare's comedies, including three we now classify as romances, are located – or at least have scenes – in greater Italy. Two of the tragedies belong in that category. We need not count the Roman tragedies, which take place in a Plutarchan sphere of their own, a model realm for reconsidering the universal problems of citizenship. As for *Cymbeline*, though its date is that of Caesar Augustus, its two non-Britons come closer to Renaissance Italians than to the ancient Romans. Out of the thirty-eight plays in the Shakespearean canon, then, these eleven constitute a significant proportion. It should be worth the trouble to walk through them briefly, watching for the commonplaces poetised, the conventional figures vitalised, and the distant regions brought home to the English repertory.

Shakespeare delighted in the diversity of the Italian city-states, the movement and interaction from one community to another, often subject to the quasi-epical intervention of their civic dynasties. *The Taming of the Shrew* is set into bold relief by its induction, which frames the play itself within a practical joke at an English alehouse. Padua, seat of learning, is saluted as 'nursery of arts' by Lucentio, arriving from Pisa – *en route* to Lombardy – at the outset (I. i. 2); later on the witty Benedick will happen to have been a local boy; and Portia, as a lawyer, will claim Paduan connections. But if Lucentio is there to study philosophy at the renowned university, emulating the student Erastrato at Ferrara in *The Supposes* (his prototype in George Gascoigne's adaptation of Ariosto's play), he is soon deflected from scholarship to courtship. And courtship is the frank intention of the mercenary Petruchio: 'I come to wive it wealthily in Padua; / If wealthily, then happily in Padua' (I. ii. 75ff.). This unromantic fortune-hunter accounts himself 'a gentleman of Verona', and *The Two Gentlemen of Verona* is not really a very romantic play (II. i. 47). Possibly the thinnest of Shakespeare's comedies, it is barely redeemed by the animal act of the clown Launce and his live dog Crab, who seem livelier than the other personages. Friendship so predominates over love that the well-named Proteus can suddenly desert his Julia for Silvia, while her gentleman, Valentine, can be perfectly willing to swing her over. In so far as true lovers should find each other unique, rather than interchangeable, Shakespeare will be doing better by them when he returns to Verona for a tragedy.

Meanwhile his landscape has extended to Sicily – or rather, to the Two Sicilies under Spain – in *Much Ado about Nothing*: a homecoming from the Spanish wars led by Prince Pedro of Aragon and an ill-fated house-party at Messina. Claudio, the misguided lover, hails from Florence. The Paduan Benedick, albeit 'the prop'rest man in Italy', is welcomed as 'Signior Mountanto' (the upward thrust in a duel) because of the verbal parries that he will exchange with the even wittier Beatrice (V. i. 172f; I. i. 30). *Twelfth Night* takes us farther afield and to sea. 'This is Illyria, lady', Viola is informed, and so are we, as the Adriatic vista opens up (I. ii. 2). This Illyrian seaport – it could well be Dubrovnick, formerly Ragusa in its more Italian days – seems to suit these Italian visitors who came from Messaline, wherever that may have been. Offhand it sounds like a dissolute Roman empress, but it is more likely a variant of Messina. If Sir Toby Belch seems virtually too English, a lesser Falstaff, Malvolio aspires towards a Machiavellian role, when he resolves to improve his mind by reading 'politic authors' (II.v.161). The sea-captain Antonio, setting foot in Illyria at his peril, reminds us that these neighbouring states were continually at war, which jeopardised the safety of any traveller from a hostile city. In this respect, he resembles the Pedant, alternately described as a Mercantant, from Mantua in *The Taming of the Shrew* (and this Italianism for 'merchant' better fits the Shakespearean metre).

Now France, the principal locale for *All's Well that Ends Well*, is at peace. But Tuscany can always play its traditional part as 'a nursery to our gentry' (I. ii. 16). At this moment 'the Florentines and the Sennoys [Sienese] are by the ears' (I. ii. 1); and the most adventurous of these young Frenchmen are off to those wars, warned by their King against 'those girls of Italy' (II. i. 19). That warning against seductive femininity would repeat itself in *Cymbeline*, where it is less needed but more heeded. The royal patient has awarded Helena, the medical lady who cured him, to her admired Count Bertram, who in his turn has fled, saying: 'I'll to the Tuscan wars, and never bed her' (II. iii. 173). It is a tortuous story from *The Decameron* and we need some reassurance along the way. Hence the title keeps up our occasionally flagging spirits with the promise of a happy ending: all will end well, if only we are patient. Bertram's Florentine lady-love will connive with Helena in what has come to be known as 'the bed-trick', a crude professional term for an old motif, an arrangement for connubial substitution under the cover of night (as in *Measure for Measure*). Well might we end by asking, with the boastful spy Parolles, 'Who cannot be crush'd with a plot?' (IV. iii. 325).

We seem to be moving in a more problematic direction with *The Merchant of Venice*, though not altogether towards romance; Bassanio too is out to wive it wealthily, and his romance will be called to the rescue of Antonio's muddled business. The Venetian empire at its height, the mercantile metropolis itself, the centralising span of the Rialto forms a busy background for sharp practice as in *Volpone*, further sharpened by – and sharpened against – the Jewish usurer Shylock. The thwarting of his revenge, the transcendence of Portia's sympathetic plea for mercy over his harsh clamour for justice, must emanate from the more leisurely region of music and moonlight, from Belmont across the water, half-way to Illyria. With Shakespearean comedy, a successful resolution often entails an incidental displacement, normally from court to countryside, but in this case from

contentious lawcourt to restorative suburb. The two gentlemen of
Verona – after a sylvan interlude – disentangle their misunderstand-
ings at the court of Milan, though Shakespeare never seems quite sure
whether its ruling figure is a duke or an emperor. More auspiciously,
as in *A Midsummer Night's Dream* or *As You Like It*, the alleviating
environment is that of a forest, where the ills of society are remedied
by turning back to nature and roaming from one 'part of the wood' to
another.

In *The Winter's Tale*, across the long temporal break, we switch
countries. Shakespeare had already switched them from the alignment
of his narrative source, thereby making his lost-and-found princess
Perdita a Sicilian, whose mythical archetype is the home-bred goddess,
the abducted Proserpina. Sicily had been the classical soil of the
pastoral; yet here it is the scene of tragicomic events, which precipitate
the characters into a Bohemian retreat, a purlieu for reversal and
renewal. This Bohemia may have a seacoast, as well as deserts, though
not as yet the special associations – gypsy or artistic – that would
accrue to it in later centuries. Still it offers a sheepcote for pastoral
antics, 'a gallimaufry of gambols' celebrating the betrothal of the
erstwhile shepherdess to her princely swain (IV. iv. 328). The
recognition scene must be staged again in Sicily, where her mother,
the supposedly defunct Queen Hermione, will come to life before our
very eyes. After some sixteen years of concealment, she makes her
reappearance as a statue.

> – a piece many years in doing and now newly perform'd by that
> rare Italian master, Julio Romano, who, had he himself eternity and
> could put breath into his work, would beguile Nature of her custom,
> so perfectly is he her ape. He so near to Hermione hath done
> Hermione that they say one would speak to her and stand in hope
> of answer.   (V. ii. 95–102)

This sculptural attribution, Shakespeare's only direct reference to an
existent artist, bypasses Giulio Romano's chief pursuits in painting
and architecture, not to mention his underground illustrations for
Aretino's *Sonetti lussuriosi*, a pornographic sequence that had provoked
some Jonsonian snickers. But as a master – in Vasari's terms – of both
disegno and *grazia*, Giulio was well qualified to exemplify the dialectic
between Art and Nature that runs through the play. It is resolved in
favour of Nature, and hopes are answered, when the living Hermione
steps down from her pedestal and embraces her daughter at last.

Where do we go from here? Where is *The Tempest* to be situated? The storm itself is magically conjured up by a pinch of dew from 'the still-vex'd Bermoothes' on the opposite side of the Atlantic (I. ii. 229). The 'uninhabited island' itself must strategically be placed in the Mediterranean, somewhere between Tunis, where his daughter has just been wedded, and Naples, whither the King and his courtiers are now returning. Pantelleria has been suggested; but we should not be all that specific; it should remain a mysterious isle, not easily spotted on any workaday map. Here conspiracy, which has previously dethroned Prospero from his dukedom of Milan, twice raises its head again and is twice put down: with the courtiers and with the clowns. It is interesting to notice – perhaps another invidious comparison – that when the drunken Stephano first sees the bestial Caliban, he wants to bring him back to Naples as a present for an emperor, whereas the jester Trinculo wants to take the servant-monster to England and make a fortune by exhibiting him there. 'Any strange beast there makes a man', he wryly comments (II. ii. 28). Banishment once more leads to restoration. The old magician will recover his duchy; but ultimately its 'gorgeous palaces' and 'solemn temples' will prove as delusive as Miranda's 'brave new world', as utopian as Gonzalo's ideal commonwealth, and as visionary as Shakespeare's world and theatre – 'the great globe itself' (IV. i. 152f.; V. i. 183).

When Shakespeare turns from comedy to tragedy, the transition is not abrupt, since love, the theme of *Romeo and Juliet,* had heretofore been mainly relegated to the comic domain. Hence the tragic treatment had to be an experiment, and it was mainly Shakespeare's innovation, though it had been preceded by *Gismond of Salerne,* an Italianate tragedy at the Inns of Court. Ever since the generation of Wyatt and Surrey, English poets had been rehearsing – as Sir Philip Sidney would put it – 'poor Petrarch's long deceased woes'. Francesco Petrarca had lived his full career as an encyclopedic scholar, an all-round humanist, a versatile innovator in many genres, and a stylist in Latin as well as a pioneer in the vernacular. But it was his intimate experience, his most personal vein as a sonneteer, his lyrical formulations of amorous feeling, the moods and phases of his transcendent passion for Madonna Laura through her life and death, that cast so far-reaching a spell over his Renaissance successors. It was, above all, his celebration of womanhood that contributed so much to the modern outlook, and that must have made it easier for Shakespeare to proceed from his own early lyricism to actual drama. Romeo is 'for the numbers that Petrarch flow'd in', according to the satirical Mercutio, who contrasts Laura unfavourably with Juliet: 'marry, she had a better love to berhyme her' (II. iv. 38–41). Sonnets are embedded in the text, most poignantly in the lovers' first encounter, and rhyme is more abundant than blank verse in the earliest scene of the play.

Parenthetically, it might be observed that there is no textual provision for a balcony scene. The word itself was never employed by Elizabethans, though the relevant function might have been served by the upper space of their formalised stage. Juliet would seem to have been standing at her window, while Romeo stood in the Capulets' garden outside. Balconies, to be sure, were more endemic to the Italian than to the English climate. Any land might have provided surroundings for an erotic rendezvous, but Italy helped to warrant the extreme youthfulness of the lovers. Conflict is inherent in dramaturgy of any kind; but in this context *'Alla stoccata* carries it away', with the stylised thrust of duelling swords at the opening, the climax, and the dénouement (III. i. 74). And, as the prologue announces in its preliminary sonnet, 'fair Verona, where we lay our scene', is notorious for its municipal blood-feuds: 'civil blood makes civil hands unclean' (2, 4). The rival families condemned by Dante to Purgatory, the Montecchi and Cappelletti, had been morally reconciled by the succession of previous storytellers, but not until their tale of faction crossed by affection had resolved itself through potion, poison and dagger. That all this had happened within a self-consciously Roman Catholic framework had a further distancing effect for Shakespeare, who had confronted and sharply defied the 'Italian priest' through *King John* (III.i.153). Yet in *Romeo and Juliet* Friar Lawrence can act as a moralistic yet sympathetic *raisonneur*.

Turning from *Romeo and Juliet* to *Othello*, Shakespeare's other Italianate tragedy, we do not leave the theme of love behind; we watch it being overpowered by an accumulation of other motives. Where Petrarchism fostered the paradigms for the earlier play, Machiavellianism preconditioned those of the later one. The spirit of Machiavelli had 'crossed the Alps' and delivered Marlowe's prologue to *The Jew of Malta*. The key-word of his statecraft, 'policy', had taken on a cynical intonation, never neutral, 'base and rotten' for Shakespeare in *1 Henry IV* (I. iii. 108). But exaggerated apprehensions of plotting and Protestant suspicions of Popery had merely prepared the way. Shakespeare was less concerned with literal poisons than with the fears that could envenom men's minds. Now Iago is not an archetypal villain, any more than Romeo is an archetypal lover; each of them, as a major Shakespearean characterisation, is highly individualised. Nor is Iago a typical Venetian, any more than that generous merchant of Venice, Antonio. Cassio, Iago's incidental victim, attests of him: 'I never knew a Florentine more kind and honest' (III. i. 40). Accordingly, he trusts him as he would a compatriot; and so does Othello, who is so far from being a compatriot. 'This is Venice', so Brabantio – one of its magnificos – confidently affirms, awakened by an unseemly hue and cry of the citizens when his daughter is carried off by a gondolier to Othello (I. i. 105). How could that ever happen here?

The peculiar topography of Venice, which gave it the most colourful of all cityscapes, made it a high point on the European grand tour. Bantering with the melancholy Jacques in *As You Like It*, Rosalind describes such tourists as having 'swam in a gundello' (IV. i. 38). More sadly, it is reported that the Duke of Norfolk, condemned to lifelong exile by Richard II, after having fought in the Crusades and retired to Italy, died and was buried at Venice. Of course, one must see that city in order to prize it – not that Holofernes ever has, but he shows off his pedantry by reciting a proverbial jingle in *Love's Labour's Lost*: '*Venechia, Venechia, / Che non te vede, che non te prechia*' (IV. ii. 97ff). From this commanding city-state-empire, so well organised under its duke and senators, Othello the Moor – like Shylock the Jew – is an outsider. Yet, far more acculturated than Shylock, through religious conversion and now through marriage, he has been entrusted by the Venetians with their naval leadership and has led them to victory against the infidel Turks. Venice functions as a point of departure, in the receding perspective of Act I. The subsequent four acts occur in its Levantine colony, swerving centrifugally with the dramatic action: this is Cyprus, not Venice. If Iago is reductive when he calls Othello 'an erring barbarian', he is even more mischievous when he invokes Desdemona as 'a super-subtle Venetian' (I. iii. 355ff.). That epithet befits not her but himself; for she is truly simple and loyal; and it is only through the madness of Othello's psychic insecurity that he can be led to mistreat her – as if she were one of those ill-famed Venetian courtesans – in the so-called 'brothel scene'. After civic order reasserts itself, with the reinforced presence of the Venetians, it is Othello who avenges his own crime by suicide, even while recalling his services to the state. And the self he kills becomes identified with the enemy, the Turkish infidel, once again and finally the outsider:

And say besides, that in Aleppo once,
Where a malignant and a turban'd Turk
Beat a Venetian and traduc'd the state,
I took by th' throat the circumcised dog,
And smote him – thus.   (V. ii. 352–6).

Regional commitments would be neutralised by the admonition of Coriolanus, when he departs from Rome to take command with its Volscian enemies: 'There is a world elsewhere' (III. iii. 135). Yet in so far as Shakespeare's creative world had a centre, Italy and the Italians were very near it, not because he had travelled there – he hadn't, and his sketchy geographical patchwork is evident when his gentlemen of Verona travel by water to Milan – but because it had animated the mainstream of humanistic civilisation as he knew it. Later English poets, settling in Italy, vainly tried to reanimate its past with their self-conscious, worked-up closet dramas, such as Byron's *Marino Faliero* or Shelley's *Cenci*. Let me quote a stage direction, not from one of them but from the pastiche that exposed them, by a playwright whom Max Beerbohm invented, known from his play as 'Savonarola' Brown:

> Re-enter Guelphs and Ghibellines fighting. SAV. [Savonarola] and LUC. [Lucrezia Borgia] are arrested by papal officers. Enter MICHELANGELO. ANDREA DEL SARTO appears for a moment at a window. PIPPA passes. Brothers of the Misericordia go by, singing a requiem for FRANCESCA DA RIMINI. Enter BOCCACCIO, BENVENUTO CELLINI, and many others, making remarks highly characteristic of themselves but scarcely audible through the terrific thunderstorm which now burst over Florence and is at its loudest and darkest crisis as the curtain falls.

What is lacking amid all this allusion and profusion? Synthesis, imagination, insight. Beerbohm's wit brings out the truth that nothing fits together, everything sticks out in different directions, depending more on historical repute than artistic recreation; and everyone, with some divergence in centuries, has been dead for several hundred years. What we miss is that organic conception which brings Romeo and Juliet or Beatrice and Benedick or Prospero and Miranda or Othello, Iago, and Desdemona to life. To life, but not necessarily to *la dolce vita*, Vernon Lee to the contrary notwithstanding. It could be accepted as a measure of Shakespeare's sustained authority, of his acceptance by Italian readers and writers, and of his continuing inter-cultural vitality that his plays engendered the *libretti* for three of Verdi's operas – two of them among the very greatest, one of these a marked improvement over its Shakespearean antecedent, *The Merry Wives of Windsor*. It is true that Falstaff started out as a thoroughly British Englishman; but, at the stage where Verdi took him up, he had reached a plane where ethnicity is outdistanced by universality.

Italy staged in English Renaissance drama

A. J. Hoenselaars

In the critical debate over the image of Italy in English Renaissance drama, several issues have commanded greater attention than others. One of these is the problem of topographical exactitude. As yet, no absolute consensus has been reached on this point, but critics now tend to agree that the outstanding geographical precision one finds in *The Merchant of Venice*, *Othello* and *Volpone* is not representative of the Italian genre.[1] In an attempt to move away from this relative critical stalemate, G. K. Hunter initiated a novel and indeed fruitful approach to the dramatic image of Italy by arguing that Italy was not important to the dramatists as a place and that 'English folly and Italian vice are in this period only complementary images to express a single vision of the human state'.[2] Following his allegations, the Italian plays increasingly came to be read as metaphors of England. As part of a pervasive attempt to domesticate the Italian settings, *The Merchant of Venice* became one of Shakespeare's city comedies, *Volpone* was described as a 'London city-comedy in a torqued way', and *'Tis Pity She's a Whore* redefined along the lines of that same London genre as a 'city tragedy'.[3] And Leah Marcus's suitably substantiated claim that 'no amount of topographical distancing could insulate a play entirely from the contemporary rage for finding homologies with events and people about London' may well herald a new attempt to bypass the problems of the Italian topography in search of more profound socio-political determinants pertaining to early modern London.[4] However fertile these alternatives have proved for the study of the Elizabethans' stage Italy, it cannot be denied that, as a consequence, the image of Italy as a location in its own right has been considerably neglected. In this chapter, therefore, I wish to redress the balance by concentrating on a range of dramatic devices consciously employed to create the illusion that the scene presented was not England but Italy. I hope to demonstrate that the stage Italy of the English dramatists was a nation in its own terms, a nation granted its own identity construct established with reference to matters Italian like topography, climate and national character, and supported by the stage Italian's relation to and experience of nations other than his own. Studied from this perspective one may eventually recognize the stage characters' sense of Italy as a correlative to the Englishman's developing sense of nationhood. Granting special attention to the clichés or stereotypes that tend to underpin the national identity construct, one may also come to read the plays as an exploration of the limitations inherent in the conception of national identity in more general terms.

Turning to Italy for their stage locations, the dramatists frequently placed that nation in an explicitly international context. The most effective means of establishing a desired sense of topographical distance and an initial identity–alterity co-ordinate, was to have the play begin in an English setting, and by means of what Leech terms the 'framing' effect, to develop the Italian location as an extension.[5] The classical example of this method is *The Taming of the Shrew*. Unlike *The Taming of a Shrew*, Shakespeare's comedy effects a transposition from the Cotswolds to the town of Padua. *The Malcontent* became a similar type of frame play when Webster wrote the *Induction* for the third impression. Here the actors of the King's Men are presented at the Globe discussing the stage history and merits of the Genoa-based play to follow. Marston introduces a deft variation on this explicit device in *The Insatiate Countess*, where Signior Rogero fears that Mendoze Foscari 'for a mess of sonnets would have given the plot of us and our wives to some needy poet, and for sport and profit brought us in some Venetian comedy upon the stage' (IV.i.32–5). The 'needy poet' is Marston himself, the stage that of Blackfriars, and the scene presented unmistakably Venice.[6] In a sardonic vein, Jonson has Peregrine in *Volpone* note about Sir Politic that

> this knight,
> Were he well known, would be a precious thing
> To fit our English stage: he that should write
> But such a fellow, should be thought to feign
> Extremely, if not maliciously.[7]

The speaker's hypothesis is countered by the stage reality he himself is part of.[8] A similar, though more complex frame of reference is established in *The Travailes of the Three English Brothers* where Will Kempe and Sir Robert Shirley meet in Venice, and discuss the hoax presentation of *England's Ioy* at the Swan Theatre in London.[9] Robert Yarington's *Two Lamentable Tragedies* consistently features an English as well as an Italian location within the context of a single play. The first of these combined plots is situated around Thames Street, London, and in an increasingly irregular pattern, the dramatist effects a number of transitions to the second scene near Padua. A detailed analysis of Yarington's unique construct, the two murder plays, the two locations and the interaction between them, could yield new insights into conceptions about the difference between Italian and English crime. In such an analysis, the play's final scene would hold a special position. Here, the allegorical Covetousness and Homicide – who do not belong to either plot but to the London stage-world – evaluate the two tragedies. In a fashion reminiscent of the interludes, Truth exiles Covetousness and Homicide from England, notably Elizabeth's England:

> No hart shall intertaine a murthrous thought
> Within the sea imbracing continent,
> Where faire *Eliza* Prince of pietie,
> Doth weare the peace adorned Diadem.[10]

The concept of assassination is thus psychologically distanced from England, and Homicide's vengeful reply points at the future: 'Truth, now farewell, hereafter thou shalt see, / Ile vexe thee more with many tragedies' (sig. K3r). Unwittingly, Homicide heralds the large body of Italian-based cloak-and-dagger tragedies that were to be produced for the London stage.[11]

Comparably, when no specific reference is made to the stage, Italy and England are implicitly distant nations. A characteristic instance may be found in the opening scene of Ford's *Love's Sacrifice* where the Pavian Roseilli is considering foreign travel. After hearing several disappointing descriptions of Spain and France, he turns to his travelled friend Fernando, and the following dialogue ensues:

> *Roseilly*: Yet, me thought,
>   I heard you and the Dutchesse, two nights since,
>   Discoursing of an Iland thereabouts
>   Call'd – let me thinke – 'twas –
> *Fernando*: *England?*
> *Roseilly*: That.[12]

England is less distant in Massinger's *The Maid of Honour*. In an attempt to convince Roberto, King of Sicily, that his country is in need of proper defence, Bertoldo first stresses the importance of the island position, and then explains its relevance to politics with reference to England. His account, marked by a familiar Stuart nostalgia for the days of Elizabeth, blends topographical and historical distance:

> if examples
> May move you more then arguments, looke on *England*,
> The Empresse of the European Isles,
> And unto whom alone ours yeelds precedence;
> When did she flourish so, as when she was
> The Mistress of the Ocean, her navies
> Putting a girdle round about the world;
> When the *Iberian* quak'd, her worthies nam'd;
> And the faire flowre Deluce grew pale, set by
> The red Rose and the white?[13]

One exceptional occasion, however, may be noted, where insularity spells homology. In Phineas Fletcher's *Sicelides* equality between England and Sicily is emphatically stated, and a comparison invited in the prologue:

> *Then let me here intreate your minds to see,*
> *In this our* England, *fruitfull* Sicely,
> *Their two twinne Iles; so like in soyle and frame,*
> *That as two twinnes they'r but another same.*[14]

In addition to such explicit references to a geographical relation between England and Italy, native Italian matters are also juxtaposed to other European nations. This is frequently established by Italian travellers whose return occupies the expository scene in a number of plays. The action of *The Duchess of Malfi* is initiated by the return from France of Antonio, and marked with triple reference to the neighbouring country in the opening lines.[15] Volterre in Shirley's *The Humorous Courtier*, too, is a 'travell'd lord' opening the play with news from France, and Sforza's account of his travels in *The Second Part of the Honest Whore* effectively sets off the Milanese setting against a broader European background in the opening scene.[16] An account of fashions and languages acquired in the course of travel does not exhaust the range of means to foil the Italian scene. Italians disguising as foreigners also establish the location by indirect means. Searching for an appropriate disguise, Pimponio in Shirley's *The Opportunity* opts for a Spanish garb on the following grounds: 'What country shall I choose to be a prince of? Italy is too well known, Spain stands convenient, and far enough, where I have been too.'[17] In Dekker's *The Wonder of a Kingdom*, Angelo, relying on his experiences in France, disguises as a French doctor, as does Picentio in *The Telltale*. Monteclaro in Massinger's *The Guardian* returns to Naples from exile in France disguised as the sophisticated and hence welcome Frenchman Laval, and in *The Double Marriage*, Massinger and Fletcher have the Duke of Sesse adopt the disguise of the servile Switzer.[18] This particular device provided Wilson with a solution to the plot of *The Swisser*, in whose Lombardy setting the banished Count Aribert adopts Swiss nationality and the appertaining costume to redeem his position.[19] Rare is Jaspero's disguise as an Indian at the court of Piacenza in *The Fatal Marriage*.

In the same way the stage Italians may travel across the Continent, a range of Europeans visit their country, thus setting off native against foreign values. An early traveller was Doctor Faustus in Marlowe's tragedy, and if the account of his journey there is not coherent, the depiction of sixteenth-century Rome has few equals in the later drama. The cowardly Frenchman Lapet and his wife enhance the Genovese setting of Beaumont and Fletcher's *The Nice Valour*, and an altogether more prominent role is reserved for the Spaniard Vasques in Ford's *'Tis Pity She's a Whore*, whereas *The Lady's Trial* features his compatriot Guzman. In *The Turk*, John Mason introduces the 'humorous trauellour' Bordello as a comic foil to the eponymous Mulleasses. As a stranger of uncertain origin, he provides a long account of Florence.[20] The devil Ruffman in Dekker's *If This Be Not a Good Play* may be a contestable addition to this catalogue. The fact, however, that he should present himself to the population of Naples in the guise of a Helvetian, confirms the assumption that the Italian setting was brought into focus, to a certain extent anyway, by the introduction of recognisable European foreigners.

Not all foreigners are like Mason's Mulleasses, who has come 'into *Italy*, to learne the language and fashions of the Countrey' (*The Argument*, lines 28–9). The other sex exerted at least as great an appeal to foreign visitors. The two Spaniards Don John and Don Fredrick in Beaumont and Fletcher's *The Chances* become involved in several Bolognese love-intrigues against their will. However, the '*French gentleman Mounsieur Laverdure*' in Marston's *What You Will* is clearly driven himself by amorous interests. He is out to woo the Venetian Celia, and on discovering that he has been unable to win her, he satisfies himself with the second best: 'Since not the Mistresse, come on Faith the maide.'[21] The Spaniard Lazarillo de Tormes in Middleton's Venice-based *Blurt Master Constable*, proves notoriously less successful.

An international variety of suitors added to the appeal of a courtship plot. Haughton's London citizen comedy *Englishmen for My Money* has a Dutchman, a Frenchman and an Italian as abortive suitors. The Italian plot of Marston's *The Insatiate Countess* is equally complicated and carried by the queue of foreign suitors to Countess Isabella.[22] They include the Count of Cyprus, Count Massimo of Venice, and the Spanish colonel Don Sago. Brome's *The Novella*, with its French, Spanish and German admirers of the putative prostitute Victoria, is conceived in a similar fashion. Like *The Insatiate Countess*, it recalls *The Merchant of Venice* with the Prince of Morocco and the Prince of Arragon as staged suitors to Portia, and an additional range of European suitors discussed by her and Nerissa.

Undoubtedly, the most remarkable category of non-Italian characters to set off the foreign scene is made up by the English themselves. With the appearance of the English, the popular identity–alterity mechanism employed to focus the Italian location, is complemented by a construct that creates an unmistakable divide between the Italian location and the London theatre scene for which the plays were originally written. In *The Merchant of Venice*, the English suitor to Portia is mentioned only in passing.[23] In a vast range of other plays, the English emerge as stage characters. In the anonymous *Thomas Lord Cromwell*, the eponymous hero and his servant Hodge visit Bologna, are beset by bandits and subsequently rescued by the Italian merchant Fryskiball whom they know from London, whereas Will Kempe tries his hand at the *commedia dell'arte* in the Venice scene of John Day's *The Travailes of the Three English Brothers*. In the second part of Heywood's *The Fair Maid of the West*, Spenser and Bess Bridges are reunited in Florence, whose duke praises the former as a 'Worthy Englishman', and the heroine as 'Fair English Elizabeth, as well for vertue As admired beautie'.[24] The Venetian setting of *Volpone* derives part of its foreign impact from the Politic Would-Bes and their countryman Peregrine. Webster's English ambassador is granted a crucial role in *The White Devil*, and if the mad English tailor in the masque of *The Duchess of Malfi* has no speaking part, his presence is conspicuous. James Shirley makes Florelli the central character of *The Gentleman of Venice*.[25] Also representatives from other parts of the British Isles make an appearance. In *Patient Grissil*, Thomas Dekker introduces the Welsh widow Gwenthyan as well as her countryman Owen ap Meredith, and the ethnic variety is even more broadly represented in Dekker's *If This Be Not a Good Play*. At the court of the King of Naples, a group of musicians is introduced, including English fiddlers, Welsh harp players and Irish bagpipers.[26] Interestingly, the traffic between the Italian location and the native English setting familiar to audiences was bi-directional. The inherent possibilities are aptly exploited in *The Fair Maid of the Inn*. Both the quack Forobosco and his Clown have already visited England on a previous occasion, because the inhabitants there are easily gulled.[27] Following their underhand practices in Florence, abortive since 'these Italians are more nimble-pated', they decide to return to the country of the theatre audience: 'We will for England thats for certaine.'[28]

When foreigners do not visit Italy in the plays, they are discussed at length. Frequent, and for our purposes also the most insightful, are the references to England, London and the English. The English are explicitly, and also flatteringly, referred to as another nation in Samuel Harding's *Sicily and Naples*. Debating the ethics of the impending battle, the Neapolitans consider that 'by *Mars's* crest it deserves not to come i'th Chronicle, though *Hollinshead* or *Hall*, those voluminous forreiners should write our annals'.[29] Allusions such as these convey a sense of familiarity, but one cannot ignore the fact that they equally establish a degree of a distance and create a sense of otherness between the stage location and the place of the stage. Reference is also extensive when in *The Cruel Brother*, following a reported row between the French and English ambassadors to Italy, Davenant's Duke of Siena compares the two quarreling nations in terms that would have appealed to Oswald Spengler. The English are 'mighty Islanders' and victorious in battle over the French because the latter are three centuries ahead of them in terms of 'perfection' and thus nearer the verge of corruption.[30] At the beginning of *The Nice Valour*, Genovese otherness is established when La Nove claims that the Duke's distracted kinsman 'will not brooke an Empresse, though thrice fairer Than ever *Maud* was; or higher spirited Then *Cleopatra*, or your English Countesse'.[31]

In many cases, reference is also made to the native population of the British Isles. Most of these are critical and satirical, as in *The*

Chances, Marston's *The Malcontent* and John Day's *Humour Out of Breath.*[32] The Italian locus was a favourite means not to set off the English nation favourably against the host nation – as had been a traditional device in the English history play – but to satirise the English seen through allegedly foreign eyes. The satire is sharpest when prejudices are heaped on to the English which they themselves had long conveniently projected on to the representatives of other nations. Satirical inversion occurs when Malevole in *The Malcontent* tells Mendoza that he is planning, after his marriage, to travel to England:

> *Mendoza*: And why for England?
> *Malevole*: Because there is no brothel-houses there.
> *Mendoza*: Nor courtesans?
> *Malevole*: Neither; your whore went down with the stews, and your
>   punk came up with your puritan.
>
> (V.iii.26–31)

The Italian duke's allusion to the absence of prostitutes signals their very existence on the London scene, and the satirical edge is best appreciated when considering that the anecdote is narrated by a spokesman of the nation that housed the brothel of Europe. A similar kind of jibe at native audiences is provided in Richard Brome's *The Novella.* Here, Swatzenburgh, the German suitor to Victoria, disguises as an English factor. This elicits a considerable degree of comment. The English, it is said, are

> Abroad, the royallst Nation of the World.
> What rich Venetian Rarity has not
> The English Money-masters purchac'd from
> Princes and States, to beare home as their triumphs?
> And for their pleasures – but i'le say no more.[33]

Via deceptive praise Brome steers toward satire, which is the more powerful for being suggestive.

The English are also repeatedly shown up for bibulousness, a vice that the English had traditionally projected on the northern peoples of Europe including the Germans, the Dutch and the Danes. In Dekker's *The Wonder of a Kingdom,* Lord Nicoletto Vanni imagines a feast and states the intention to 'drinke as hard yet as an Englishman'. The Duke of Florence and the Prince of Pisa, however, reply that he might be too ambitious, given the fact that the English are the heaviest drinkers, outdoing even the Dutch.[34] Comparable references may be found in *The Captain*, in the arcadian setting of Lyly's *Sapho and Phao*, and in Shakespeare's *Othello* where Iago claims to have learnt his drinking song in England where they are 'most potent in potting.'[35]

This mode of reference to alleged English alterity in proverbial terms raises the issue of those traits attributed to the Italians. The plays readily yield their cliché assumptions since, as Praz has noted, the Italians are highly self-conscious about their supposed characteristics.[36] A deceptive and scheming nature is suggested in Shirley's *The Bird in a Cage*, where Bonamico informs the audience that 'Italy is full / Of juggling mountebanks, that shew tricks with oils, / And powders'.[37] Fernando in Ford's *Love's Sacrifice* singles out adultery as a common practice when he states that 'three honest women in our courts here in Italy, are enough to discredit a whole nation of that sex [...] for a chaste wife, or a mother that never stept awry, are wonders, wonders in Italy', thus also illustrating the proverbial Italian penchant for jealousy (I.ii). Vengefulness, too, is a self-conscious national trait which, once addressed, cannot be halted. As Baptista puts it in *The Fair Maid of the Inn*: 'An *Italians* revenge may pause, but's ne're forgot' (II.ii.30–4). The connection between this acknowledged urge and its dire consequences is best captured in *Blurt Master Constable*, where Camillo calls on his countrymen to give the Frenchman Fontinelle his due: 'he that has any drop of true Italian bloud in him, thus vow (this morning) to shed others, or let out his owne.'[38] Given such self-referential allegations for the purpose of establishing the Italian's stage identity, one is tempted to concur with Praz who interprets them as 'commentary intended for the use of English audiences' (p. 156). Still, Praz ignores the fact that information of this kind was not new to English audiences. The Italian national character had provided an effective frame of reference to Englishmen since the mid-fourteenth century, and its stamp on English-based drama dates from the 1550s.[39] This state of affairs explains how, in *The Insatiate Countess*, Marston may evoke Claridiana's vengefulness merely by having him announce in a rhyming couplet ending the first act:

Rogero shall know yet that his foe's a man,
And what is more, a true Italian.[40]

Moreover, views on ethnic distinctions derived support from the climate theory, particularly following its revival by Bodin and Huarte.[41] This theory was founded on the assumption that the climate of a particular region profoundly affected the appearance, character and temperament of its inhabitants. Dividing the Continent into three climatic zones – hot, cold and temperate – inhabited by southerners, northerners and inhabitants of the temperate zone respectively, the character of the northerners was diametrically opposed to that of the southerners, placing a privileged group in the heavily contested temperate middle region. In a number of plays, the climate theory is openly relied on to support Italian stereotypes. In *The Antiquary*, Lorenzo's wife Aemilia falls in love with her male page, who happens to be Angelia in disguise. Angelia's subsequent generalisation both about her own sex and about the proverbially jealous Italian male grants climate equal status with national character:

> I cannot blame
> These just Italians to lock up their wives,
> That are so free and dissolute: *they labour*
> *Not with their country's heat more than their own.*[42]

Climate is also the frame of reference for foreign travellers, and in the anonymous *Thomas Lord Cromwell*, the hero describes the generous Florentine merchant Fryskiball with the words, 'Theres few such men within our climate bred'.[43] A number of plays allude to the Anglo-Italian climate contrast more explicitly, notably when characters discuss dull or nimble minds. In Davenant's *The Just Italian*, jealous Altamont justifies his claim to revenge with the words: 'Let Italy avouch the just demean / Of my revenge. Dull Britons know no wrath'.[44] A deft variation on the theme is found in Shakespeare's *Cymbeline*, where Iachimo ironically acknowledges defeat in Britain with reference to the climate of the northern country.[45]

The wide currency of Italian stereotypes in all locations of the drama argues in favour of the view that for English audiences the identity of the Italians was established much more firmly than the characters' self-conscious utterances might suggest. Moreover, the popularity of the newly-revived climate theory would have contributed to fix not only the Italian national character, but also the Italian location riddled with its topographical inaccuracies.

Once we recognise that the information content of such clichés as commented on by Praz was minimal, we may begin to appreciate the stereotypes as diegetic elements in the literary construct of the plays, capable of conveying information beyond their questionable mimetic content. Frequently, stereotyped traits are evoked not to establish Italian identity but, paradoxically, to mark the fact that an Italian character deviates from the assumed norm. In Day's *Law Tricks*, the Genovese Countess rejects an invitation to adultery from Horatio, thus eliciting the page's surprising response: 'Hart, a new fashion! A Lady poore, beautifull and chast? cleane From the bias of Custome. To be poore, painted, and proud is as common in Genoa as felt and feather in the fortunate Iland.'[46] In *The City Night Cap*, Lodowick is told he should not let his wife be kissed by strangers since, unlike in England, "tis against our nation's custome'; yet, Lodowick refuses to behave like his countrymen: 'I care not; let naturals [i.e. natives of a country, but also fools] love nations. My humour's my humour' (I.ii.259–65). The irony is that, refusing to be jealous at the outset, he proves unable to preserve his poise once he finds himself cuckolded; Lodowick re-asserts the stereotype he set out to disprove. In *The Gentleman of Venice*, this device underlies the very conception of Cornari. In the 'small characters of the persons', functioning as the *dramatis personae*, Shirley describes him as one who 'against the nature and custom of the Italian, endears an English gentleman' to use him as a stud for his wife.[47] In the event, the disinterested gesture conflicts with Cornari's Italian sense of honour, and he ousts the 'dull islander' who thought that he could 'mount madonas' in Venice 'and not pay for the sweet career' (V.ii., p. 73). Also the climate theory is mobilised for ironic strategies. Iachimo's paradoxical attribution of revenge traits to the dull British climate is a case in point, and in *The Humorous Courtier*, Shirley's Duchess of Mantua describes Foscari in the following terms:

> Foscari is a foreigner, born in
> A climate not so temperate as our's;
> And I am yet to know whether his mind
> Be different from such as please me here,
> At home.

> (vol. 4, I.i., p. 540)

The irony is best appreciated when considering that Foscari is the Duke of Parma. Given the proximity of Mantua and Parma, the Duchess's attempt to establish difference by means of the climate theory is tantamount to an absurdity, a fact also evidenced by their marriage which ends the play.

In none of these cases is any theory of the Italian national character undermined. Instead, the dramatists' move eventually contributes to establish it more clearly. Surprise tactics of this kind belong to the realm of comedy; yet they also bring into focus an aspect of the Italian-based drama that is often overlooked. It is an aspect which involves not merely the frequent clichés about national character, but the stereotyped nature of the Italian stage genre as a whole. Allusion to the genre as a stereotype is explicit in Robert Davenport's Verona-based *City Night Cap*. It opens on a situation, familiar from other plays, with the Italian meaning to establish his wife's chastity by means of a trial. The Venetian lord Lorenzo asks his friend Philippo to tempt his symbolically named wife Abstemia for a third time. Philippo, convinced by now of her fidelity, objects:

> Try your fair wife?
> You know 'tis an old point, and wonderous frequent
> In most of our Italian comedies.

(I.i.5–7)

No less significant is Lorenzo's answer:

> What do I care for that? Let him seek new ones
> Cannot make old ones better; and this new point,
> Young sir, may produce new smooth passages,
> Transcending those precedent.

(I.i.8–11)

Lorenzo and Philippo refer to a theatrical tradition spanning decades, and alert one to the operation of the principles of *imitatio* and *aemulatio* behind the established genre. The avowedly generic status of the Italian plays – operating on the principle of imitation – is coupled with the necessity of emulation. It is this awareness which accounts for experimental departures like Shirley's in *The Gentleman of Venice*, and for those occasions on which the validity of the Italian national character is temporarily suspended.

The Italian's explicit references to an assumed national identity signal yet another, related problem. Here, one of Praz's examples listed to illustrate the self-consciousness of Italian stage characters may serve to demonstrate that, perhaps, critics have tended to underestimate the dramatists' conscious use of national stereotypes, and by extension their attempts to transcend them. In *The Devil's Law-Case*, Webster's Contarino addresses his rival suitor Ercole with the words:

> I vow,
> By the essentiall front of spotlesse Vertue,
> I have compassion of both our youths;
> To approve which, I have not tane the way,
> Like an Italian, to cut your throat
> By practise, that had give you now for dead,
> And never frownd upon you.[48]

It may be noted that Contarino is not self-consciously Italian, but self-consciously un-Italian. He disowns proverbial Italian vengefulness in an attempt to claim a virtue considered alien to Italians, namely compassion. The dramatist realised that too strict a reliance on stereotyped traits for stage Italians stood in the way of more profound character portrayal. Like Webster, Ford was conscious of this problem. Thus in *Loues Sacrifice*, Fiormonda establishes her brother's gentle character by questioning the country of his nativity: 'Thou an Italian. I could burst with rage, / To thinke I haue a brother so befool'd, / In giuing patience to a harlots lust' (sig. H2r). More comic is the solution Ford devises in *The Lady's Trial*. Adurni wants to apologise to Auria for having endangered the reputation of his wife. In this matter of marital honour, Auria eschews the option of retaliation by violent means. Instead, he consciously chooses for amicable dialogue, and comments on his uniqueness in terms that recall the concerns over emulation voiced in the opening scene of Davenport's *City Night Cap*: 'Sure, Italians hardly / Admit dispute in questions of this nature. / The trick is new'.[49] In order to distinguish the Genovese hero from his fellow Italians, the dramatist is forced to grant him a code of behaviour that is un-Italian, and it is appropriate that he should have the character himself comment on it.[50] The inference that may be drawn on the basis of this type of phenomenon in Ford as in Webster is that, paradoxically, the *most* distinctive stage characters in the Italian-based drama are the *least* Italian. This also explains the ironic twist in Marston's *The Fawn*, where Hercules (alias the Fawn) fails to understand his fellow Italians once they refer to endogenous national stereotypes. Nymphadoro, fearing that Prince Tiberio may dash his hopes for advancement, initiates the following dialogue:

Nymphadoro: How? the prince? Would he only stood cross to my
    wishes, he would find me an Italian.
Hercules: How, an Italian?
Herod: By thy aid, an Italian.[51]

Only following Herod's explanation 'in direct phrase' (II.i.101) that it
concerns revenge to be effected by means of poison does Hercules seem
to be enlightened. His surprised response is feigned, but the situation sets
him off against the typical villains. In this sense, Webster, Ford and
Marston's main characters also resemble Jonson's Celia in *Volpone*,
about whom Jonas Barish has noted in appropriately geographical
terms that: 'Where Lady Would-be strives to adopt Italian vices for
her own, Celia's gestures as well as her name demonstrate her
alienation from the moral and spiritual province of Venice.'[52]

Finally, it is worth noting that the manipulation of stock traits
considered part of the Italian's national character – whether for comic
or serious purposes – was not motivated solely by generic require-
ments or by the need to set off main characters from more or less
stereotyped extras. The late sixteenth and early seventeenth centuries
witnessed the sceptical reappraisal of national stereotypes. Bacon's
propagation of scientific experiment as a means of countering Aristo-
telian generalization is echoed both in the prose of the period and in
the work of playwrights like Ben Jonson, where cliché assumptions are
reassessed and, for lack of an alternative, often satirically debunked.[53]
The tendency may also be observed in the Italianate drama. A sardonic
instance blending the perennial issue of geographical exactitude and
an undue reliance on clichés may be found in Davenant's *The Cruel
Brother*. In this tragedy, with its notably sparse reliance on Italian
topography, Castruchio interrogates the courtier Cosimo. In order to
facilitate the cross-examination, Castruchio gives his informant
Cosimo money, thus eliciting the latter's response: 'A little more of
this mettle would puzzle / My geography; Is this Italy or the Indies?'[54]
More philosophical is Chapman in his Florence-based *All Fools*. At the
end of this comedy, Valerio holds a long speech about cuckoldry, a
proverbially Italian trait which determines the action of *All Fools* as it
does many of the plays with Italian settings. In his speech, Valerio
eloquently argues for the universal applicability of the phenomenon.
Referring to women, he notes:

> For their power, it is general over the world: no nation so
> barbarous, no country so proud, but doth equal homage to the horn.

Europa, when she was carried through the sea by the Saturnian bull, was said (for fear of falling) to have held by the horn: and what is this but a plain showing to us, that all Europ[e], which took name from that Europa, should likewise hold by the horn. So that I say it is universal over the face of the world, general over the face of Europe, and common over the face of this country.[55]

With the acknowledgement of vice not as a specific but as a universal fault grew the awareness that its attribution to a specific other was no more than a convenient and distorting projection of common human error, an error rooted in ethnocentic thought patterns. This also explains Dekker's forceful thrust at Signior Emulo, the 'foolish gallant visiting Italy' in *Patient Grissil* (p. 212), and who inveighs against the Italian nation after being ousted from the court:

> How *Italy*? away you ideot: *Italy* infects you not, but your owne diseased spirits: *Italy*? out you froth, you scumme, because your soule is mud, and that you haue breathed in *Italy*, you'll say *Italy* haue defyled you: away you bore, thou wilt wallow in mire in the sweetest countrie in the world.   (III.ii.92–7)

Indeed, this praise of Italy echoes Sir Owen ap Meredith's no less patriotic view of Wales expressed earlier in the play: 'By Cod *Wales* is better countrie then *Italie*, a great teale so better.'[56] The validity of neither allegation is explicitly questioned, but the friction is unmistakable. Instances such as these argue in favour of a reassessment of the Italian-based drama of the English Renaissance focusing on the southern country not as a conglomerate of stereotypes, but as a distant nation in its own right, as a locus different from that of the history plays or London city comedy, in which the dramatists rehearsed, more objectively, the energies that stirred the early modern sense of nationhood and the concomitant behaviour patterns of the individuals involved.

Notes

1 See Robert C. Jones, 'Italian settings and the "world" of Elizabethan tragedy', *Studies in English Literature*, 10, 1970, pp. 251–68. Marlene Soares dos Santos, 'Theatre for Tudor England: an investigation of the ideas of Englishness and foreignness in English drama, c. 1485–1592, with particular reference to the interludes', Ph.D. dissertation, The Shakespeare Institute, Birmingham, 1980, chapter 2 (pp. 110–80). David C. McPherson

argues for accuracy on the basis of intertextuality in *Shakespeare, Jonson, and the Myth of Venice*, Newark, 1990.

2 G. K. Hunter, 'English folly and Italian vice: the moral landscape of John Marston', in his *Dramatic Identities and Cultural Tradition: Studies in Shakespeare and His Contemporaries*, Liverpool, 1978, pp. 103–21; see also his 'Elizabethans and foreigners', in *ibid.*, pp. 3–30.

3 See respectively Gail Kern Paster, *The Idea of the City in the Age of Shakespeare*, Athens, Ga., 1985, pp. 180–219; Gale H. Carrithers, 'City-comedy's sardonic hierarchy of literacy', *Studies in English Literature*, 29, 1989, pp. 337–55 (p. 339); and Verna Foster, "*Tis Pity She's a Whore* as city tragedy', in *John Ford: Critical Re-Visions*, ed. Michael Neill, Cambridge, 1988, pp. 181–200 (p. 183). Melchiori recognises 'typical City Comedy situations' also in the Italian setting of *The Insatiate Countess*. See: John Marston and Others, *The Insatiate Countess*, ed. Giorgio Melchiori, The Revels Plays, Manchester, 1984, pp. 36–7. To Samuel Schoenbaum, *The Revenger's Tragedy* is 'akin' to city comedy (*Middleton's Tragedies: a Critical Study*, New York, 1955, p. 4). On the metaphorical reading see also Murray J. Levith, *Shakespeare's Italian Settings and Plays*, Houndmills and London, 1989, p. 11, and George H. McWilliam, *Shakespeare's Italy Revisited*, Leicester, 1974, p. 17.

4 Leah S. Marcus, *Puzzling Shakespeare: Local Reading and Its Discontents*, Berkeley, 1988, p. 161.

5 Clifford Leech, 'The function of locality in the plays of Shakespeare and his contemporaries', in *The Elizabethan Theatre*, ed. David Galloway, London, 1969, pp. 103–16 (p. 107).

6 Another instance of framing is that of the kind found in *The Tragedy of Tancred and Gismund, 1591–2*, where the 'Epilogus' to the play based in Italy addresses the English women in the audience (ed. W. W. Greg, Malone Society Reprints, Oxford, 1914, ll. 1877–80).

7 Ben Jonson, *Volpone*, ed. Philip Brockbank, The New Mermaids, London, 1968, II.i.56–9.

8 In *Love's Cruelty*, Shirley inverts Jonson's device by having Hippolito speak of a masque under preparation as follows: 'a masque is prepared, and music to charm Orpheus himself into a stone; numbers presented to your ear that shall speak the soul of the immortal English Jonson.' See *The Dramatic Works and Poems of James Shirley*, eds William Gifford and Alexander Dyce, 6 vols., London, 1833, 2, II.ii, p. 213.

9 John Day, *The Works of John Day*, ed. A. H. Bullen (1881) and introduced by Robin Jeffs, London, 1963, p. 370. See also H. Neville Davies, '*Pericles* and the Sherley brothers', in *Shakespeare and his Contemporaries: Essays in Comparison*, ed. E. A. J. Honigmann, The Revels Plays Companion Library, Manchester, 1986, pp. 94–113.

10 *Two Lamentable Tragedies ... by Rob. Yarington*, London, 1601, *STC* 26076, sig. K3r.

11 I can agree only in part with Martin Wiggins's theory developed in *Journeymen in Murder: the Assassin in English Renaissance Drama*, Oxford, 1991. He effectively demonstrates that the stage type of the hired assassin was largely a native English product. Unconvincing is the argument that

the type's disappearance from the English scene and 'the shift towards the Mediterranean' should represent a waning interest in the type, paralleled by the declining frequency of political assassinations in England (*Journeymen*, p. 207). The alienation of the type may suggest that there 'was little place for murderous intrigue in the cultivated *beau monde* that was the England of Caroline drama', but as the vast range of Italian as well as Spanish-based plays performed on the popular and private London stages suggests, there was certainly no lack of interest.

12 *Loues Sacrifice. A Tragedie*, London, 1633, *STC* 11164, sig. B2r.

13 *The Plays and Poems of Philip Massinger*, ed. Philip Edwards and Colin Gibson, 5 vols, Oxford, 1976, 1, I.i.220–9.

14 *Sicelides: a Piscatory*, in Giles and Phineas Fletcher, *Poetical Works*, 2 vols, ed. Frederick S. Boas, Cambridge, 1908, 1, p. 190. It is doubtful whether the parodic irony that Michele Marrapodi discerns in the play was also meant to apply to England. See *La Sicilia nella drammaturgia giacomiana e carolina*, Facoltà di Magistero dell'Università di Messina, Quaderni dei Nuovi Annali, 18, Rome, 1989, pp. 54–5.

15 John Webster, *The Duchess of Malfi*, ed. John Russell Brown, The Revels Plays, London, 1964, I.i.1–4 (italics added). Webster provides a variation on this theme in the opening scene of *The Devil's Law-Case*, where merchant Romelio speaks of his trade relations with Spain, the Low Countries and the East Indies.

16 James Shirley, *The Dramatic Works and Poems of James Shirley*, vol. 4, I.i, pp. 541 and 542. See also *The Fair Favourite*, in *The Dramatic Works of Sir William D'Avenant*, eds James Maidment and W. H. Logan, Edinburgh, 1872–74, 4, I.i, pp. 207–8.

17 *The Opportunity* in *The Dramatic Works and Poems of James Shirley*, 3, II.i, p. 389.

18 He notes that "'tis the profession / Of all our Nation, to serve faithfully'. See *The Double Marriage*, in *The Works of Francis Beaumont and John Fletcher*, ed. Arnold Glover, 10 vols, Cambridge, 1905–12, 6 (1908), IV.i, p. 375.

19 Arthur Wilson, *The Swisser*, ed. Linda V. Itzoe, The Renaissance Imagination, 7, New York and London, 1984, I.i.56–7. Also Ascanio in Shirley's *The Opportunity* adopts a Swiss disguise to keep an eye on Pimponio in Spanish garb. In Beaumont and Fletcher's *The Double Marriage*, the patriotic Neapolitans disguise as mercenary 'Switzers' in the final act.

20 John Mason, *The Turk*, ed. Fernand Lagarde, Salzburg Studies in English Literature, Jacobean Drama Studies, 30, Salzburg, 1979, II.iii.

21 *The Plays of John Marston*, ed. H. Harvey Wood, 3 vols, Edinburgh and London, 1934–39, 2 (1938), p. 294.

22 See also Lewes Machin, *The dumbe Knight: a historicall Comedy*, London, 1608, *STC* 17398. Here the main action, involving the Queen of Sicily courted by foreign suitors, is set off by a plot in which orator Prate learns that his wife is 'sounded by the plumes [= plumbs] of forrainers' (sig. K1r).

23 *The Merchant of Venice*, I.ii.63–73. Equally unsuccessful is the Englishman discussed in *The City Night Cap*, who once tried to kiss Lodovico's wife Dorothea ('as ye know their custome [...] it be none of ours'). See Willis J. Monie, *A Critical Edition of Robert Davenport's 'The City Night Cap'*, New

York, 1979, I.ii.185–6.

24 Thomas Heywood, *The Fair Maid of the West, Parts I and II*, ed. Robert K. Turner, Jr, Regents Renaissance Drama Series, London, 1968, V.iv.190–2.

25 In the Genovese setting of Day's *Law Tricks*, Ioculo claims to have spoken with an English messenger who has 'a most strange discourse'. The messenger is alleged to have brought miraculous tales of a flood in London, ships landing in the middle Isle of Paul's, fishermen catching red spurlin and she mackerel at the Royal Exchange, and a quarrel between personified 'Westminster', 'Winchester', and 'Charing Cross' (*The Works of John Day*, pp. 177–9).

26 *The Dramatic Works of Thomas Dekker*, ed. Fredson Bowers, 4 vols., Cambridge, 1953–61, vol. 3 (1958), II.i.39–42. See also the Irishman Bryan in the second part of Dekker's *The Honest Whore*. On the rich potential inherent in the Irish element presented in the foreign, Italian context, see Ann Rosalind Jones, 'Italians and others: Venice and the Irish in *Coryat's Crudities* and *The White Devil*', *Renaissance Drama*, n.s. 18, 1987, pp. 101–19.

27 *The Complete Works of John Webster*, ed. F.L. Lucas, 4 vols, London, 1927, 4, II.ii.95–6.

28 *The Complete Works of John Webster*, vol 4, V.ii.37. A comparable decision is taken by the beggars in the Flemish setting of *Beggars Bush*. See John Fletcher and Philip Massinger's *Beggars Bush*, ed. John H. Dorenkamp, Studies in English Literature, vol. 37, The Hague, 1967, V.ii.223–4.

29 Samuel Harding, *Sicily and Naples, or The Fatal Vnion: a Tragedy*, Oxford, 1640, p. 85 (sig. K1r).

30 *The Dramatic Works of Sir William D'Avenant*, 1, II.i, pp. 146–8.

31 *The Nice Valour*, ed. George Walton Williams, in *The Dramatic Works in the Beaumount and Fletcher Canon*, ed. Fredson Bowers, 10 vols, Cambridge, 1966–, 7 (1989), I.i.56–8.

32 See *The Chances*, ed. George Walton Williams, in *The Works in the Beaumont and Fletcher Canon*, 4 (1979), III.i.8–9; *The Malcontent*, III.i.71–2; and *The Works of John Day*, II.ii, p. 431.

33 *The Novella*, in *The Dramatic Works of Richard Brome Containing Fifteen Comedies Now First Collected in Three Volumes*, 3 vols, London, 1873, 1, V.i, p. 162.

34 *The Dramatic Works of Thomas Dekker*, vol. 3 (1958), I.i.22–4.

35 *The Captain*, ed. L. A. Beaurline, in *The Dramatic Works in the Beaumont and Fletcher Canon*, 1, Cambridge, 1966, III.ii.39–46; John Lyly, *Sapho and Phao*, in *The Complete Works of John Lyly*, ed. R. Warwick Bond, Oxford, 1902, 2, III.ii.75–8; and *Othello*, ed. M. R. Ridley, The New Arden Edition, London, 1962, II.iii.71–2. See also Henry Glapthorne, *The Lady's Privilege*, in *Plays and Poems, now first Collected with Illustrative Notes and a Memoir of the Author*, ed. R. H. Shepherd, 2 vols, London, 1874, 2, p. 128.

36 Mario Praz, 'Shakespeare's Italy', in *The Flaming Heart: Essays on Crashaw, Machiavelli, and Other Studies in the Relations between Italian and English Literature from Chaucer to T. S. Eliot* [1958], New York, 1973, p. 156.

37 *The Dramatic Works and Poems of James Shirley*, vol. 2, II.i, p. 385.

38 *Blvrt Master-Constable: or The Spaniards Night-Walke*, London, 1603, *STC* 17876, sig. G2v.

39 A. J. Hoenselaars, *Images of Englishmen and Foreigners in the Drama of Shakespeare and his Contemporaries: a Study of Stage Characters and National Identity in English Renaissance Drama, 1558–1642*, Rutherford, N.J., 1992, pp. 16–20.

40 Melchiori, I.i.460–1. Rogero, in turn, prides himself on his 'Venetian spirit' (IV.i.62). Guido, facing the Spaniard, also presents himself as 'A true Italian' (V.iv.45).

41 Waldemar Zacharasiewicz, *Die Klimatheorie in der englischen Literatur und Literaturkritik von der Mitte des 16. bis zum frühen 18. Jahrhundert*, Wiener Beiträge zur Englischen Philologie, 77, Vienna, 1977.

42 *The Antiquary* in *The Dramatic Works of Shackerley Marmion, with Prefatory Memoir, Introductions, and Notes*, London, 1875, IV.i, p. 257.

43 *The True Chronicle Historie of the whole life and death of Thomas Lord Cromwell*, London, 1602, STC 21532, sig. C3r

44 *The Dramatic Works of Sir William D'Avenant*, 1, IV.i, p. 264.

45 *Cymbeline*, ed. J. M. Nosworthy, The New Arden Edition, London, 1969, V.ii.1–4.

46 *The Works of John Day*, Act 2, p. 149. For explicit, self-conscious references of Italians to this custom, see *The Fair Maid of the Inn*, in *The Complete Works of John Webster*, 4, I.i.58–60.

47 *The Dramatic Works and Poems of James Shirley*, 5, p. 4.

48 *The Complete Works of John Webster*, 3 (1927), II.i.266–72.

49 'A Critical, Modern-Spelling Edition of John Ford's "The Lady's Trial"', ed. Katsuhiko Nogami, unpublished Ph.D. dissertation, The Shakespeare Institute, Birmingham, 1989, IV.ii.112–14.

50 For a more extensive re-assessment of Auria's character along similar lines, see Katsuhiko Nogami, 'The rationalization of conflicts in John Ford's *The Lady's Trial*', *Studies in English Literature*, 32, 1992, pp. 341–59 (pp. 342–4).

51 John Marston, *The Fawn*, ed. Gerald A. Smith, Regents Renaissance Drama Series, London, 1964, II.i.95–8.

52 Jonas Barish, 'The Double Plot in *Volpone*', *Modern Philology*, 51, 1953, p. 88.

53 See my 'Broken images of Englishmen and foreigners in English Renaissance drama', *Germanisch-Romanische Monatsschrift*, n.s. 41, 2, 1991, pp. 157–73; and *Images of Englishmen and Foreigners*, pp. 21–5, 109–10.

54 *The Dramatic Works of Sir William D'Avenant*, 1, III.i, p. 172.

55 George Chapman, *All Fools*, in *the Plays of George Chapman: the Comedies*, 2 vols, ed. T. M. Parrott [1910], New York, 1961, V.ii.290–8.

56 *Patient Grissil*, in *The Dramatic Works of Thomas Dekker*, 1 (1953), II.i.200–1.

Italian vices:
cross-cultural constructions of temptation and desire in English Renaissance drama

Andreas Mahler

O me! this place is hell.

(The White Devil, V.iii.181)

1

On his grand tour through Europe, Thomas Nashe's unfortunate traveller, Jack Wilton, accused of murder and with the rope already round his neck, meets a banished English earl who begins to reflect on the educational value of such journeys:

> Italy, the paradise of the earth and the epicure's heaven, how doth it form our young master? It makes him to kiss his hand like an ape, cringe his neck like a starveling, and play at heypass, repass come aloft, when he salutes a man. From thence he brings the art of atheism, the art of epicurising, the art of whoring, the art of poisoning, the art of sodomitry. The only probable good thing they have to keep us from utterly condemning it is that it maketh a man an excellent courtier, a curious carpet knight; which is, by interpretation, a fine close lecher, a glorious hypocrite. It is now a privy note amongst the better sort of men, when they would set a singular mark or brand on a notorious villain, to say he hath been in Italy.[1]

This is not a realistic view, it is a semantic construct. Having been to Italy means to indulge in sins of all sorts and to hide misbehaviour under the gloss of refined manners; it is a metonymy for leading a sinful life, a cultural signifier for a precisely defined signified. 'Italy', to an average Elizabethan, therefore means, above all, two things: the absence of true faith and religion and the presence of interactional dishonesty. As Roger Ascham puts it, referring to a purported saying among the Italians themselves: 'Inglese italianato è un diavolo incarnato.'[2] How does Italy form our young master? It makes him a devil – a highly civilised debauchee, a criminal with excellent manners, urbane and polite, a 'lecher', a 'hypocrite', and a 'villain'.

Such a view stands in sharp contrast to the humanist idea of Italy as the legitimate heir to Roman virtue. Much earlier in the novel, Wilton's master, Henry Howard, Earl of Surrey, expresses precisely this other view in his desire to travel and to discover the 'fame of Italy': ' "Go and seek Italy", with Aeneas', says his love Geraldine, sending him away on a grand tour of perfection and education.[3] Such hopes and expectations are still referred to in the banished Earl's use of terms like 'paradise' and 'heaven'. But the 'fame' of Italy seems for him to have turned into notoriety: the positive model has been replaced by the fascinating horrors of the 'myth of Italian wickedness'.[4] What remains, though, is the use of religious terms: if Italy is not virtuous, it surely must be vicious; if it does not bring forth human beings like the 'more than celestial Geraldine', it is bound to produce devils incarnate.[5] This reversal in the religious connotations accompanying the word 'Italy' is typical of the turn from the sixteenth to the seventeenth century. The humanist fascination with everything Italian changes into an overall 'Italophobia' which identifies Italy with evil and vice.[6] The sources for this are, however, widely anachronistic. They depict the times of the 'Sforza, Gonzaga, d'Este, and Medici, [...] a world long vanished', as described by historians such as Guicciardini: 'The real Italy of the turn of the seventeenth century is not one that appears in the plays.'[7]

Elizabethan and Jacobean Italies, then, have to be seen as mental constructs, as possible dramatic worlds to be filled with meaning by the Elizabethans and Jacobeans themselves.[8] Their semantic content varies accordingly from 'topographically more or less vaguely defined Mediterranean regions',[9] from 'un generico mezzogiorno',[10] which forms the background of most of the comedies, to locales with a precisely specified meaning, in which the setting is no longer a mere point of reference for the localisation of the action, but one of the essential semantic sources for the construction of the fictional world presented by the drama. In medieval drama, the repertoire of world-creating elements had been largely sacred; the world of the mystery and morality plays is dominated by the ethical values of a ubiquitous religious discourse which invariably divides world and characters into good or bad. In the early modern process of secularisation, however, religiously dominated strategies of world-making find themselves more and more replaced by other techniques.[11] The semantic identification of Italy with vice makes it possible for Renaissance dramatists to avoid immediate Christian and overtly didactic connotations by placing their dramatic worlds outside the traditional religious context. What had to be shown in highly abstract allegorised form as a conflict between humankind and supernatural good and bad forces can now be represented as social interaction between more or less ordinary people. Vice finds itself secularised into a form of human behaviour,[12] and it is projected on to a constructed Italianness that has become one of the dominant myths of Elizabethan/Jacobean society.[13]

The Italian on stage, therefore, is a dramatic signifier whose signified is largely informed by cultural meanings already at hand. However, the word 'Italy' does not only comprise the semantic features of an Italy long passed away as seen by an English public eager to project its fears and desires on to distant lands. If one accepts that meaning is constructed differentially, the cross-cultured perception of everything Italian also reveals itself to be the reverse of everything English.[14] Perception is always determined by 'the beholder's share',[15] and this share can be traced in the very Englishness of Elizabethan/Jacobean Italies: '"Italian" vices are metropolitan vices and in fact duplicate those in the home life of their own dear Queen. [...] Italy became important to the English dramatists only when "Italy" was revealed as an aspect of England.'[16] It is precisely this otherness, which had once served to construct vice as the negative side of virtue, that now determines the view of Italy as the negative side of England. Overtly Italophobic world-making consequently opens up the possibility of covert thematisation of indigenous problems; what normally had to remain on the margins of early modern official discourse can now be brought into the centre. Fictitious worlds, then, can never be regarded as mere mirrors of society; rather they represent reactions to deficient realities whose weak points are, in the terms of Wolfgang Iser, either 'reinforced' or 'revealed'.[17] In focusing largely negated problems of early modern urbanisation and their impact on interpersonal relations, fictitious Italies fulfil this very function of 'answer by revealing and balancing out the deficiencies of the systems that have created the problem'; they achieve the 'imaginary correction' of a deficient England.[18]

Elizabethan and Jacobean stage Italies can thus be understood as imaginary complements to the complex realities of early modern England. Their semantic content is a significantly heterogeneous amalgamation of a projected early sixteenth-century Italy, of a negated late sixteenth-century England, and of the dramatic tradition of the Vice which manages to combine the two aspects of fascination and horror with which the English experience the 'radical change' of Renaissance society.[19] On the early modern stage, this 'dual quality' of the Vice is manifested on two levels.[20] Dramatic horror finds itself counterbalanced by theatrical fascination, thus turning semantic negativity into a pragmatic ambivalence.[21] In the process of secularisation, the structure as well as the functions of the Vice – 'the Vice as protagonist and opponent to the figures of Virtue; the Vice as intriguer and manipulator of the representatives of humanity; and the Vice as producer, manager, and commentator'[22] – are in this way preserved within a social setting: 'By becoming part of the dramatic representation of society, the Vice's descendant turns both *provocateur* and victim, not merely of his own doings and undoings, but of those social relationships of which the dramatic action is a poetically heightened image.'[23] The figure of the Italian on stage as one of the Vice's heirs is consequently also predetermined by the 'Italian' setting which surrounds him. He is not only one of the vital forces of the dramatic action; he is always already semantically characterised by the setting as an 'Italian', sexually over-active, morally corrupt, theologically dubious, a representative of sex and crime and atheism who manages to compensate for his intrinsic negativity by the use of an exaggerated 'impression management',[24] an Italianate *dissimulazione onesta*,[25] which the English cannot help interpreting but as deliberate dishonesty.

The English Italian is, therefore, already characterised before he first appears on the stage. His main field of action is tragedy, since it is there that his semantic potential finds itself fully deployed in the construction of a conflictual dramatic world. 'Tragedy' as has been argued, 'places gender issues in centre stage.'[26] The secularisation of the Vice consequently brings forth gendered variants of Italianness. Among these, two of the most typical ones are temptation and desire, which are figurally specified into the tempting male and the desiring female. It is on these that I want to concentrate in the following sections of this chapter. As examples for the male/masculine variant of temptation, I will select Iago and Bosola; as examples for the female/feminine variant of desire, Desdemona, Vittoria Corombona and the Duchess of Malfi.[27] The dramatic constructions of temptation and desire serve to problematise the seemingly obvious analogy between the sex-related categories of maleness and femaleness and the gender-related categories of masculinity and femininity. They show the stage Italians as transgressors consequently to be punished. It is thus that they trace a problem of early modern English society by conceiving a fictitious Italy which serves to reveal what the English themselves try to negate.

2

Early modern Italian society has been called a *società spettacolo*,[28] a society in which face and façade play an important part in interpersonal communication.[29] It is certainly not by chance, then, that in Shakespeare's *Othello* this aspect is the first to be addressed in the world-creating process. When Iago complains to Roderigo about his not being accepted for the post of lieutenant, he refers to models of behaviour to which the stranger Othello obviously does not respond:

> three great ones of the city,
> In personal suit to make me his lieutenant,
> Oft capp'd to him, and by the faith of man,
> I know my price, I am worth no worse a place.
>
> (I.i.8–11)

The intervention of three well-to-do Venetian citizens in favour of Iago's seemingly just cause would normally guarantee him the desired place. However, their studied politeness fails to achieve the desired result: Othello refuses the 'mediators' (I.i.16) and chooses the Florentine Cassio,

> A fellow almost damn'd in a fair wife,
> That never set a squadron in the field,
> Nor the devision of battle knows,
> More than a spinster, unless the bookish theoric,
> Wherein the toged consuls can propose
> As masterly as he: mere prattle without practice
> Is all his soldiership.
>
> (I.i.21–7)

Semantically, the text begins to construct an opposition between intrinsic value and mere show. From Iago's perspective, Cassio seems to represent exactly the type of Italian whose outward appearance manages to impress his fellow citizens. In contrast to this, Iago posits himself as a brave and faithful soldier who expects Othello to know his true worth as someone, 'of whom his eyes had seen the proof', / At Rhodes, at Cyprus, and on other grounds' (I.i.28–9). This view is confirmed by the more general conclusion:

> But there's no remedy, 'tis the curse of service,
> Preferment goes by letter and affection,
> Not by the old gradation, where each second
> Stood heir to the first.
>
> (I.i.35–8)

In a world that begins to lose its fixed hierarchical structure, it becomes very hard to distinguish between 'natural' order and culturally produced value. Ironically, though, it is not Cassio who is the representative of interactional dishonesty, rather it is Iago himself. There is no big difference between preferment 'by letter and affection' and the action of 'capping'. Iago's complaint, then, is not so much about the loss of truth and order as about what he considers to be Cassio's better social play. It is in this vein that he formulates his allegiance to Othello:

> I follow him to serve my turn upon him:
> We cannot all be masters, nor all masters
> Cannot be truly follow'd. You shall mark
> Many a duteous and knee-crooking knave,
> That, doting on his own obsequious bondage,
> Wears out his time much like his master's ass,
> For nought but provender, and when he's old, cashier'd,
> Whip me such honest knaves: others there are,
> Who trimm'd in forms, and visages of duty,
> Keep yet their hearts attending on themselves,
> And throwing but shows of service on their lords,
> Do well thrive by 'em, and when they have lin'd their coats,
> Do themselves homage, those fellows have some soul,
> And such a one do I profess myself.
>
> (I.i.42–55)

This confession to Roderigo also constitutes an explicit figural self-characterisation for the spectator.[30] In his addiction to 'forms', 'visages' and 'shows', and his refusal to count himself among the 'honest knaves', Iago reveals himself as a thoroughly Machiavellian figure ready to play his part as ruthlessly and self-interestedly as possible:

In following him, I follow but myself.
Heaven is my judge, not I for love and duty,
But seeming so, for my peculiar end.
For when my outward action does demonstrate
The native act, and figure of my heart,
In complement extern, 'tis not long after,
But I will wear my heart upon my sleeve,
For doves to peck at: I am not what I am.

(I.i.58–65)

This divide between essence and social existence is characteristic of a *società spettacolo*, in which identity and role-playing tend to become indistinguishable. In neglecting what Watzlawick, Beavin and Jackson have called the aspect of content, and in foregrounding the aspect of relationship, Iago posits himself as a typical representative of an Italianate world, where people are never what they pretend to be. This explicit self-commentary tallies with the expectation of the spectators. The mentioning of Venice in the title has already promised them a titillating signified for which Iago now seems to be the appropriate stage signifier. If one accepts that dramatic figures should first of all be considered as empty signs to be filled with meaning, one can see clearly how Shakespeare uses the exposition of *Othello* to combine Elizabethan and Jacobean ideas of Italianness with the name of Iago.[31] He explicitly reminds the audience that 'this is Venice' (I.i.105), and he insists on thematising more than once that the society depicted is one dominated by a form of early modern impression management which communicates with the help of dishonest social signs:

Though I do hate him, as I do hell's pains,
Yet, for necessity of present life,
I must show out a flag, and sign of love,
Which is indeed but sign.

(I.i.154–7)

The ensign's characteral features and his programmatic dissimulation align him more closely with the semantics of the background than any other figure in the play. Through figural and authorial characterisation techniques, Iago is soon recognisably established as a prototype of the early modern stage Italian, as lecher ('an old black ram / Is tupping your white ewe', I.i.88–9), as 'seeming' hypocrite (I.i.60), and as villain.[32] For an English audience, the deceptive nature of his Italianness becomes even more awe-inspiring through Othello's similarly non-Italian perspective. For a long time, Othello '[t]hat thinks men honest that but seems to be so' (I.iii.398) continues to see him as 'honest Iago' (I.iii.294), and it is only right at the end of the play that he discovers him as the 'demi-devil' (V.ii.302) and 'hellish villain' (V.ii.369) that he has always been for the spectators. That Iago is conceived as a *diavolo incarnato*, a sort of secularised vice, is above all made clear in the most explicitly Machiavellian passage of the play, in which he sets himself in marked contrast to the idea of virtue:

> Virtue? a fig! 'tis in ourselves, that we are thus, or thus: our bodies are gardens, to the which our wills are gardeners, so that if we will plant nettles, or sow lettuce, set hyssop, and weed up thyme; supply it with one gender of herbs, or distract it with many; either to have it sterile with idleness, or manur'd with industry, why, the power, and corrigible authority of this, lies in our wills. If the balance of our lives had not one scale of reason, to poise another of sensuality, the blood and baseness of our natures would conduct us to most preposterous conclusions. But we have reason to cool our raging motions, our carnal stings, our unbitted lusts; whereof I take this, that you call love, to be a sect, or scion. (I.iii.319–33)

This is not only to console the lovesick Roderigo; it also reveals the strategy Iago is about to employ against Othello. Instead of cooling down his 'raging motions', he stirs them up; instead of appealing to reason, he tries to eclipse it; instead of placating the Moor's rashness, he rouses the 'blood and baseness' of his nature in order to bring him not only to 'most preposterous conclusions', but to a most precipitate action. It is in this sense that the 'super-subtle Venetian' (I.iii.357) Iago turns out to be the tempting male, whose words and actions do not only characterise him as legitimate heir to the Vice, but also serve to instigate others to actions which they will soon regret. The text constructs him as an amoral intriguer and a manipulator, as an early modern secular equivalent to Temptation.

3

In Webster's *Tragedy of the Duchess of Malfi*, the strategies of world-making are similar to the ones in *Othello*. The place-name of the title already suggests an Italianate world, and Webster is quick in taking up this expectation in the first scene of the first act. The text begins by constructing a difference, opposing Amalfi to France:

You are welcome to your country, dear Antonio,
You have been long in France, and you return
A very formal Frenchman, in your habit.
How do you like the French court?

(I.i.1–4)

The two perspectives addressed by Delio – Italian and non-Italian –
can in a way be seen as structurally equivalent to the difference
between Iago's and Othello's interpretation of the complexities of
Venetian society. Antonio's reply consequently takes up the distinction
and semanticises the French court as a positive counter-model to the
court at Amalfi:

I admire it;
In seeking to reduce both State and people
To a fix'd order, their judicious King
Begins at home. Quits first his royal palace
Of flatt'ring sycophants, of dissolute,
And infamous persons, which he sweetly terms
His Master's masterpiece, the work of Heaven,
Consid'ring duly, that a Prince's court
Is like a common fountain, whence should flow
Pure silver-drops in general. But if 't chance
Some curs'd example poison't near the head,
Death and diseases through the whole land spread.

(I.i.4–15)

This almost Tillyardian vision of providential order and harmony, 'of
an ordered universe in a fixed system of hierarchies', indirectly
projects the idea of chaos on to the Italian world which will form the
background of the play.[33] The text calls up prototypical elements of the
early modern myth of Italianness – 'flatt'ring sycophants', 'dissolute,
[a]nd infamous persons' – and establishes Amalfi as a locale with a
typically Italian semantics. It is not surprising, then, that the first
figure to enter the stage after this characterisation should be Bosola,
the 'court-gall' (I.i.23), who

rails at those things which he wants,
Would be as lecherous, covetous, or proud,
Bloody, or envious, as any man,
If he had means to be so.

(I.i.25–8)

Similar to Iago, his first complaint is one of neglected merit. Bosola turns to the Cardinal, for whom he has spent several years in the galleys, to protest against his lack of attention: 'I have done you better service than to be slighted thus. Miserable age, where the reward of doing well, is the doing of it!' (I.i.31–3). The Cardinal's cool retort to this motivates Bosola to take up a more active part in the game of self-interest and social flattery: 'slighted thus? I will thrive some way: blackbirds fatten best in hard weather: why not I, in these dog-days?' (I.i.38–9). This intention to 'thrive' is commented upon by the Cardinal as not 'honest' (I.i.40), but, indeed, it is the Cardinal who seems to be everything but honest himself: 'Some fellows, they say, are possessed with the devil, but this great fellow were able to possess the greatest devil, and make him worse' (I.i.45–7). With a successful *diavolo incarnato* in front of him, Bosola decides to become a devil himself. The world thus depicted is a world of dishonesty, dissimulation, hypocrisy and sin. It is the Italianate counterpart to the imaginary France celebrated at the beginning of the play by Antonio, a land of 'death and diseases' brought about by Machiavellians like the Cardinal who – some 'curs'd example' poisoning the State 'near the head' – destroys its 'fix'd order' by ruthlessly exploiting others. The Italianate world of *The Duchess of Malfi* consequently italianises Bosola, making him a 'familiar' (I.ii.183) 'a very quaint invisible devil in flesh: / An intelligencer' (I.ii.184–5), 'a villain' (I.ii.197), and an expert in Mediterranean impression management who knows what one needs to 'be taken for an eminent courtier': 'a reasonable good face', 'good grace', and 'set speech' (II.i.1–7). It is precisely the ineluctable role-play of the *società spettacolo* which makes 'this world a tedious theatre', in which the Duchess, like many others, has to 'play a part [...] 'gainst my will' (IV.i.83–4) and where Bosola turns out to be 'an actor in the main of all' (V.v.85). It is a world of hardly understandable *dissimulazione onesta*, of 'as Tasso calls / *Magnanima mensogna*: a noble lie' (III.ii.179–80), which often ignobly leads to 'seeming / Honour' (V.ii.302–3) confusing the English audience like the 'English tailor, craz'd i'th' brain / With the study of new fashion' (IV.ii.50–1). The perspective which falls on Italy is thus not only opposed to the French ideal conjured up at the beginning, it is also informed by the beholder's 'share'. This English beholder who would like to imagine English society as dominated by the aspect of content projects all interactional role-play on faraway lands. Bosola formulates this desire for himself:

Do I not dream? Can this ambitious age
Have so much goodness in't, as to prefer
A man merely for worth: without these shadows
Of wealth, and painted honours? possible?

(III.ii.276–9)

But he also spoils it with his actions: 'What an excellent / Honest man
might'st thou have been', says Ferdinand in the face of his dead twin-
sister, the Duchess, and he continues,

For thee, (as we observe in tragedies
That a good actor many times is curs'd
For playing a villains's part) I hate thee for't:
And, for my sake, say thou hast done much ill, well.

(IV.ii.271–2; 286–7)

Bosola's vice-like quality is instrumental for the theatre society of
Amalfi. He is the intriguer and tempter who keeps. the action going,
until his 'revenge is perfect' (V.v.63). At that moment, the Italianate
universe of discourse constructed in *The Duchess of Malfi* collapses:

These wretched eminent things
Leave no more fame behind 'em, than should one
Fall in a frost, and leave his print in snow;
As soon as the sun shines, it ever melts
Both form and matter.

(V.v.113–17)

Delio's emblematic way of expressing the ephemeral quality of
interactional grandeur does not only bring the gruesome action to a
halt; it also admonishes the English audience to 'make noble use / Of
this great ruin' (V.v.110–11) by committing them to substantial values
like 'truth' and '[i]ntegrity of life' (V.v.119–20). The end of the *società
spettacolo* thus reveals to the English the destruction of their own
society unless they manage to recuperate 'English' honesty and replace
appearance by 'reality' again.

4

The figure of the tempter is a world-maker himself. He creates figural
universes of discourse which are informed by personal interest and
distinct from the general universe of discourse of the play.[34] It is in this

sense that Iago has been called 'the artificer of a *destructive projection*' and 'a prisoner of his own *imaginaire*',[35] because he deflects on others obsessions and desires which he does not seem able to cope with himself. His role as tempter makes him want to transform imagined appearances into reality; his discourse is consequently imbued with projections of repressed desire: 'The obscenity of his language is constantly designed [...] to represent Othello as the repulsive black champion of a degraded hyperbolical sexuality, and to expose Desdemona as an insatiable whore.'[36] The idea of the 'old black ram / [...] tupping your white ewe' (*Othello*, I.i.88–9), of Desdemona being 'cover'd with a Barbary horse' (I.i.111) and 'making the beast with two backs' (I.i.116–17), may serve as examples. The representation of Desdemona as a woman is thus closely tied to the notion of desire. Later in the play, this notion is connected with the idea of Italianness. In Iago's discourse, Desdemona turns out to be a specifically 'Italian' woman acting mainly 'for her body's lust' (II.iii.348):

> Look to your wife, observe her well with Cassio;
> Wear your eye thus, not jealous, nor secure.
> I would not have your free and noble nature
> Out of self-bounty be abused, look to't:
> I know our country disposition well;
> In Venice they do let God see the pranks
> They dare not show their husbands: their best conscience
> Is not to leave undone, but keep unknown.
>
> (III.iii.201–8)

For the English audience, as for the stranger Othello, Italian women are represented as instances of lust and desire who, in the 'country disposition' of a *società spettacolo*, manage to keep up the façade of virtue even though everyone suspects it to be nothing but façade. It is in this way that Desdemona appears to be 'that cunning whore of Venice, / That married with Othello' (IV.ii.91–2). In the construction of early modern man as a unified, autonomous subject, female desire is thus a threatening element since it is beyond male control. Catherine Belsey has shown that in the Renaissance the gender terms of Man and Woman began to differentiate themselves in the sense that '[w]oman was produced in contradistinction to man' and consequently defined man by her difference.[37] This meant that her semantics had to remain fixed for man to feel secure. Desire is potential action and potential change; therefore, it is in man's interest to discredit it from the start, for example by turning 'virtue into pitch, / And out of her own goodness make the net / That shall enmesh 'em all' (II.iii.351–3). Iago's strategy of ensnaring Desdemona's actions, 'so that every external sign becomes a simulacrum of his vision',[38] is an act of male semantic appropriation; it fixes the idea of desire on to her, disqualifies it as unfeminine and consequently demands that the discursively produced 'transgression' be punished.

The cross-cultural construction of the Italian woman as subject with a will of her own can also be seen in the figure of the Duchess of Malfi. Her autonomous decision to remarry is not only opposed to the male intention of keeping her under control: 'she's a young widow / I would not have her marry again' (*Duchess of Malfi*, I.ii.178–9); it is also a provocative act because it throws into relief two of the central assets of the Italian stage society at Amalfi, the necessity of role-play and the observance of social hierarchy:

> The misery of us, that are born great,
> We are forc'd to woo, because none dare woo us:
> And as a tyrant doubles with his words,
> And fearfully equivocates: so we
> Are forc'd to express our violent passions
> In riddles, and in dreams, and leave the path
> Of simple virtue, which was never made
> To seem the thing it is not.
> [...]
> I do here put off all vain ceremony,
> And only do appear to you, a young widow
> That claims you for her husband.
>
> (I.ii.360–7; 375–7)

The Duchess's marriage to her steward Antonio is thus perceived by her surroundings as transgression in more than one way. Her behaviour is semanticised as un-Italian, and it is her body which first betrays this un-Italianness:

> I observe our Duchess
> Is sick a-days, she pukes, her stomach seethes,
> The fins of her eyelids look most teeming blue,
> She wanes i'th'cheek, and waxes fat i'th' flank;
> And, contrary to our Italian fashion,
> Wears a loose-bodied gown: there's somewhat in't.
>
> (II.i.67–72)

This lack of dissimulation discloses her act; it makes public what the Duchess considered to be entirely private:

> Why might not I marry?
> I have not gone about, in this, to create
> Any new world, or custom.

(III.ii.110–12)

Ania Loomba has argued that one of the dominant strategies to keep women under control is to mingle the public and the private spheres and to treat active female sexuality in terms of public transgression as a threat to order: 'Patriarchal legality conceives of female sexuality as criminal.'[39] Consequently, the Duchess's act and her almost shatteringly innocent defence ('I have youth, / And a little beauty'; III.ii.139–40) are immediately transformed into subversive action ('So you have some virgins, / That are witches'; III.ii.140–1). Whatever she does is discursively perceived as 'contrary to our Italian fashion'; her private desire is made a public issue which then threatens the stable semantics of a male-dominated society. Desire is thus constructed as unfeminine, since it 'is inscribed […] at every level (social, economic, political, sexual) as the motivation for change, upheaval, disruption, and […] female tragic transgression'.[40]

In the figure of Vittoria Corombona, the 'famous Venetian Curtizan' (*sic*) as the title-page calls her, temptation and desire find themselves combined. *The White Devil* constructs an Italianate *società spettacolo* which is not only based on a large number of Italian references making it quite clear that '[*t*]*he action takes place in Italy, first at Rome, but in the final act, at Padua*' (*The White Devil*, p. 36), but which is also semantically endowed by everything 'Italian': 'Courtly reward, / And punishment' (I.i.3–4), 'damnable degrees / Of drinkings' (I.i.18–19), 'ruin' (I.i.28), 'murders here in Rome, / Bloody and full of horror' (I.i.31–2), 'violent sins' (I.i.35), and 'crimes' (I.i.36). It is characterised by a complicated system of impression management which always makes sure that 'some great men 'scape' (I.i.38) and the idea of revenge threatening to 'make Italian cut-works in their guts / If ever I return' (I.i.51–2). 'In no other play', as Jonathan Dollimore has remarked, 'is the identity of the individual shown to depend so much on social interaction.'[41] As a typical 'daughter of Eve',[42] Vittoria is first presented in the function of temptress telling her lover Brachiano a dream, which is immediately interpreted by the vice-like figure of Flamineo as an attempt to talk him into murdering Camillo and Isabella:

Excellent devil.
She hath taught him in a dream
To make away his Duchess and her husband.

(I.ii.254–6)

This brings into play the Renaissance idea that 'at the root of all transgression is woman'.[43] Transgressive acts question the present order and consequently entail legal action. In the ensuing 'arraignment of Vittoria' (III.ii), temptation and desire serve as the main ground for the accusation: 'You know what whore is; next the devil Adult'ry, / Enters the devil, Murder' (III.ii.108–9). Vittoria counters this ('your names / Of whore and murd'ress, they proceed from you, / As if a man should spit against the wind, / The filth returns in's face'; III.ii.147–50), but what is more important is her refusal to accept that desire equates with vice:

> Grant I was tempted,
> Temptation to lust proves not the act,
> *Casta est quam nemo rogavit.*

(III.ii.197–9)

For the Cardinal Monticelso, the main representative of Renaissance sexual politics, the identification of Vittoria with 'vice' (III.ii.249) and the interpretation of private desire as 'public fault' (III.ii.256) remain, however, unshattered: 'If the devil / Did ever take good shape behold this picture' (III.ii.215–16). This Italianate construction of Vittoria as white and female devil is commented upon in an exchange between the French and English ambassadors: 'She hath lived ill.' – 'True, but the cardinal's too bitter' (III.ii.106–7). The introduction of an English perspective serves to distance the English audience from the negativity of the *società spettacolo* depicted in the play: 'You are happy in England, my lord', says Flamineo, affecting distraction, 'here they sell justice with those weights they press men to death with. O horrible salary!' (III.ii.28–30). For an English audience, this remark of a seemingly distracted stage Italian projecting happiness, truth and justice on the English society and its legal system, however, can only be taken ironically. It establishes a link between the fictitious Italy and the real England of the spectators. In foregrounding the aspects of temptation and desire, the dramatic world of *The White Devil* addresses problems of early modern English society which can be brought more sharply into focus than in non-fictional discourses.

5

Italian vices are English problems. Temptation and desire constitute points of negotiation for the early modern readjustment of gender relations. In Elizabethan and Jacobean times, temptation was normally considered to be female: 'From the outset and especially in the middle ages, Christianity had a strong misogynist streak. Woman was the sinful temptress, lustful, vain, and the bane of man.'[44] In opposition to this, desire was treated as male, and female desire was consequently perceived 'as a disease and as a monstrous abnormality'.[45] For Elizabethan and Jacobean drama to stage tempting males and desiring females was to probe part of the traditional hierarchy by subverting its usual semantic order. The myth of 'Italy' offered an ideal imaginary place for this. Iago, Bosola, Desdemona, Vittoria and the Duchess of Malfi are all constructed as stage Italians; they are also constructed as transgressors: 'Desdemona, [...] the Duchess of Malfi and Vittoria all act autonomously and in doing so become "unruly"';[46] Iago and Bosola are descendants of the Vice and, consequently, threats to order. As transgressors, the men are semanticised as non-masculine, the women as non-feminine. 'Disprove this villain, if thou be'st a man' (*Othello*, V.ii.173), says Emilia to Iago, and since he cannot, she knows that she is free to speak: ''Tis proper I obey him, but not now' (V.ii.197). Iago unwittingly questions his masculinity himself when he asserts that '[m]en should be what they seem, / Or those that be not, would they might seem none!' (III.iii.130–1). This annulment of masculinity, however, does not entail femininity; despite their roles as tempters, neither Iago nor Bosola is a feminine man, rather they are no men at all. In the end, they turn out to be devils, or beasts: 'O Spartan dog, / More fell than anguish, hunger, or the sea, / Look on the tragic lodging of thy bed: / This is thy work' (V.II.362–5). In a world which still 'intends to show man at the centre of the Ptolemaic cosmos',[47] male transgression is constructed not as feminine, but as non-human; it is a step outside: 'Mine is another voyage' (*Duchess of Malfi*, V.v.105).[48] In contrast to this, female transgression is unambiguously perceived as masculine; it is a step towards the centre. Desdemona's decision to get married with Othello against her father's will suggests that '[o]ur general's wife is now the general' (*Othello*, II.iii.305–6). This strategy of masculine semantisation engenders in the Duchess of Malfi the desire to actually be 'a man' (*Duchess of Malfi*, III.v.116), which finally comes true when, in the face of death, she decides to put off her 'last woman's fault' (IV.ii.226). Vittoria Corombona, eventually, manages to formulate the conceptual trap which early modern woman falls prey to:

> Humbly thus,
> Thus low, to the most worthy and respected
> Lieger ambassadors, my modesty
> And womanhood I tender; but withal
> So entangled in a cursed accusation
> That my defence of force like Perseus,
> Must personate masculine virtue.
>
> (*The White Devil,* III.ii.129–35)

In order to assert herself, she is forced by men to act as a man and is then condemned. Early modern woman is thus caught in a double-bind between feminine, defenceless speech, 'woman's poor revenge / Which dwells but in the tongue' (III.ii.282–3), and masculine, forbidden action; between inefficient '[f]eminine arguments' (V.vi.67) and transgressive 'masculine virtue' (V.vi.243). Female existence finds itself placed on the margins of the male subject. 'Who am I?', the Duchess of Malfi asks the seemingly mad Bosola (*Duchess of Malfi,* IV.ii.123), and the answer seems to come from Brachiano in *The White Devil:* 'Woman to man / Is either a god or a wolf' (IV.ii.91–2).

Early modern theatre was an instrument of 'probing [...] the processes of signification that served to legitimate power as authority';[49] it constituted a place of vital semantic exchange before becoming re-monologised again in the Restoration period. In staging Italianate constructions of temptation and desire, English Renaissance drama addressed and probed virulent social, moral and gender-related problems of early modern English society: the problem of impression management, the problem of appearance and reality, the problem of sin, the problem of modern subjectivity. The early modern English myth of Italy ideally lent itself to the semantics needed for the representation of such issues. Italy was, therefore, a privileged site for creating alternative worlds that could be used for such discussion without being too close to English reality. English Italies reveal an 'Italian' England.

Notes

1 Thomas Nashe, *The Unfortunate Traveller and other Works*, ed. J. B. Steane, Harmondsworth, 1985, p. 345.
2 Roger Ascham, *The Schoolmaster*, ed. L. V. Ryan, Ithaca, N.Y., 1967, p. 66.
3 Nashe, *Unfortunate Traveller*, p. 289.
4 Mario Praz, 'Shakespeare's Italy', *Shakespeare Survey*, 7, 1954, pp. 95–106 (p. 96).
5 Nashe, *Unfortunate Traveller*, p. 289.
6 G. K. Hunter, 'English folly and Italian vice: the moral landscape of John Marston', *Jacobean Theatre*, eds J. R. Brown and B. Harris, Stratford-upon-Avon Studies 1, London, 1960, pp. 85–111, p. 94.
7 Hunter, 'English folly', p. 95.
8 For an application of the theory of possible worlds to drama and the world-creating aspects of dramatic texts see Keir Elam, *The Semiotics of Theatre and Drama*, New Accents, London, 1980, pp. 99ff.
9 Manfred Pfister, *The Theory and Analysis of Drama*, trans. J. Halliday, European Studies in English Literature, Cambridge, 1988, p. 260.
10 Mario Praz, 'L'Italia di Ben Jonson', *Machiavelli in Inghilterra ed altri saggi*, Rome, 1942, p. 173.
11 For a development of this idea see N. Goodman, *Ways of Worldmaking*, Indianapolis, 1978, pp. 10ff.
12 For the various functions of the Vice in medieval and Renaissance drama see Robert Weimann, *Shakespeare and the Popular Tradition in the Theater*, ed. R. Schwartz, Baltimore, 1978, pp. 151ff.
13 For the idea of myth as secondary (connotative) signification see Roland Barthes, *Mythologies*, trans. A. Lavers, London, 1972, pp. 109ff.
14 Catherine Belsey, *Critical Practice*, New Accents, London, 1980, pp. 47ff.
15 The phrase is E. H. Gombrich's, see *Art and Illusion: a Study in the Psychology of Pictorial Representation*, Oxford, 1988, pp. 153ff. For an historical application of Gombrich's theory of perception see Peter Burke, *The Historical Anthropology of Early Modern Italy*, Cambridge, 1987.
16 Hunter, 'English folly', pp. 94ff.
17 W. Iser, *The Act of Reading: a Theory of Aesthetic Response*, Baltimore, 1978, p. 83.
18 Iser, *Act of Reading*, p. 85.
19 Michael Hattaway, 'Drama and society', *The Cambridge Companion to English Renaissance Drama*, eds A. R. Braunmuller and Michael Hattaway, Cambridge, 1990, pp. 91–126 (p. 95).
20 Weimann, *Popular Tradition*, p. 154.
21 For the distinction between a world-creating dramatic discourse and a performance-oriented theatrical discourse see Elam, *Semiotics*, pp. 2ff.; for the idea of ambivalence see also Weimann, *Popular Tradition*, pp. 154ff.: 'The Vice, in coping with the inherent tensions between terror and laughter, completely offset the structural balance of the original homiletic allegory of the Psychomachia.'
22 Weimann, *Popular Tradition*, p. 156.
23 Weimann, *Popular Tradition*, p. 160.

24 E. Goffman, *The Presentation of Self in Everyday Life*, Harmondsworth, 1976, pp. 203ff.

25 This term refers to Torquato Accetto, *Della dissimulazione onesta* (1641) where it is used in a positive sense as a principle of interactional politeness which collides with the Protestant idea of transactional sincerity; for further details see Burke, *Historical Anthropology*; for the distinction between interactional and transactional communication see G. Brown and G. Yule, *Discourse Analysis*, Cambridge Textbooks in Linguistics, Cambridge, 1983, pp. 1ff. and, in more general terms, P. Watzlawick, J. H. Beavin and D. D. Jackson, *Pragmatics of Human Communication: a Study of Interactional Patterns, Pathologies, and Paradoxes*, New York, 1967.

26 D. Callaghan, *Woman and Gender in Renaissance Tragedy: a Study of 'King Lear', 'Othello', 'The Duchess of Malfi' and 'The White Devil'*, London, 1989, p. 1.

27 All citations are to William Shakespeare, *Othello*, ed. M. R. Ridley, The Arden Shakespeare, London, 1975, and to John Webster, *Three Plays: 'The White Devil', 'The Duchess of Malfi' and 'The Devil's Law-Case'*, ed. D. C. Gunby, Harmondsworth, 1972.

28 For the use of this term, first employed by V. Titone, see Burke, *Historical Anthropology*.

29 For the notion of 'face' in interpersonal behaviour see P. Brown and S. C. Levinson, *Politeness: Some Universals in Language Usage*, Studies in Interactional Sociolinguistics 4, Cambridge, 1987, pp. 13ff. and 61ff.

30 For a systematic presentation of dramatic characterisation techniques and the terminological distinction between 'figural' and 'authorial' characterisation see Pfister, *Drama*, pp. 183ff.

31 Elam, *Semiotics*, p. 132.

32 The term 'villain' is used several times in the play for Iago, the most explicit lines perhaps being those in which Emilia unwittingly describes her husband with foreboding accuracy: 'I will be hang'd, if some eternal villain, / Some busy and insinuating rogue, / Some cogging, cozening slave, to get some office, / Have not devis'd this slander' (IV.ii.132–5).

33 E. M. W. Tillyard, *The Elizabethan World Picture*, Harmondsworth, 1978, p. 13.

34 For worlds-within-the-world and characters' sub-worlds see Elam, *Semiotics*, pp. 114ff.

35 A. Serpieri, 'Reading the signs: towards a semiotics of Shakespearean drama', in *Alternative Shakespeares*, ed. John Drakakis, New Accents, London, 1985, pp. 119–43 (pp. 136 and 138).

36 Serpieri, 'Reading the signs', p. 138.

37 Catherine Belsey, *The Subject of Tragedy: Identity and Difference in Renaissance Drama*, London, 1991, p. 9.

38 Serpieri, 'Reading the signs', p. 137.

39 Ania Loomba, *Gender, Race, Renaissance Drama*, Cultural Politics, Manchester, 1989, p. 107.

40 Callaghan, *Woman and Gender*, p. 140.

41 Jonathan Dollimore, *Radical Tragedy: Religion, Ideology and Power in the Drama of Shakespeare and his Contemporaries*, London, second edition, 1989, p. 231.

42 Callaghan, *Woman and Gender*, p. 52.
43 Callaghan, *Woman and Gender*, p. 55.
44 Dollimore, *Radical Tragedy*, p. 239.
45 Callaghan, *Woman and Gender*, p. 140.
46 Callaghan, *Woman and Gender*, p. 59.
47 Callaghan, *Woman and Gender*, p. 1.
48 Significantly, Bosola has to semanticise all mankind as 'womanish' (V.v.102) in order to save his own manhood, somewhere else.
49 Hattaway, 'Drama and society', p. 96.

The fictional world of *Romeo and Juliet*: cultural connotations of an Italian setting

Angela Locatelli

In this chapter I shall be looking at the problem of 'Shakespeare's Italy' from the point of view of the 'semiotic theory of culture' proposed by Yuri M. Lotman.[1] In particular, I shall be exploring the epistemic dimensions and the ideological aspects that are implicit in Shakespeare's settings, but which have rarely been made explicit.

I shall also be taking Shakespeare's depiction of Verona and Mantua in *Romeo and Juliet* as a model of cultural exchange. Specifically, I wish to provide a definition of Verona and Mantua by looking at the setting of *Romeo and Juliet* as a cultural space, a space in which meanings are created, values established, and both are constantly negotiated, inside and outside the space itself.

I believe that representing another country is always a complex act of 'mirroring' one's culture in another, and that 'the exotic', a term which applies to Italy when perceived through Elizabethan eyes,[2] far from being a mere escapist category, can be seen as a means of confronting anthropological 'otherness', or forms of cultural difference.

It is against this background that describing and referring to another country becomes an act loaded with ideological nuances, rather than a mere act of 'curiosity', or an amused and 'neutral' indulgence in the exotic.

Moreover, the dramatist's choice to play on both the fantastic and the realistic lies at the root of his art and at the root of our enjoyment of it. The power of transcending reference, or, rather, the social construction of reference, is omnipresent in cultural exchange and is extremely relevant in literature, as well as in the shaping of any world picture.[3] That is why the habitual lack of physical detail or cartographical correctness in Shakespeare does not seem to harm, at

least from the point of view of rhetorical persuasiveness, the characterisation of Shakespeare's towns and cities. They do not need to be
'true' as long as they are 'believable'; but, of course, verisimilitude is
intrinsically a matter of cultural agreement, a semiotic convention.[4]

I have chosen, therefore, to speak of a 'fictional world' and not of
'setting' because I wish to foreground the fictional rather than the
referential dimension of dramatic settings. It is an obvious, but
sometimes disregarded, fact, that the knowledge provided by poetry
and drama is not of the same sort as that provided by maps, and
therefore the reconstruction of the minutest details of topography can
be of little relevance when assessing the truth of a play.

As Tony Tanner aptly remarked in the 'Series Preface' to his
Venice Desired:

> A city's representational life is quite different from its historic,
> economic, demographic, cartographic, political, ceremonial, cultural
> life, though of course it may draw on and indirectly reflect or
> transcribe elements from all of these dimensions of the city's
> existence.[5]

If we look at a city through a text, that is at an image of it, in a
painting, a play or a poem, what comes into play is both the object
depicted and the hand of the 'painter'. They are of equal importance,
as framing in photography daily teaches us.

The strategies by which descriptions of a city 'reflect' or
'transcribe' one or more of a city's dimensions are one of the proper
concerns of the semiotics of culture, and will be the main object of my
discussion. I believe that these strategies are often based on the
creation of cultural analogies, as well as on recurring processes such as
renaming, mythmaking and stereotypic labelling.

Each culture represents itself by idealising itself, and by asking
its members to 'read' facts in a certain key. This process of 'self-
fashioning', to use Stephen Greenblatt's terminology,[6] has been richly
dealt with in Lotman's 'semiotic theory of culture'.

Different mechanisms have thus emerged which are responsible
for the effectiveness of self-representation. Two of these mechanisms,
'renaming'[7] and mythmaking, seem to me to figure prominently, not
only in Shakespeare's 'description' of Italy but in the 'geography' of the
entire canon.

More precisely, 'renaming' consists in attributing the name of a
glorious city to a less known city, thus endowing it with the same

positive qualities. The lesser place automatically inherits the prestigious qualifications of the famous site. In other words, if Rome is universally known as 'the eternal city' and I call London Britain's Rome I am implying that London has achieved Rome's eternal fame.

This is exactly what happens for Shakespeare's London, the city which is turned into Venice, as well as several other glorious ancient places, through a series of well chosen attributes and through the many analogies, both implicit and explicit, that the dramatist creates between London and Venice, Verona or Milan.

London is keenly creating its own myth in the Elizabethan age because this is the period in which it is fast moving, beyond national relevance, towards international recognition. By appropriating certain myths, London is striving to acquire a new status. It is trying to be recognised both as capital and as a city of world significance. Being the seat of the court, it is also defining itself symbolically as the centre of the State,[8] as demonstrated by the analogy between ancient Rome and London in the Roman plays. The equation with contemporary Rome remained more problematic, given the strong antagonistic connotations of 'Popish' rule within Elizabethan England.

I believe that analogies powerfully fill the semiotic void in the Shakespearean canon. Analogies provide meanings to social and political realities, hitherto 'unreadable' because 'unread'. This happens not only in geography but also in certain uses of history, particularly when history is perceived as exemplary and the past is called upon to 'explain', clarify, and justify current events.

Shakespeare builds the myth of London by borrowing the history and the mythology of Venice, Verona, Mantua and other foreign cities. Significantly he disregards relevant 'facts' like the conspicuous relationship between the Mantua of the Gonzaga and the English court, because fiction is all he needs to empower both his tale and the city it celebrates.

Moreover, he 'describes' Verona but he 'means' Stratford or London. I would also suggest that every setting, no matter how distant and exotic, is meant as analogous (whether a similarity or opposition is created) to London, and its strangeness is given as the equivalent of London's own booming diversity, a diversity which was absolutely necessary to its acquisition of the status of 'capital' or primarily significant 'locus' in the state.

In *Romeo and Juliet* the dramatist writes about Verona but signals to his audience that London is the implied referent. Recent studies, such as David C. McPherson's *Shakespeare, Jonson and the Myth of Venice*,[9] or Murray J. Levith's *Shakespeare's Italian Settings and Plays*,[10] provide ample documentation on Shakespeare's settings and thus corroborate, from another angle, my theoretical observations on 'mythmaking' and 'renaming' in Shakespeare's plays.

Shakespeare's geography seems to me to be very far from documentary, but can be even more 'convincing' than an actual travel journal. This happens because Shakespeare's geography unfolds along a double axis: it lingers between information and utopia, social criticism and idealisation, and above all between description and prescription. Just like the greatest satirists, Shakespeare often monitors home customs and behaviour, but pretends to be talking about the remotest realities in time and space.

We must stress the specific fictional nature of Shakespearean 'histories' and 'geographies' as we realise that mythmaking means that *via* his exotic lands 'Shakespeare creates England'.[11]

Another mechanism which very effectively promotes national identity is stereotypic labelling. It probably begins with an original cultural 'split', with the dichotomy of 'us' and 'them'. As Lotman puts it:

> Every culture begins by dividing the world into 'its own' internal space and 'their' external space. How such binary division is interpreted depends on the typology of the culture. [...] This space is 'ours', 'my own', it is 'cultured', 'safe', 'harmoniously organized', and so on. By contrast 'their space' is 'other', 'hostile', 'dangerous', 'chaotic'.[12]

This dichotomy is central to the 'epistemic double' foregrounded in Puritan theology and in Elizabethan culture.[13] Its power in the elaboration of a national identity makes the use of stereotypes a frequent strategy to meet 'otherness', as non-European characters in the Shakespearean canon amply demonstrate. Caliban comes to mind, as well as the doctrine of 'the white man's burden', and a parallel may be drawn, as far as stereotypic labelling is concerned, between the situations and ideology of Elizabethan colonisation and Victorian imperialism. In both instances stereotypes favour the namer's claim to 'superiority' over the named, and they justify oppression and exploitation.

Stereotypes are also the main road to demonisation and scapegoating mechanisms.[14] The scapegoat is the 'unabsorbed other' that is represented as radically different, while being, on the contrary, a vital part of a given society and culture. Othello, Shylock, Poor Tom,

Caliban, Joan of Arc, Ophelia, but also, to some extent, Tybalt, Romeo and Cleopatra embody the various forms of the unabsorbed and irreducible 'other' in the Elizabethan context. They are practically synonyms of the foreign, the poor, the mad, the heretic, the woman, the 'excessive' character. Lotman fully confirms this proposition:

> the barbarian is created by civilization and needs it as much as it needs him. The extreme edge of the semiosphere is a place of incessant dialogue. *No matter whether the given culture sees the 'barbarian' as saviour or enemy*, as a healthy moral influence or as a perverted cannibal, *it is dealing with a construct made in its own inverted image.* It is entirely to be expected, for instance, that the rational positivistic society of nineteenth century Europe should create images of the 'pre-logical savage', or of the irrational subconscious as anti-spheres lying beyond the rational space of culture.[15]

Lotman puts forward some considerations which may help us in answering a question that is vitally related to Shakespeare's perception of foreign lands like Italy: 'What is the voyage for him, and for his contemporaries?'

> In the medieval thought system earthly life itself was a value category in opposition to heavenly life. So the earth as a geographical concept [...] acquired a religious and moral significance which is unknown to modern geography. [...] Movement in geographical space meant moving in the vertical scale of religious and moral values.[16]
>
> Notions of moral value and of locality fuse together: places have a moral significance and morals have a localized significance. Geography becomes a kind of ethics.[17]

Clearly, the voyage for Shakespeare is no longer a pilgrimage, at least not in a religious sense; the grand tour of Elizabethan education is a type of cultural lay pilgrimage, but the pilgrims are rapidly losing their devotion. The central aspect of the tour to Italy is a paradoxical acquisition, in Roger Ascham's opinion, of a strange mixture of atheism and pompous ritual.[18] No longer a pilgrimage, the tour becomes an earthly experience and provides a pretext to compare home values to foreign values.

Geography is still symbolic, and renaming it just one aspect of this symbolism, since, in the age of discoveries, geography is charged ideologically, albeit no longer according to a religious perspective. The foreign country is perceived primarily as an open space, a space to explore and to conquer, or as the space of 'the other', from whom to differentiate or perhaps even to 'copy', but always clearly to distance oneself from. The most fascinating voyage for Shakespeare and his contemporaries is the exploration of the New World and the marine adventure. This voyage is a pragmatic (as opposed to religious) way of 'chartering' the world, in the sense of both mapping out and colonising it. 'Writing' the world and 'conquering' the world are one and the same thing for an age where indeed the Baconian adage 'knowledge is power' 'made sense'.

Given this theoretical frame, we may now test its significance in a closer analysis of *Romeo and Juliet*. As we explore the connotations of the fictional world of the play, we register an ambivalent attitude throughout the text, an attitude which could be defined as an act both of praising contempt and of disparaging admiration. Far from being an ephemeral, and subjectively psychological, Shakespearian mood, this approach is indeed typical of a very long tradition and of a widespread cultural stance. We should in fact recall that among the premises that have shaped, up to our times, the English perception of Italian culture, we find a fairly constant mixed attitude of alternating praise and execration, together with the need to establish a clear sense of difference between these two worlds. Whether the difference between English and Italian culture was felt as corrupting – as in the case of Roger Ascham, Thomas Nashe, John Webster, the writers of Gothic novels, a large number of Victorians – or liberating – as in the case of Fynes Moryson, Sir John Harington, Ruskin, E. M. Forster or D. H. Lawrence – it was invariably 'explained' as an expression of the excessively 'hot' temperament of a 'primitive' race.

The same point of view is foregrounded in *Romeo and Juliet*. Several instances of unruly pride and childish rage are represented in the play, and violence is the attribute that primarily connotes city life in Verona.

The Prologue is one of the most explicit statements in the play on the close links between the 'star–cross'd lovers' and their fellow citizens' 'civil hands unclean'. The effect of the Prologue is that the innocent lovers' doom is explained at the outset as a consequence of the general mood of civil unrest among the citizens of 'fair Verona', a mood which includes 'parents' rage', 'parents' strife', and an 'ancient grudge':

Chorus: Two house holds, both alike in dignity,
  In fair Verona, where we lay our scene,
  From ancient grudge break to new mutiny,
  Where civil blood makes civil hands unclean,
  From forth the fatal loins of these two foes
  A pair of star-cross'd lovers take their life;
  Whose misadventur'd piteous overthrows
  Do with their death bury their parents' strife.
  The fearful passage of their death-mark'd love,
  And the continuance of their parents' rage,
  Which, but their children's end, nought could remove
  Is now the two hours' traffic of our stage;
  The which if you with patient ears attend,
  What here shall miss, our toil shall strive to mend.

                    (Prologue, 1–14)

The adjective 'fair' may even be ironic, given its presence in the context of the many negatively charged lexical items denoting strife and unrest. 'Fair' indeed states and contributes to create a powerful ambivalence towards this world. Verona may be fair, but who would feel safe there?

Whether or not we are to think of the Chorus as Shakespeare's authorial voice, we nevertheless notice that 'fair' and 'unclean' are subtly counterbalanced in the very first 'description' of this fictional world. This duplicity continues to mark the qualifications of Shakespeare's Italy in *Romeo and Juliet.*

The Prince's early appeal to social goodwill (I.i) is also significant in so far as it portrays a strong and authoritarian figure, trying to control, even at the cost of torture and death, his riotous subjects:

  Rebellious subjects, enemies to peace,
  Profaners of this neighbour-stained steel, –
  Will they not hear? What ho! you men, you beasts,
  That quench the fire of your pernicious rage
  With purple fountains issuing from your veins,
  On pain of torture, from those bloody hands
  Throw your mis-tempered weapons to the ground,
  And hear the sentence of your moved prince.
  Three civil brawls, bred of an airy word,
  By thee, old Capulet, and Montague,
  Have thrice disturb'd the quiet of our streets,

And made Verona's ancient citizens
Cast by their grave beseeming ornaments,
To wield old partisans, in hands as old,
Canker'd with peace, to part your canker'd hate.
If ever you disturb our streets again
Your lives shall pay the forfeit of the peace.

(I.i.87–103)

The opening scene of Act III, where 'hot' becomes a keyword, makes explicit reference to the themes of pride, of boasting, and of a general impatience and mistrust. In the dialogue between Benvolio and Mercutio the Italian stereotype turns into a self-fulfilling prophecy of violence,[19] with the entrance of Tybalt:

> *Benvolio*: I pray thee, good Mercutio, let's retire:
> The day is hot, *the Capulets abroad.*
> *And, if we meet, we shall not 'scape a brawl;*[20]
> For now, these hot days, is the mad blood stirring.
> *Mercutio*: Thou art like one of those fellows that when he enters the confines of a tavern claps me his sword upon the table and says 'God send me no need of thee!' and by the operation of the second cup draws him on the drawer, when indeed there's no need.
> *Benvolio*: Am I like such a fellow?
> *Mercutio*: Come, come, thou art as hot a Jack in thy mood as any in Italy; and as soon moved to be moody, and as soon moody to be moved.

(III.i.1–14)

The conversation continues, along the same pattern, explaining that Italians need no reasons to enter a quarrel, since almost any flimsy motive more than suffices for their choleric temperament.

Mercutio's previous 'description' of Tybalt in Act II is almost a caricature, but it introduces another attribute of the Italian character: excessive refinement. It closely recalls Ascham's contempt for the sophisticated manners of the Italian(ate) gentleman as a 'diabolo incarnato':

> *Mercutio*: More than prince of cats, I can tell you. O! he is the courageous captain of compliments. He fights as you sing prick-songs, keeps time, distance, and proportion; rests me his minim rest, one, two, and the third in your bosom; the very butcher of a silk button, a duellist, a duellist; a gentleman of the very first house, of the first and second cause. Ah! the immortal passado! the punto reverso! the hay!

Benevolio: The what?

Mercutio: The pox of such antick, lisping affecting fantasticoes, these new tuners of accents! – 'By Jesu, a very good blade! – A very tall man! a very good whore' – Why, is not this a lamentable thing, grandsire, that we should be thus afflicted with these strange flies, these fashion-mongers, these *pardonnez-moi*, who stand so much on the new form that they cannot sit at ease on the old bench? O, their *bons*, their *bons*!   (II.iv.20–38)

Despite the obvious mistaking of French idioms for Italian ones in Mercutio's punning – a mistake which is always typical of inaccurate and disrespectful labelling in cultural contacts – the down-playing of foreign refinement remains clear in Mercutio's speech. The allusion to the 'fantasticoes', in his disparaging portrait of Tybalt, is yet another attribution endorsing Italian weakness of character and unreliability. It is interesting to notice that 'fantasticoes' relates Shakespeare's play to other contemporary texts: to Sir Philip Sidney's *Apologie for Poetrie* (1581), and more specifically to George Puttenham's *Arte of English Poesie* (1589):

For as well Poets and Poesie are despised, & the name become of honorable infamous, subject to scorne and derision [...] for commonly who is studious in th'Arte or shewes him selfe excellent in it, *they call him in disdayne a phantasticall; and a light head or phantasticall man (by conuersion) they call a Poet.*[21]

In order to 'defend' Poets, Puttenham · proceeds to draw a distinction between 'phantasticoes' and 'euphantasioti', between 'disordered phantasies' and correct 'iudgement'. 'Euphantasioti' are those 'in whose exercises the inuentive part is most employed and is to the sound and true judgment of man most needful'.[22]

Sidney had drawn a similar opposition in his *Apologie for Poetrie*, where 'eikastike' and 'phantastike' correspond to Puttenham's 'euphantasioti' and 'phantasticall': 'Mans wit may make Poesie (which should be Eikastike, which some learned have defined, figuring foorth good things) to be Phantastike: which doth contrariwise, infect the fancie with unworthy objects.'[23] Puttenham's distinction, as well as that of Sidney (who was acquainted with the works of Minturno, Scaliger and Castelvetro), derives from Mazzoni and Tasso, and clearly draws its water from the well of the debate on Aristotle's *Rhetorica* and *Poetica*, which was playing such a prominent part in Renaissance Italian culture.[24]

Since we are dealing with *imitatio* of the works of the rival culture, let us mention both Petrarch and the *novelle* and notice the way in which they were 'mirrored' in English culture. Mario Praz has shown the relevance of Petrarchan rhetoric in *Romeo and Juliet* and of several 'traditional *concetti*' in Romeo's passionate speeches.[25] In terms of stereotypic labelling such rhetoric, and especially Romeo's frequent recourse to oxymoron, make him as much of a stock character as Tybalt. The two most 'valiant' Italian youths in the play are both impulsive and ruled by passion: Romeo is the emphatic and shallow 'Latin-lover', Tybalt is the 'lusty', 'raging', 'Latin-hater'.

As we have seen, 'hot' is one of the attributes which are foregrounded in *Romeo and Juliet* when the Italian temper is defined. Rage seems to be a dominant mood, choler a national humour, together with a fondness for duelling and great ability in this skill, which translates into the notorious brawls and rivalry that mar the life of the citizens of Verona.

Even if this recalls the conflicts of our own metropolitan life, we are with Shakespeare quite distant from the sly and deceitful politics of the Italian courts of Jacobean drama. Instead of a 'white devil' here we have a show of princely authority invoked as the remedy to social unrest and dissolution. It is the familiar Shakespearean ideology of the histories, implying that a tyrant is better than civil war.

The operation of 'renaming' is apparent: the peace of Verona streets stands for the peace of London streets, the fear that 'airy words' would provoke murder rather than mere disputes must have seemed 'real' to many Elizabethans living at a time of high ideological tension.

Luigi da Porto's *Historia novellamente ritrovata di due nobili amanti* (1530) traces the parental feud in *Romeo and Juliet* back to the rule of Bartolomeo della Scala in 1302, and thus partly confirms the picture of a violent Verona. His *novella* travelled a long way:

> from Italy across the Alps to England – over a period of six decades [...] From its composition by da Porto to the English translations of the 1560s by Arthur Brooke and William Painter, it arranged the same characters, situations, and events in the same order. Allusions to the story in England between 1567 and 1595 reveal that this plot circulated unchanged among the Elizabethans.[26]

It may be worth comparing the fictional world of Shakespeare, as it is outlined in the Prologue to *Romeo and Juliet*, with Arthur Brooke's 'description' of Verona:

There is beyonde the Alps, a towne of auncient fame
Whose bright renoune yet shineth cleare, Verona men it name,
Bylt in a happy time, bylt on a fertile soyle,
Maynteined by the heavenly fates, and by the townish toyle.
The fruitfull hilles above, the pleasant vales below,
The silver streame with chanell depe, that through the towne
    doth flow,
The store of springes that serve for use, and eke for ease
And other moe commodities which profite may and please,
Eke many certaine signes of thinges betyde of olde,
To fyll the hungry eyes of those that curiously beholde
Doe make this towne to be preferde above the rest
Of Lumbard townes, or at least compared with the best.[27]

Shakespeare's emphasis on 'civil blood' is not confirmed in Brooke's 'description'. Fame, prosperity, laboriousness and the felicity of Verona's geographical location are foregrounded instead. 'Auncient fame', 'bright renoune', 'a fertile soyle', the 'heavenly fates', the 'townish toyle' are, not surprisingly, the same elements that English travellers of the age were to notice and note in their reports. The atmosphere of Lombardy and the Veneto regions seemed idyllic and hospitable to the English travellers of the age of Shakespeare. A famous first-hand laudatory report is that of Coryat, who also explicitly compared Mantua to London.[28]

In view of this what is even more striking in Shakespeare's setting is the lack of specific geographical detail and the emphasis on city violence. The dramatist seems totally uninterested in physical geography and instead prefers history, or what we could call anthropic geography. And yet he mentions 'civil hands unclean', but not the 'townish toyle', which could become an exemplary virtue for English audiences, or could be recognised by them as an asset in both rural and city life at home.

Speculation as to Shakespeare's actual visit to Mantua in 1593, with the Earl of Southampton, is still inconclusive, as well as his actual sight of Giulio Romano's famous frescos there.[29] Shakespeare never mentions the Palazzo Ducale, the Palazzo del Capitano, the Domus Magna, the Castle of San Giorgio and the Basiliche of Santa Barbara and Sant'Andrea. He ignores the important waterways linking the town to the Adriatic and simply sets the Mantua scene in the obscure apothecary shop, where Romeo buys the poison. Mantua was renowned for being the birthplace of Virgil and the home of Baldassare

Castiglione and many other accomplished courtiers. Between 1627 and 1628 Charles I sent Daniel Nys to Mantua in order to examine the art gallery of the Gonzaga, in view of buying it: acquiring such treasure would 'attract the eyes and envies of the major European governments'.[30] The Italian historian Luzio tells us that in 1437, Henry VI had even given the first marquis Gianfrancesco Gonzaga the permission to confer the Lancastrian collar on fifty noble knights.[31] Later 'the common love of horses' strengthened the ties between Henry VIII and Francesco and Federico Gonzaga. How could Shakespeare simply ignore this, had he been there?

I am not saying that it is essential for Shakespeare to mention specific aspects of what would have been his visit to the region, including, for example, the obviously important Roman amphitheatre in Verona, which is alluded to by Fynes Moryson;[32] nor do I believe that the complete lack of detail as to the splendours of the Gonzaga palaces in Mantua, to which Coryat makes enthusiastic reference, seriously undermines the rhetorical effectiveness of Shakespeare's 'description'.

As I have said, the credibility of a dramatist does not depend on factual evidence: it is a matter of rhetorical verisimilitude. As long as the fictional world of the artist has internal cohesion and coherence, it is bound to be accepted by the audience. Its 'reality' is determined by its 'credibility', and not the other way around. That is why Italy, or any other location in the canon, is primarily (if not exclusively) fictional and as such beyond the need of verification. If we understand that Shakespeare was 'textualising' these towns, and how and for what purposes, the relevance of the actual truth of his visit to Mantua with the Earl of Southampton becomes secondary. Incidentally, the Earl of Southampton's claim to be a descendant of the Montagues[33] reinforces the reading of the complete identification of the English nobility with the Italian aristocracy, as well as the analogy between Italy and England in terms of mythmaking.

We can appreciate the correspondence of some elements in *Romeo and Juliet* with 'factual truth', and enjoy the masked ball at the Capulets' (I.iv) together with the allusion to the custom of masked balls at Carnival made by Moryson. Similarly the pestilence that delays 'barefoot brother' John (V.ii) and prevents him from delivering Friar Laurence's message to Romeo does reflect a historical situation in vivid detail. Murray Levith remarks that the family tomb of the Capulets corresponds to one of Coryat's observations on Italian burial customs.[34]

However, the dramatist is not bound to geographical, cartographic or even historical correctness. Whether he acknowledges it or not, ideology or taste determines his connotations of people and places, and connotations in art are much more important than in ordinary speech, where denotations are more relevant.

Having said this, the connotations of Friar Laurence and Brother John are worth noticing, mostly because they contradict a prevailing Elizabethan qualification of the monasteries as seats of corruption, and possibly because they confirm, at least in *Romeo and Juliet*, Shakespeare's philo-Catholic feelings. Friar Laurence is iconographically convincing, in his knowledge of medicinal plants; his Christian–Stoic posture greatly ennobles him, as well as his love of balance and his quiet temper in a city that is full of hasty and overbold action. Friar Laurence and Brother John's readiness to give help and advice must be noticed as relevant positive connotations attributed to them by the dramatist. And yet the unfortunate mishap of the undelivered letter is caused by clearly charitable and generous intentions. The fact that Brother John is devoted to 'visiting the sick' is ultimately the cause of the fatal delay.

This shows a significant ambivalence, a twofold attitude that generally marks Shakespearean connotations of the fictional worlds of Verona and Mantua. Favourable qualifications are usually overshadowed by negative ones, whereas the negative ones clearly remain. In *Romeo and Juliet* elegance is portrayed as affectation, fantasy as lightheadedness, duelling skills are attributed to 'hot' temperaments, tenacity becomes stubbornness, and declarations of love prove a childish prattle or ridiculous bellowing. 'Fighting by the book of arithmetic', as Mercutio remarks, is deemed not a valuable skill but a display of bragging affectation. Sidney's *sprezzatura* comes to mind, in contrast to Tybalt's cynical vein.

Ambivalence, then, is the main tone of the Italian qualifications on the Shakespearean stage: admiration and depreciation go hand in hand.

Are we to detect in this ambivalence a sign of the cultural competition between Elizabethan England and Italy? A touch of envy prevails, even in this 'romantic' play, which undoubtedly sounds full of praise for Italy if compared to the spite that is expressed in the lurid settings of Jacobean drama. This explains the 'Italian tone' as well as the 'Englishness' of the play, the keen interest and the manifest contempt towards Italy throughout the Elizabethan age.

Shakespeare 'records' the shift in attitude, the movement from praise and *imitatio* to rivalry and *vituperatio*, which is evident in the emblematic difference between the enthusiasm for Italian culture of the early humanists and the English scholars who had studied in Italy, including Thomas Linacre, John Cheke, Thomas Hoby, William Thomas, Sir Philip Sidney, Edward de Vere, Robert Toft, Gabriel Harvey, Sir John Harington, and the horrified contempt of Roger Ascham, Thomas Nashe, but also of Kyd, Tourneur, Middleton, Marston, Dekker and Webster.[35]

In Shakespeare we perceive the coexistence of all the elements of a specific cultural tension. We find a basic identification (London as Venice) as well as a perplexed and critical distancing (towards Verona).

The duplicity of the attributes in *Romeo and Juliet*, where when a favourable trait is described an unfavourable trait is connoted, signals the dominant mood of cultural *imitatio* in terms of a 'mirroring' and a differentiating. This is not just Shakespeare's approach in this play; it is a widespread outlook in his own age, when imitating the Italians.

Notes

1 Yuri M. Lotman, *Universe of the Mind: a Semiotic Theory of Culture*, trans. Ann Shukman, Bloomington and Indianapolis, 1990, pp. 123–204.

2 The Elizabethan and Jacobean perception of Italy as an 'exotic' country has been illustrated in: L. A. Sells, *The Italian Influence in English Poetry: from Chaucer to Southwell*, London, 1955, pp. 82–102; G. H. McWilliam, *Shakespeare's Italy Revisited*, Leicester, 1974, pp. 3–24; K. R. Bartlett, 'The strangeness of strangers': English impressions of Italy in the sixteenth century', *Quaderni d'italianistica*, 1, 1980, pp. 46–63; S. Rossi and D. Savoia (eds), *Italy and the English Renaissance*, Milan, 1989, pp. 7–24.

3 M. Pagnini, *The Pragmatics of Literature*, trans. N. Jones-Henry, Bloomington, Ind., 1987, pp. 94–107.

4 For a discussion of literary 'verisimilitude', see my *Una coscienza non tutta per sè: Studio sul romanzo dello 'Stream-of-consciousness'*, Bologna, 1983 pp. 13–36.

5 Tony Tanner, *Venice Desired*, Oxford, 1992, p. vi.

6 The process of 'self-fashioning' is defined in Stephen Greenblatt, *Renaissance Self-Fashioning: From More to Shakespeare*, Chicago and London, 1980.

7 Lotman finds examples of 'renaming' in the works of Richelieu, Mademoiselle de Scudéry and Tallemant. He says that they 'create an image of space with many levels: *real Paris turns into Athens*, through a series of conventional renamings', Y. M. Lotman, *Universe of the Mind*, p. 136 (emphasis mine).

8 Lotman suggests that: 'the city may be isomorphous with the state, and indeed personify it' ... 'Jerusalem, Rome, Moscow have all been treated as centres of their worlds'. See Y. M. Lotman, *Universe of the Mind*, p. 191.

9 David C. McPherson, *Shakespeare, Jonson, and the Myth of Venice*, Newark, London and Toronto, 1990, pp. 17–50. McPherson deals extensively with 'the Myth of Venice'. He acknowledges his debt to Franco Gaeta's 'Alcune considerazioni sul mito di Venezia', *Bibliothèque d'humanisme et Renaissance*, 23, 1961, pp. 58–75.

10 Murray J. Levith, *Shakespeare's Italian Settings and Plays*, Houndmills and London, 1989, pp. 1–11.

11 Of course, England (or better the English educational institutions) recipro-cated, by 'creating Shakespeare', as brilliantly argued recently by cultural materialism and deconstruction. The point is made, for example, in Terence Hawkes, *That Shakespeherian Rag*, London and New York, 1986; in Howard Felperin, *The Uses of the Canon*, Oxford, 1990, and in *Alternative Shakespeares*, ed. John Drakakis, London, 1985.

12 Y. M. Lotman, *Universe of the Mind*, p. 131.

13 Angela Locatelli, 'Doubles and doubling as Shakespearian difference', *Saikoanaritikaru Eibungaku Ronso/Psychoanalytical Study of English and Literature*, 15, Tokyo, 1992, pp. 20–36.

14 Angela Locatelli, *L'eloquenza e gli incantesimi: Interpretazioni Shakespeariane*, Milan, 1989, pp. 73–88 and pp. 58–70.

15 Y. M. Lotman, *Universe of the Mind* p. 142 (emphasis mine).

16 Y. M. Lotman, *Universe of the Mind*, p. 171.

17 Y. M. Lotman, *Universe of the Mind*, p. 172. Lotman goes on to say: 'How easily we metaphorize concepts such as East and West, how significant the renaming of geographical places seems to us, and so on. It is so easy to make geography symbolic' (p. 177).

18 Roger Ascham, *The Scholemaster* (1570/71), ed. Lawrence V. Ryan, Ithaca, N.Y., 1967.

19 Angela Locatelli, 'Profezia e performance in *Romeo and Juliet*', in *Romeo and Juliet: Dal testo alla scena*, ed. Mariangela Tempera, Bologna, 1986, pp. 39–50.

20 *Romeo and Juliet*, I.i.1–14 (emphasis mine).

21 George Puttenham, 'The Arte of English Poesie' (1589), quoted in O. B. Hardison, *English Literary Criticism: the Renaissance*, New York, 1963, p. 155–6 (emphasis mine).

22 George Puttenham, 'The Arte of English Poesie', p. 157.

23 Sir Philip Sidney, *An Apologie for Poetrie* (1554–86), in *The Prelude to Poetry*, ed. Ernst Rhys, London, 1970, p. 42.

24 Paul O. Kristeller, 'Rhetoric in medieval and Renaissance Culture', in *Renaissance Eloquence: Studies in Theory and Practice of Renaissance Rhetoric*, ed. J. J. Murphy, Berkeley, 1983, pp. 1–19; Joel E. Spingarn, *Literary Criticism in the Renaissance*, New York, 1963, pp. 3–106.

25 Mario Praz, *The Flaming Heart*, New York, 1958, p. 158. On the issue of Italian literary influences see also R. J. Murray, *The Influence of Italian upon English Literature during the XVI and XVII Centuries*, London, 1886, pp. 15–38 and 43–61; L. A. Sells, pp. 68–82 and 103–244.

26 Jill L. Levenson, *Romeo and Juliet*, Shakespeare in Performance, Manchester, 1987, p. 4.

27 Arthur Brooke, quoted in Murray J. Levith, *Shakespeare's Italian Settings and Plays*, pp. 43–4.

28 Thomas Coryat: 'It is most sweetly seated in respect of the marvailous sweete ayre thereof, the abundance of goodly meadows, pasture, vineyards, orchards and gardens about the city, that I thinke London which both for frequencie of people and multitude of howses doth trise exceed it, is not better furnished with gardens'; quoted in *Gazzetta di Mantova*, 318th year, complimentary copy, special edition, 1982, p. 1.

29 Mario Praz, *The Flaming Heart*, p. 162.

30 Rino Bulbarelli, 'Mantua and London: an ancient link', in *Gazzetta di Mantova*, 1982, p. 1.

31 Rino Bulbarelli, 'Mantua and London', p. 1.

32 Fynes, Moryson, *An Itinerary Containing His Ten Yeares Travell* [1617], 4 vols, Glasgow, 1907.

33 Murray J. Levith, p. 56.

34 See Murray J. Levith, pp. 54–5.

35 R. W. Dasenbrock, *Imitating the Italians: Wyatt, Spenser, Synge, Pound, Joyce*, Baltimore and London, 1991, pp. 1–84.

PART II

Themes and tradition

5

History and myth in *The Merchant of Venice**

J. R. Mulryne

1

The myth of Venice casts a long shadow over the stage history of *The Merchant of Venice*.[1] Since the beginning of the nineteenth century, directors and designers have made repeated and variously successful attempts to convey through settings and stage images the play's cultural ambience. It is natural and right that they should. No play of Shakespeare's more specifically evokes a particular location, and no location in the history of western thought has proved more rich and evocative in its associations than Venice. Directors, designers and actors are therefore faced with the necessary task of interpreting the play's local and historical allusions in the idiom of their own day; matters would be the same with any stage play that remained in the performance repertoire. Yet *The Merchant* constitutes a special case, for the myth of Venice, already a potent imaginative construct in Shakespeare's own day, has so come to dominate subsequent stagings that, while it has enriched, it has also perhaps obscured, something of the play's structure and significance.

The emotional and cultural associations of the myth have varied over time. Shakespeare's audience brought to his theatre an awareness of the heady mix of political order, mercantile success and sexual glamour that made up the popular image of Venice for the Elizabethans. The Victorians saw Venice in the afterglow of the Fall of the Republic, coloured by the poems of Wordsworth and Byron and the paintings of Turner, but suffused also with the attribution to Venice of

*Revised version of an article included in *Mélanges offerts à Marie-Thérèse Jones-Davies: L'Europe de la Renaissance. Cultures et Civilisations*, eds Jean-Claude Margolin and Marie-Madeleine Martinet, Paris, Touzot, 1988.

87

a cultural supremacy that found expression, with whatever differences, in the writings of Ruskin, Pater and Burckhardt. After the terrors of the Holocaust, we in the middle and late twentieth century have found ourselves preoccupied with justice and the Jew, while remaining conscious of the enormous cultural reputation of the Venetian Renaissance.[2]

It may be that Shakespeare saw behind the costly veneer of the myth to something closer to the actual human and cultural conditions of late sixteenth-century Venice. It may therefore help us to respond to his script more accurately, and even perhaps to re-balance our theatre productions, if we set *The Merchant* alongside some glimpses of Venetian social and cultural life such as Shakespeare might have derived for himself from reading, from travellers' tales, from his Italian acquaintances in London, or even, it has sometimes been thought, from personal travel. This undertaking is not a novel one, though I have taken advantage of some recent historical research that has more decisively than ever separated Venetian fact from Venetian myth. Nor does it, of course, offer to be exhaustive, either in regard to the play or in regard to history; and not only because of the limits of my own knowledge. As a brief discussion, the essay comments on no more than two aspects of *The Merchant* that have troubled critics and theatre practitioners: the unease that permeates the opening scenes (and may be thought to condition the temper of the piece thereafter) and the evocative, and perhaps disquieting, ambience of the Belmont of Act V, especially in its initial moments.

2

The main features of the myth of Venice, a cocktail of fact and propaganda, are well known. James S. Grubb's summary puts matters succinctly:

> the prevailing vision of Venice has been remarkably consistent and persuasive and has been transmitted substantially unaltered in guide books and histories since its full articulation in the sixteenth century: a city founded in liberty and never thereafter subjected to foreign domination; a maritime commercial economy; a unified and civic-minded patriciate [...]; a republic of wisdom and benevolence, provider of fair justice and a high degree of toleration.[3]

The myth offers us, that is, a vision of the city transfigured, an ideal counter-pastoral, with Venice as a miracle of civilisation rising from the waters, serene, stable and rich. Such a vision is unquestionably an aspect of Venice in Shakespeare's play. No less a critic and man of the theatre than Harley Granville Barker thought so, when he wrote in 1930 of Shakespeare's Venice as 'a city of royal merchants trading to the East, of Jews in their gaberdines [...] and of splendid gentlemen rustling in silks'. 'To the lucky young Englishman who could travel there,' he went on, 'Venice stood for culture and manners and the luxury of civilisation; and this − without one word of description − is how Shakespeare pictures it.'[4] We may check at the illogicality; or we may understand that Granville Barker is paying implicit tribute to the performance reality, in the audience's imagination and on stage, which exists in the play-script merely as allusion − and which for the 1920s and 1930s was supplied by post-Victorian notions of Venice, and by the art of scene and costume designers. More recently, in a brilliant essay, Philip Brockbank has found analogies between *The Merchant of Venice* and the St Ursula cycle of the Venetian painter Carpaccio, which to a large degree certify the visionary role of the city in regulating men's understanding of themselves, and of their communal life. Brockbank shows that:

> analogous principles of perspective and order are at work on our ethical imagination in certain paintings of Carpaccio and plays of Shakespeare, and that painting performed for fifteenth-century Venice some of the functions that theatre performed in sixteenth-century London and had performed in the fourth century BC for the 'crowded magnificent cities' celebrated by Sophocles.[5]

This vindication of the city, endorsed and extended as a function of Venetian Cinquecento painting in art-historical studies by David Rosand, Patricia Fortini Brown and others,[6] must strike us as a powerfully allusive presence in any full reading of Shakespeare's play.

Yet the opening speeches of the play that give us, in C. L. Barber's phrase, 'the gorgeous opulent world of the Venetian gentleman' where we find 'a ceremonial social feeling for wealth'[7] give us also a competing sense of the life of the city as fragile, anxiety-ridden and characterised by surface not substance. It is as though the city were undergoing a crisis of morale that separated behaviour from conviction. The grandeur of the Venetian merchants, the wealth of their argosies, the proud social order that functions through accepted precedence, all of these offer a composite image of great persuasiveness. It is not difficult to transpose the references into equivalents in the ceremonial court of Elizabeth: the 'pageants of the sea' which in a concise phrase interpret the sense of the whole vision, readily equate to progress entertainments and pageantry and the Elizabethan iconography of power. But there is a counter-movement too. Antonio's saddened mind is, we hear, 'tossing on the ocean', the ocean which also supports these magnificent pageants; by a device that is almost surreal, mind and attributed significance are parted. There is also, surely, more than a hint of insolence in phrases such as 'overpeer the petty traffickers', an isolating arrogance that comes between rank and merchandising, in place of the 'ceremonial social feeling' of Barber's phrase. Such hints culminate in Salerio's speech (I.i.29–36) where rocks administer to the trading ship what amounts to a respectful caress ('touching but my gentle vessel's side') only in so doing to spill the merchandise unprofitably in the sea. No visual oxymoron could be more powerful or more acutely suggestive than the image of precious silk and wild ocean, the supremely civilised and the untameable, as the spilled merchandise attempts to 'Enrobe the roaring waters with my silks'. The achievements of Venetian civilisation come to seem not merely precarious but perhaps unachievable.

Molly Mahood has discussed the ways in which the Venetian speeches 'so strangely trivialise and fictionalise the hazards of the sea trade'; the term she applies to them is 'fantasy'.[8] Her choice of phrase is surely right, for the speeches convey the sense, not of a coherently imagined vision, but of a social ideal, based on merchant enterprise, that fails to convince because its component terms are awkwardly related, even contradictory. Critics have pointed to the unsettling structure of values elsewhere in the play. Barber, for example, remarks that 'Shylock is the opposite of what the Venetians are; but at the same time he is an embodied irony, troublingly like them.'[9] The unreason of Christian behaviour towards Jews in the play, with its disquieting conflicts of value, has its source in historical circumstances; the sophistical nature of traditional arguments about usury and the Jew is well documented. But the unease that characterises this thinking historically may be rooted deeper still in conflicts within the Venetian self-image, both in reality and as *The Merchant of Venice* discloses them. Unease about the relation of the terms that in ideal circumstances made for social cohesion readily explains unreasoning aggression against outsiders. The want-wit sadness of the play's opening, so often a puzzle to critics and performers, could be thought of as stemming not from sources within the individual, but from a general crisis, a loss of morale, as the elements of a sustaining myth fall apart.

It is impossible to document in a brief essay the historical changes that seem in the real world to correspond to the play's uneasy ambience. I can only refer to professional historians, and invite the reader to explore and assess their work. There is general acceptance, it appears, that the irreversible decline of Venice as a maritime commercial power can be convincingly dated to the mid–sixteenth century and after.[10] Even if alternative investments offered a degree of compensation, losses to the Venetian economy, and self-esteem, that in the second half of the century went with failing commercial opportunities, with piracy, and with loss of influence to other, emergent, European powers, bit deep into Venetian confidence.[11] J. H. Plumb employs, it may be thought, an unfashionably emotive vocabulary when he writes that by 1550 Venice was 'still strong, still rich, still capable of sacrifice, but essentially an empire in defence, wishing for a secure isolation in which to enjoy her immoderate riches.' The city, he adds, had 'lost the future' and 'this feeling of the future lost was already pervading much of the attitude to life of Venetian men and women.'[12] The judgement, if not the terms, would meet with general agreement. Ugo Tucci narrows the frame somewhat, and brings our own concerns more sharply into focus, when he discusses the widening split in the later sixteenth century between the patrician ideal of merchant venturing, so characteristic of traditional thinking about Venetian social structures, and the bourgeois values increasingly taken to be characteristic of trade. Tucci writes that:

> The nobles' insufficient ability to assimilate the new factors which were transforming the nature of mercantile activity revealed them as feeling progressively less like merchants and more like nobles. Those of them who in the *cinquecento* did remain in the breach [as merchant venturers] kept firmly to the old mentality, even though they were trying to keep it alive in a world infused with a radically changed approach.[13]

An effort such as this to keep alive an increasingly irrelevant mentality (and one felt to be such) provides a certain recipe for unease and self-mistrust.

Tucci pursues his point in a direction which, we may think, takes

91

us even further into the world of contradictory values which *The Merchant of Venice* also embraces. 'What counts', he writes, 'is the split which has developed between the patrician and mercantile mentalities, and the growing conviction that their respective moral and behavioural rules are incompatible which has widened it.'[14] Such felt incompatibility, expressed in the play as an inexplicit conflict of values, may be thought to underline not merely the unease of Antonio and the others, but the unreason and on occasion the aggression of the play's high-bred youths. It could even be that the 'idleness' of this group in *The Merchant*, which Shakespeare finds various strategies for expressing, corresponds to what contemporaries saw as an unpleasing social phenomenon among the young Venetian patriciate. W. H. Auden, in a brilliant essay, complains of Portia as well as the young Venetians (and Jessica) as 'frivolous members of a leisure class, whose carefree life is parasitic upon the labours of others, including usurers.'[15] The terms may be jarringly modern, though arguably apt to an age of nascent capitalism, but they do evoke both something recognisable in *The Merchant of Venice* and, rather strikingly, the social circumstances which Tucci tells us came into being as Venice lost its way commercially, and, in a broad sense, culturally:

> The spectacle of the inactivity in which youth was growing up aroused ['commentators'] greatest concern; it was to this that they attributed the quarrels and turbulence which – no more seriously, perhaps, than in the good times past – were troubling them. Where trade, with structural characteristics that played so important a part in the framework of society, had been abandoned, it was replaced by the idleness of many sections of the upper class because, in effect, no new activity had been substituted for the old.[16]

For the youth of Shakespeare's Venice, or at least the most prominent of them, the quest for a golden fleece at Belmont becomes the 'new activity' which substitutes for self-indulgent lethargy. But, so far as the first scenes are concerned, the overwhelming impression is the *inactivity* of which Venetian commentators complained: the oddly unprogressive, almost plotless dramatic rhythms of the early scenes at Venice and at Belmont have frequently irritated directors and actors. Unexplained comings and goings, the depressive *ennui* of Antonio and Portia, idle chatter from Gratiano and Nerissa, inexplicable switches of focus from everyone, including the nonentities Salarino and Solanio – all this creates in an audience's mind a perplexed sense of theatrical indecision and indirection. Perhaps it is putting one's finger on the balance too overtly to express it in this way, but the scenes do appear to offer a remarkable dramatic equivalent a society such as that of late sixteenth-century Venice afflicted by an absence of positive values, and the inertia that accompanies it.

3

The unease that expresses itself so insistently in the play's Venice touches the life of Belmont also. Portia's first speech refers to a weariness that recalls Antonio's, and thereafter at many points we are conscious of the fragility, even the equivocal nature, of the rituals of order that regulate social life in Portia's world. Yet Belmont and its lady are a prize, a golden fleece for the voyaging Jason, partly because they represent a world of wealth that is alternative to anxious and risk-laden Venice. At Belmont, life is characterised by a seeming security that offers a strongly marked contrast to the competitiveness, if also the high spirits, of Venice. Its imaginative space is that of the great house, domestic though opulent, as opposed to Venetian out-of-doors business and social activity. A sense is conveyed of graciousness, or potential graciousness, of a life that is aristocratic in setting, in confidence, in tempo. When the action at Belmont moves outside in Act V, it moves into elaborate gardens where Lorenzo and Jessica exchange amorous mythologies by moonlight, where there is a sense of ease and spaciousness, and where the action is permeated by unseen music. The impression we draw of Belmont, that is, superficial as it may be, is of a leisured society based on inherited wealth, a 'beautiful mount', secure and landed, in contrast to the insecure society of Venice, uneasily dependent on, and ambivalent about, the risks of commerce and the sea.

The play's balanced opposition of Venice and Belmont parallels in a remarkable way a profound development in the cultural history of sixteenth-century Venice. 'To continue to think of Venice in the sixteenth-century as a maritime republic', writes Sir John Hale, 'illuminates neither its psychology nor its culture'.[17] As Hale and others have demonstrated, the mind of the Venetian nobility was at this period turning away from maritime affairs and commerce, and turning instead towards the pleasures and profits of life on the mainland. Though the development was partial and discontinuous, it was obvious to contemporaries:

> When the Venetian nobles and citizens had become rich, they
> wanted to celebrate their success, and live and attend and give
> themselves up to pleasure and delight and the green of the
> countryside on the mainland [...] so abandoning navigation and
> seafaring, which were more vexatious and arduous.[18]

The motives this contemporary sees for mainland living are entirely
hedonistic, but there were commercial motives too, for investment in
land offered returns generally more secure, if less spectacular, than
merchant venturing.[19] Many of the rich of Venice were drawn in; as
Brian Pullen has shown, improvement and reclamation of mainland
properties took as the century went on an increasing proportion of
Venetian capital.[20] Yet significant as the financial attractions were,
they were in a more profound way symptomatic of a change in habit
of mind, a process of cultural self-fashioning which James S. Grubb has
called 'a change in *mentalité* ... towards aristocratisation of a formerly
mercantile patriciate.'[21] In Shakespeare's play, the journey to Belmont
represents for the former merchants of Venice just such a process of
re-making, the acceptance of an aristocratic lifestyle that without
abandoning Venetian wealth contrasts in a marked way with the style
of their former existence.

The impressions of Belmont we derive from the play offer us, as
we have noted, a sense of aristocratic confidence and ease, in contrast
to Venetian anxiety. But there is a sense also of a brittleness of lifestyle
that carries with it its own anxious undertow. In particular, the mood
of Act V, with its pastoral setting, and its blend of romantic sentiment
and worldly jest, has frequently, as Molly Mahood remarks, proved
disturbing to audiences. The mythological references at the scene's
opening, to Troilus and Cressid, Thisbe, Dido, Medea and Jason, are
each weighted with references to disaster, thus compromising
Lorenzo's and Jessica's love-idyll. 'From very early in the act,' writes
Professor Mahood, 'there occur sudden quick disturbances of our
feelings, sudden almost subliminal recollections of the fear and pain of
past events.'[22] It is as though we are invited to read these moments
back into the contradictory feelings about wealth and worth earlier
scenes have dealt in. The sense of disturbance is intensified by the
unusual dramatic strategies Shakespeare employs. The rhythms of the
Lorenzo–Jessica exchange are extraordinarily relaxed; the management of space as Portia and Nerissa approach the house insists in a
quite surprising way on distance and perspective; the scene is lit by

moonlight that comes and goes, and music from an unseen source filters through the dialogue. These atmospheric qualities unsettle an audience, as do the mythological allusions and the uncertain temper of the Jessica–Lorenzo exchange. Shakespeare seems intent on creating an ambience that is indeed aristocratic, but one which in its leisurely expansion and indirection matches by similarity and contrast the play's busy but equally indirect opening scene. Belmont is figured as a lifestyle that replaces, and from certain standpoints perfects, the dissatisfactions of the Venetian world. But it carries with it its own uncertainties and dissatisfactions; the two locations are locations in counterpoint, but as in counterpoint there are shared if antithetical patterns.

If we look in the history of sixteenth-century Venice for a counterpart to Portia's Belmont, we may find ourselves struck by parallels to Belmont in the structure and design of the Palladian villa, the defining instance in architectural terms of the new culture on the mainland.[23] Given the differences between real world and play world, the parallels can scarcely be exact, and given the inexplicitness of Elizabethan plays on matters of location, the evidence cannot be directly visual. Yet the impressions of Belmont we derive from indications in the script do suggest that (in the context of the cultural change from Venice to Belmont) Shakespeare may have had the Palladian villa in mind as the model for Portia's 'hall'. In his source, Ser Giovanni Fiorentino's *Il pecorone*, Belmont has the characteristics of a small, late-medieval city-state, with knights and ladies and tournaments and rejoicing in the streets. The lady's house is a castle overlooking a harbour, and into this harbour Giannetto, the Bassanio-figure, sails his ship, pennants fluttering in the breeze.[24] Shakespeare transforms this setting into that of a great house, characterised, as we have said, by ordered ceremonial space, and set in gardens where mythological thoughts come to mind. The circumstances of the house, and it may be suggested the unsettling nature of its ambience, recall features of the Palladian villas built in such numbers on the *terrafirma* in the middle years of the sixteenth century.

By no means all the villa-building in the Veneto between the 1530s and 1570 came from Palladio's hand or even under his inspiration, yet his is the characterising outlook as well as that of the best-documented and most prolific creator. His famous manual, *The Four Books of Architecture (I quattro libri dell'architettura)*, offers in its second book a conception of the villa as a place of cultural self-fashioning that identifies very accurately the interplay between practical and aesthetic motivations that occupied the minds of the Venetian (and Vicentine) would-be aristocracy who were his patrons. The villa is to be reminiscent of the noble's town house in its 'great splendour and conveniency', but it will also provide facilities for 'industry and the art of agriculture'. It will offer a setting for exercise and hunting, 'and finally, where the mind, fatigued by the agitations of the city, will be greatly restor'd and comported, and be able quietly to attend the studies of letters, and contemplation.'[25] The villas themselves translate this practical idyll into living arrangements that reconcile the management of land with opportunities for a high-bred lifestyle. They are remarkable examples indeed of architecture that is at once aesthetically imposing, and thoroughly well-adapted to practical ends. And they provide precisely the setting for contemplation and aristocratic ease for which the rich Venetian, successful in trade, was seeking.[26]

The sober and utilitarian basis of much of Palladio's thinking about architecture is somewhat at odds however with the purpose he and his patrons had in mind in building the villas. The most ambitious houses (and by implication all the houses) represent statements about social caste and wealth which contrast sharply with the land-management purposes for which the villas were also ostensibly created. The embellishment of many of them by painters and stuccoists, acknowledged in the Four Books, transforms the sobriety of much of the architectural thinking into altogether more eye-catching forms. Not only do the villas provide suitable spaces for aristocratic intercourse and display, their decoration denotes in its visual style something of the ambition and something of the nervousness of the would-be aristocrats. The underlying idiom of the whole enterprise is of course pastoral – the transfer to rural surroundings of urban values – but as so often in pastoral the contrary elements of ordinariness and sophistication, rustic and citified, prove difficult to reconcile. The particular form this struggle takes in the Palladian villa is the interplay between architecture and embellishment, function and fantasy, that in characteristic cases makes for uneasy connections between the real world and the imaginary.

At the Villa Barbaro at Maser, for instance, built for Daniele Barbaro, humanist scholar, diplomat, editor of Vitruvius, and for his brother Marcantonio, both of them Venetian patricians rich as a result of commercial enterprise, the frescos by Veronese and his assistants elaborate the rooms into settings for a dialogue between present and past, interior space and the world outside, the actual and mythological, solidity and space. The walls are opened by landscapes of places real and imaginary, mythological deities turn ceilings into heavens, *trompe l'oeil* effects conflate the painted world with the architecturally structural, fictional people (possibly identifiable with real) step through painted doors, and down long perspectives painted figures of the master and mistress of the house greet each other over the heads of the real company within. Outside the villa, the gardens continue the artificial conversation, placing free-standing mythological figures within the mannered naturalism of Renaissance garden-design.[27] In the Barbaros' day, no doubt, music parties, such as that in Pozzoserrato's *Music in a Villa Garden*,[28] were on hand to complete this exercise in the sophistication of wealth and practical life that is the villa's contribution to the 'aristocratisation of a formerly mercantile patriciate'.[29] If Maser is untypical of Palladio's villas (Howard Burns, for example, stresses its 'uniqueness'),[30] its illusionistic strategies do represent in an especially refined and developed form some of the aesthetic qualities associated with the cultural self-image adopted by Venetian nobility in their new setting on the mainland.

This new self-image may appear characterised by strain, and an anxiety to impress; and this is unsurprising given the cultural circumstances which brought it into being. The conscious effort to create a newly-aristocratic lifestyle inevitably led to aesthetic forms that, whatever their appeal to antiquity and to literary and visual tradition, must strike the observer as anxious and raw. To extrapolate from such a self-image to Portia's uneasy if leisured garden, with its mythological reminiscences and its music, and to her 'hall' and its formal rituals, can scarcely be a direct procedure, and perhaps not a convincing one. Yet if we find the life of the play's Venetian merchants plausibly related to the cultural circumstances of historical Venice, it may be worth considering whether the alternative life they created for themselves on the mainland may not provide the cue for Shakespeare's Belmont. What is incontestable is that productions of the play have found difficulty in securing an image for Belmont, in visual terms, that could offer the same persuasiveness as the overwhelming eloquent visual language of the locations in Venice. The same is true of the myth of Venice itself. The land-based culture never made its way into the language of the myth which, as Innocenzo Cervelli remarks, 'continued to be defined as urban polity alone, leaving relations between city and mainland without theoretical definition'.[31] The myth of Venice, so powerful in cultural influence down the centuries, never became the myth of Venice and the Veneto. Perhaps such a dual myth or dual reality is necessary to the understanding and the presentation of Shakespeare's play; and perhaps if the myth of the Veneto has no shadow to cast we need to create one, even if we should also need, as with the myth of Venice, to see behind the surface to the actual circumstances that brought it into being.

Notes

Since this essay was written, two studies have appeared which corroborate some of its findings, even if they approach the play with different interests. In the more substantial of the two, David C. McPherson (*Shakespeare, Jonson and the Myth of Venice*, Newark, University of Delaware Press, 1990) lays emphasis on the decline of Venetian power in the sixteenth century, and draws attention to the range of published accounts and maps of Venice available to English purchasers in the 1590s especially. He also gives a good account of the ownership of mainland villas, and the social strains between land-owning 'aristocrats' and merchants that followed. Murray J. Levith (*Shakespeare's Italian Settings and Plays*, London, Macmillan, 1989) draws attention to possible parallels between the social conflicts in the play and strains in Shakespeare's own society, a topic that invites more theoretically developed consideration.

1　For a discussion of this see Margaret Shewring, 'A question of balance: Shakespeare's *The Merchant of Venice* on the nineteenth and twentieth century stage', in *L'Image de Venise au Temps de la Renaissance*, ed. M.-T. Jones-Davies, Paris, 1989, pp. 87–111.

2　See Margaret Shewring, 'A question of balance'.

3　James S. Grubb, 'When myths lose power: four decades of Venetian historiography', *Journal of Modern History*, 58, 1986, pp. 43–4.

4　Harley Granville Barker, *Prefaces to Shakespeare*, 4 (1930).

5　From a transcript of the lecture delivered at the Shakespeare Conference of the Shakespeare Institute, University of Birmingham, August 1988.

6　See David Rosand, *Painting in Cinquecento Venice*, New Haven and London, 1982, and Patricia Fortini Brown, *Venetian Narrative Painting in the Age of Carpaccio*, New Haven and London, 1988.

7　C. L. Barber, *Shakespeare's Festive Comedy*, Princeton, 1959; Cleveland and New York, 1963, p. 170.

8　*The Merchant of Venice*, ed. M. M. Mahood, Cambridge, 1987, p. 25.

9　Barber, *Shakespeare's Festive Comedy*, p. 168.

10　See Grubb, 'When myths lose power', p. 61.

11　See, for example, Brian Pullen, 'The occupations and investments of the Venetian nobility in the middle and late sixteenth century', in *Renaissance Venice*, ed. J. R. Hale, London, 1973, pp. 379–408.

12 J. H. Plumb, *The Penguin Book of the Renaissance*, Harmondsworth, 1964, pp. 235, 242.

13 Ugo Tucci, 'The psychology of the Venetian merchant in the sixteenth century', in Hale, *Renaissance Venice*, p. 358.

14 Tucci, 'The psychology of the Venetian merchant', p. 359.

15 W. H. Auden, *The Dyer's Hand*, London, 1963, reprinted in *Shakespeare, 'The Merchant of Venice': a Casebook* ed. John Walden, London, 1969, p. 239.

16 Tucci, 'The psychology of the Venetian merchant', p. 349. ᾽

17 Sir John Hale (ed.), *The Genius of Venice*, London, 1981, p. 15.

18 Cited by Lionello Puppi in Hale, *Genius of Venice*, p. 21.

19 See Pullen, 'Occupations and investments'.

20 Brian Pullen, *Rich and Poor in Renaissance Venice*, London, 1971.

21 Grubb, 'When myths lose power', p. 65.

22 Pullen, 'Occupations and investments'.

23 See, for example, James S. Ackerman, *Palladio*, Harmondsworth, 1966; Howard Burns, Lynda Fairbairn and Bruce Boucher, *Andrea Palladio 1508–1580: the Portico and the Farmyard*, London, 1975; and Renato Cevese, *Le ville del Palladio*, Treviso, 1985.

24 For a translation of *Il pecorone*, see Geoffrey Bullough, *Narrative and Dramatic Sources of Shakespeare*, 2, London, 1958, pp. 443–514.

25 Andrea Palladio, *The Four Books of Architecture*, trans. Isaac Ware, London 1738; facsimile edition, Ontario and London, 1965, p. 46.

26 See A. Richard Turner, *The Vision of Landscape in Renaissance Italy*, Princeton, 1966, pp. 206ff., for a comparison with the Villa d'Este and the Roman villa generally.

27 See Roy Strong, *The Renaissance Garden in England*, London, 1979, chapter 1.

28 The painting was exhibited in the Arts Council Exhibition in 1975; see Burns *et al.*, *Andrea Palladio*, p. 203.

29 See note 21 above.

30 Burns *et al.*, *Andrea Palladio*, p. 196.

31 Innocenzo Cervelli, cited in Grubb, 'When myths lose power', p. 73.

6

'In fair Verona':
commedia erudita into romantic comedy*

Giorgio Melchiori

In the first phase of his playwriting activity, Shakespeare was a tireless experimenter in all theatrical genres current at the time on the Elizabethan stage, from history to Senecan tragedy, from comedy on the classical model to the exquisite euphuism of *Love's Labour's Lost*, to the happy conflation of at least three distinct dramatic genres in *A Midsummer Night's Dream*. Though it is practically impossible to establish the exact order in which they were written and presented on the stage, each early play of his, whether history, tragedy or comedy, explores, or rather creates, a new theatrical sub-genre. Two of the early comedies have Italian locations. But while *The Taming of the Shrew* is based on a traditional comic pattern,[1] renewed by the original device of being enclosed in a contemporary realistic typically English frame, *The Two Gentlemen of Verona*, by general agreement, is the forerunner, or rather the first Shakespearean example, of yet another dramatic genre, which was to characterise Shakespeare's production of comedies from 1595 to at least 1601, from *The Merchant of Venice* to *Twelfth Night* and beyond: the so-called 'Romantic comedy'. This is a genre close to that of the 'romances', identified with Shakespeare's last plays, from *Pericles* to *The Tempest*, but differing from them because it lacks the elements of wonder, while the festive mood prevails (in spite of the reminders of the darker side of comedy in the Hero plot of *Much Ado*, in Jaques in *As You Like It* or in Malvolio in *Twelfth Night*), together with the constant play on disguise and the celebration of young love, so that each of the romantic comedies ends not with a single marriage but with the union of a number of happy couples.

*This chapter develops, with a different approach, suggestions contained in my book *Shakespeare's Garter Plays*, forthcoming from the University of Delaware Press.

What is puzzling is that the plot, the themes, the situations of *The Two Gentlemen of Verona* have been traced to a number of sources, both classical and modern, narrative and dramatic, but in none of them are the background, the places of the action, Venetian, or even modern Italian.[2] Why did Shakespeare transfer (albeit rather confusedly) these characters to purely imaginary Venetia and Lombardy, Verona and Milan, with Mantua thrown in for good measure, and, in between, a forest which is undoubtedly Sherwood Forest, peopled as it is by gentlemen outlaws who choose the Veronese nobleman Valentine as their new Robin Hood? Why did he want to mention Verona in the very title of the play? In show business, then as now (and Shakespeare and his fellow players were the leading experts of their time in the trade), the choice of the title is of crucial importance for the success of the enterprise. Shakespeare and the players must therefore have counted on the appeal of that foreign place-name, Verona, on their potential audience, *before* the tragic story of Romeo and Juliet had made of it a familiar password to the world of – indeed – 'romantic' love to any theatregoer.

The explanation of the choice is to be looked for, I believe, on two levels. One, the most obvious, is connected with the origin of the tragedy which I have just mentioned: there is no doubt that, at the time of 'inventing' *The Two Gentlemen of Verona*, Shakespeare was reading Arthur Brooke's poem *The Tragical History of Romeus and Juliet*, which is his one source for the Veronese tragedy, and the places mentioned in that poem must have appeared to him suitable imaginary locations for a story of love intrigues with a happy ending. But there is also another type of explanation, which requires a different approach. It is the approach implicit in the first paragraphs of the present chapter.

In other words, I suggest that Shakespeare, from his very first experiment in the genre, conceived of the love comedy – the romantic comedy – as of something typically Italian, and for this reason he favoured the choice of Italian names for the main characters and, at least in the earliest examples, of Italian locations for the action. The reason must be looked for in the origins of romantic comedies on the English stage, and the key to it may be provided by the title itself of *The Two Gentlemen of Verona*. It has been noticed that this title was perhaps meant to recall that of another comedy that had enjoyed the privilege of being performed at court before Queen Elizabeth some ten years earlier.[3] The only extant edition of it is dated 1585, and the full title runs: *Fedele and Fortunio. The deceites in Loue: excellently discoursed in a very pleasant and fine conceited Comoedie, of two Italian Gentlemen. Translated out of Italian, and set downe according as it hath beene presented before the Queenes moste excellent Maiestie.*[4]

Though the comedy of *The Two Italian Gentlemen* was published anonymously, there is no doubt about its author: that exceptional Jack of all trades called Anthony Munday – an extremely versatile playwright, a novelist in his own right and translator of voluminous French romances, pamphleteer and historian, deviser of pageants for the London City guilds, and government informer against English Roman Catholics.[5] A man who, while on the one hand had caused through his accusations the execution of Edmund Campion and other Catholics (and boasted of the fact), on the other presented in such a favourable light the figure of Sir Thomas More, in the best play ever written about the Catholic martyr, that Elizabethan censorship prevented its performance;[6] a man, finally, who in two very successful plays, *The Downfall of the Earl of Huntingdon* (1598) and *The Death of the Earl of Huntingdon* (1599), enriched the Robin Hood legend, by identifying the outlaw who robbed the rich to help the poor with a nobleman forced to retire to the forest by the evil practices of court and clergy.

Fedele and Fortunio; or, The Two Italian Gentlemen was written when Munday was hardly twenty-five, possibly as his first attempt at playwriting. Intended mainly as a literary exercise, the play is now remembered, if at all, as one of the rare Elizabethan translations of Italian plays,[7] though Leo Salingar,[8] after quoting Stephen Gosson's well-known statement in his *Plays Confuted* (1582), 'bawdy Comedies in Latin, French, Italian and Spanish have been thoroughly ransacked to furnish the Play houses in London', comments: 'though only one sure example is known, Anthony Munday's *Two Italian Gentlemen* (c. 1584), from a comedy by Pasqualigo'. The plot is based on the rivalry between the two young gentlemen Fedele and Fortunio for the love of a gentlewoman, Victoria; the supporting roles are provided by Virginia (a young lady secretly in love with Fedele), Attilia and Pamphila (the maids of Victoria and Virginia respectively), Fedele's tutor Pedante, the braggart Captain Crackstone, the go-between Medusa, an expert in magic arts; exactly as in the later Shakespearean comedies, after a whole sequel of errors, disguises and love deceits, the story ends in no fewer than four happy marriages: Victoria with Fedele, Virginia with Fortunio, Attilia with Captain Crackstone, and Medusa with Pedante.

It is my contention that, inadvertently, by devising this play, Munday had founded a new dramatic genre, and that this is the original model of Shakespeare's romantic comedies. I say *inadvertently*, because his initial aim had been that of providing a fairly sophisticated and partly Italianate English audience with a recent example of Italian comedy: hence the words 'Translated out of Italian' on the title-page of the printed text. In 1579, when he was nineteen, Munday had spent some months as a pupil in the English College in Rome, with the deliberate intention, as he was to claim upon his return, of reporting on his fellow students, refugee English Catholics considered guilty of high treason.[9] On his way back he stopped briefly in Venice, and it was there that he must have come across a newly printed book: the second edition of *Il Fedele, comedia del clarissimo Luigi Pasquàligo*, that is to say the Venetian nobleman Count Alvise Pasqualigo – a *commedia erudita* first published in 1576, then in 1579, and again later in 1589 and 1606, a play that enjoyed the distinction of a faithful Latin translation by Abraham Fraunce, published in England in 1582 under the title of *Victoria*.[10]

Munday wanted to present the English court, surely highly literate, but not to the point of listening for hours to the Latin text diligently prepared by Fraunce, with an English version not devoid of literary refinements, but closer to Elizabethan theatrical practices. A serious misunderstanding is engendered by those words 'Translated out of Italian' on the title-page. In fact Munday's is not a translation, but a verse adaptation with radical changes of Pasqualigo's original.[11] Pasqualigo's play is far from being a romantic comedy on the deceits in love happily concluded by the union of four loving couples. Vittoria is no simple maid uncertain in her choice between two suitors: she has a husband significantly called Cornelio, and freely dispenses her favours alternately to her lovers Fedele and Fortunio, so that, when one of them, jealous of the other, threatens to reveal her behaviour to her husband, she makes no scruple of offering herself to the boastful henchman Frangipietra in order to have the inconvenient lover suppressed. On the other hand, lustful Virginia has a tryst with Fortunio, mistaking him for Fedele in the dark, and only the unexpected arrival of her father forces a marriage between the two. The only other marriage in the Italian play is that between Vittoria's maid Attilia and Fedele's servant Narciso. And in the end Vittoria accepts again Fedele as her lover, in spite of her earlier attempt at having him killed; her change of mind results from her gratitude to him, who manages to hoodwink her husband into believing in her innocence and married chastity. All this is seasoned with the menial loves and intrigues of a number of servants, and with lengthy tirades on the nature of love and on female inconstancy and promiscuity, placed mainly on the lips of the pedant Onofrio. Verbosity, a tendency to use quotations and sententious arguments, are shared by all characters, branding *Il Fedele* as a typical *commedia erudita*.

Munday's so-called translation is in fact a total metamorphosis. In order to present the comedy to the English court, Munday has shorn it of minor characters and intrigues, preserving only what must have seemed to him the most amusing situations, translated into a different context determined by the suppression of a fundamental theme: that of adultery. For instance, in Pasqualigo's comedy Fedele, in order to convince Cornelio of Vittoria's infidelity, shows him his servant Narciso in disguise coming out of Vittoria's house, where he had met her maid Attilia. The disappearance in Munday's version not only of Cornelio but also of Narciso forces a substantially different solution: in the English version Fedele, in order to get rid of his rival Fortunio, must make him believe that Victoria is promiscuous, and therefore shows him Pedante disguised coming out of Victoria's house (which he had entered as a beggar) and boasting of having enjoyed her. This is a return to the traditional situation of the pretended love meeting in order to discredit an innocent woman, the most famous example of which is the story of Ariodante and Ginevra in the fifth canto of *Orlando Furioso*, a situation that was to be reproduced in every detail in Shakespeare's *Much Ado about Nothing*.

What matters is that Munday gave the English public the impression that the new kind of comedy which he had inadvertently *invented* was a faithful reproduction of the Italian model. The play of the Venetian nobleman Pasqualigo stood as the model for romantic comedy, while in fact such comedy was native to England, the more or less casual result of Munday's endeavours at cleansing for an English audience the loose morality of Italian *commedia erudita*. It was therefore natural for English playwrights to think of the new 'romantic' plays as Italian-style comedies, and not only to locate them in Italy or other southern countries but also to draw their plots and situations from Italian *novelle* or at least from stories of obvious Italian origin. Hence such titles as *The Two Gentlemen of Verona* or *The Merchant of Venice*, the whole plot of which comes from a *novella* in *Il pecorone* by Ser Giovanni Fiorentino,[12] untranslated at the time into English (but

Shakespeare must have had some knowledge of Italian), though the trial scene is surely reminiscent also of an episode in an English romance, another work of Anthony Munday, *Zelauto or the Fountain of Fame*, based in turn on the same Italian story; and *Much Ado about Nothing* is directly derived from a novella by Bandello of which there was no English translation.[13]

But in spite of the Italian or Italianate background of romantic comedies, a common characteristic of them all is the introduction of openly and strictly English elements in the comic roles. Such is the case of the typical London night watch appearing in the Messina of *Much Ado*, or of Speed and Launce in *The Two Gentlemen of Verona*. In most romantic comedies the clowns, the astute or silly servants, have English names in contrast with the Latinised forms of those of the main characters, and use a language which characterises them as belonging to the small world of Elizabethan London. In other words, the very *lazzi* ultimately derived from the *commedia dell'arte* are metamorphosed, are translated bodily into the language of the society in which Shakespeare and his audience moved.

Once again, it was Munday's comedy *The Two Italian Gentlemen* which provided the model for this conflation of English humour and Italian romantic comedy. One character that he created deserves attention. In reducing the acting roles and re-orientating the plot of Pasqualigo's original version, Munday developed only two of the secondary characters in the Italian play at the expense of all the others. The longest role, in his version, is that of Pedante – the counterpart of Onofrio, whose irrepressible verbiage had already been emphasised by Pasqualigo; but the second longest role in Munday's play is that of a character who, in Pasqualigo's, put in appearances only in two or three scenes: the braggart Frangipietra, presented by Pasqualigo along the traditional line of *commedia dell'arte* rather than that of *commedia erudita*. For him Frangipietra is a 'bravo' ready to sell himself to the highest bidder, rough in behaviour and language, meant only to expose Vittoria's unscrupulousness in hiring him as an assassin. By 'translating' Frangipietra into Crackstone, Munday created a fully rounded character, who, though on the one hand modelled on the traditional *miles gloriosus*, on the other is based on contemporary experience of English life: Crackstone, as he himself tells the audience, is an army sutler who, by 'nicking them of their measure [...] got so much gain / That I bought this apparel of a captain that was slain', so that he is now accepted by everybody as a captain and, by telling his imaginary war exploits, moves among the better sort and considers himself irresistible for 'proper gentlewomen', even if at times he has to seduce their maids first.[14]

In order to stress his new status Munday has invented for him a high-sounding language, mixing together military boasts, dog Latin, new polyvalent word coinages, inversions and adaptations of proverbial expressions and long soliloquies revealing a kind of misdirected self-knowlege. For instance, immediately after having sworn to Victoria that he will kill Fedele, he begins: 'Now shall my valerosity appear unto all', and boasts of having 'put cities into sacks and make thousands to yield'. But then he thinks it over:

> To bring Fedele to the counter is but to fight with a fly;
> There is neither praise, pride nor providence in the victory.
> Therefore take heed, Crackstone, what you do.
> You hazard your good name; your honour stands on tip-toe.
> To kill a gentleman that never ought me malice is more than cruelty,
> And to kill him for a woman will bring me utterly to infancy.
> Shall I kill him then? Peradventure yea. Shall I let him go?
> Peradventure I may, peradventure no.
> O single device! Here is a brain, I believe,
> Able to shoot birdbolts of inventions from my hand into my sleeve.
> I will make a great noise before Victoria's door in the street,
> As though at this present with Fedele I did meet.
> Then will I run to her house amain
> And make her believe that Fedele is slain.
> Then before that she hear any news of his life,
> I'll have her to the priest and make her my wife.

(IV.vi.1–22)

This speech cannot fail to call to mind the soliloquies and the posturing of a much more complex and endearing character, one of the greatest creations of Shakespeare for all time. Munday, by transforming the common braggart of Pasqualigo's comedy into the eloquent, self-important Crackstone, familiar counsellor of adventurous young men, created the prototype of a typically English character – the boon companion of Prince Hal – that Shakespeare enriched by making him more mature in years and much ampler in size, as well as by compounding the *maschera* of the Italian 'bravo' with the Morality vice and the Lord of Misrule out of the native English tradition. Sir John

Falstaff is the direct heir of Captain Crackstone. Besides, the language that Munday devised for him provided Shakespeare with a number of suggestions for the 'irregular humourists' surrounding Prince Hal in the two Parts of *Henry IV*. Crackstone suggested the general outline of the character of Falstaff, but he also provided Pistol with his emphatic doggerel and his high-sounding misquotations, and Mistress Quickly with her gift for transforming pretentious malapropisms into ever new polysemic creations.

I have tried to trace the route from the Italian *commedia erudita* of a Venetian man of letters to English romantic comedy, considered (in view of the ignorance of Munday's role in transforming the Italian original) as Italian-style comedy; that is why English romantic comedy is generally set in an imaginary Italy, which may at times be called Illyria, or even, when the romantic comedy pattern became a vehicle for a more complex inner dialectical process, Roussilion (*All's Well that Ends Well*) or Vienna (*Measure for Measure*). It should be kept in mind, though, that from its first appearance the Italian-style romantic comedy bears an admixture, mainly in the comic or clownish roles and in the representation of everyday life, with characters, attitudes and allusions closely connected with the small world of Elizabethan street life: details that are so obviously English that Shakespeare, finding in the prototype of romantic comedy – Munday's *Two Italian Gentlemen* – the character of Crackstone (the only Italian name translated into English[15]) did not transfer him into one of his romantic Italianate comedies, but promoted him to the role of leading character in two of his *English* histories, the two parts of *Henry IV*.

In spite of the fact that Salingar had pointed out thematic affinities between *The Two Italian Gentlemen* and *The Two Gentlemen of Verona*,[16] and Daniel Boughner had underlined the kinship between Pasqualigo's Frangipietra and Falstaff, showing how both, when in danger, discourse on the subject of honour,[17] this aspect of Falstaff's ancestry has been obscured even by some of the supporters of the direct or indirect Italian origin of the play that saw Falstaff's last reincarnation, *The Merry Wives of Windsor* – a claim contested by recent critics who see it as Shakespeare's one and only thoroughly English comedy.[18] In a paper significantly entitled 'The Italianate background of *The Merry Wives of Windsor*',[19] Oscar James Campbell hit on the analogy with Munday's *The Two Italian Gentlemen*, but saw the character of Falstaff not as developing from that of Crackstone, but as a laborious adaptation of that of Pedante: noticing what he considers relics of pedantic forms in Falstaff's language – the result, in his opinion, of the process of adaptation from the original pedant to the boastful knight. Campbell does not seem to realise that such rhetorical flourishes were traditionally shared, though with subtle differences, by the pedant and the *miles gloriosus* – witness the two champions of high-falutin' rhetoric in *Love's Labour's Lost*, Holofernes and Armado.

The fact remains that, outside England, Sir John Falstaff is seen not so much against the background of English history, but rather – and Verdi's opera based on Arrigo Boito's excellent libretto is largely responsible for it – in the context of the farcical comedy located in the village of Windsor. The legend according to which Shakespeare wrote *The Merry Wives of Windsor* in a fortnight because Queen Elizabeth, amused by the previous appearances of the character, wanted to see 'Falstaff in love' has no historical foundation, but represents effectively the general attitude towards the contents of that play. In fact *Merry Wives* bears all the marks of improvisation, reintroducing, apart from the hero himself, a number of other characters (Mistress Quickly, Justice Shallow, Lieutenant Bardolph, Ancient Pistol and Corporal Nym) already familiar to Elizabethan audiences from their previous exploits in the histories; but the author seems to have no idea of how to use them – they are there merely as supporting roles, while the main action takes a different turn, bringing to the fore new and different characters. On the other hand *Merry Wives*, because of the constant mention in it of local place-names and customs (the most brilliant invention being the Garter Inn, where Falstaff lodges, which entitles him to be called a 'knight of the Garter'), and of the final celebration of the Queen and of the Order of the Garter, justifies the claim that it is the only one of Shakespeare's comedies that forsakes the Italian models, entering the mainstream of English domestic or city comedy, a genre which was to find its most gifted practitioners in Ben Jonson and Thomas Dekker, Thomas Heywood and Thomas Middleton.

But when we compare the work of the latter with that of Shakespeare, what strikes us is not the similarity, but the substantial difference in character behaviour. Main plot and subplot (the merry wives and the love story of Fenton and Anne Page), once short of local reference, have little in common with the loving presentation of the life and interests of the English middle class offered by the authors of city comedies. The English local colour and the celebration of some national institutions appear in *Merry Wives* as hardly more than a decorative superstructure, and its superficial nature is revealed as soon as we try to explore the origin of the main plot line of the play. The situation is the exact opposite of that presented by *The Two Gentlemen of Verona*: there the Italian background could not be traced to any of the possible sources; in the case of the Windsor comedy, on the contrary, source hunters looking for the models on which Shakespeare had based it have been unable to find any, apart from some marginal details,[20] in the native English narrative or dramatic tradition. The most obvious source of the main plot of *Merry Wives* is a *novella* (with no known English translation) from *Il pecorone* by Ser Giovanni Fiorentino,[21] in the same way as the supporting structure of *The Merchant of Venice* is another story (also untranslated) from the same collection. Characteristically, in Shakespeare's adaptation the Italian story undergoes the same cleansing process that Pasqualigo's *Il Fedele* had received at the hands of Anthony Munday when he 'translated' it into *The Two Italian Gentlemen*: for all the talk of 'horns', no adultery is consummated in the English versions.

The Merry Wives of Windsor, then, built on the basic scheme of the multiple *beffa* (so typically Italian a feature that there is no exact English equivalent for the word), is an Italian-style comedy in English dress. What singles it out from Shakespeare's other romantic comedies is not only and not so much the Windsor locale as the insistence on the *beffa* (something more than a merry trick or a practical joke) not as subsidiary or incidental but as the central theme of the plot. Another distinguishing feature is the invention of diversified languages for the different characters (from the Frenchified English of Doctor Caius to the Welsh accent of Sir Hugh Evans, the pompous rhetoric of the Host of the Garter, the equivocations of Mistress Quickly during the Latin lesson to little William Page): these linguistic mannerisms, beyond the schemes of the romantic comedy developed in England thanks to Munday's remarkable feat in the art of 'translation', are the direct inheritance of the Italian *commedia erudita*, a genre in which Count Alvise Pasqualigo was but a follower in the steps of Pietro Aretino and of Cardinal Bibbiena, of Ludovico Ariosto and of the Sienese Accademici Intronati, as well as of Nicolò Machiavelli.

Shakespeare had started by 'Italianising' alien subject-matter in order to create a new genre of comedy, but ended by 'Anglicising' Italian subject-matter when turning comedy into farce. The road from Verona (in Shakespeare's first romantic comedy as well as in his one lyrical tragedy) to Windsor is in fact a circular route: after calling at Padua, Venice and Messina, with diversions to imaginary Arden and

109

Illyria, it leads back to the starting point – Windsor is but a new name for that Italian ground from which Anthony Munday had bred English romantic comedy out of *commedia erudita.*

Notes

1 The 'Bianca' plot is based on George Gascoigne's *Supposes* (1556), adapting Ariosto's *I Suppositi,* while the Petruchio–Katharina plot exploits traditional stories of female shrewishness. See *Narrative and Dramatic Sources of Shakespeare,* ed. G. Bullough, I, London, 1957, pp. 57–68.

2 The only two 'possible sources' indicated by Bullough (*Sources,* I, pp. 203–66) are the stories of Titus and Gisippus taking place in ancient Rome (included in Sir Thomas Elyot's *The Governour*), and of Felix and Felismena, from Jorge de Montemayor's *Diana Enamorada,* located in pagan Portugal. The 'scenario' by Flaminio Scala, *Flavio Tradito,* located in Florence, is mentioned merely as an analogue, since it appeared in print, in Italian, only in 1611.

3 The connection between *The Two Italian Gentlemen* and *The Two Gentlemen of Verona* is remarked upon by Leo Salingar, *Shakespeare and the Traditions of Comedy,* Cambridge, 1974, p. 225

4 *Fedele and Fortunio the Two Italian Gentlemen,* ed. Percy Simpson, MSR, 1910 for 1909.

5 On the career of Anthony Munday see Celeste Turner, *Anthony Munday: an Elizabethan Man of Letters,* University of California Publications in English II, no 1, 1928.

6 It was apparently on that occasion that Shakespeare's and Munday's paths crossed for the first time, when Shakespeare was called upon to rewrite a scene of the play which might have disturbed the censor; see *Sir Thomas More,* a play by Anthony Munday and others, eds V. Gabrieli and G. Melchiori, Manchester, 1990. Several years later it was Munday who severely castigated Shakespeare and his fellow Chamberlain's Men for their disrespectful presentation on the stage of the Protestant martyr Sir John Oldcastle in the original version of *Henry IV.*

7 Louise George Glubb, *Italian Drama in Shakespeare's Time,* New Haven, 1989, p. 50, in a footnote mentions it in a list of such translations: 'Pasqualigo's *Il Fedele* in Fraunce's Latin *Victoria* and Munday's *Fedele and Fortunio, the two Italian Gentlemen'.*

8 Salingar, *Traditions,* p. 189.

9 See especially his *The Englishe Romayne Life* (1581).

10 Ed. G. C. Moore-Smith, in *Materialen zur Kunde des älteren englischen Dramas,* 14, Louvain, 1906.

11 For a close comparison between *The Two Italian Gentlemen* and *Il Fedele* see the Introduction to *A Critical Edition of Anthony Munday's 'Fedele and Fortunio',* ed. Richard Hosley, New York, 1981.

12 Giornata IV, Novella i.

13 The story of Timbreo and Fenicia (Bandello, *Novelle,* I, xxii) is located, like

the play, in Messina. Bullough, *Sources*, II, London, 1958, pp. 61–81, quotes the episode of the night meeting at Victoria's house in Munday's *The Two Italian Gentlemen* as an analogue.

14 All quotations are from Richard Hosley's already mentioned critical edition of the play. I have modernised the spelling.

15 In the later French adaptation of *Il Fedele* by Pierre Larivey (*Le Fidelle*, 1611), Frangipietra's name is translated 'Brisemur' (Crackwall); see Daniel C. Boughner, *The Braggart in Renaissance Comedy: a Study in Comparative Drama from Aristophanes to Shakespeare*. Minneapolis, 1954, pp. 264–5.

16 Salingar, *Traditions*, p. 232.

17 Boughner, *Braggart* , p. 88. Boughner had not seen Munday's adaptation of *Il Fedele*, but only the Italian original.

18 See for instance Jeanne Addison Roberts, *Shakespeare's English Comedy: 'The Merry Wives of Windsor' in Context*, Lincoln, Nebr., 1979.

19 University of Michigan Publications in Language and Literature 8, Ann Arbor, 1932, pp. 81–117.

20 In stories such as those in Barnabe Riche's *Farewell to the Militarie Profession* (1581), and in *Tarltons Newes out of Purgatorie* (1590), reprinted with many misgivings in Bullough, *Sources*, II, pp. 3–38.

21 Giornata I, Novella ii. The most recent editor of *Merry Wives*, T. W. Craik, Oxford, 1990, pp. 14–15, acknowledges that 'No other proposed source for elements of the play comes anywhere near so close as this [*Il pecorone*], which may be taken to be the point from which Shakespeare's plot grew'.

7

Duelling in the Italian manner:
the case of *Romeo and Juliet*

Sergio Rossi

This chapter is intended to complement an earlier study in which I emphasised the progressive spread in England of the duel according to the rules which had been codified in France, in Spain but above all in Italy between 1540 and 1570.[1] The attempt to provide norms for the encounter of two contestants was one of the aspects of the lively debate on the legality of duelling, on the right of a gentleman to obtain satisfaction on his own account for insults sustained and on the necessity for observance of precise forms so as to avoid the degeneration of such encounters into brawls involving the seconds of the duellists, as indeed occurred. From this followed the necessity of establishing who had the right to bear arms, in what cases satisfaction for an offence might be entrusted to single combat and what type of offence might receive such satisfaction. A number of treatises were published on the topic in Italy, France and Spain, though not in England where, perhaps for historical reasons, the problem was not debated, but merely adumbrated in translations and adaptations of Italian originals.[2] These treatises were intended for anyone who, considering himself a gentleman by birth or education, might best understand the prescriptions they contained.[3]

The spread of the duel as a means of resolving private quarrels was an epidemic which involved all the countries of Europe one by one. It signalled the continued decline of spectacular encounters between contestants sheathed in heavy armour. In the Elizabethan age, the colourful aspects of the latter type of contest were manifested above all in the grandiose annual commemorations of the Accession Day tilts.[4] The diffusion of the duel, moreover, fostered the development of theories of method and of what type of arms were best adapted for duellists. In these matters also the most authoritative treatises were the work of Italians, who set out to make of fencing a new art and to raise it to become a component in the education of a gentleman, on a level with the accomplishments of poetic composition, conversation, dancing and riding he was already obliged to master. The sword, therefore, was no longer reserved for use solely in war. It became part of a gentleman's dress, to serve, at least in principle, as a means of defence only and not of offence. Italian masters of arms imparted to the whole of Europe their notions of the way of wielding their weapon, basing themselves on the principle of striking the opponent with the point (*stoccata*). The consequences of such a blow were much more lethal than the wounds inflicted by the cut of the older fashion. These masters set up school at various courts, London among them, where the presence of a number of 'professours' of fence is recorded. These were not slow to come into opposition with the local masters of arms, jealous of their own traditions and above all of the high fees demanded by the foreigners, with which they could not compete.[5]

The best known Italian master of arms in London was Vincentio Saviolo, seemingly the author of the fencing manual *Vincentio Saviolo his Practise* of 1595. I have my doubts about Saviolo's paternity in this case, because we are dealing here with a work born in the ambience of the ceaselessly active John Florio, whose friend Saviolo was. It is no accident that the volume is dedicated to the Earl of Essex, known as the 'English Achilles' since, after Sidney's death, he best embodied in his person the new type of knighthood.[6] If we consider the publication dates of manuals such as Sir William Segar's *The Book of Honour and Armes* (1590), the translation of di Grassi, *Di Grassi his True Arte of Defence* (1594), and *Vincentio Saviolo his Practise*, in relation to John Florio's connections during those years with the Earl of Southampton and therefore with the Earl of Essex, we shall realise that the time about 1595 corresponds to the moment when Florio and Shakespeare are most likely to have met. Shakespeare, in turn, because the plague had closed the theatres, was in contact with Southampton, to whom he dedicated his poems. It is not by chance that Florio appears in *Love's Labour's Lost* (1598) with characteristics that are to be found in other sources.[7] To this controversial personage can also ultimately perhaps be attributed certain Shakespearean interpretations of the Italian scene, including fencing, in *Romeo and Juliet.*

To connect Shakespeare with the problem of duelling is to propose a new key to the reading of many plays in which an armed encounter between two persons is not a matter of spectacle only but rather an important element in the drama itself. This is the more so because spectators in England also were able to understand the sad actuality of the motivation for single combats, to appreciate the ritual which accompanied them and, when they saw them on the stage, could discern their role in the drama and their character. In the greater proportion of cases, indeed, the duel was not extraneous to the text, though it is sometimes indicated merely by a stage direction, but rather an integral part of the action, a moment of dramatic violence corresponding to the violence of the society in which the spectator lived and in which he was also liable violently to die.

The behaviour of the contestants in the duels and encounters which take place in *Romeo and Juliet* is drawn directly from the text of Saviolo, which is divided into two parts: *The First Intreating of the Use of the Rapier and Dagger, The Second of Honor and Honorable Quarrels*, which is, as Ruth Kelso long ago established, a faithful translation, with some adaptations designed for the English reader, of *II Duello* of Muzio Giustinopolitano (1551).[8] Shakespeare used the manual attributed to Saviolo for his technical terminology as well as to explain the situations in which the contestants find themselves. Though giving proof that he knew both the practical part concerning the use of arms and the theoretical part concerning the code of honour which governs them, he seems to reveal a distinct attitude to the duel, in the sense that, rather than accepting it as a manifestation of his time, he expresses a veiled conviction of its uselessness. Such uselessness is underlined, from another angle, in the complex and ambiguous thematic of *Romeo and Juliet*, so much the more in that the futility of the encounters is accentuated by their violence, as well as by the unreasonableness and the desire to kill of the contenders, who sometimes infringe the rules which ought to govern their encounters. In response to the demands of the public, to the events of the day, and to the Italianising ambience with which he was in contact at the time, Shakespeare gives us an Italian drama in which duels and encounters intensify the dramatic situation. This particular position is limited to *Romeo and Juliet*, and does not recur in later plays such as *King Lear*, *Hamlet* or *Macbeth*, in which the duel is accepted without reserve, though with various nuances.

The encounters in *Romeo and Juliet* are four: the street brawl between the two factions of Capulets and Montagues, with its first exchange of blows between Benvolio and Tybalt (I.i), the true duel between Tybalt and Mercutio, followed at once by the encounter between Romeo and Tybalt (III.i) and finally, in the last act, the brief exchange of blows between Paris and Romeo, at night, in the graveyard, where Paris falls (V.iii). If we look at these four encounters closely, we shall see that they mark a like number of determining moments in the drama.

As usual in the greater part of Shakespearean drama, the opening scene gives the key to a reading of the entire text; its twin themes, of violence and of love destined to tragic wreck, are already announced here. In the brawl between the two factions, provoked for common-place motives by the servants (servants are not persons suited for duelling but only for scuffling, so that they are armed with swords and bucklers), the theme of violence provoked by pointless causes is already apparent.[9] The encounter of honour is reduced to a vulgar affray, which Tybalt futilely seeks to raise to an encounter between gentlemen. This can be deduced from the triviality of the serving-men's blows, which is also the announcement of another of the drama's themes, that of bawdy, which is much more marked here than in other Shakespearean contexts. In the first scene, moreover, are enumerated all the arms which are alluded to in the drama. They are few and they are those that are most frequently alluded to in the manuals: sword, rapier, club, bill, partizan, long sword. Shakespeare uses 'sword' and 'rapier' interchangeably to describe the arms suited to the duellists, while the other arms are well fitted to the persons who arrive successively on the scene to make up the encounter.[10] They begin with the clubs that were the regular weapons of the London apprentices and journeymen and end with the long sword loudly demanded by the aged Capulet. This was an old-fashioned two-handed sword ill fitted for hand-to-hand fighting and still less for duels with skilled wielders of the rapier. All were outmoded arms, despised by up-to-date duellists who put their trust in the Italian-style sword and dagger.[11] All the duels in the play are *all'italiana*, since the *dramatis personae*, as one can gather from the final scene, bear arms of this sort.

The dagger gets no mention in the first scene. The omission is perhaps deliberate if account is taken of the symbolic value which it assumes in the course of events as the instrument of Juliet's death, as indeed in all classic theatre. This significance emerges clearly in the second part, after the duels of the third act, as we pass from a context of sarcastic wit to one that is purely dramatic, where the dagger dominates the symbolism of arms.[12] In the scene in the Friar's cell, as the stage direction tells us but as we can also easily divine from the context, Romeo 'offers to stab himself, and the Nurse snatches the dagger away' (III.iii.110), when he is afraid he has lost Juliet's love by killing Tybalt. Juliet, desperate and undecided whether to drink the potion given her by Friar Laurence, places a dagger beside her: 'Lie thou there' (IV.iii.23), as an alternative decision, thus anticipating the final scene of her suicide. The dagger, together with the sword, is the arm that Romeo carries with him and, in the final scene, both these arms, which bring death in the duel, become the symbol of death for the whole tragedy. Mercutio, Tybalt and Paris all perish by the sword, which, to conclude the cycle, is abandoned at the entrance to Juliet's tomb. With Romeo's dagger Juliet takes her life.

The other fencing terms used by Shakespeare in the play, appearing in the first edition of John Florio's dictionary *A World of Words* in 1598 as well as in the fencing treatises in English, confirm the dramatist's familiarity with Florio's work.[13] Shakespeare nevertheless made a much reduced selection limiting himself to the words that would contribute most to the dramatic impact of the text. He avoided those, such as *stramazone, inbroccata, incartata*, which were less well adapted to creating an atmosphere of tension, and which also phonetically carry a suggestion of rhetorical eloquence and had been subjected to criticism by Silver,[14] to add to those he could acquire from the international vocabulary of fencing, such as *stoccata, punto reverso* (back-handed thrust) and *passado* (thrust with one foot forward).[15]

The opening scene's importance is not exhausted by the description of the encounters and the use of arms. It introduces new elements which determine the course of the drama, for example the motive of reason and the attempt at control through Benvolio (the symbolism of the name is obvious), the world which has been disturbed by the art of Tybalt. Above all, however, the affirmation of authority is introduced in the person of Escalus, because the brawls disturb the order not only of the two rival families but also that of the city in general and so of the State: the old world of the long swords is menaced by that of the sword and dagger. Escalus, the incarnation of the State, has been interpreted as a weak prince, who delays applying the law. Seen in the perspective of his time, however, he behaves as princes behaved in analogous situations, sending the surviving duellists into exile. This punishment is consonant with the rank of the defeated.[16] In condemning the duel, Shakespeare may also have known the work of Bertrand de Loque, *Discourses of Warre and Single Combat*, translated by John Eliot in 1591, the more so because echoes of de Loque are to be found in *Henry V.* In an encounter without deadly consequences such as that in the first scene, the prince's intervention can only be admonitory. Escalus, as representing power and therefore the common good, attempts to apply a brake to behaviour that is becoming more and more uncontrollable and against which the law established by the king can do little.[17] The condemnation to death with which he threatens the duellists is an anticipation in time: Richelieu was to arrive at that position, but not until 1627. One can read in Muzio other cases of condemnation to death which had certain resonances. The peace with which the play concludes anticipates that: 'Some shall be pardoned, and some punished' (V.iii.308), though the order reintroduced by Escalus is not the same as that of other tragedies where it is restored by the blood of innocent persons who bring it to life again. Here the victims are certainly the two young people, guilty in their turn however of having destroyed an equilibrium. The peace of Escalus is the peace of Elizabeth, who exacted obedience from her subjects and preferred to the duel her own exaltation as Gloriana and the pageants of the tournament. One can read between the lines and see Shakespeare taking up a critical position in the face of this violent behaviour, which breaks the law and is 'bred of an airy word' (I.i.88).

This first scene has precise references to London life.[18] It would therefore be readily comprehensible to the spectators, especially because it offers the first key to a reading of the play and establishes the two levels on which it operates, the violent one of the encounter and the sophisticated one which can be found in the conversation between Romeo and Benvolio immediately after the first affray in the streets of Verona.

The other aspect in which the duel is a determining factor for the rest of the play and gives it a decisive dramatic turn and, in consequence, a change of linguistic register, comes in the first scene of the third act, in which we are present at the double encounter and the deaths of Mercutio and Tybalt. Once again Shakespeare uses the Italian manuals to delineate the duel, as he also does in the fourth scene of the second act. Mercutio describes to Benvolio the figure of Tybalt, who has sent Romeo the letter of challenge to appear masked at the Capulets' feast. The sending of the cartel observes the rules of the code of honour but Mercutio profits by the presentation of Tybalt to play ironically not only with the name of the challenger (Tybalt is the name of the prince of cats according to English folklore) but also with the concept of the duel and duellists. Up to now, Tybalt has made only two fleeting appearances on the scene. In one, Benvolio emphasises to Montague Tybalt's violence in the first affray: 'with his sword prepared / Which [...] he swung about his head' (I.i.108–9). This is confirmed by Tybalt himself at the banquet, when he warns old Capulet of the presence among them of Romeo, 'this intrusion shall / [...] convert to bitterest gall' (I.v.91–2). Mercutio's ironic characterisation of the violent Tybalt uses a series of allusions and phrases which are once again taken from fencing manuals certainly known in the circle of Essex. He is opposed to the new school and his Tybalt echoes the controversy about the Italian school. Above all, and in addition to certain specific allusions such as 'captain of compliments', or 'keeps time'; or 'the very butcher of a silk button' which can be traced to the manuals already mentioned, Mercutio's description is an ironic version of English fashion-mongers and their following of the dictates, and even more the displays, of the Italian school. To be ironic about Tybalt is also to be ironic indirectly about the person who had been promoter, among so many other enterprises, of the diffusion of the art of fencing: John Florio, whom Shakespeare ridicules directly or indirectly in other plays also.[19] Tybalt's aggressiveness may recall Florio and his well-known threatening actions against the sheriff Laurence Grose, made under the aegis of Southampton. Leaving aside this detail, Florio was the embodiment of the negative view of a bombastic, rhetorical Italian world, and so readily vulnerable to attack, especially as representing a distorted and superficial vision of Italy, very different from that obtained, for example, by travellers and the students who attended Italian universities.

Mercutio is not only making a witty jest: his strokes are sometimes also premonitory of what is to come in the third act. There is for instance the list of irrational provocations of duels at all costs, attributed to the pacific Benvolio ('Thou wilt quarrel with a man for cracking nuts'; III.i.19). As he makes a series of allusions to the conduct of Romeo, who has not returned home the previous night, having just heard of Tybalt's challenge, Mercutio is preoccupied, as is shown by his remark: 'And is he a man to encounter Tybalt?' (II.iv.17). In his eyes, Romeo is still a boy and will so remain in the duel and the rest of the drama. At the beginning of the third act the premonitions of the preceding scenes reach their tragic conclusion. What had been adumbrated in the encounter between the servants and then in that between Benvolio and Tybalt, interrupted by the arrival of the prince, becomes a tragedy of fatality, of pointless death. This is owed to a series of equivocations. For Tybalt too Romeo, in refusing to fight, shows himself a boy and not a man. Mercutio's anger, excited by this refusal, the greatest falling short in the code of honour, forces him to brand his friend's attitude as 'dishonourable, vile submission' (III.i.72), and he takes Romeo's place in the encounter. It is certainly observance of the code of honour that forces him to this decision, for the code forbade the duel to those who, like Romeo, were still young.[20] There is also something else. First of all, Mercutio is not cognizant of the secret marriage of his friend and dies without knowing it; he is bound to the youth above all and cannot allow him to be accused of cowardice. He takes the position to which he is impelled by the quintessentially Renaissance concept of *amicitia*, raised to the level of one of the most exalted forms of human relationship. This in turn determines Romeo's decision to challenge Tybalt after the death of his friend. That Romeo remains essentially a boy, in spite of what Mercutio says to Tybalt before the formal encounter – 'Your worship in that sense may call him "man"' (III.i.58) – is confirmed by his irrational conduct in the duels he undertakes. The death of Mercutio transforms him from a peacemaker into a furious duellist who, impelled solely by anger, like lightning kills an expert swordsman such as Tybalt. Similarly, after the presumed death of Juliet, he kills Paris with a few blows in a duel which contravenes the code by taking place in a consecrated spot and at a time at which the rules forbade such encounters. They were required to take place in full daylight. In each case, too, his conduct is far from that prescribed by the manuals, which recommended control and coldness for good results in single combat.

Until the moment when Romeo withdraws from the encounter with Tybalt, ritual has been respected. Tybalt has given Romeo the lie; Mercutio, on Romeo's arrival, exhorts the challenger to 'go before to field, he'll be your follower' (III.i.57), an allusion to the form according to which the duel ought to take place in an unfrequented place. Benvolio also suggests that they 'withdraw unto some private place' (III.i.50) to dispute, but Romeo's refusal to fight forces the situation. The dispute, so far contained within the limits of the rules, degenerates and Mercutio, who had woven a subtle web of words to give the encounter the character of a dance executed to the sound of a fiddlestick (the sword) fights immediately after Romeo's refusal.[21] In the duel the rules are set aside, and the norms immediately infringed by Benvolio and by Romeo, who ought not to have interfered to separate the duellists once the encounter had begun.[22] The context at this point enters the ambiguous realm of fatality: chance has Mercutio killed by Tybalt through the involuntary fault of Romeo, and by a faithless stroke, so that the dramatic character of the situation is increased. Mercutio, too, dies in a way that is consistent with the personality he incarnates. He speaks in prose, the register of concreteness and reality, as death descends upon him. Romeo, on the other hand, operates in the other register, deciding to die on Juliet's tomb, raising death to a higher pitch as he expresses himself in verse. Imminent death, owed to a *stoccata* sustained in a duel *all'italiana* (a slash *all'inglese* might well not have been fatal) forces Mercutio to curse not only the families to whose enmity he is a victim, but also his adversary, who has sought the encounter at all costs: 'A braggart, a rogue, a villain that fights by the book of arithmetic' (III.i.100).[23] This is the final allusion to the manuals and to the Italian school of fence.

Why does Mercutio die in so absurd a mode, the victim of chance and of the aid he has given unasked to Romeo? The best reply is John Dryden's: 'Shakespeare showed the best of his skill in his Mercutio, and he said himself, that he was forced to kill him in the Third act, to prevent being killed by him'.[24] In effect, the death of Mercutio closes the first part of the play and from that moment all moves towards the final catastrophe. The end of this character, an entirely Shakespearean creation, who has up to this moment dominated the stage as the most novel and dynamic, leaves Romeo as the only male protagonist. The play had been balanced between wit and tragedy. Now it turns decisively towards the fatal consequences of a 'death-marked love'. The plot, with its suggestions of dramatic potential and the undercutting of this by irony, now moves directly towards its tragic solution. Mercutio is not mentioned again. He can no longer hold the play in libration, and for this reason too he must disappear.

Tybalt, on the other hand, continues to be intermittently present as a symbol of death: freed from Mercutio's irony, he has a tragic connotation only in the words of Juliet, as she expresses fear of a lonely awakening in the tomb, 'Where bloody Tybalt, yet but green in earth / Lies festering in his shroud' (IV.iii.42–3), and again in the obsessive vision of a 'mangled Tybalt' searching for the Romeo who has slain him 'upon a rapier's point' (IV.iii.57). And finally Romeo, in the chapel of the Capulets before killing himself and completing the fatal series of dead lovers, refers to Tybalt enwrapped in a 'bloody sheet' (V.iii.97).

In *Romeo and Juliet*, then, brawls, riots and duels are not matters of chance, inserted to make the play more of a spectacle and give the audience greater satisfaction. They *are* the drama, together with a series of other components which confer on the tale of the two lovers an Italian character, mediated by an interpretation of the Italian world as Shakespeare knew it in London. For this reason Shakespeare's sources for the encounters also cannot fail to have been Italianate, like the duels that mark the stages of the tragedy. The reference point for documentation, as always when problems of Anglo-Italian influence in the Elizabethan and Jacobean age are in question, is again John Florio. Florio had a decisive part in the publication of Saviolo's manual and made himself the promoter of other new aspects of Italian civilisation, precisely in the ambience frequented by Shakespeare. Florio's own limitations, however, conditioned his interpretation of this world. Shakespeare, as a good subject of the English realm as well as a man of the theatre, always filtered his sources through the sieve of the ever-present demands of a strongly nationalistic audience. He had, more-over, certain reservations about the Italian duel. Tybalt, a practitioner of the Italian mode, is a negative character, and Mercutio deals ironically with certain aspects of his dangerous practice. Mercutio is the antagonist who engages the audience's sympathies, however much his chance death leaves him incomplete as character.

What appears in *Romeo and Juliet*, therefore, is an incomplete Italy, acting as a frame to a marvellous and ambiguous love story. The distinguishing mark of this drama is the encounter, the duel, in which is reflected a particular problem, raised by Florio and considered critically by Shakespeare.

Notes

1 S. Rossi, '*Vincentio Saviolo his Practise* (1595): a problem of authorship', in *England and the Continental Renaissance: Essays in Honour of J. B. Trapp*, eds E. Chaney and P. Mack, Woodbridge, 1990, pp. 164–75.

2 Rossi, '*Vincentio Saviolo*', p. 164, n. 4.

3 Rossi, '*Vincentio Saviolo*', p. 166, n. 8.

4 F. A. Yates, 'Elizabethan chivalry: the romance of the Accession Day tilts', in *Astræa: the Imperial Theme in the Sixteenth Century*, London, 1975, pp. 88–111: and see, among others, *The Progresses and Public Processions of Queen Elizabeth*, ed. J. Nichols, London, 1823, vol. II, pp. 312–36. See also *The Progresses, Processions and Magnificent Festivities of King James I*, ed. J. Nichols, London, 1828, vol. III, p. 471.

5 The Italian mode of fencing was diffused in Europe through France as a result of contact between the French armies, who had invaded Italy to dispute with the Spaniards the hegemony of the peninsula, and the civilisation of the Italian Renaissance. One Pompeo, an Italian, was master of arms to Charles IX (1563); Henry III, considered one of the best

swordsmen in his kingdom, was a pupil of Silvio, another Italian. In London about 1570, according to the witness of George Silver, an Italian identified only as 'signor Rocco' and his son Ieronimo taught fencing; and in the 1590s he was succeeded by Vincentio Saviolo. My quotations from Silver, *Paradoxes of Defence*, London, 1599; *Vincentio Saviolo his Practise*, London, 1595; and *Giacomo di Grassi his True Art of Defence*, London, 1594, are taken from the reprint: *Three Elizabethan Fencing Manuals*, New York, 1972.

6 John Eliot had dedicated to the Earl of Essex his translation of Bertrand de Loque, *Discourses of Warre and Single Combat*, 1591, in which the right of duelling was denied 'as a thing contrary to the profession of Christians' (p. 51). In the light of the quarrel between Eliot and Florio, it was perhaps this translation that led Florio to present Essex with the interpretation of the legality of duelling maintained in Muzio's work (cf. Rossi, '*Vincentio Saviolo*', p. 167). In addition, Essex had taken part in the battle of Zutphen, where Sidney received the wound of which he died; he had also fought several duels, in one of which, against John Blount, he had been slightly wounded in the leg. The Queen banished them both from court until their reconciliation; she also prevented a duel between Essex and Sir Walter Raleigh.

7 F. A. Yates, *John Florio*, Cambridge, 1934, p. 334. There is also a description of Florio in the conversation-manual of another Italian, Benvenuto Italiano, *Il passagiere*, 1612, Dialogo Secondo, parte I, pp. 140–2, and Dialogo Secondo, parte II, pp. 516–20.

8 R. Kelso, 'Saviolo and his Practise', *Modern Language Notes*, 39, 1924, pp. 33–5.

9 Sword and buckler were considered outmoded arms, derived from the tournament and little adapted for duelling (*Vincentio Saviolo*, p. 399). The translator of di Grassi believes: 'The sworde and Buckler fight was longwhile allowed in England (and yet practise in all sortes of weapons is praisworthie) but now being layd downe, the Sworde but with Serving-men is not much regarded, and the Rapier fight generally allowed' (*Giacomo di Grassi*, an advertisement to the curteous reader, p. 10).

10 The words are both used to translate Italian *spada*, though 'rapier' was originally a shorter sword and 'sword' signified in fairly recent times a sort of long sword wielded with both hands and therefore difficult to thrust with. To make it manageable the armourers substantially reduced its weight, making the blade narrower and adding grooves. Shakespeare commentators use 'rapier' to indicate an arm of Spanish origin, on the basis of Cotgrave (1611), who gives: 'Espee Espagnole: a Rapier, a Tucke', though the manuals which Shakespeare had at his disposal give no indications of this kind.

11 The Italian and the English styles in fencing are different in one single respect. The Italian school, and the European in general, sought to pierce the adversary with the point and was therefore more murderous; the English, founded on the possibility of using a technique effective in battle, privileged the cutting stroke. It is worth remarking that nowhere in Europe was an English style ever spoken of and that no manual gives an example of an English duel.

12 At one point only (IV.v.100–40) the dramatic tension is reduced, in the dialogue between Peter and the musicians, after the apparent death of Juliet,

and 'dagger' is given a comic sense.

13 In the list of works consulted in compiling his dictionary, Florio includes the treatise of Pietro Grizio, *Il Castigliano overo dell'arme di nobiltà*, Mantua, per Francesco Osana, MDLXXXVI, in which, however, arms are spoken of as devices of noble families.

14 An augmented list is polemically furnished by Silver: 'Now; o you Italian teachers of Defence, where are your Stocatas, Imbrocatas, Mandritas, Puntas, & Punta reversas, Stramisons, Passatas, Carricados, Amazzas, & Incartatas' (*Paradoxes*, p. 55).

15 A propos *stoccata*, Mercutio challenges Tybalt with the cry 'Alla stoccata!' (III.i.73), which can be interpreted in various ways. H. E. Cain, in *Shakespeare Association Bulletin*, Jan. 1942, suggests that *stoccata* should be understood as *steccata*, but has not found much support. 'Alla stoccata!' nevertheless, though it might signify 'after the manner of', is not recorded in the word-lists and is not used in Italian manuals of the Cinquecento, while 'alla steccata' might be justified as an invitation by Mercutio to Tybalt to fight in a place removed from public view, as the rules required, and 'walk' might mean 'Let us go' as well as 'come'. *Steccato*, according to Florio's dictionary, could mean 'also a combate'; in the part of Saviolo's manual translated from Muzio, we read:'After the defie it is not lawfull that the one Gentleman should offend the other, but in the steccata, which is the place of Combat' (p. 373). The *steccato* hypothesis gains strength if it is remembered that the Prince had announced that the rigours of the law would be applied if fresh encounters 'disturb'd the quiet of our streets' (I.i.90). It is true that the rhythm of the action is such as to make one think differently and that the encounter is precipitated by heightened emotion and uncontrolled behaviour encouraged by the heats of summer, all factors which force the opponents towards disrespect for the laws.

16 The intervention of Escalus and the punishment of the duellists reflect what some of the treatises say, e.g. F. Albergati, *Trattato del modo di ridurre a pace l'inimicitie private*, Rome, 1583; G. B. Pigna, *Il duello*, Venice, 1554; M. A. Possevino, *Trattato nel quale s'insegna a conoscere cose pertinenti l'honore*, Venice, 1559. Albergati devotes much space to relations between duellist and prince; and whether the defence of personal honour can justify disobedience to the prince's order. The problem is seen from another angle by Muzio (*Il Duello*, ch. xxi) and faithfully translated into English: 'Whether the subject ought to obey his Soveraigne, being by him forbidden to Combat'. Here he seems to understand that the gentleman ought always to consult his private honour: 'they will retire into some secrete place, where it shall not consist onely in theyr Princes power to forbidde, or staie them from it, and so laying aside all respect either of their Princes favour or losse of goods, or banishment from their countrie, they take the combate in hande' (*Vincentio Saviolo*, p. 378).

17 In France between 1588 and 1608 some thousand gentlemen were killed in matters of honour (cf. P. Lacaze, *En garde*, Paris, 1991, p. 37), or rather two thousand according to de Loque (*Discourses of Warre*, introd. p. viii). There is information concerning some twenty official duels fought in England in the 1590s, while only five are known from the preceding decade (cf. R.

Lacey, *Robert Earl of Essex: an Elizabethan Icarus*, London, 1971, p. 126).

18 Many incidents in the chronicles may have given Shakespeare inspiration; the problem is only to choose from them. See, for instance, Lacey, *Robert Earl of Essex*, pp. 124–5; George Silver's 'A brief Note of three Italian Teachers of Offence', in *Paradoxes*, p. 67: and *Vincentio Saviolo his Practise*, p. 323. The affinities with *Romeo and Juliet* are evident and, since Shakespeare could have had the Saviolo text at his disposition, it is very probable that he used this page as a model for the behaviour of Escalus, or for III.i.52–4.

19 The Holofernes–Florio connection in *Love's Labour's Lost* is well known. So is the use of the *Vincentio Saviolo* manual for *As You Like it* (V.iv.67). Cf. also *As You Like It* (I.ii.140) and *Vincentio Saviolo*, pp. 333–4.

20 The familiar manual *Vincentio Saviolo*, in the chapter 'touching the appointing of champions', remarks that 'there are also such manner of cases that in respect of persons it is lawfull to appointe Champions, as if a man shall not bee of eighteene yeeres' (p. 446).

21 In these images of duel/ballet can be found another allusion to the rhythm and precise co-ordination in the movement of the feet in the Italian method (Saviolo was also a dancing master). There is another in the transposition to another key of the bawdy jests of Sampson and Gregory in the first act where the sword is called 'tool', with an obvious sexual significance.

22 Separation of the duellists was not orthodox, though not entirely forbidden. Certain illustrations suggest that the arbitrator could do it with a long stick. Muzio is not categorical: 'I like not the custome which some men have in medling with other mens weapons, especiallye with theirs that professe armes, neither can I thinke it an ouer-wise parte for men to be viewing one the others Rapiers, whereof may this inconuenience rise, that a man may so take occasion to kill his enemie' (*Vincentio Saviolo*, p. 324). This last case applies better to the final duel in *Hamlet*. A duel which had a similar outcome was fought on 18 September 1589 between Marlowe and Bradley, in which Thomas Watson, intervening to separate them, killed Bradley (Eccels, *Christopher Marlowe in London*, London, 1934, pp. 9–10, 35–6).

23 All the fencing manuals, including those in English which Shakespeare could more easily have consulted, emphasise the need to co-ordinate and harmonise in duelling the movement of the body, the play of the legs and the management of the sword, as one can read in *Vincentio Saviolo*, pp. 211–13, and further in the translation of di Grassi (ch. 'Of paces', p. 133). Fencing, considered an art by the Italians, surely took this preoccupation from the study of painting which looked for such proportions. This is evident in the illustrations which complete the manuals, which are of high quality.

24 Dryden resolves the question in an entirely different way: 'But, for my part, I cannot find he was so dangerous a person … He might have lived to the end of the play, and died in his bed, without offence to any man.' 'Defence of the epilogue: or an essay on the dramatic poetry of the last age', in *Essays of John Dryden*, ed. W. P. Ker, 1, Oxford, 1990, p. 174.

8

Merchants and madcaps: Dekker's *Honest Whore* plays and the *commedia dell'arte*

Viviana Comensoli

In her seminal work on the influence of Italian popular comedy on the English stage, Kathleen Lea has noted that while there is no direct evidence that English Renaissance dramatists came into actual contact with Italian comedians, the earliest recorded visit of Italian players in England occurred in 1546; by 1578 six more visits had been documented and 'by 1591 the visits ... were ... common enough for spies to choose the habit of tumblers as a safe disguise'.[1] More recently, Ninian Mellamphy has suggested that the 'incidence of references to improvising comedians, magnificoes, pantaloons, pedants, and zanies in later Elizabethan literature', together with historical accounts of Italian players in England and of English actors in Europe, 'make it virtually certain that Shakespeare's contemporaries had a more than casual knowledge of the commedia dell'arte'.[2] Louise George Clubb has noted Shakespeare's various 'means of acquaintance with the improvised comedy and its popular masks'.[3] And Andrew Gurr, relying on clear evidence from Elizabethan records attesting to the English public's familiarity with Italian comedy, has concluded that 'as early as 1590 many of the actors who were to work with Shakespeare – and perhaps Shakespeare too – were not only acquainted with the stock characters of the commedia dell'arte, but may actually have been using its comic conventions and the technique of improvisation in the plays they were performing'.[4] Although the scant amount of scholarship that exists on the influence of the *commedia dell'arte* on English popular comedy has focused on Shakespeare, a cursory survey of Elizabethan and Jacobean plays that employ Italian dramatic motifs suggests considerable intertextuality between the plots and character types of the *commedia dell'arte* and those of Shakespeare's contemporaries.[5] One notable example is the exploitation of Italian comedic structures by one of Shakespeare's most prolific contemporaries, Thomas Dekker.

Until recently, critical appraisal of Dekker's plays has been cautious and frequently apologetic. In the 1960s Harold Toliver voiced a common sentiment when he wrote: 'Dekker will not likely share the lot of rediscovered minor figures' as he 'had the misfortune of being overmatched by Jonson in satire and overshadowed by Shakespeare in romantic comedy'.[6] During the past decade, however, the complexity of Dekker's stagecraft has become increasingly evident, to the extent that he has been recently designated 'a major playwright of both Elizabethan and Jacobean London'.[7] In her reassessment of Dekker's Protestant plays, Julia Gasper has challenged the prevailing view of Dekker as a genial purveyor of popular culture; instead, Gasper has found a dramatist whose keen interest in contemporary politics is inscribed within a sophisticated dramaturgy.[8] And Larry Champion has argued that Dekker needs to be revaluated for his 'persistent determination to experiment in form and, in some instances, to expand the traditions of English drama'.[9] Dekker's acquaintance with Italian dramatic traditions, however, has generally eluded critics. With respect to his debt to Italian popular comedy, Kathleen Lea has noted that in *The Whore of Babylon* (1607) and again in *If This Be Not a Good Play, the Devil is in It* (1612) Dekker was familiar enough with the *commedia dell'arte* to utilise for comic effect the Italian *zanni* or clownish servants.[10] But it is in *The Honest Whore*, Parts I and II (*c.* 1604–5) that the influence of the *commedia dell'arte* is especially pronounced. In both plays Dekker employs an Italian setting and dramatic paradigms from the *commedia dell'arte* for ironic effect, distinguishing the plays as the first to convey the satirical temper of the private theatres through an adult company and a popular play-house.[11]

Both parts of *The Honest Whore* are set in contemporary Milan, but the thematic relevance of the Italian setting has not been explored. Concurring with the view that 'Dekker's Milanese court' is merely 'a thin disguise for the Jacobean court',[12] critics have generally treated the two plays as morality-patterned comedies exalting English middle-class values, which are most fully embodied by the merchant Candido. Paralleling the conversion of the courtesan Bellafront (Part I) and her persistence in virtue (Part II) is the fortitude of Candido, a Milanese linen-draper and long-suffering husband. In both plays

Candido undergoes a series of bizarre, often farcical, trials of his virtue, culminating in his wrongful incarceration either in an asylum (Part I) or in the house of correction (Part II). Following these ordeals, he supposedly emerges as a model of patience for the entire community. Yet critical commentary is divided about the dramatic value of the merchant plot. On the one hand there are those who view the linen-draper as evidence of Dekker's obeisance to middle-class spectators, Candido's exemplary behaviour contrasting sharply with the dissolution that permeates the underworld of panders and bawds in the Bellafront plot. According to Larry Champion, in Part I of the play Candido 'survives the role as comic butt to emerge as a kind of middle class hero who delivers an encomium on the virtues of patience at the end of the play'; and in Part II Candido's wrongful arrest for stolen goods in the final act is a test of his enduring patience which is extolled by the highest authority figure in his world, namely the Duke of Milan.[13] R. J. Palumbo praises the linen-draper as the embodiment of 'the highest values of [...] citizen morality',[14] while Douglas Bruster has proposed that in 'Dekker's bourgeois world view, the cuckold merchant is a kind of Christ figure. [...] Rather than an object of derision, Candido serves as role model'.[15] For others, on the other hand, the linen-draper and the farcical stage action surrounding him are the source of more qualified judgements and even scepticism. Peter Ure, for example, has observed that 'Candido's humour [...] makes him seem ridiculous and touchingly *good* at one and the same time; we look up to him with one auspicious and one dropping eye'.[16] For Alfred Harbage, the patient Candido is 'an absurd figure' whose eccentric behaviour is couched in 'an aura' of humility.[17] And Larry Champion has cautioned that if the Candido action is not 'played broadly, [...] the spectator would understandably begin to question not only Viola's motivation in her determination to infuriate her husband but also Candido's willingness to be mocked and bludgeoned in the name of patience which by any realistic standard smells either of cowardice or of stupidity'.[18]

I propose that the comic admixtures of the Candido plot contain an impulse which Northrop Frye ascribes to ironic comedy, both classical and Renaissance, namely the 'tendency [...] to ridicule and scold an audience assumed to be hankering after sentiment, solemnity, and [...] approved moral standards'.[19] The *Honest Whore* plays' ironic impulses are in part influenced by the scepticism that characterised the early Jacobean theatre, and that contributed to the shift towards satirical drama in the private playhouses following the reopening of the theatres in 1604 (all playhouses had been closed during a major outbreak of plague in 1603).[20] The preference for satire peaked between 1600 and 1613 when most plays written for the coterie theatres were satirical comedies. Few tragedies were staged here and virtually no chronicle plays or romances. The subject of most of these satires is sexual infidelity 'coupled [...] with cupidity and fraud'.[21] There is an overriding interest in sexual transgression within a money economy, and in the exposure of folly and hypocrisy, usually of characters from the merchant class. The Italian setting of the *Honest Whore* plays, together with Dekker's employment of characters and situations resembling those commonly found in Italian popular comedy, clarifies his satirical intent. The signal example of influence is the portrait of the self-satisfied merchant, suggesting that Candido is deliberately modelled after the comic mask of Pantalone, the old magnifico of the *commedia dell'arte* and the prototype of the merchant madcap. The striking parallels between the two characters, and between the numerous stage motifs and *topoi* that surround them, strongly indicate that, rather than catering to his middle-class audience's complacency, Dekker, like the Italian creators of Pantalone, satirises an unbridled mercantile ethic.

Pantalone is a self-fashioned eminent citizen (usually of Venice, but sometimes of Naples, Rome or Milan), whose chief pursuit, like Candido's, is the linen trade. Italy was one of the largest European centres of trade, and by the mid-sixteenth century had, like England, built up an energetic cloth industry among many others.[22] In comedies such as *Il pedante, Il ritratto* and *La travagliata Isabella* the Pantalone mask reveals a notable duality: Pantalone is a shrewd and intelligent man of affairs whose 'demeanour is appropriately discreet',[23] at the same time that he is greedy and credulous. In many other plays Pantalone's comic aspects revolve chiefly around 'the contradictions of senility',[24] foremost of which is his fondness for moral platitudes combined with a love of riches. In the later years of the *commedia dell'arte* Pantalone's miserliness was a constant source of derision: 'In punishment for his avaricious nature, which is evidently only an atavism, and which [...] affects no one but his near and dear ones, the fates combine to rain down all manner of ill-luck and calamity on his venerable head'.[25] But Pantalone is rarely discouraged by humiliation or calamity, stoically accepting his misfortunes as temporary and setting out to pursue more riches. The overriding obsession with and perseverance in accumulating money, the senility and the fondness for moralising are among the distinguishing features of Dekker's linen-draper. Like Pantalone's eminence and habitual modesty, which are overshadowed by greed, Candido's public image as an upstanding citizen and 'the mirror of patience' (Part I, I.iv.15) is counterbalanced by his preoccupation with wealth and reputation. Indeed, the linen-draper's understanding and practice of patience are so focused on the virtue's application to the business of selling cloth that before the dénouement in both Parts I and II of the play it is virtually impossible to differentiate between Candido the successful tradesman and Candido the patient man. Just as Pantalone is an old magnifico who is both avaricious and gullible, Candido is an 'old fellow' (Part II, I.ii.15) and 'a very noble Citizen' (lines 13–14) who is subjected to a series of bizarre tests exposing his compulsive greed and limited understanding of the virtue he represents. Candido's trials are remarkable for their absurdity; rather than mirroring the struggles of the afflicted soul toward virtue as, for example, Patient Griselda's tests do, they reveal the merchant as an opportunist. Like Pantalone, who is inevitably duped either by a family member, a gallant, or a *zanni* (a servant-clown or trickster), Candido is victimised by his wife Viola and the gallants who cheat him in his shop. There are additional parallels between Viola's impoverished, cynical and outspoken brother Fustigo, who delights in practical jokes, and the *zanni*, who is always of humble birth and who is 'the cleverest, the most plain-spoken, [...] and the most cynical of the Italian Masks';[26] and similarities in the use of farcical stage jests (or *lazzi*) whose function is to expose Candido and Pantalone as comic butts.

In Part I of *The Honest Whore* the tricking of Candido is initiated by the arrival of the rascal Fustigo. Like his counterpart *zanni*, Fustigo is the confidant of a principal character (in this case Viola), his function being to set the plot in motion. Fustigo introduces the linen-draper to the audience as one who is as tight-fisted as he is stoic – 'Troth sister I heard you were married to a verie riche chuffe [i.e., miser]' (I.ii.30)[27] – and therefore worthy of scorn. Fustigo further describes Candido as a senile 'whiblin' (I.ii.61), that is, an 'impotent creature' (a 'term of contempt' in Elizabethan slang).[28] Candido's lack of sexual virility is mentioned again moments later when Viola's 'strange longing' (lines 81–2) to make her husband 'horne mad' (line 91) is portrayed as stemming from sexual frustration. Viola complains that while she lacks none of the material comforts which a citizen's wife may desire, her husband has 'not all things belonging to a man' (lines 58–9). In a number of the Italian analogues Pantalone's impotence (an effect of greed) is also the object of his wife's and *zanni*'s derision. When Pantalone is duped by his wife and her confidant their deception involves insult, mockery and usually cuckoldry. In this context, Candido's and Pantalone's senility is a variant of the familiar carnival figure of classical comedy, the cuckold or senex. Viola, like Pantalone's wife, plays an active role in her husband's humiliation, but whereas in both classical comedy and the *commedia dell'arte* the wife's adultery is unequivocal, Viola's commission of her brother to play her lover so as to dupe her husband into believing he is being cuckolded forestalls the moral complication. This departure from the convention suggests Dekker's compliance with the general rule of decorum in the English public theatres never to play a comedy of adultery.[29]

In both Part I of *The Honest Whore* and the sequel the gallants who abuse Candido's patience directly recall the gallants who trick Pantalone. Indeed, Dekker's names for the gallants – Castruchio, Pioratto, Fluello, Beraldo and Pandulfo (who appears in name only in Part I, III.i.88–9) – are all variants of minor characters in the *commedia dell'arte*, cases in point being Coviello, Pincastro, Ubaldo and Pandolfo. During the first test of his patience in Part I, Candido eagerly complies with a gallant's request for a 'pennyworth' of 'lawne' cut from the centre of an expensive seventeen-yard piece (I.v.63–8). Viola's incredulous remark, 'What will he spoile the Lawne now?' (line 87), is calmly reproached by Candido in his reply, 'Patience, good wife' (line 88), the rationale for Christian steadfastness being that by allowing even one customer to get away 'We get by many' (line 123). 'Deny a pennorth', he warns his wife, and 'it may crosse a pound' (line 126). Candido's supplication of his sniggering customers underscores his opportunism:

> Pray Gentlemen take her [Viola] to be a woman,
> Do not regard her language. – O kinde soule:
> Such words will driue away my customers.
>
> (lines 92–4)

Unruffled even by his journeyman's warning that the gallants are 'some cheating companions' (line 98), Candido implores them to bring him further business:

I haue your mony heare; pray know my shop,
Pray let me haue your custome. [...]
Let me take more of your money.

(lines 100–3)

The scene builds in such a way that it undercuts Candido's 'quiet sufferance' (line 218) by its *reductio ad absurdum* in Candido's motto: 'he that meanes to thriue, with patient eye / Must please the diuell, if he come to buy' (lines 127–8). In 'pleas[ing] all customers, / Their humours and their fancies' and 'offend[ing] none' (lines 121–2) one finds the way to wealth.

While Candido's and Pantalone's love of riches makes them likely prey for the *zanni* and gallants, their dupability also stems from a weak understanding. It was a frequent practice of Elizabethan and continental dramatists to represent a dull-witted, gullible character as a foolish Pantaloon,[30] a practice that survived as late as the eighteenth century. In 1728, the actor and improvisator Luigi Riccoboni wrote a treatise on the history of the Italian theatre in which he advised actors assuming the Pantalone mask to 'try to provoke laughter at appropriate junctures by his [Pantalone's] self-importance and stupidity, and in this manner represent a man ripe in years who pretends to be a tower of strength and good counsel for others', but who 'goes on being tricked by everyone he knows'.[31] In his study of deception as a common motif of Renaissance comedy in general, John Curry observes that the degree of susceptibility depends on the extent of the victim's intelligence:

At the lowest level lie the fatuous and the lumpish; then come those who are not stupid but who, because of lack of education and culture, are ignorant and superstitious; above these are victims who, while not entirely stupid or ignorant, are egoistic or self-deceived with respect to some particular phase of their own character or powers; we find next some who are not justly classified with any of the above groups, but are shown as unwary and overtrusting; and finally there are those who are rather cunning and deceitful and quite experienced.[32]

Candido's and Pantalone's opportunism excludes them from the category of blind trust; instead, their credulity is partly an effect of a weak understanding that equates acquisitiveness with virtue. In Italian comedy deception is also often used in relation to the theme of madness. As Louise Clubb notes, 'real madness, supposed madness, assumed madness, fear of madness, and obsessions bordering on madness were familiar both as phenomena and as structural key signatures'.[33] Dekker's portrayal of the slow-witted merchant madcap is foregrounded in Acts III and IV of Part I, where the word 'mad' permeates the dialogue.[34] Before being committed to Bedlam asylum, Candido goes to absurd lengths to test his conception of virtue as the endowment of wealth. Viola, who has been unsuccessful in inciting her husband's passion, has locked away his senate gown, which he has patiently replaced with a fine table cover (a mark of social status)[35] cut through the middle so that it may fit cape-like over his head. Candido's costume – 'something fashioned like a gowne, / With my armes out' (III.i.187–8) – suggests a comic variation of the *zimarra* or black gown for which Pantalone was famous. Exasperated with Candido's resolve, Viola cries out in disbelief: 'Grit about him like a mad-man: what: has he lost his cloake too: this is the maddest fashion that ere I saw' (IV.iii.29–30). Viola's pronouncement that her husband has lost his ability to reason would be less convincing were it not for the fact that Candido's ludicrous garb is unnecessary – Candido himself has admitted that he could have attended the senate meeting without a gown, had he been willing to pay a higher fine:

> Out of two euils hee's accounted wise,
> That can picke out the least; the Fine imposde
> For an vn-gowned Senator, is about
> Forty Cruzadoes, the Carpet [table cloth] not 'boue foure.
> Thus haue I chosen the lesser euill yet,
> Preseru'd my patience. [ ].

> (III.i.202–7)

Candido's boast that he has kept his patience intact through his 'wise' choice of a lesser 'evil' attests to a feeble understanding of the very concepts he invokes, namely wisdom and evil. In *The Book named the Governour* (1531) Sir Thomas Elyot defines the faculty of understanding as 'the most excellent gift that man can receive in his creation, whereby he doth approach most nigh unto the similitude of God, which understanding is the principal part of the soul.' Elyot also emphasises that understanding is alien to the concern for material reward: those with true understanding 'nothing do acquire by the said influence of knowledge'.[36] And in 1428–29 the Italian humanist Poggio Bracciolini, citing Seneca's *De tranquillitate animi* ('On the Tranquility of Mind'), wrote of the necessity of combining public duty with active virtue, which includes 'resist[ing] or restrain[ing] those who rush about in pursuit of money and luxury'.[37] But wisdom, according to the mercantile ethic, is not the spiritual capacity of judging rightly in matters pertaining to moral conduct or soundness of judgement; rather, it is sound sense in practical affairs. Evil, by the same token, is anything that disrupts those affairs.

In this context Candido reveals significant parallels with Simon Eyre, the tradesman-hero of Dekker's citizen comedy *The Shoemaker's Holiday* (1599–1600). Joel Kaplan has observed that Eyre 'is as much merchant as madcap', and that his 'opportunism and madness are most often inseparable'.[38] While in *The Shoemaker's Holiday* the merchant's vitality obscures morally questionable behaviour, Candido's acquisitiveness suggests a growing scepticism on Dekker's part towards the merchant code, a scepticism notable in the *commedia dell'arte*, in which Pantalone, rather than enhancing the social order, distorts it through *cupiditas*.

Related to Candido's and Pantalone's dull wit, self-deception, and *cupiditas* is their comic use of contrasting discourses. The parallels between the two characters' linguistic variations clarify what critics have perceived as a puzzling duality in Candido's demeanour and language.[39] On the one hand, Candido is well known for his sober maxims and proverbial wisdom: 'The straightest arrow may flye wide by chance' (Part II, I.iii.132); 'all [wars] are bad, yet wars doe good, / And like to Surgeons, let sicke Kingdomes blood' (III.iii.103–4). And when public occasion warrants, his language is appropriately elevated: in Part I, he delivers an encomium on patience (V.ii.493–514) described by the Duke as having 'liuely colours' (line 515); Part II features Candido's long litany honouring the history and variety of 'Caps', especially those worn by London citizens – 'And that's the Cap which you see swels not hye, / For Caps are Emblems of humility; / It is a Citizens badge' (I.iii.40–2). The speech is a solemn but thoroughly predictable reflection on degree, and delineates an ideal world devoid of struggle and conflict: 'Each degree has his fashion, it's fit then, / One should be laid by for the Citizen' (lines 38–9). On the other hand, the linen-draper is mocked even by his trusty journeyman for his bombast and babble – 'he talkes like a Iustice of peace, of a thousand matters and to no purpose' (Part I, V.i.26–7); he 'talkes like a young Gentleman, somewhat phantastically' (lines 72–3). We may compare Candido's discrepant language with Pantalone's discursiveness which ranges in tone from formal to vulgar. Gianrenzo Clivio, in his essay on 'The languages of the *commedia dell'arte*', has noted that Andrea Perrucci's treatise *Dell'arte rappresentativa premeditata ed all'improvviso* (Naples, 1699) is 'the only [...] reasonably reliable source that we possess to investigate the problem of language [...] within the commedia dell'Arte'.[40] In his discussion of the Pantalone mask, Perrucci 'refer[s] to vertical varieties of Venetian, intending to have Pantalone speak in a more vulgar or more elevated form according to circumstances'.[41] Perrucci cites three examples of typical speeches by Pantalone, all in Venetian. In all three passages Pantalone selects from the stock of maxims and platitudes for which he was famous; they are differentiated only by modulations in vocabulary and tone. In the first, the 'Conseglio' ('Counsel'), Pantalone advises a prince that sound judgement is a necessary corollary to efficient political rule. The vocabulary is highly stylised and the syntax formal: 'chi vol raccoger el fruto da quel c'ha semenao l'è necessetae, che se vada dal semmenaor del consegger per cogniosser el tempo che sia ben a farlo. Chi vol alzar l'Edifizio della Politica, el se serva del fondamento de la rason perché senza questa anderà per tera tuta la machina' ('Whoever wishes to gather the fruit of that which he has sown must go to the sower of the Counsellor to know the time when it is good to do so. Whoever wishes to raise the Edifice of policy must use the foundation of reason for without this the whole building will fall to the ground.')[42] In the 'Persuasiva al Figlio' ('Admonishing the Son'), in which Pantalone chastises his son for loose living, the vocabulary is more mundane: 'e no ti cognosi che i Buli xè tante sansughe, che tanto le te sta tacae, in tanto che le te ha zupegao el sangue e dale vene, e dela scarsela'. ('and do you not know that the knaves are so many leeches that remain attached to you until they have sucked your blood from your veins and from your skin'). The final example, the 'Maledizione al Figlio' ('Cursing the Son'), is both prosaic and ribald: 'se ti vorrà nuar te posi niegar coma le Simie, se ti vorà magnar le Arpie te caga into a le vivande; le Mosche te cortezi come una carogna, le Zeraste quando ti bevi te posa pisar in tel vin' ('if you want to swim may you drown like Monkeys, if you want to eat may Harpies cack into your food; may Flies hover about you like a corpse and, when you drink, may Mosquitoes piss in your wines'). As Clivio suggests, although 'stylistic differences, especially in the matter of vocabulary, are quite striking, the three passages do have in common certain rhetorical devices, especially the use of metaphors and comparisons, which are of a grandiloquent and almost bombastic nature in the first passage, more down to earth in the second and frequently vulgar or obscene in the third'.[43] Just as Pantalone modulates lexicon, register and syntax for comic effect, Candido's language, we have seen, is also marked by extreme variations, ranging from magniloquent to plebeian. In Part I of the play the comic shifts in phrasing, vocabulary and tone culminate in the linen-draper's grand, exemplary tribute to Patience – 'It is the sap of blisse / Reares vs aloft; makes men and Angels kisse' (V.ii.511–12) – a tribute that climaxes absurdly in the linen-draper's crass reduction of the virtue to 'the hunny gainst a waspish wife' (line 514). The encomium is further undermined by the speaker's vanity: rather than assigning the commendation of Candido's virtue to another character, Dekker gives it to the linen-draper himself, who in the course of extolling his own virtue makes a startling comparison between himself and Christ, venerating 'the best of men' (line 496) in a barrage of adjectives ('meeke', 'patient', 'humble', 'tranquill') that Candido's admirers have typically applied to him:

> Patience my Lord; why tis the soule of peace:
> Of all the vertues tis neerst kin to heauen.
> It makes men looke like Gods; the best of men
> That ere wore earth about him, was a sufferer,
> A soft, meeke, patient, humble, tranquill spirit,
> The first true Gentle-man, that euer breathd.
>
> (lines 494–9)

In the sequel, Candido's wise saws are displaced by a preponderance of earthy, often bawdy language, and by farcical scenes that closely approximate the *lazzi* or comic stage business of the *commedia dell'arte*. Viola has died, and we meet Candido on the day of his wedding to a much younger woman who is merely called Bride or Wife. Whereas in Part I Candido's preoccupation with wealth is an adjunct to impotence and senility, in Part II Dekker exploits another stock-in-trade of the Pantalone mask, namely the old magnifico's infatuation with a much younger woman. Although he is sometimes impotent, Pantalone is more frequently lecherous, seducing and impregnating Franceschina or Olimpia, or else avenging his cuckoldry with his own adulterous liaisons. Indeed, his avarice more often coextends with lust, two vices frequently paired in Renaissance treatises as the most pervasive of human afflictions. Bracciolini, for example, declares that 'avarice and lust are [...] the seat and foundation of all evils', and he cites Cato's warning that these two sins 'have been the destruction of every great empire'.[44] (Once again, however, Dekker yields to theatrical decorum in that Candido does not court a much younger woman until Viola has died.) As authorial recompense for their desire for younger women, Candido and Pantalone are scolded and ridiculed by their termagant brides and, in Pantalone's case, by his mistresses. In an episode informed by verbal coarseness and farce, Candido, upon the advice of the gallant Lodovico, sets out to tame his Bride: 'A curst Cowes milke I ha drunke once before, / And 'twas so ranke in taste, Ile drinke no more. / Wife, Ile tame you' (II.ii.72–4). As Alexander Leggatt has noted, Candido's efforts to tame his bride are 'conducted on the level of slapstick, with symbolic overtones: they prepare to fence, he with a yard and she with an ell. "Yard" being a common term for the male sex organ, its use here suggests an elemental sexual conflict'.[45] Although the farcical tussle between senex and shrew resembles the popular improvised mock-fights and the 'appeals to a primitive sense of fun'[46] that informed the *lazzi* or 'harlequinesque raillery'[47] of the *commedia dell'arte*, it also has its roots in a medieval theatrical tradition of laughter-inducing brawls. This long tradition is ultimately employed by Dekker for satirical purposes. As a portrait of a 'world [...] vpside downe' (Part I, IV.iii.63) the Candido scenes of *The Honest Whore* plays ironically counterpoint the Duke's cheerful pronouncement at the end of Part II that Candido's patience is 'a Patterne for a King' (V.ii.497).

Numerous details of *The Honest Whore* plays point to Dekker's more than passing engagement with Italian popular comedy. Rather than suggesting gratuitous borrowings, the plays illustrate the appropriation of dramatic conventions of the *commedia dell'arte* in ways which helped shape the satirical vision of an English Renaissance dramatist whose craft has been too often belittled or misunderstood.

Notes

1 K. M. Lea, *Italian Popular Comedy: a Study in the commedia dell'arte, 1560–1620, with Special Reference to the English Stage*, 2 vols, 1934; rpt New York, 1962, 2, pp. 357 and 352–74. Louise George Clubb, in 'Italian comedy and *The Comedy of Errors*', *Comparative Literature*, 19, 1967, suggests that 'Royal interest' in Italian comedy is also 'proved by Queen Elizabeth's request that her courtiers organize a performance of one' (p. 241).

2 Ninian Mellamphy, 'Pantaloons and zanies: Shakespeare's "apprenticeship" to Italian professional comedy troupes', in *Shakespearean Comedy*, ed.

Maurice Charney, New York, 1980, p. 141.

3 Louise George Clubb, *Italian Drama in Shakespeare's Time*, New Haven and London, 1989, p. 256. For other general accounts of the evolution and impact of the *Commedia dell'arte* see Winifred Smith, *The Commedia dell'Arte*, 1912; rpt New York and London, 1964; Allardyce Nicoll, *The World of Harlequin: a Critical Study of the Commedia dell'Arte*, Cambridge, 1963, and *Masks, Mimes and Miracles: Studies in the Popular Theatre*, London, 1949; Pierre Louis Ducharte, *The Italian Comedy*, trans. Randolph T. Weaver, New York, 1966; Roberto Tessari, *La Commedia dell'Arte nel Seicento: 'Industria' e 'Arte Giocosa' della civiltà barocca*, Florence, 1969; and *The Science of Buffoonery: Theory and History of the Commedia dell'Arte*, ed. Domenico Pietropaolo, University of Toronto Italian Series 3, Ottawa, 1989.

4 Andrew Gurr, 'The clowning zanies: Shakespeare and the actors of the *commedia dell'arte*', *Shakespeare in Southern Africa: Journal of the Shakespeare Society of Southern Africa*, 3, 1989, p. 15.

5 See Lea, *Italian Popular Comedy*, 2, pp. 339–455; Smith, *The Commedia dell'Arte*, pp. 170–99; and Gurr, 'The clowning zanies', pp. 14–15.

6 Harold Toliver, '*The Shoemaker's Holiday*: theme and image', *Boston University Studies in English*, V, 1961, p. 208.

7 Anne Lancashire, 'Recent studies in Elizabethan and Jacobean drama', *SEL: Studies in English Literature*, 31, spring 1991, p. 388.

8 Julia Gasper, *The Dragon and the Dove: the Plays of Thomas Dekker*, Oxford, 1990, *passim*.

9 Larry S. Champion, *Thomas Dekker and the Traditions of English Drama*, New York, 1985, pp. 5–6.

10 Lea, *Italian Popular Comedy*, II, pp. 376 and 390.

11 Peter Ure notes that Part I of *The Honest Whore* 'was performed by the Henslowe/Alleyn company, Prince Henry's Men (formerly the Admiral's), at (presumably) the Fortune playhouse, [...] in 1604; the second Part followed hard upon the success of the first, presumably in 1605' ('Patient madman and honest whore: the Middleton-Dekker oxymoron', *Essays and Studies*, n.s. 19, 1966, p. 21). Part I of the play is a collaboration with Middleton, but it is generally agreed that Dekker's is the controlling hand. Cyrus Hoy writes that 'the play is largely Dekker's [...] Middleton's contribution may have consisted principally in touches given to individual passages throughout the play' (*Introductions, Notes, and Commentaries to Texts in 'The Dramatic Works of Thomas Dekker' Edited by Fredson Bowers*, 4 vols, Cambridge, 1980, 2, pp. 5–6). Part 2 is entirely by Dekker.

12 Martin S. Day, *History of English Literature to 1660*, Garden City, New York, 1963, p. 343.

13 Larry S. Champion, 'From melodrama to comedy: a study of the dramatic perspective in Dekker's *The Honest Whore*, Part I and II', *Studies in Philology*, 69, 1972, pp. 195–6, 202.

14 R. J. Palumbo, 'Trade and custom in 1 *Honest Whore*', *American Notes and Queries*, 15, 3, 1976, p. 34. Norman Muir praises the linen-draper in similar terms: 'Candido's patience is no simple, one-dimensional comic humor', but 'a Christianized version of the classical cardinal virtue of fortitude' ('Middle-class heroism and the cardinal virtue fortitude in Thomas Dekker's *Honest*

Whore plays', *Explorations in Renaissance Culture*, 15, 1989, p. 83).

15 Douglas Bruster, 'The horn of plenty: cuckoldry and capital in the drama of the age of Shakespeare', *Studies in English Literature*, 30, spring 1990, p. 206.

16 Ure, 'Patient madman and honest whore', p. 26.

17 Alfred Harbage, *Shakespeare and the Rival Traditions*, New York, 1952, p. 143.

18 Champion, 'From melodrama to comedy', p. 195.

19 Northrop Frye, *Anatomy of Criticism*, Princeton, 1957, p. 48.

20 On the development of satirical comedy in Jacobean England see O. J. Campbell, *Comical Satyre and Shakespeare's 'Troilus and Cressida'*, San Marino, Cal., 1938, *passim*; Alfred Harbage, *Shakespeare and the Rival Traditions*, pp. 71–80; Alan Dessen, *Jonson's Moral Comedy*, n.p.: Northwestern University Press, 1971, *passim.*; and Andrew Gurr, *Playgoing in Shakespeare's London*, Cambridge, 1987, pp. 158–9.

21 Harbage, *Shakespeare and the Rival Traditions*, p. 71.

22 See Pierre Jeannin, *Merchants of the 16th Century*, trans. Paul Fittingoff, New York, 1972, pp. 16, 24.

23 Nicoll, *The World of Harlequin*, p. 51.

24 Giacomo Oreglia, *The Commedia dell'Arte*, trans. Lovett F. Edwards, New York, 1968, p. 78.

25 Ducharte, *The Italian Comedy*, p. 181.

26 Smith, *The Commedia dell'Arte*, p. 13.

27 Thomas Dekker, *The Honest Whore*, Part I, in *The Dramatic Works of Thomas Dekker*, ed. Fredson Bowers, 4 vols, Cambridge, 1953–61, 2. Further references to Parts I and II of the play are to this edition and volume.

28 Hoy, *Introductions, Notes, and Commentaries*, 2, p. 19.

29 Harbage, in *Shakespeare and the Rival Traditions*, p. 249, notes that the 'single exception' is Chapman's *Blind Beggar of Alexandria* (1598).

30 Middleton's Doctor in *The Changeling*, for instance, has in his cure an idiot-patient whose intelligence, Lollio sarcastically notes, 'will hardly be stretch'd up to the wit of a magnifico' (*The Changeling*, ed. George Walton Williams, Regents Renaissance Drama Series, Lincoln, Neb., 1966, I.ii.119). For further examples of how Shakespeare, Middleton and Brome employ Pantalone's various names 'as terms of contempt for some exemplar of old age's folly', see Smith, *The Commedia dell'Arte*, p. 178.

31 Luigi Riccoboni, *Histoire du théâtre italien* (1728), cited in Ducharte, *The Italian Comedy*, p. 185.

32 John V. Curry, *Deception in Elizabethan Comedy*, Chicago, 1955, p. 99.

33 Clubb, *Italian Drama in Shakespeare's Time*, p. 60.

34 Charlotte Spivack, in 'Bedlam and Bridewell: ironic design in *The Honest Whore*', *Komos*, 3, 1973, p. 12, notes that Part I of the play 'contains over twenty references to madness prior to the madhouse scene in the last act'.

35 See William Harrison's inventory of the 'great provisions' (for example, 'tapestry' and 'fine linen') which may be found in the houses of 'wealthy citizens' (*Description of England* [1577, 1587], ed. Georges Edelen, Ithaca, N.Y., 1968, p. 200).

36 Sir Thomas Elyot, *The Book named the Governour*, ed. S. E. Lehmberg, New York, 1962, pp. 4–5.

37 Bracciolini, 'On avarice', trans. Benjamin J. Kohl and Elizabeth B. Welles, in *The Earthly Republic*, ed. B. Kohl and R. Witt, Philadelphia and Manchester, 1978, pp. 241–89 (p. 247).
38 Joel Kaplan, 'Virtue's holiday: Thomas Dekker and Simon Eyre', *Renaissance Drama*, n.s. 2, 1967, p. 113.
39 See above, notes 16, 17 and 18.
40 Gianrenzo P. Clivio, 'The languages of the *commedia dell'arte*', in *The Science of Buffoonery*, p. 212.
41 Clivio, p. 216.
42 The three passages are found in Perrucci, pp. 196–8, and are cited in Clivio, p. 217. The translations of all titles and passages are mine.
43 Clivio, p. 217.
44 Bracciolini, 'On avarice', p. 246. Bracciolini's citation from Cato is taken from Livy's *Ab urbe condita*, 34.4.2–3.
45 Alexander Leggatt, *Citizen Comedy in the Age of Shakespeare*, Toronto and Buffalo, 1973, p. 92.
46 Smith, *The Commedia dell'Arte*, pp. 3–4.
47 Mellamphy, 'Pantaloons and zanies', p. 146.

PART III

Venice: spectacle and polis

9

The Veneto, metatheatre, and Shakespeare*

Agostino Lombardo

'All the world's a stage' says the melancholy Jaques in *As You Like It*, and he goes on to draw a detailed comparison between the life of man, with his entries and exits, and the various acts of a play. The speech is rightly praised and frequently quoted although its concepts are not original. The metaphor – which was also inscribed at the entrance of Shakespeare's Globe Theatre (*Totus mundus agit histrionem*) – runs right through classical times, the Middle Ages and the Renaissance; in Spain it is a commonplace, from *Don Quixote* to Calderón's *gran teatro del mundo*. Neither does it constitute an exception in Shakespeare's own plays; on the contrary it is the most conspicuous thread woven into the texture of the playwright's works. If every artistic expression is also and always metalanguage – if the artist, when representing a human situation, always represents his own condition as an artist, and reflects on his own means of expression – this is even more so in the case of Shakespeare and his language. For this great man of theatre the stage is not only the vehicle to which he entrusts his own perception of reality; it is metatheatre, itself the object of reflection and representation, and also a permanent source, an inexhaustible reservoir of words, metaphors, characters, situations and conventions to apply to the representation of life. Through metatheatre certain aspects of drama, which only the twentieth century – through Pirandello, Brecht and Beckett – was to rediscover and appreciate in their extensive possibilities, are grafted on to the language of the theatre. It is thus that behind a character who sets up a particular dramatic situation, we may often identify the 'producer' of theatrical shows – what nowadays we would call the director. Such is the case of *The Tempest*, which is

*An earlier version of this paper was given in an International Shakespeare Conference at Verona in 1986.

played out entirely in a metatheatrical dimension, and in which Prospero is in fact duke, magician, coloniser, father, but above all a man of theatre – a dramatist who, with the help of Ariel (a spirit of the air but also and especially actor, mime, singer, dancer, the very symbol of theatre) invents the show of the tempest, makes objects and characters appear and disappear, in short, plays at theatre. If, therefore, the island is a symbol of America, England, the world, it is above all a symbol of the world as a stage and of the very theatre in which Shakespeare, himself actor and playwright, sets up the production of *The Tempest*. Even when the metatheatrical element is less explicit, the image of the 'director' behind certain characters is still present. This is so in the case of *Hamlet* (as Goethe pointed out in *Wilhelm Meister*), in which the prince, in the crucial and central part of the play, absolves the role of stage director, giving directions to the actors who have arrived at Elsinore, watches their rehearsal, writes part of the script, and then, when the play-within-the-play is about to be performed, sees also to the seating arrangements of the audience. And besides the director there are the actors, not only those represented as such, as in *Hamlet* or in *A Midsummer Night's Dream*, but also those other characters who 'play a part', such as certain kings in the history plays, or as Macbeth who, being a usurper, has to act throughout the role of king 'in borrow'd robes', so that at the end he is made to soliloquize the famous passage identifying man's life with an actor's task (V.v.24–8), or Edmund and Edgar in *King Lear*, Iago in *Othello*, and Antony both in *Julius Caesar* and in *Antony and Cleopatra*. The same applies to the female characters: Cleopatra, who with her 'infinite variety' and her very gestures stands out and seems to symbolise the actress; Juliet, Portia, Lear's daughters, Lady Macbeth; all those many female characters who disguise themselves as men – disguise, in fact, and its moral counterpart, simulation, run throughout the whole canon.

My aim in this chapter is to underline the fact that Shakespeare's preoccupation with metatheatre is particularly evident, and in effect originates in the plays set in Italy, and particularly in the Veneto and in Venice. Nor is this surprising. In spite of certain fantastic affirmations to the contrary, it is hardly credible that Shakespeare had ever been to Italy. Shakespeare's Italy is a country in which the 'real' features – social, historical, geographical, political, cultural – are inextricably intertwined with the imaginary. His Italy is the product of the written and oral traditions, and of the imagination, and is itself a mask behind which are hidden the features and problems of London and England. Italy is an Elizabethan myth fed by a thousand sources, not least by the travellers who 'narrate' it. Italy is the Papal State, the courts of the Renaissance, Machiavelli; it is desire, nostalgia, utopia; it is the stage on which anything can happen – loves, murders, political intrigue, tragedies, comedies. If this is true of all Italy, it is even more so of the Veneto, owing to the close and solid economic and commercial relations between England and Venice, as well as to the fact that Venice was emblematic of the 'mythical' qualities of Italy. The Veneto, it must also be remembered, was the land of the *teatro all'italiana*, of Palladio introduced to England by Inigo Jones, of the *commedia dell'arte*, therefore possessing, to Shakespeare's imagination, a theatricality that other Italian localities, ancient Rome and Sicily included, did not have.

Shakespeare looks on the Veneto as on a stage. *The Taming of the Shrew*, one of the earliest comedies, is proof of this. Largely inspired by Ariosto's *I suppositi* as translated by Gascoigne, *The Taming of the Shrew* moves along the lines of the Latin and Italian comic tradition. Here, as in *The Comedy of Errors*, mistaken identities and misunder-standings, *quid pro quo*, are at the very basis of the dramatic structure. However, the note of originality introduced by *The Taming of the Shrew*, surpassing in interest the vivid and exhilarating characterisa-tion of Katharina, is the way in which the work is transformed into a discourse on the theatre and on theatrical illusion. The importance of this procedure is already evident in the Induction: it cannot be sufficiently stressed that *The Taming of the Shrew* is constructed as a play-within-the-play, that it starts with a 'prologue' (sometimes sadly left out) set in England and in which a troup of actors, out to play a joke on the tinker Sly, put on a play for him so as to make him think he is a nobleman. The process is continued to great effect in the sub-plot: Lucentio disguises himself as a tutor to woo Bianca, while Tranio presents himself under the guise of his master. We will remember that the Veronese Petruchio wants to marry 'richly' in Padua, and decides to face the shrew Katharina Minola, known to everyone, her own father included, as 'the pest'. After a scene that is theatre at its purest, in which everybody pretends to be somebody else, Petruchio decides to make use of theatrical illusion and of disguise, and especially of verbal simulation, to achieve his aim. He himself expounds his method to the audience:

> I'll attend her here,
> And woo her with some spirit when she comes.
> Say that she rail, why, then I'll tell her plain
> She sings as sweetly as a nightingale:
> Say that she frown, I'll say she looks as clear
> As morning roses newly wash'd with dew.
> Say she be mute, and will not speak a word,
> Then I'll commend her volubility,
> And say she uttereth piercing eloquence.

(II.i.169–77)

His method works and Petruchio wins Katharina. His performances, however, do not end there. On the very day of the wedding, the bridegroom adds physical, gestural and behavioural disguises to verbal simulation. He wears slovenly clothes, vaunts the manners of a rascal, hurls insults at everyone, offends and beats his wife, forces her to refrain from food for paltry reasons, whisking away the dishes from under her very nose, orders dresses for her which he then refuses to pay for, and deprives her of sleep. He indulges in a series of performances which culminate in his imposing on her a 'fictive reality', no more nor less than what the theatre does – what Eduardo De Filippo did in *La Grande Magia*:

> *Petruchio*: Good Lord, how bright and goodly shines the moon!
> *Katharina*: The moon? The sun! It is not moonlight now.
> *Petruchio*: I say it is the moon that shines so bright.
> *Katharina*: I know it is the sun that shines so bright.
> *Petruchio*: Now by my mother's son, and that's myself,
>   It shall be moon, or star, or what I list. [...]
> *Katharina*: Forward, I pray, since we have come so far,
>   And be it moon, or sun, or what you please.
>   And if you please to call it a rush-candle,
>   Henceforth I vow it shall be so for me.

(IV.v.2–15)

Soon afterwards the old Vincentio makes his appearance and Petruchio greets him as if he were a young lady and invites his wife to do likewise; Katharina obliges and plays the game. Besides writing an extremely vivacious and amusing comedy, with *The Taming of the Shrew* Shakespeare also laid the basis for a theme which was not only to recur in his works, but which was to constitute a distinctive aspect of his dramaturgy. Shakespeare suggests here that the theatre can identify with life – it is life itself. This gives rise to a joyous exploitation of the means offered by the theatre to conjure up autonomous worlds. Space and time, actions, and gestures are all ruled by a demiurge playwright who creates new worlds with his words.

The Two Gentlemen of Verona expresses, though perhaps less intensely, the same playful joy. Set in a more or less imaginary Verona, from which one can set sail for Milan, the play centres on the deception practised by the enamoured Proteus on his friend Valentine for the love of Silvia. It is richly metatheatrical, profuse in all kinds of theatrical misunderstanding and pretences, and in disguises of female characters as male which anticipate similar disguises in comedies such as *As You Like It* and *Twelfth Night.* The metatheatrical element in these plays is heightened by the fact that in the Elizabethan theatre the female roles were performed by male actors (this makes the Petruchio–Katharina–Vincentio episode, quoted above, acquire further meta-theatrical complexity). In *The Two Gentlemen of Verona,* side by side with the playful joy at making theatre, a more problematic view of the theatre may be found. The greatest playwright of the modern age begins to express in this play an awareness of the negative potentialities of the theatre, and to consider that its possibilities can be destructive as well as creative; the power of the dramatist can be diabolic as well as divine. The fairy-tale world of theatre may transform itself into a nightmare of intrigue and deceit. Other Shakespearean plays will develop more fully and elaborate on this motif, which is already present in this early work, as it was present in *Titus Andronicus* (Aaron comes immediately to mind). With Proteus Shakespeare creates, as the name of the character already suggests, one of his many portraits of actors. For Proteus is indeed proteiform: he continually pretends and 'acts'; the whole play is a stage for his performances, for his theatre-within-the theatre. As he abandons Julia in Verona and joins Valentine in Milan and falls in love with Silvia, his actions develop into a series of deceptions, pretences and fictions. As he himself put it: 'I cannot now prove constant to myself, / Without some treachery us'd to Valentine' (II.vi.31–2). He immediately betrays his friend to the Duke to whom he reveals the plans for Valentine's and Silvia's elopement, with the result that Valentine is exiled. Then he plays the part of the faithful friend:

Thy letters may be here, though thou art hence,

> Which, being writ to me, shall be deliver'd
> Even in the milk-white bosom of thy love.
>
> (III.i.248–50)

He continues role-playing with the Duke and with Thurio, another rival for Silvia's hand. He plants into the Duke's mind the idea of slandering Valentine to Silvia and agrees to do it himself, pretending to do so unwillingly:

> You have prevail'd, my lord: if I can do it
> By aught that I can speak in his dispraise,
> She shall not long continue love to him.
>
> (III.ii.46–8)

As Iago does in *Othello*, Proteus weaves a complex web of intrigue in which he himself ends up entangled. Yet, since *The Two Gentlemen of Verona* belongs to the world of comedy, everything ends well; deceit does not end in bloodshed and death; the repentant Proteus is welcomed back among the 'honest', as Valentine (who in the meantime has 'played' the bandit and thus has himself adopted the role of a Robin Hood) puts it. The final reconciliatory words of the Duke include 'all jars, / With triumphs, mirth, and rare solemnity' (V.iv.158–9). Nevertheless the metatheatrical element in this Verona-based comedy tends to steer the action to the confines of tragedy; the playacting-within is tinged with melancholy; something much less light-hearted and joyously playful is taking shape.

Shakespeare's first tragedy, *Romeo and Juliet*, also draws inspiration from various Italian sources (Masuccio Salernitano, Luigi da Porto, Matteo Bandello), but goes a step further than *The Two Gentlemen*. This *tragedia della giovinezza*, as Benedetto Croce defines it, set in 'beautiful Verona', is too well known, often for the wrong reasons, and too 'mythical' to require an outline of its qualities. However, a reading of this play from the metatheatrical perspective I am here suggesting for the Veneto plays will highlight a few structural elements too often overlooked. For in *Romeo and Juliet* the metatheatrical device (of which the Chorus, so rare in Shakespeare, is an example) evolves further and decisively from metatheatre as play to a probing of the more problematic and tragic aspects of reality intimated in *The Two Gentlemen*.

Think of the feast at the Capulets' house (I.v). The feast is 'theatrical' throughout; there is singing and dancing; the guests are masked. It is primarily an occasion for pleasure and enjoyment. It is on this occasion, moreover, that the love between Romeo and Juliet is born. Yet, it is also a scene heavy with premonitions of grief and of death, and with an inner theatricality rich in ambiguity. Although, for instance, the masks which Romeo and his friend wear form part of the conventions of the 'masked ball', they are necessary as a disguise in the hostile, family-feud context. They are weapons of defence, interpreted as 'offensive weapons' by Tybalt:

> What, dares the slave
> Come hither, cover'd with an antic face,
> To fleer and scorn at our solemnity?

> (I.v.54–6)

Metatheatrical playfulness degenerates, breaks down and turns to tragedy through Mercutio, perhaps the most interesting, poetical, and theatrical character of the play. Already memorable for his account of Queen Mab, Mercutio not only enlivens the stage with the youthful fervour that characterises the play; he can also carve out, within its structure, room for that special kind of freedom and inventiveness that are proper of the poet, and more still of that emblematic figure: the fool. Indeed Mercutio stands for the theatre as imagination, as play, as the joy of make-believe, of making up situations. His diversity, his eccentricity, his non-belongingness are in fact due to his forming part entirely – as the fool and certain characters of the *commedia dell'arte* to whom he owes his creation do – of the life of the theatre, to his going through life with the lightness, the irony and the detachment of the *maschera*. The result is that he is the first to die; reality rejects the transgressions and the liberties of the theatre (in the same way that it will not accept the transgressions and the liberties of youth), and, therefore, has to destroy their symbol or emblem. Metatheatre brings about tragedy. The streets of Verona, which had been a stage for the playfulness of its youth, now become the scene of bloodshed. Mercutio's death results in Romeo killing Tybalt and in Romeo being exiled from that Verona of which he says:

> There is no world without Verona walls
> But purgatory, torture, hell itself;

> Hence 'banished' is banish'd from the world,
> And world's exile is death.

(III.iii.17–20)

The room for playfulness becomes ever more restricted; the long series of metatheatrical elements that succeed each other in this play (and of which the balcony is one) gradually lose their ludic quality and begin to accompany and underline the progress towards tragedy. What follows after the killings and Romeo's exile itself takes the form of playacting, but this time the playacting moves towards the final catastrophe. Let us follow this trail of simulation which frequently passes unnoticed. The first character to put on an act is Juliet, who has secretly married Romeo in Friar Laurence's cell. Juliet's mother, thinking that she is mourning her cousin Tybalt, beseeches her to resign herself to his death; Juliet plays up to her mother by railing against Romeo, but in a way that lets the audience in on her pretence. Then Juliet learns that she is to be married to Paris; she seeks Friar Laurence's help and the latter adopts the role of playwright and 'director' (albeit a rather unsuccessful one) and puts on the show of Juliet's death. The Friar's cell itself becomes a stage:

> If, rather than to marry County Paris,
> Thou hast the strength of will to slay thyself,
> Then it is likely thou wilt undertake
> A thing like death to chide away this shame,
> That cop'st with death himself to scape from it.

(IV.i.71–5)

The solution to Juliet's problems is proffered in instructions that sound much like a series of stage directions:

> Hold, then. Go home, be merry, give consent
> To marry Paris. Wednesday is tomorrow;
> Tomorrow night look that thou lie alone.
> Let not thy Nurse lie with thee in thy chamber.
> Take thou this vial, being then in bed,
> And this distilling liquor drink thou off;
> When, presently through all thy veins shall run
> A cold and drowsy humour, for no pulse
> Shall keep his native progress, but surcease.

(IV.i.89–97)

Juliet will be buried; she will then reawake and will go off with Romeo who in the meantime will have been informed about everything. So much according to Friar Laurence's script (Shakespeare must have been inspired by the character's 'popishness' in having him endowed with histrionic qualities), and the obedient 'actress' Juliet complies. She returns home and there she pretends to be happy, acts according to Friar Laurence's instructions, says that she will marry Paris, calls for her dresses and costumes to prepare herself for the occasion. She then sends away her mother and her nurse because, as she herself puts it, 'My dismal scene I needs must act alone' (IV.iii.19). And, though frightened and anguished, she performs her act, drinks the contents of the vial, *'falls upon her bed'* and is believed dead by the household, so that Friar Laurence can come along and proceed with the performance of his script. The whole scene, including the Friar's words of comfort to the grief-stricken household and his 'stage directions' are pure theatre-within:

> Dry up your tears, and stick your rosemary
> On this fair corse, and, as the custom is,
> All in her best array bear her to church.
>
> (IV.v.79–81)

As we know, the script of the playwright-within is successful only in part; Friar Laurence does not succeed in 'directing' Romeo's part, or in fitting the two segments of his 'script' together. Juliet's performance deceives Romeo, who views it as reality and not as 'theatre'. He therefore continues the performance on the plane of the inner fictive-reality and drinks 'real' poison so as to die beside his Juliet. In the final scene, different levels and planes of theatricality and reality, fiction and truth intermingle in a fatal embrace. Romeo goes to Juliet's tomb, kills Paris who tries to bar his way, and dies near his beloved who then wakes up – she is still performing the Friar's script – and is thus brusquely faced with 'reality' in the form of the dead Romeo. In the meantime Friar Laurence has himself been faced with 'reality', first in the form of Paris's and then of Romeo's corpse, the tragic result of his 'invention', for 'A greater power than we can contradict / Hath thwarted our intents' (V.iii.153–4). Juliet refuses to go away with him; she then opts out of the Friar's deranged script and the performance-within, sucks the poison from Romeo's lips and stabs herself. The pretence of death has become 'real' death; the monument that was to

151

have served as a stage for a pretended death reverts to its original role of tomb; the stage is turned into a churchyard into which the whole community is gathered; Verona itself has become both stage and tomb. Quite apart from the many implications in *Romeo and Juliet* as to the nature of theatre and as to its relations and its shifting boundaries with reality, the play also presents a clear example of metatheatre as an integral and essential structural part of the action, as well as of the movement from a ludic to a tragic reality.

Although a comedy, *The Merchant of Venice* moves largely in the same direction. In the opening scene of the play Antonio introduces the theme:

> I hold the world but as the world, Gratiano,
> A stage, where every man must play a part,
> And mine a sad one.

(I.i.77–9)

To this, it is well to remember, Gratiano replies: 'Let me play the fool'. Metatheatre abounds throughout; the play teems with disguises, pretences, masks, *coups-de-théâtre*. Belmont is itself a theatrical invention, whereas Venice – which here makes its appearance for the first time in Shakespeare – is not a 'mythical' city but a ruthless commercial centre in which the power of money holds sway, very like the real Venice and the London of the rising merchant classes. Belmont is the creation of the artistic imagination: purportedly situated on the mainland, it is in fact one of Shakespeare's islands; the alternation of scenes between Venice and Belmont in the play highlights the diversity between the two locations. Belmont is utopia, nostalgia, artistic invention par excellence; it is, in fact, theatre. Only in this location – and not in the middle-class Venice of the play, one of the first bourgeois plays – can the fairy-tale ritual of the caskets be performed; only in this setting can A-Thousand-and-One-Nights princes make their appearance, or such courtings and love contests, and games and concerts, and dances and masques take place. It is in this splendidly isolated world, against this painted background, that Portia moves and acts; it is from this theatre that for love of Bassanio and to defend Antonio against Shylock she ventures out to Venice and to 'reality'. But when she faces 'reality', she does so with the instruments of her own world: those of the theatre. She faces the world of the merchant city by becoming an actress, adding another example to the long line of female equivalents to inner-play male actors that culminates in Cleopatra. Although Portia is no Cleopatra, she is none the less a magnificent actress; she scarcely does anything else but act; she acts with her suitors, but most of all she puts on a show when she has to leave Belmont for Venice. With her household she pretends that she has to retreat to a monastery together with Nerissa until Bassanio's return, then sets about plotting her 'script' according to which she will assume the role of lawyer and Nerissa that of her assistant. Then Portia and Nerissa appear at Antonio's trial. Now a trial is both ritual and theatre, with its own inner audience, so that 'representing' a trial always involves theatre-within. In this case the scene is loaded with irony because the audience knows that Portia is impersonating a male lawyer and that they are therefore watching a 'double' performance. It is precisely this metatheatrical element which casts an ambiguous light on the 'real' trial, and on those very values which it upholds. Thanks to Portia's forensic skill, the trial comes to a 'just' conclusion: with Shylock not only not obtaining his 'pound of flesh', but punished, stripped of his property, humiliated and pushed aside in a series of pronouncements of increasing harshness. The sentence inflicted on Shylock already casts doubts on the way the 'city' administers justice; the metatheatrical elements increase these misgivings. The heavy intrusion of pretence into the court proceedings put into bold relief the ambiguity and the perplexity surrounding human and social values – already felt in the portrayal of Antonio – which constitute the hidden key to the play. This ambiguity threatens the rediscovered harmony precisely through metatheatre: the technique, in fact, is not abandoned once the trial is over, although it is henceforth used in a lighter vein. Portia – and with her Nerissa – rids herself of her legal robes, but does not immediately reveal herself to Bassanio. Instead she makes use of a stage property – the ring which she had persuaded Bassanio to give her when she was still disguised as a lawyer, which had been in its turn a gift from her as Portia to Bassanio – to play still another 'sketch' with him. Love, almost lost and found again, now feels the tremor of ambiguity; Belmont will never be the same again. The old harmony seems lost for ever; Antonio, whom Bassanio's marriage leaves in a loneliness similar to that of Shylock, is the expression of this loss. The use of the metatheatrical device in *The Merchant of Venice* leaves us with a final impression of human fragility, precariousness and ambiguity; it is not only for Antonio or for Shylock that the 'mercy' exalted by Portia should be invoked, but for all those who, like them, are cast in the 'clay' of the human condition.

The fact is that with *The Merchant of Venice* we are very close to that group of plays that revolve round *Hamlet*; close, that is, to that supreme moment in Shakespeare's art in which the playwright perceives and represents, defines and delves into the great transformation that is taking place in English culture and society. This revolution is collective and historical; it involves the passage from the Middle Ages to the modern era, the birth of a new conception of man and his place and role in society and in the universe. This 'new' man is, however, more liable to anguish, to tensions and contradictions, to dreams of utopias and to delusions. Ambiguity, the sense of precariousness, doubts about the world, about reality, about man, about language, about theatre itself, which the metatheatrical device exposes in *The Merchant of Venice*, blossom out in all their rich and tragic form in plays such as *As You Like It, Julius Caesar, Hamlet, Troilus and Cressida, Measure for Measure,* all plays in which metatheatre is widely utilised, as it is in Shakespeare's last Veneto play, to which I shall now turn my attention.

In *Othello, the Moor of Venice,* the most complex of Shakespeare's Veneto plays, the moral and material evil that produces the tragic outcome is nurtured by and consummated with the instruments of the theatre. Moreover, the character who moves events to their tragic end, the 'honest' Iago – like the Aaron of *Titus Andronicus,* or the eponymous hero of *Richard III,* or partly like Proteus in *The Two Gentlemen of Verona* – sums up the qualities of man as a man of the theatre.

We are made aware of this right at the very opening, when he expounds his philosophy to Roderigo in the 'I am not what I am' speech. He then immediately assumes the role of 'director', giving detailed 'acting' instructions to Roderigo:

> Call up her father,
> Rouse him, make after him, poison his delight,
> Proclaim him in the street, incense her kinsmen,
> And though he in a fertile climate dwell,
> Plague him with flies.

> (I.i.67–71)

After which he becomes the actor who, by the power of words, evokes in front of Brabantio's eyes a theatrical illusion, reporting Desdemona's elopement with Othello by means of obscene visual imagery: 'Even now, very now, an old black ram / Is tupping your white ewe'

(I.i.88–9). Having 'put on this show' for Brabantio, he then proceeds to develop his web of intrigue with Othello and with Roderigo in a series of histrionic performances until, in line with a technique common to other Shakespearean characters–actors–directors, he expounds his 'script' to the audience:

> Cassio's a proper man, let me see now,
> To get this place, and to make up my will,
> A double knavery ... how, how? ... Let me see,
> After some time, to abuse Othello's ear,
> That he is too familiar with his wife:
> He has a person and a smooth dispose,
> To be suspected, fram'd to make women false:
> The Moor a free and open nature too,
> That thinks men honest that but seems to be so;
> And will as tenderly be led by the nose ...
> As asses are.
> I ha't, it is engender'd; Hell and night
> Must bring this monstrous birth to the world's light.
>
> (I.iii.390–402)

The Venice in which the first part of the play is set is a hard, ruthless city, the seat of great political and economic power. From the second act onwards, the scene is Cyprus, another island stage, this time for the enactment not of comedy but of tragedy, for a theatre of cruelty. The alternation between Venice and another location, common to both *The Merchant* and *Othello*, between two separate stage-worlds, that of 'reality' and that of theatre – which however in the end tend to intersect, merge and mingle, interacting with each other – is extremely effective. At one and the same time actor and director, Iago adapts his art to suit each of the characters he interacts with – Desdemona, Othello, Roderigo, Cassio, Emilia – and the situation. All his words are 'fiction', except when he confides with the audience. Iago, in fact, gives us a double performance: the performance with which he deceives and dominates the other characters, and that by means of which he exults in his histrionic abilities and takes the audience into his confidence, almost making an accomplice of them. We might call Iago's part doubly metatheatrical. However, Iago is not only actor, but also director and playwright; his strategy is to create a 'reality' out of nothing, as when he convinces Roderigo to provoke Cassio during his watch. The 'performance' takes place according to

Iago's 'script', with all the characters becoming actors in his 'play'. Cassio is coaxed to get drunk and is then provoked into a brawl by Roderigo; Othello demotes Cassio on hearing Iago's 'fictive' reconstruction of the incident; Iago advises Cassio to ask Desdemona to plea for him with Othello. As Iago explains to the audience:

> And by how much she strives to do him good,
> She shall undo her credit with the Moor;
> So will I turn her virtue into pitch,
> And out of her own goodness make the net
> That shall enmesh 'em all.

(II.iii.349–53)

The 'temptation' of Othello is the next act of the tragedy constructed by Iago's language; words are his weapons as they are the actor's and the biblical serpent's. It starts with the insinuation 'Ha, I like not that' (III.iii.35) at the sight of Cassio and Desdemona seen together at a distance, proceeds with a series of allusive remarks about their friendship, and is crowned by the intolerable innuendo: 'O, beware jealousy; / It is the green-ey'd monster, which doth mock / That meat it feeds on' (III.iii.169–71). Having sketched out the 'script', the rest follows almost automatically, except that Iago directs, controls, injects new elements to propel its movement forward. Thus he introduces the handkerchief, flimsy enough as proof but a useful stage-prop, or the dialogue between Cassio and Iago about the courtesan Bianca, with Othello eavesdropping and 'hearing' and reading this *mise-en-scène* according to Iago's intentions. The negative potentialities of theatre and of fiction come out forcefully in these scenes; theatre as deceit at the service of evil. Othello as the spectator of a double illusion, as victim of a deceit and of a scenic fiction stretched to its extreme limits, creates in the audience a state of anguish to which there is no catharsis: the tragic condition of modern man.

Like an impotent chorus, no longer an accomplice but turned victim, the audience watches helplessly the terrible succession of killings. Corpse upon corpse is piled on the Cyprus stage: Roderigo is killed by Iago (who now does not use only words to buttress his 'script'), Desdemona is killed by Othello, Emilia is killed by Iago, Othello kills himself. Othello's death is itself a theatrical performance; through it – by means of words and gestures rich in theatricality – he tries to leave behind him in his last speech that noble image of himself which his actions in Cyprus had obfuscated (V.ii.349–57). By the force of words and of theatre, Iago has succeeded in bringing to pass what he had wanted, and can therefore well say, 'Demand me nothing, what you know, you know, / From this time forth I never will speak word' (V.ii.304–5). And yet in the end something has gone wrong in what had looked like a perfect construction; at a certain point something had not gone according to his script. He had had to kill Emilia, in fact, because she had revealed the truth, had refused to be led by him any more, to act according to his directions; the actress had rejected the author. The author has therefore been constrained to return to his role in the play as laid on by others, and to reinsert himself in the interaction conducted by Venice, to which the final victory goes.

In *Othello* Shakespeare's use of the metatheatrical device reaches its most complex and suggestive level. It will be made further use of in all his successive works, from *King Lear* to *Antony and Cleopatra*, to *Timon of Athens* and *Pericles* and *The Tempest*, right up to the most recent addition to the Shakespearean canon, *Henry VIII*. But there is no doubt that it is through the plays set in the Veneto – the mythical land of the imagination, the theatre of the Elizabethan and Jacobean mind – that the metatheatrical device takes form and is developed into an essential Shakespearean dramaturgical technique. Metatheatre – especially in maturer works – is not simply a technical virtuosity, a *divertissement*, an extrinsic quality or dramatic accessory. There metatheatre has increasingly become the very essence of Shakespearean drama and gradually merges with Shakespeare's reflections on life and on its rhythms, movements and forms. For Shakespeare the world is a stage because the nature of theatre, its fragility and ambiguity, its power of illusion, its daily birth and death, its perpetual metamorphosis, are the very elements which the dramatist recognises as characteristic of the human condition in a world in transition that has lost its certainties.

(translated by Bernadette Falzon)

Note

All references to the plays are to the *New Arden Shakespeare*, gen. eds Harold F. Brooks, Harold Jenkins and Brian Morris, London, 1951–.

10

Streets, squares and courts: Venice as a stage in Shakespeare and Ben Jonson

Roberta Mullini

1   Venice and the sense of spectacle

Writing home from London in November 1617, Horatio Busino – the Venetian ambassador's chaplain – tries to help the recipient of his narrative to visualise London life by drawing comparisons with his own country. The Thames 'runs through the city like our Grand Canal, but [is] as wide as the Giudecca Canal'. The small boats on the river accompanying larger vessels are 'like the gondolas about the Bucintoro', and guildsmen's gowns during the Lord Mayor's entry 'resemble those of a Doctor of Laws or the Doge'.[1] The comparative procedure is not so strange as it first appears, since it derives from the traveller's necessity to offer his addressee an analogical way of understanding the foreign reality. What strikes one most in Busino's chronicle is the special attention he gives to spectacular aspects of English life, apart from his curiosity for agriculture, the recently imported use of tobacco, and other minor features of early seventeenth-century English habits. As a Venetian, he was accustomed to living in a town which, famous all over Europe for its law system and for its state organisation, had also built its internal cohesion on a diplomatic use of ceremonies, rites and spectacles. In other words, Busino's attention to London festivals derived from his being bred in a 'spectacular' town where authority had employed the already showy nature of the place, enriched by lavish architecture and art, as a means to affirm political power. Actually, in Venice festive culture played a very important role 'because everybody considered feasts as moments of glorification of the myth of the town'.[2]

Triumphs, processions, performances inside the palaces of the aristocracy and in the squares, but also along the streets, made Venice a complex *machina theatralis*. Canals, bridges, buildings and various types of floating vessels opened up vistas and perspectives in a rich, natural and architectural scenery. Religious and civic festivals underlined everyday city life, while on special occasions Venice showed all its fascination by building festive structures and apparatuses. Every year on Corpus Christi Day a sumptuous procession gathered in St Mark's Square; on Ascension Day, the marriage of the town to the sea was celebrated by the whole citizenship, which accompanied the Doge's Bucintoro off the Grand Canal; a lot of other feast days dotted the year and offered opportunities for celebration. When foreign visitors arrived in town, Venice exhibited all its magnificence: in 1574 for Henry III, king of France, a loggia and a three-vaulted triumphal arch after Palladio's drawings were raised at the Lido, so that 'they could be enjoyed and admired by those who arrived there [...] because the watery perspective augmented the fascination of the structures'.[3] Contemporary artists recorded the event in pictures and drawings, in the same way as they witnessed the solemn entry of the dogaressa Morosina Morosini Grimani in 1597. This lady arrived at the Palazzo Ducale on the Bucintoro, followed by hundreds of smaller boats and gondolas, while in front of St Mark's Square a 'teatro del mondo' had been built on the water (based on Vincenzo Scamozzi's drawing). The 'theatre of the world' was a floating circular apparatus made of timber and stucco, towed by ships or barges along the Grand Canal. Its origin goes back to the end of the fifteenth century: though its decorations had been modified, it nevertheless kept its round structure and its function as a scenographic apparatus, which had been invented to add special effects to the urban spectacle, mainly because of its mobility which affected the perspective of the city like an item of changeable scenery.[4]

But the Venetian landscape of small squares, minor canals and narrow streets was also the scene against which popular (even aristocratic) entertainments were performed. There, mock fights with sticks and bullfights took place, street fools sang, mountebanks sold their goods, actors performed their *commedia improvvisa*, and masked people flowed by during Carnival. These are the forms of entertainment that Giacomo Franco reproduced in his engravings.[5] Carnival was the time during which popular festivals were concentrated. P. Molmenti states that it dates back to the end of the eleventh century and that masks are attested as early as 1268, in a document which prohibits them.[6] But once disguise was allowed, masks became very popular, so that 'mask makers prospered as to be able to found a special branch of the painters' guild'.[7] On these occasions St Mark's Square itself was the main 'stage' on which maskers 'performed'. Nevertheless, they also used to sing serenades in the streets and to frequent minor sites. An engraving by Pietro Bertelli (1589) shows a company of masked people under some ladies' windows, in the act not of singing but of throwing 'odorous eggs'.[8] A particularly noteworthy activity took place on Shrove Thursday: on a stage in the Piazzetta, near the Palazzo Ducale, built between two sets of steps for spectators – including the Doge – acrobats created high human pyramids of various shapes called 'Forze d'Ercole' (Hercules' Labours) to celebrate the Venetian victory over the Patriarch of Aquileia in 1164.[9]

The local performance which kept its original flavour well into the sixteenth century, despite the development of 'regular' forms such as comedy and tragedy, is the *momaria*. Appearing in the fifteenth century when the first 'Compagnie della Calza' were formed, a *momaria* was a highly symbolic spectacle in which pageantry and lavish costumes were used.[10] Music and dance played a relevant role in it, whereas, even if some lines were spoken, dramatic texts did not, a *momaria* being 'a secular pantomime, where the performers' movements were nearly always ruled by music, and where the language of gestures substituted words'.[11] The 'Compagnie della Calza' were also responsible for the construction of the 'teatri del mondo', at least till 1564, when the 'Compagnia degli Accesi' built one of them ('the most complex one') in honour of Francesco Maria della Rovere, Duke of Urbino.[12]

The status of Venice, as it appeared to the inner citizens and as it was exported abroad, certainly rested on the political system of the town, but it also resulted from the ample and complex visual machinery of its spectacular festivals: Venice the town was a set of multiple stages on which Venice the State acted its inward and outward politics.[13]

2 Political and legal 'stages'

As stated above, the Republic's authorities were well aware of the power of public ceremonies to enhance both the interior and the exterior idea of the town as an ancient, independent, tolerant and righteous state. But the fame of Venice also rested on less ephemeral elements: actually what contributed to it, apart from the well-known status of Venetian commerce, was the legal system through which justice was administered and power controlled. As early as 1480 Bartholomew Glenville (Bartholomeus Anglicus) wrote:

> Venetia itaque in Italia est provincia quae multarum terrarum et civitatum dominium habuit ab antiquo in mari et in terra, cuius potestas hodie per longissimos maris protractus usque in Graeciam se extendit. Germanorum fines usque in Aquileiam tangit. Dalmatum et Sclavorum piratarum predam tyrannicam reprimit et compescit. Insulas et portus, promunctoria maris et sinus sub eius dominio existentes *iustissime* regit. Subditos protegit ab hostibus potentissime ac defendit. Rem publicam et civilem *iustis legibus* subicit. [...] Huius gentis referre singulas probitates estimo superfluum, cum de gentis Venetorum virtute et potentia, circumspectione et prudentia, unitate civium et concordia, *amore totius iustitiae* et clementia *omnibus fere nationibus iam sit notum.*[14]

The land of Venice is then an Italian province which has governed many a town and territory over land and sea since ancient times. Its present power reaches very distant places and extends as far as Greece. It touches the German land as far as Aquileia. It restrains and represses the tyranny of Dalmatian and Slavonian pirates. It reigns *very righteously* over islands, ports, and all promontories and creeks in its dominion. It protects and defends its subjects from their enemies with all its strength. It rules the commonwealth with *equitable laws.* [...] I deem it superfluous to report individual examples of the probity of its people, since *almost all nations already know* the virtue of the Venetian population; the circumspection, the prudence, the harmony and the unity of Venetian citizens, their love for *complete justice* and mercifulness. (my translation)

It is noteworthy that Glenville finds it superfluous to relate other details about Venice, since they are 'already known to all nations', and that he uses the word 'justice' (or its derivatives) three times in a relatively short passage. From the quotation we understand that by the end of the fifteenth century the fame of Venice had spread all over Europe and was defined mainly in terms of righteous power.

The government of the Republic was in the hands of a patrician oligarchy from which not only the Doge was chosen but also the members of the various administrative and judicial boards. The Doge was assisted and controlled by the two main groups of state magistracy, that is the Council of Ten and the 'Avogaria di comun', whose chief task was to see to the observance of the law:

> To sum up [...] the opposition between the Council of Ten and the
> Avogaria, one could say that the Avogadori represent the law as a
> guarantee of justice and equality, whereas the Council of Ten
> represent the law as an expression of authority.[15]

The legal procedures of these two levels of magistracy varied. The
Avogadori held their trials publicly and defendants were allowed to
have their own lawyers, who disputed with an 'Avogadore di comun'
and were permitted to read the recorded proceedings of previous days.
The Council of Ten, on the other hand, worked in an atmosphere of
utmost secrecy and defendants were alone in front of the court, no
lawyer being admitted. It is not difficult to believe that the procedure
of the Venetian law administration that mainly appealed to foreigners
was the Avogadori's (especially after the Reformation, since the
Council's procedures too closely resembled those of the Inquisition).
Foreigners admired the guarantees offered by a fair trial and the lively
debates which took place in courts where 'spectators' were admitted
and where the skilful oratory of both sides was to be witnessed.[16]

While members of the Avogaria were patricians, lawyers came
principally from the University of Padua, although a degree was not
considered absolutely necessary. In any case the fame of Venetian
judges ranked very high and they themselves were proud of their
office, so much so that Pietro Bodoaro (a patrician lawyer at the end
of the sixteenth century) wrote that 'Venetian judge'

> vuol dire in linguaggio di chi'l conosce, giudice per disposizione di
> volontà giusto, per bontà d'animo incorrotto, per isperienza delle
> humane attioni prudente, per fede catolico, et per dolcezza et facilità
> di natura, di carità, di pietà et di misericordia ripieno.[17]
>
> [The phrase 'Venetian judge'] means, to those who understand
> the language, a judge righteous because of the disposition of his will,
> incorrupt because of his good-heartedness, prudent because of his
> knowledge of human actions, catholic because of his faith, and full of
> charity, piety, and mercy because of the ease and meekness of his
> nature. (my translation)

Of course we are allowed to doubt the truth of this flattering portrait,
especially concerning the honesty of the judges and their unbribability.
In any case, this was the state of self-consciousness of those who
worked inside the Venetian law courts, when they assembled robed in
crimson velvet gowns trimmed with ermine.[18]

3 The role of Venice in Shakespeare and Jonson

The solemn aspects of the administration of justice were part of the widespread idea of Venice: they contributed to the myth of the town in the same way as its private and public ceremonies. It is no wonder, then, that these two Venetian 'spectacles' were of great interest to the Elizabethan dramatists. Other Italian places were chosen by playwrights both to distantiate the events of their plays from local English problems (and avoid censorship by doing so), and to reproduce a stereotyped idea of Italy as the land of corrupt power and lost glory. But many of these towns and cities (Ferrara, Padua, Naples, Parma, Florence and perhaps Rome itself) often lack authenticity on the Elizabethan stage: they are neutral locations, an 'Italian anywhere', so to speak, ready to justify the plots which take place in them. Venice, on the other hand, is used very specifically, even if differently, by both Shakespeare and Jonson, who know how to authenticate their 'Venices'. In fact, only the knowledge (even if sometimes imprecise) of what makes Venice famous at the turn of the sixteenth century allows the two playwrights to render the town a protagonist of their plays, together with the *dramatis personae*, and not simply a backdrop against which the action takes place.

The image of Venice which Shakespeare evokes in *The Merchant of Venice* and *Othello* stresses the multi-cultural dimension of the town, its worldwide commercial interests, its political role against the Turks in the Mediterranean and its equitable administration of justice. Venice is the place where different ethnic groups live together (though with reciprocal prejudices and racial hatred), where legal commerce ennobles citizens' life and usury is censored, where law courts meet to judge private cases which have deep public and political implications. Jews are tolerated, Moors can reach the top of a military career, mixed marriages are celebrated, and European Christianity is upheld and defended. It would seem a utopian ideal, were it not cracked by obscure, individual flaws which spoil this idealistic vision. The government of the town, as it were, is represented as positive, righteous and far-sighted, whereas the behaviour of individuals shows hatred, jealousy, greed and vindictiveness. What Shakespeare compares is a public and a private image, the contrast between State politics and individual misbehaviour.

That Venice lives on international commerce reaching as far as the then-known world is clear from what Bassanio says about Antonio's misfortunes:

> But is it true Salerio?
> Hath all his ventures fail'd? what not one hit?
> From Tripolis, from Mexico and England,
> From Lisbon, Barbary and India
> And not one vessel scape the dreadful touch
> Of merchant-marring rocks?
>
> (III.ii.265–70)[19]

City life itself articulates around streets, canals (a 'gondola' is mentioned in II.vii.8), the Ghetto and 'the Rialto'. This last place was not only the famous extant stone bridge but also a *loggia* nearby, where merchants assembled to discuss their transactions.[20] Actually it is the place from where the news about the fortune of ships spreads (I.iii.17 and 34; III.i.1), and where Shylock is abused by Antonio (I.iii.101–2).

Street revels are hinted at in II.v and II.vi, when Lorenzo abducts Jessica from her father's house. Even if the text calls it 'a masque' repeatedly, it resembles more a *momaria*, with revellers masked and disguised, leaving a private house and going along the streets. According to Shylock, these revels are accompanied by drum and fife music leading 'Christian fools with varnish'd faces' (II.v.33).

The primary focus in *The Merchant of Venice*, however, is the way in which justice is administered in the town. Trials have always been associated with spectacle as occasions on which orators wearing their rich robes show their ability to manipulate words and concepts.[21] And English drama has always made skilful use of trial scenes since the 'Parliament of Heaven' episode in the N Town cycle and in *The Castle of Perseverance*. The highly dramatic potential of the trial against the Christian debtor is already present in the sources of *The Merchant*, especially in the *novella* from *Il pecorone*. However, the Italian story does not locate the trial inside the institutional magistracy (the dispute takes place in an inn) and does not involve any public authority. Shakespeare's court, on the other hand, is chaired by the Duke himself (the Doge) and 'magnificoes' act as judges, while the trial resembles one held by the *Avogadori di comun*. The historical imprecision of this situation is evident: the Doge was originally part of the Council of Ten, but in the sixteenth century he had already gradually lost his power over the other magistrates. The procedure followed seems to be that of a law case dealt with by the *Avogadori*, but incongruously located in a Council of Ten session. This typical Shakespearean inaccuracy does not affect the plot, since it focuses the play's attention on the law itself and on the role of Venice as a righteous distributor of justice.

Once more Venice and its sense of justice stand out as *the* judge, because, as Antonio stresses:

> The duke cannot deny the course of law:
> For the commodity that strangers have
> With us in Venice, if it be denied,
> Will much impeach the justice of the state,
> Since that the trade and profit of the city
> Consisteth of all nations.

(III.iii.26–31)

The meeting in *Othello* (I.iii) is more similar to a Council of Ten session. The Duke and 'senators' are assembled to discuss matters of state and war, when Brabantio enters to have the Moor convicted of sorcery. There is no lawyer to defend Othello, as the defendant is alone in front of his accuser, nor is there any audience. There is nothing of the terrifying secrecy historically imputed to this Council, which, on the contrary, is shown by Shakespeare as humane and just. Other details of Venetian life do not appear in the tragedy, but here, too, the town has a well-defined role as a benevolent character in charge of its citizens' well-being. Therefore, it is no wonder that Othello, in order to divert his controllers' attention in the last scene and to kill himself, 'performs' a short play where he acts as a defender of Venetian honour by killing a Turkish slanderer.

When, during the 1986–87 season, the Compagnia del Teatro Eliseo performed *Volpone*, directed by Gabriele Lavia, the first scenes of the second act were expunged and Scoto the Mountebank's speech ending with Celia's courtship was replaced by a scene in a church where she was shown holding a love letter from Volpone.[22] In doing this, the performance eliminated the most Venetian of all episodes and it transformed the play into a cynical and satirical fable about human greed 'for all places'. All other Venetian hints were also abolished, while the setting was a type of dark gold mine containing Volpone's bed. But Jonson had not chosen Venice as the place for his play haphazardly: the dramatist reversed Shakespeare's idealistic view of the town, which, through the mirror of private affairs, appears to be the den of general corruption.

What in Shakespeare is a multi-cultural society becomes in Jonson's *Volpone* a bad example which foreigners come to imitate. Lady

Would-Be is in Venice to learn a courtesan's ways, and her husband is proud to be taken 'for a citizen of Venice' (IV.i.38).[23] The law is continually neglected and justice corrupted. Law courts and their 'Avocatori', as well as lawyers, far from being righteous, are subject to corruption. Merchants are selfish and sell their wives; patricians are depraved. Old 'magnificoes' are gulled and new upstarts centre on stage. In this town, 'riches, the dumb god that giv'st all men tongues' (I.i.22) represents the only value, barren in itself since there is no Bassanio asking for money to court a lady. Romance is impossible here, even between Celia and Bonario, since they are too naive. But this is Venice, nevertheless. It is the town where the problem of money has become urgent, where since the 1530s to obtain wealth has been a state business and a political tool. Marin Sanudo tells in his *Diaries* that on the pageants built in 1526 to celebrate the Cognac League the following sentences were written: 'Aurum belli materia', 'Per aurum victoria', 'Obediunt omnia pecuniae'.[24] In this society gold and money were the means of obtaining public offices.

Discussing Jonson's choice of Venice as the setting for *Volpone*, Dutton highlights the role of the Italian town in the first decade of the seventeenth century as 'middle ground in the struggle between the Protestants and the Catholics in the Counter-Reformation', since 'the city was Catholic but maintained its independence of the Papacy and of other Catholic powers to such an extent that Sir Henry Wotton, an English ambassador at this time, even entertained hopes of its turning Protestant'.[25] The dramatist's decision to set the action in Venice would answer a hope of English diplomacy on the one hand, and, on the other, offer, as ever, a safer ground for satire and parody.[26]

However, Jonson's Venetian setting was not only 'exotic and fantastic', that is exotic to avoid censorship, and fantastic because unrealistic.[27] His Venice retains much of the real town's characteristics, especially its spectacularity, even if seen by a more disillusioned eye. Presenting a long and intriguing series of disguisings, the play often focuses on the town's spectacles of disguise which mingle with the plot.[28] The mountebank scene takes place in the 'Piazza' (St Mark's Square), near 'the Portico to the Procuratia' (II.ii.36), that building already provided with arches even before the new addition by Vincenzo Scamozzi in the second half of the sixteenth century. It is the 'Serenissima's maximum "theatre"', where mountebanks and street players usually performed.[29] A character of the *commedia dell'arte* is explicitly mentioned, namely *zanni* (II.ii), the nickname for ridiculous male servants of Pantalone, the 'magnifico' in the *scenari*.[30] When Volpone disguised as Scoto enters to start his performance, he orders Nano to mount the trestle stage calling him 'Zany' (II.ii.28). Later Nano is addressed as 'Zan Fritada', when asked to 'sing a verse' (lines 114–15). It is worth noticing that one of Giacomo Franco's engravings is devoted to these daily Venetian performances: in it, with the title 'Intartenimento che dano ogni giorno li Ciarlatani in Piazza di S. Marco al Populo d'ogni natione [...]', musicians, masked *commedianti* of the *commedia improvvisa* and quacks can be seen performing even on the same raised platform, surrounded by people. An old Pantalone is portrayed in the foreground while possibly courting a lady. Actually it could be an illustration to the third scene of the second act of *Volpone*.

Famous Venetian authorities are also mentioned in the play: there seems to be no Doge in Jonson's Venice, but the 'Great Council' (Maggior Consiglio?), 'the Forty' (Quarantie), 'the Ten' (Council of Ten) are quoted as the addressees of Sir Politic's plans 'unto the state of Venice' (IV.i.71–5).

Jonson's text gives ample space to the administration of justice by locating two great scenes in a Venetian court (IV.v and V.x). The playwright is well aware of the dramatic and theatrical power of legal cases, and employs it skilfully in both episodes. Volpone's trial seems to take place during an Avogadori session, not only because the judges are called 'Avocatori' in the speech headings but because the defendant is represented by an 'advocate'. The justice administered by this court – even if, in the end, truth triumphs – is severely impaired by the Avocatori's gullibility and by their inclination to value money above everything. Venetian justice, notwithstanding Pietro Bodoaro's self-confident words quoted above, has degenerated in its theatrical reproduction as well.

Jonson, too, appears inaccurate: in fact, in 1571 an act had been approved which gave the Council of Ten (and not the Avogaria) the power to decide about all patricians' cases.[31] But, as with Shakespeare, this is not the kind of verisimilitude requested of a playwright. Both Shakespeare and Jonson understood the relevance of Venice in European culture and the fascination of its being a 'theatre of the world'. The idea of Venice resulting from their plays keeps to international stereotypes about the town. However, both playwrights used this idea functionally: Venice was a kind of imperfect Utopia for Shakespeare, for Jonson its grotesque reversal. Theatricality was already there (in the streets, squares and law courts) as an inherent quality of the town. Venice was for them an active background for narratives that had to, and actually did, interact with its reality.

Notes

1 In *Calendar of State Papers: Venetian*, eds H. F. Brown and Allen B. Hinds, 37 vols, London, 1864–1939; 15, 1909, pp. 59 and 61.

2 M. Teresa Muraro, 'La festa a Venezia e le sue manifestazioni rappresentative: le Compagnie della Calza e le *momarie*', in *Storia della cultura veneta*, eds G. Arnaldi and M. Pastore Stocchi, 6 vols, Vicenza, 1976–86; 3/III, 1981, p. 315 (my trans.). See also D. C. McPherson, *Shakespeare, Jonson, and the Myth of Venice*, Newark, 1990 (esp. chap. 2).

3 L. Padoan Urban, 'Gli spettacoli urbani e l'utopia', in *Architettura e utopia nella Venezia del Cinquecento*, Catalogo della Mostra, Venezia Palazzo Ducale, luglio-ottobre 1980; Milan, 1980, p. 146 (my trans.).

4 More detailed information about Venetian spectacles is included in the many editions of P. Molmenti, *La storia di Venezia nella vita privata*, 3 vols, Bergamo, especially vol. 2 (the edition I consulted dates 1910–12). See also E. Benini Clementi, 'I "teatri del mondo" veneziani', *Quaderni di teatro*, 25, 1984; *Il teatro italiano nel Rinascimento*, eds F. Cruciani, and D. Seragnoli, Bologna, 1987; *Teatro e culture della rappresentazione: lo spettacolo in Italia nel Quattrocento*, ed. R. Guarino, Bologna, 1988; L. Padoan Urban, 'Teatri e "Teatri del mondo" nella Venezia del Cinquecento', *Arte veneta*, 20, 1966, and 'Le feste sull'acqua a Venezia nel secolo XVI e il potere politico', in *Il teatro italiano del Rinascimento*, ed. M. de Panizza Lorch, Milan, 1980; B. Tamassia Mazzarotto, *Le feste veneziane*, Florence, 1980; L. Zorzi, *Il teatro e la città*, Turin, 1977.

5 *Habiti d'huomeni et donne venetiane*, a collection of prints published in Venice in 1610, many of which are reproduced by Molmenti, *La storia di Venezia*, and by L. Zorzi, 'Spettacoli popolari veneziani del tardo Cinquecento (dagli *Habiti* di Giacomo Franco)', in *L'attore, la commedia, il drammaturgo*, Turin, 1990.

6 Molmenti, *La storia di Venezia*, 1, 1910, p. 255.

7 Molmenti, *La storia di Venezia*, 1, 1910, p. 256 (my trans.).

8 The engraving is reproduced in Molmenti, *La storia di Venezia*, 2, p. 60.

9 The 'Forze d'Ercole', too, are reproduced in one of Franco's prints. In it the human pyramid stands out against the lagoon background and, particularly, the two columns marking the land's end.

10 The 'Compagnie della Calza' were not formed by professional actors, but by aristocratic youths who, united by a special 'coat of arms' embroidered on their stockings, gathered to offer spectacles both on private and on public occasions. Marin Sanudo, in his *Diaries* testifies to ceremonies such as nuptials which were celebrated with *momarie* as early as the end of the fifteenth century.

11 M. Teresa Muraro, pp. 330–1. Many critics underline the resemblance of the Venetian *momaria* to the French *mommerie*, to the English 'mumming' and to the Iberian *momo*, especially for the omnipresent use of masks. But

there are individual aspects which differentiate one type of spectacle from another, notwithstanding the similar names. See J. Oliveira Barata, *História do Teatro Português*, Lisbon, 1991, pp. 69–71; G. Wickham, *The Medieval Theatre*, London, 1974, p. 136; and S. Westfall, *Patrons and Performance*, Oxford, 1990, p. 33.

12 M. Teresa Muraro, p. 340.

13 In a widely discussed document dated about 1561 Alvise Cornaro advanced his ideas 'per conservare la virginità a questa mia cara patria et il nome di Reina del mare' ('so that this dear country of mine may preserve its virginity and the title of Queen of the sea'). Among minor proposals, he suggested that a 'Theatro di pietra grande' ('a large stone theatre') should be built in the lagoon, so that 'tale edificio si vederà commodamente stando nella piazza di San Marco e sarà un bellissimo vedere' ('this building will easily be seen by those standing in St Mark's Square, a wondrous sight'). The new vista should also have been enriched by 'una fontana di acqua dolce viva e pura' ('a lively and pure fresh-water fountain') and by 'un monte' ('a mountain') to be created as two artificial islands (the document is reproduced in M. Tafuri, *Venezia e il Rinascimento*, Turin, 1985, Appendice, pp. 242–3). M. Tafuri observes that, according to Cornaro's ideal, 'the emersion of a theatre *all'antica* from the water of the lagoon would have underlined the link between the specific spectacularity of the town and antiquarian culture. As a place for spectacles, the theatre itself would have become a spectacular object [...]: the building was imagined as a fantastic object, a scenographic apparition to be appreciated *commodamente* from the major "theatre" of the Serenissima, the Piazzetta' (*ibid*, p. 226; my trans.). On Venice as a 'virgin city', see McPherson, pp. 33–4.

14 *De proprietatibus rerum*, liber XV, 'De provinciis', Lyons, 1480. Quoted by F. Gaeta, 'L'idea di Venezia', in G. Arnaldi and M. Pastore Stocchi, *Storia della cultura veneta*, 3/III, 1981, pp. 567–8 (my italics).

15 G. Cozzi, *Repubblica di Venezia e stati italiani: politica e giustizia dal secolo XVI al secolo XVIII*, Turin, 1982, p. 100 (my trans.).

16 Cf. Cozzi, *Repubblica di Venezia*, pp. 103–4.

17 *Orazioni civili*, Bologna, 1744, p. 144. Quoted in Cozzi, *Repubblica di Venezia*, pp. 218–19.

18 Cf. *'Tre Avogadori di Comun e tre notai'* (end of the sixteenth century), a picture painted by Paolo de' Freschi, Venice, Palazzo Ducale.

19 Quotations are from the Arden editions of the plays: *The Merchant of Venice*, ed. J. Russell Brown, London, 1985 (1959); *Othello*, ed. M. R. Ridley, London, 1979 (1962).

20 Also Coryat, in his *Crudities* (2 vols, London, 1611), endorses this piece of information (1, p. 312). An idea of what the Rialto looked like may be grasped from Vittore Carpaccio's *Miracolo della croce* (1494, Venice, Gallerie dell'Accademia) where both the ancient wooden bridge and the *loggia* are portrayed.

21 I will not discuss here the relationship between drama and trial, nor the often analysed trial scene in the play. See C. Dente, *La recita del diritto: saggio su 'The Merchant of Venice'*, Pisa, 1986.

22 The title role was played by Tino Carraro, Mosca by Umberto Orsini;

scenery and costumes were designed by Paolo Tommasi.

23 Quotations are taken from C. H. Herford and P. and E. Simpson's edition of Jonson's *Works*, 11 vols, Oxford, 1925–52, 5, 1937. Spelling is modernised.

24 *I Diarii di Marin Sanudo (MCCCCXCVI–MDXXXIII)*, 58 vols, ed. R. Fulin, F. Stefani, N. Barozzi, G. Berchet and M. Allegri, Venezia, 1879–1903 (rpt. Bologna, 1969–70), 43, p. 67.

25 R. Dutton, *Ben Jonson*, Cambridge, 1983, p. 150.

26 Dutton discusses the relationship between *Volpone*, the Gunpowder Plot and Lord Salisbury (pp. 147–8, and 151–3).

27 N. Grene, *Shakespeare, Jonson, Molière: the Comic Contract*, London, 1980, p. 140.

28 I have dealt with the problems of the play as a continuous performance of disguising in '*Volpone* di Ben Jonson: la teatralità della simulazione', *Rivista di Letterature Moderne e Comparate*, 43, 4, 1990.

29 Tafuri, *Venezia e il Rinascimento*, p. 226.

30 'Franciscina' (Franceschina) and 'Pantalone di Besogniosi' (de' Bisognosi) are the *commedia dell'arte* characters quoted later by Corvino in II.iii.4 and II.iii.8, when he stops Scoto's speech. For the use of *commedia dell'arte* characters in Jonsonian masques, and especially for the relationship between Inigo Jones's costumes and the Italian/Venetian dramatic practice, see K. Richards, 'Inigo Jones and the Commedia dell'arte', in *The Commedia dell'Arte from the Renaissance to Dario Fo*, ed. C. Cairns, Lewiston, 1989.

31 Cf. Cozzi, *Repubblica di Venezia*, p. 169.

11

The idea of Venice in Shakespeare and Ben Jonson[*]

Leo Salingar

By the early seventeenth century imaginary foreign settings were very familiar on the English stage. An Italian court was the favoured setting for Jacobean tragedies of intrigue and revenge. And from the last years of Shakespeare's career, from about 1610 onwards, when peaceful relations had been resumed with Spain and Spain's cultural prestige was gaining ground, John Fletcher and others were beginning to turn to Spanish short-story writers, notably Cervantes, as previously they had turned to Italians, to furnish them with raw material for plots. Several of their comedies of romantic adventure are derived from one or a couple of Spanish *novelas* and were set in Spanish cities; for example *The Spanish Gypsy* (1623) by Middleton and Rowley, where the action, combining two stories by Cervantes, takes place in or near Madrid; or Fletcher's *Rule a Wife and Have a Wife* (1624), set in Valladolid. These and similar plays capture something of the spirit of Spanish cape-and-sword romances. Again, the action of Middleton and Rowley's outstanding tragedy, *The Changeling* (1622), is derived mainly from an English but partly also from a Spanish narrative source and is set in Alicante. But although these nominally Spanish or nominally Italian plays contain allusions to national manners and carry some local or topical references, none of them builds up a distinct impression of a particular foreign city. The sense of place in them is vague and generalised. In contrast, our impression of Venice is distinctive and strong in Shakespeare's *The Merchant of Venice* (produced about 1596), in *Othello, the Moor of Venice* (1604) and in Ben

[*]This article is the second of two papers on 'Images of Europe on Shakespeare's Stage', read at Paris in September 1991 in the International Seminar on *Image de l'Europe des nations sur scène* organised for the Council of Europe by the Centre National de la Recherche Scientifique. The text, with a change of title, is published here by courtesy of the CNRS.

Jonson's *Volpone, or The Fox* (1605). These three plays belong, of course, to three different genres – romantic comedy, tragedy and satire – and none of them aims at a thoroughgoing local actuality or at a symbolical realism in the vein of Thomas Mann. But in each of them the image or, better perhaps, the idea of Venice is more than a nominal location or a background; it becomes a pivotal factor in the whole unfolding of the play. The only other foreign city to be given a similar prominence in Elizabethan drama is classical Rome. But these three plays stand apart from the rest of Elizabethan and Jacobean drama in their portrayal of anywhere from the continental Europe of their own day. For the Elizabethans, Venice held a unique and complex significance; as Parker sums it up in his edition of *Volpone*, it was 'the exemplar of wealth, sophistication, art, luxury, political cunning, and stringent government'.[1]

One broad reason for its significance lay in the expansion of English trade. By the end of the sixteenth century, London was a major international business centre, and since the 1570s English merchants had been active in the Mediterranean as well as the Baltic. The English were now trading directly in oriental luxury goods; English seamen fell captive to the Moors or the Turks, from Algiers to the Greek islands (and it is worth noting that the Witches in *Macbeth* intend some of their malice for a shipman 'to Aleppo gone, master o'th *Tiger*'); finally, there were English ambassadors at Venice and Constantinople, consuls at Tripolis, in Syria and Aleppo.[2] All this meant continuous contact and competition with the Venetians. By 1600, London had overtaken her Mediterranean rival in population, with perhaps 200,000 inhabitants as compared with some 140,000 urban inhabitants in Venice.[3] And Venice, no longer a major power in the western Mediterranean, was beginning to lose her eastern empire as well, especially with the fall of Cyprus to the Turks in 1571, a loss only partly offset by her share in the victory at Lepanto the same year. But, as Fernand Braudel tells us, her home industries were expanding 'in silk and woollen manufacture, glassmaking and printing', and Venice still dominated the trade of the eastern Mediterranean, with perhaps 'seven or eight hundred' ships entering and leaving her port every year about the turn of the century, and with a huge volume of monetary exchange that made the city what the historian calls 'a sort of "capitalist empire"' – quoting a contemporary to the effect that the Rialto was perhaps the best-stocked centre for exchange in Europe ('forse in Europa, non si trova altra piazza più commoda').[4]

Visitors were impressed by the exceptional variety of nationalities to be seen in Venice, both travellers and alien residents. Montaigne commented that 'la liberté de la police de Venise, et utilité de la trafique la peuple [sic] d'étrangiers', and Shakespeare's merchant, Antonio, enlarges upon the same theme:

The duke cannot deny the course of law:
For the commodity that strangers have
With us in Venice, if it be denied,
Will much impeach the justice of the state,
Since that the trade and profit of the city
Consisteth of all nations.[5]

Much the same might be said about Antwerp. But Venice was unique. While the rest of Italy was labouring under internal repression or foreign control, she maintained her comparative toleration and her independence as a city-state, thanks to her strict, efficient and secretive administration and thanks, it was said, to her strange but enduring form of government, described by an Englishman as 'a compounded form of state, containing in it an Idea of the three principal governments of the ancient Athenians and Romans, namely the Monarchical, the Oligarchical, and Democratical'.[6]

Above all, perhaps, sightseeing tourists, already becoming frequent, were impressed by the unique townscape of Venice and the increasing splendour of her palaces. Montaigne, in 1580, was even disappointed because her famous 'rarities' were not as striking as he had imagined. But Shakespeare makes the pedant in Love's Labour's Lost air his knowledge of the saying 'Venetia, Venetia, / Chi non to vedi, non ti pretia.' And Thomas Coryat, after touring the Continent in 1608, lauded Venice as 'the Queen of the Christian world [...] the most resplendent mirror of Europe', and 'the most glorious and heavenly show upon the water', with 'her incomparable situation, surpassing wealth, and most magnificent buildings'.[7]

Shakespeare and Jonson, however, make little or no dramatic use of the city's reputation for visual splendour. They concentrate rather on the idea of Venice as an aristocratic republic and cosmopolitan centre of capitalism, with her exceptional freedom for strangers and her exceptional attraction for travellers in search of sophistication. The image of Venetian society in their three plays is a refracted projection of London.

In Shakespeare's narrative source for *The Merchant of Venice*, the medieval story by Giovanni Fiorentino, Venice is presented as a port with many merchants and 'fine ships', with festivities and 'a reputation as a place of strict justice', but no other descriptive characteristics.[8] Ansaldo, named as 'the richest Christian merchant there', who is to sacrifice himself for the sake of his godson, the orphan hero, is introduced simply in his 'counting house', without further elaboration. But Shakespeare opens his play in the middle of a dialogue between Antonio and his friends, breathing an atmosphere of patrician leisure and introducing Antonio's 'argosies' with their cargo of 'spices' and 'silks', their 'portly sail' outstanding from the multitude of 'petty traffickers' on the sea and 'overpeer[ing]' them – a sharply realistic image, if we go by the analysis of contemporary Venetian shipping given by Braudel.[9] We hear later that his ships are bound severally for Tripolis, the Indies, Mexico and England (I.iii.16) and, subsequently, for 'Lisbon, Barbary, and India' as well (III.ii.267). The list, reminiscent of Marlowe's *Tamburlaine*, strains probability but fits the heightened colouring of romance. Similarly, we learn that suitors from 'every coast' in 'the wide world' (at least, of Europe and the Mediterranean) have 'come in quest' of Portia (I.i.167–72). More prosaically, we learn of Shylock buying a diamond in Frankfort and grasping at 'news' of his daughter 'from Genoa' (III.i.72 and 77). And through Shylock or in connection with Shylock we hear repeatedly of the Rialto as the focus of Venetian 'news' and business – three times in his first scene (where 'What news on the Rialto?' is a mechanical, evidently habitual, phrase of his), and twice again in the middle scene where he is torn between vindictiveness over Antonio's losses and misery over the loss of his own daughter.[10] Although some of these passages are poetically heightened, what is striking about the others is the way Shakespeare makes the speakers take their background naturalistically for granted, without any emphasis on local colour.

Shakespeare ignores such famous sights in Venice as St Mark's Square, the Doge's Palace, the Arsenal and (although he mentions a gondola) the Grand Canal. What counts for him dramatically in the idea of Venice is the theme of 'venture' (or 'ventures') and 'hazard' – words he uses more often here than in any other play; and secondly, the presence of Shylock, as a moneylender and a Jew.

In his first dialogue with Antonio, Bassanio compares Portia's suitors with Jason (I.i.172), and Gratiano triumphantly echoes him later, in the scene of the double betrothal: 'We are the Jasons, we have won the fleece' (III.ii.240). Throughout the comedy, the 'ventures' of love and of commerce interchange and coalesce.[11] As we hear, in the opening speeches, of Antonio's merchant 'ventures' (I.i.21 and 42), we hear also of the typical risks at sea that they entail (a topic absent from Shakespeare's narrative source), though Antonio is confident that his risks are safely distributed. Then Bassanio touches on the admitted irrationality of 'hazard' in the 'childhood proof' he adduces – the analogy from his 'school-days', of shooting one arrow to retrieve another – as an embarrassed apology to Antonio for requesting yet another loan (I.i.130–4 and 140–52). The second scene, of Portia with Nerissa, extends the idea of risk by introducing the 'lott'ry' of the caskets which, rather than any considered choice, is to determine who will be Portia's husband. Instead of the motif from his source story of the sexual trap set by the widowed Lady of Belmont, Shakespeare has his series of wooers' casket scenes, with their emphatic refrain of 'lott'ry,' 'chance' and 'hazard'. Meanwhile, the third scene has introduced Shylock, with his sternly calculated 'thrift', as opposed to reckless 'ventures' at sea – and likewise, to Antonio's trust in 'the hand of heaven' (I.iii.88). The tension between the differing human beings in 'venture' tightens through the middle scenes (partly by way of the episode of Jessica's elopement, one of Shakespeare's additions to the story) to the point in the trial scene where Portia defeats Shylock, not with a lover's intuition, such as had apparently led Bassanio to choose the right casket, but with literal-minded logic, the weapon Shylock himself has favoured. Shakespeare turns what had been little more than a clever quibble in the original story (where the Jew had been given no character to speak of) into a stunning theatrical revolution. Even then, in his *decrescendo* after the trial scene, Shakespeare dwells on lovers' irrational yet binding commitments, first through Lorenzo and Jessica's litany of classical legends and then through the comic byplay over Portia and Nerissa's rings.

Hostility between the Jew and the Christian is of course central to Shakespeare's play, but it is hostility within a framework of comparatively free and frequent intercourse, wherein Shakespeare apparently reflects without exaggerating the real conditions in the Venice of his day. It was the freedom of Venetian institutions that attracted the Jews there, forming a relatively large community (over 1,600 by the 1580s).[12] And over and above purely financial relations, some Italian Jews sought and found social relations with Gentiles, in spite of occasional prohibitions by the Church and the Jewish authorities alike. 'In 1592,' we are told, 'it was [...] necessary to reissue a ban in Rome forbidding Jews to teach Hebrew, *singing, dancing, and other arts* to Christians' (my emphasis); and 'the Jewish community in Padua in 1599 had to forbid the Jews to dance with Christians'. Shakespeare's invented episode of Jessica's elopement with Lorenzo and her subsequent conversion was not unthinkable, therefore; such liaisons apparently occurred in fact.[13]

On the other hand, Shakespeare seems not to have heard about the ghetto; he seems to assume that Shylock lives in the midst of the Christians – as when Old Gobbo asks Launcelot, 'which is the way to Master Jew's?' (II.ii.31). And he dresses Shylock in a 'Jewish gaberdine' (I.iii.107), possibly a standard theatrical costume for Jews, but unknown to social historians. Thomas Coryat was to observe that the wealthy Venetian Jews and Jewesses dressed resplendently, the men being distinguished from Christians by their headgear (red hats, he says, for the Italian- and western-born Jews, yellow turbans for the Levantines).[14] Coryat also says that in Italy converted Jews forfeit their goods (as a penalty for their usury), so that 'they are left even naked, and destitute of their means of maintenance' – which explains, he adds, why 'there are fewer Jews converted [in Italy], than in any country of Christendom'.[15] There would have been no need, then, to inflict two distinct punishments on Shylock, as in Shakespeare's trial scene. (In the original story, the frustrated Jew had simply '[taken] his bond and [torn] it in pieces in a rage'). Shakespeare's Jew is a superbly powerful dramatic creation, firmly grounded in the play's idea of Venice, but not in precise circumstantial knowledge.

So too with the Venetian aristocrats. Shylock sneers at their prodigality (II.v.15); Bassanio admits his past extravagance, and we see him distributing liveries to his servants, including the newcomer, Launcelot, and giving them orders for the provision of a feat for his friends before he sets out to Belmont (II.ii). But in sixteenth-century Venice, for all her public pomp and display, private extravagance was frowned upon. Indeed, the Venetians had a reputation for domestic meanness, which William Thomas alludes to in his *Historie of Italie* in 1549; while Montaigne remarked that although food was as dear as in Paris, Venice was extremely cheap to live in ('c'est la ville du monde où on vit à meilleur conte'), there being no need for attendants.[16] Fynes Moryson, travelling abroad at the time of Shakespeare's play, noted that the Venetians were 'covetous' in spite of their aristocratic pride, thought Italians generally were 'viciously frugal in housekeeping' and commented on the absence of menservants. Similarly, Coryat was shocked to see wealthy Venetian Senators buying their own provisions, and observed that they kept 'no honourable hospitality [...] but a very frugal table', far removed from 'that noble state and magnificence' of the English aristocracy.[17] In Shakespeare's medieval source-story the hero dines out and gives dinners in Venice.[18] But the operative factor for the dramatist must surely have been the contrast between a lavish and a parsimonious style of living, not documentary accuracy.

There is also the broader contrast in the play between the tension in the city and the atmosphere of fairy-tale prevailing at Belmont. The effectiveness of the romance depends upon the contrasting thrust of comparative realism in the scenes at Venice.

In *Othello*, also drawn from Italian sources, this time a sixteenth-century tale by Giraldi, Shakespeare again makes dramatic use of the idea of Venice as an exceptional city-state. Again, the play involves conflict between insiders and a radical outsider, the Moor, turning again, therefore, on relative institutional freedom. Only the first act is set in Venice, and in the main action, in Cyprus, the imagined environment belongs to a military garrison rather than a town. But Venice was noted for giving military commands to foreigners, and Giraldi explains that because of his personal merit as a soldier, the Moor 'was very dear to the Signoria, who in rewarding virtuous actions ever advance the interests of the Republic'.[19] The theme of promotion on merit, not on the strength of family or status, becomes a central thread in the tragedy, as in Iago's resentment towards his commander and Cassio. There is no threat to Cyprus in Giraldi's story, written before the Turkish conquest of the island, but Shakespeare supplies a fictionally altered version of the Turkish attack.[20] This, with their escape from the play's invented tempest, lends an ironic sense of security to Othello and Desdemona – whom Shakespeare, unlike Giraldi, hurries to Cyprus immediately after the wedding. The Turkish threat also gives added force indirectly to the idea of Venice, which runs through the play.

Shakespeare provides Othello with royal ancestry in addition to pride in his personal values and with a history of exotic adventure that becomes both a credible source of fascination to Desdemona and a source of contrast to the other native, city-minded Venetians. Giraldi mentions in passing that the heroine's 'relatives' had tried to dissuade her from marrying the Moor. Shakespeare builds this hint into the

177

figure of Brabantio, as a self-important senator, just as he builds Iago into a subordinate officer hardened by urban as well as military experience; and he adds the idle gallant, Roderigo, to the group of native Venetian characters. Iago is jealous of Cassio partly for the very reason that his rival officer is a Florentine. When in the opening scene Iago and Roderigo set out to rouse Brabantio against his daughter's secret elopement, they harp on social and racial prejudice; Iago, with vicious allusions to 'an old black ram', 'a Barbary horse', and Roderigo, more tamely, with reference to 'a lascivious Moor', 'an extravagant [i.e. *wandering*] and wheeling stranger, / Of here, and every where'.[21] Brabantio follows this lead, accusing Othello of seducing Desdemona by witchcraft, seeing that she had 'shunned / The wealthy curled darlings of our nation' (I.ii.67); and he repeats the charge before the Duke in the Senate scene, insisting that her defection is 'Against all rules of nature' (I.iii.101). In contrast to the impartiality and the State interest represented by the Duke, Brabantio expresses a socially confined mentality – a mentality that Iago, for his part, well knows how to exploit. He keeps his dupe, Roderigo, hopeful of an easy breach in the 'frail vow, betwixt an erring barbarian, and a super-subtle Venetian' (I.iii.356); and when the time is ripe he poisons Othello himself with the same insidious thought of cultural incompatibility:

> I would not have your free and noble nature
> Out of self-bounty be abused, look to 't;
> I know our country disposition well;
> In Venice they do let God see the pranks
> They dare not show their husbands.[22]

(III.iii.203–7)

And further:

> Ay, there's the point: as, to be bold with you,
> Not to affect many proposed matches,
> Of her own clime, complexion, and degree,
> Whereto we see in all things nature tends;
> Fie, we may smell in such a will most rank,
> Foul disproportion; thoughts unnatural.

(III.iii.232–7)

On which Othello, in soliloquy, naively comments, 'This fellow's of exceeding honesty, / And knows all qualities, with a learned spirit, / Of human dealing' (III.iii.262–4). He leaves the remote moral eminence of his military 'occupation' – (a word to which Othello gives exceptional weight (III.iii.363)) – for the role of a jealous husband according to Italian convention.

There is attraction and repulsion between Othello and the idea of Venice, and a dramatic rhythm in the naming of Venice or the Venetians as the play goes forward. The city is named only once in the first scene, but with special emphasis. Iago discourses to Roderigo about the service he has seen, 'At Rhodes, at Cyprus, and on other grounds, / Christian and heathen' – suggesting the city's sphere of power (I.i.29–30). Next, he proposes to 'call up' Brabantio, Roderigo says he will 'call aloud', and Iago incites him with a vivid urban image: 'Do, with like timorous accent, and dire yell, / As when, by night and negligence, the fire / Is spied in populous cities' (I.i.75–7). All this prepares for Brabantio's exclamation as he listens to their story incredulously from his window: 'What, tell'st thou me of robbing? this is Venice, / My house is not a grange' (I.i.105). Not merely a built-up city, as opposed to the countryside, but a capital, renowned for government and justice.

Venice and Venetians are named seven times in all in the first half of the play; then, fifteen times after Othello's crisis of jealousy. While Othello's character breaks down, the state reasserts itself from a distance. 'Something from Venice', 'the great messengers of Venice' – Lodovico and Gratiano, who have come to recall Othello from Cyprus – are twice announced on the stage to the sound of trumpets (IV.i.208, IV.ii.171). This resonates, as it were, through the last words of Othello, where he seems to wish to justify himself to the messengers as the champion of Venice and Christianity. It helps us to measure the force of Othello's words if we notice that Fynes Moryson reports that Christians in the Turkish empire might not carry arms, and that the aggressiveness and arrogance of the Turks was such that a Christian traveller dared not look them in the face.[23] No doubt some similar report lies behind Othello's last words before he kills himself:

> And say besides, that in Aleppo once,
> Where a malignant and a turban'd Turk
> Beat a Venetian, and traduc'd the state,
> I took by the throat the circumcised dog,
> And smote him thus.

> (V.ii.353–7)

Not only is the Moor now once again charming the attention of Venetian listeners – the listeners who have been forced to arrest him

– with a story of his remote adventures, but he is doubly yet paradoxically identifying himself with Venice; once in the past and again by his present gesture, as he treats himself like the malignant Turk and assumes to himself the execution of Venetian justice. The tragic interplay between heroic outsider and the idea of the city continues until the end.

Evidently Shakespeare was deeply interested in the exceptional individual at odds with society. In a sense, Shylock and Othello are simply two of the strong-minded outsiders, villains or heroes, who follow in varied succession through his work, from Richard of Gloucester to Timon of Athens. They belong to their Venetian setting in that the social position of each of them would have been virtually inconceivable elsewhere, especially in London; but it could be said that Venice was provided as a setting by each of the *novelle* he was working from. *Volpone* likewise follows a main line in the author's thinking. But with Ben Jonson the location at Venice results from a deliberate choice.

Volpone, or the Fox, is a magnifico, without direct heirs, who gives it out that he is sick and dying so that clients will flock to him with extravagant gifts, each incited by the hope that he will be chosen to inherit Volpone's entire wealth. Aided by Mosca, his parasite, Volpone exploits the greed of his dupes until the two plotters overreach themselves, fall out and betray each other to justice. As a satiric moralist, Jonson was concerned with the motives at work in an acquisitive society and the pretensions it stimulated, in fantastic speculation, social adventurism, deception and self-deception.[24] Before writing *Volpone*, he had set out his basic scheme of two cunning scoundrels plotting against their world and then against each other in his Roman tragedy *Sejanus*; and the same scheme reappears in his later comedies, notably *The Alchemist*. But *Sejanus* was grounded in classical history, and Jonson's later comedies are set in the London of the day. When he revived his early success, *Every Man in His Humour*, he transposed the setting of the comedy from Florence to London without altering the plot; and the basic scheme in *Volpone* is independent of an Italian setting. Indeed, Jonson took suggestions for the specific details of his plot partly from classical satire on legacy hunters in Horace, Petronius and Lucian, and partly from medieval beast fables and *Reynard the Fox*, having no connection with Venice. He apparently chose Venice for his setting because Venice was both the supreme type of a modern commercial city like London and by repute a parallel with the decadent splendour of classical Rome. And, more of a self-conscious scholar than Shakespeare, Jonson documented his Venetian background thoroughly from contemporary writers, John Florio, for example.[25] (In his preface to the published play, Jonson asserts that he shows the punishment of his rogues at the end, unlike the usual procedure of comedy, in order to silence those who complain of the immorality of the stage; and the reputation of Venice for strict justice may have been a secondary reason for his choice of setting. But the judges in his comedy are of doubtful integrity, like nearly everybody else.)

The play opens with Volpone's hymn to gold and his dialogue with Mosca stressing his intellectual superiority – 'I glory,' he says, 'More in the cunning purchase of my wealth / Than in the glad possession, since I gain / No common way' (I.i.30). Venice is first named, in connection with the thought of conspicuous wealth, towards the end of the first act, when Volpone's third visitor, the merchant Corvino, says he has brought an orient pearl, 'Venice was never owner of the like' (I.v.10). Similarly, in the central episode, where Volpone tried to seduce Corvino's wife Celia, he offers her 'a carbuncle / May put out both the eyes of our St Mark', as opening to an amazing list of allurements of cosmopolitan origins, ancient and modern (III.vii.192). Meanwhile the play is thick with allusions to Italian authors and ideology in general (*'ragion des stato'*, for example IV.i.141), and specifically to Venetian places, institutions, ranks and customs. We hear, for instance, of the Piazza and 'the portico to the Procuratia', of the Arsenal and the Lazaretto, of Volpone's 'long row of houses / By the Piscaria' (including a 'pretty [...] bawdy-house', it seems), and of his final, and fitting, relegation 'To the hospital of the Incurabili'.[26] Much is said about *chequins* and other Venetian coins. There are comically knowing references to the Great Council and the Senate by the English visitors, Sir Politic Would-Be and his Lady, who furnish the sub-plot (IV.i.74 and IV.iii.1). When Volpone's attempt at seduction collapses he fears the intrusion of 'officers, the *Saffi*' (III.viii.16); then, regaining his *élan*, he adopts the disguise of another grade of police, 'One o' th' *commandatori*' (V.iv.114) – a whim that leads to his own arrest. Earlier, for his initial approach to Celia, Jonson has given him a disguise as Scoto Mantuano, the famous mountebank, in a superb, prolonged display of a charlatan's eloquent ballyhoo, thickly larded with expressions from colloquial Italian (II.ii). This mountebank scene is a striking application of local colour. At the same time, it is a development and an exposure of Volpone's essential role, as he throws himself into the part of a charlatan vending impossible gratifications.

181

The superlative 'cunning' of Volpone and Mosca starts from and ends in self-delusion, like the gross expectations of their dupes. Such is the guiding principle of the action: Venice is a solidly imagined city, but its glamour is a mirage. The satire is extended on a lower register by way of the English couple, the Politic Would-Bes. The wife is a vociferous bluestocking; the husband, as his name implies, a mindless copier of others (Sir Pol, the parrot), a ridiculous amateur of statecraft. They both represent contemporary types that Jonson was to use again, in his London comedies. Here they are caricatures of fashionable travellers and, through their gullibility, parodies of the Venetians. They have come here 'to draw the subtle air' of the place (IV.i.66). The wife spouts Italian writers' names indiscriminately, but also she 'Lies here in Venice for intelligence' (a sharply appropriate term) 'Of tires, and fashions, and behaviour / Among the courtesans' (II.i.27); her credulity about the famous courtesans (another touch of local colour) leads her to farcical disarray. Her husband is equally credulous about mountebanks and their momentous secrets; access to hidden subtleties is part of his vanity. In the approved style of a fashionable traveller he delivers 'instructions', adapted to 'this height of Venice', and keeps a diary.[27] He makes 'observations' and writes 'essays', and his talk is full of 'news', financial 'projects', 'policy', plots, spies and the guarded behaviour a foreigner needs in Venice – on the possession of which he absurdly deceives himself. The foolish Would-Be couple underline the empty grasping behind the 'cunning' of the leading characters. Also, beyond implicit analogies, they anchor the play in London through satire on the type of traveller attracted to Venice precisely by its reputation for exotic and distinguished subtlety.

For all his use of local colour, then, Jonson as well as Shakespeare, adapts his image or idea of Venice to his own dramatic purpose. Neither dramatist sets out to make knowledge about a foreign city, or even knowledge about the experience of travel, a theatrical subject in itself. Both, essentially, are reacting to English life and thought. On the other hand, English self-awareness in Shakespeare's time was stimulated (if not provoked) by the new voyages and increased contacts with Europe. And, apart from indulging nationalistic prejudice, the theatre valued a sense of foreignness, either for the sake of an aesthetic distancing useful for satire, a kind of Brechtian alienation, or else for the sake of the raised emotions of romance. The idea of Venice constituted the keenest and firmest meeting between English knowledge about Europe and the English dramatic imagination.

Notes

1 *Volpone*, ed. R. B. Parker, Manchester, 1983, p. 89.
2 *Macbeth*, ed. Kenneth Muir, The Arden Edition, London, 1962, I.iii.7. See also Edward P. Cheyney, *A History of England from the Defeat of the Armada to the Death of Elizabeth* [1914], New York, 1948, 1, chapter 17; Ralph Davis, 'England and the Mediterranean, 1570–1670', in *Essays in the Economic and Social History of Tudor and Stuart England*, ed. F. J. Fisher, Cambridge, 1961, pp. 117–37; Fernand Braudel, *The Mediterranean and the Mediterranean World in the Age of Philip II* (2nd edition 1966), translated by Siân Reynolds (1972), 1, pp. 612–29.
3 Roger Finlay, *Population and Metropolis: the Demography of London, 1580–1680*, Cambridge, 1981, pp. 51–69; and Braudel, *The Mediterranean*, 1, p. 421.
4 Braudel, *The Mediterranean*, 1, pp. 390–1. Cf. Gino Luzzatto, 'L'economia veneziana nel sec. XVI', in *Rinascimento europeo e rinascimento veneziano*, ed. Vittore Branca, Venice, 1967.
5 Michel de Montaigne, *Journal de voyage en Italie par la Suisse et l'Allemagne en 1580 et 1581*, ed. Charles Dédéyan, Paris, 1946, p. 242; *The Merchant of Venice*, ed. John Russell Brown, The Arden Edition, London, 1955, III.iii.26–31.
6 Thomas Coryat, *Coryat's Crudities* [1611], Glasgow, 1905, vol. 1, p. 418. John Julius Norwich, *A History of Venice*, London, 1985, pp. 462 and 525.
7 Montaigne, *Journal*, p. 173; *Love's Labour's Lost*, ed. Richard David, The Arden Edition, London, 1956, IV.ii.95; Coryat, *Crudities*, 1, pp. 2, 300, and 303; Norwich, *A History of Venice*, p. 521.
8 Giovanni Fiorentino, *Il pecorone*, translated by Geoffrey Bullough, in *Narrative and Dramatic Sources of Shakespeare*, ed. Geoffrey Bullough, 8 vols, London, 1957–75, 1, pp. 463–76.
9 Braudel, *The Mediterranean*, vol. 1, pp. 308–11.
10 Cf. *The Merchant of Venice*, I.iii.17, 33 and 102, and III.i.1 and 40.
11 John Russell Brown, *Shakespeare and his Comedies*, London, 1957, pp. 65–7.
12 Moses A. Shulvass, *The Jews in the World of Shakespeare*, trans. by Elvin I. Kose, Leiden, 1973, pp. 16 and 355; Braudel, *The Mediterranean*, 1, p. 641.
13 Shulvass, *The Jews in the World of Shakespeare*, pp. 164 and 184.
14 Coryat, *Crudities*, vol. 1, pp. 371–3; Shulvass, *The Jews in the World of Shakespeare*, p. 187; *The Merchant of Venice*, ed. Brown, I.iii.107n.
15 Coryat, *Crudities*, vol. 1, pp. 373–4.
16 William Thomas, *The Historie of Italie* (1549), p. 85r; Montaigne, *Journal*, pp. 173–4.
17 Fynes Moryson, *Shakespeare's Europe: Unpublished Chapters of Fynes Moryson's 'Itinerary'*, ed. Charles Hughes, London, 1903, p. 152; Coryat, *Crudities*, 1, pp. 397 and 415–17.
18 *Sources*, ed. Bullough, vol. 1, p. 464.
19 Giraldi, in *Sources*, ed. Bullough, 7 (1973), p. 242; cf. Moryson, *Shakespeare's Europe*, pp. 132 and 139.
20 *Sources*, ed. Bullough, 7 (1973), pp. 211–14.
21 *Othello*, ed. M. R. Ridley, The Arden Edition, London, 1962, I.i.88, 111, 126 and 136.

22 *Othello*, III.iii.203–7. See also Richard Marienstras, *Le Proche et le lointain*, Paris, 1981, pp. 202–18.
23 Moryson, *Shakespeare's Europe*, pp. 53 and 62–4.
24 See L. C. Knights, *Drama and Society in the Age of Jonson*, London, 1937.
25 See Mario Praz, 'Ben Jonson's Italy' [1937], in *The Flaming Heart*, New York, 1958, pp. 168–85; *Volpone*, ed. Parker, 'Introduction', pp. 11–44; and R. B. Parker, 'Jonson's Venice', in *Theatre of the English and Italian Renaissance*, eds J. R. Mulryne and Margaret Shewring, London, 1991, pp. 95–112.
26 *Volpone*, ed. Parker, II.ii.35 and 36; IV.i.91 and 106; V.vii.8–12; and V.12.120.
27 *Volpone*, ed. Parker, notes on IV.1.1–8 and 133.

12

Dobbin on the Rialto:
Venice and the divison of identity

Avraham Oz

The identity riddle by which Launcelot Gobbo is 'try[ing] confusions' with his blind father to the utmost force of comic cruelty is supposed to be resolved in measuring Launcelot's apparently non-existent beard against the hair of Gobbo's 'fill-horse', Dobbin, as a test case by which the father can truly recognise his son. Has Launcelot, a talking animal of humble origins, developed similar traits to mute Dobbin, whose name and the measure of his hair are the only parts in him which talk in the course of the play? Are their physical delineations, and hence their identities, interchangeable? Though these questions remain unanswered, the analogy itself turns out to be misleading: Dobbin's tail cannot serve, as it happens, to measure Launcelot's imaginary beard, unless it 'grows backward' (*The Merchant of Venice*, II.ii.35, 89–93).[1] Unlike the case of the former comic entry in the canon, *A Midsummer Night's Dream*, this latter anomaly is unacceptable within the dramatic framework of *The Merchant of Venice*, in which the only mysteries, it seems, relate to maritime and other commercial contingencies that find their economic representation by the rise and fall of rates in the Rialto: these, rather than natural organisms, are the only phenomena in Venice that can grow backward or leap forward, as Shylock's purely economic account of Biblical mysteries such as Jacob's sheep would attest. And yet in an English play about Italy presented before an English audience, in which an Italian peasant named Gobbo would call his horse Dobbin, both measures and identities are rather strange and admirable than growing to something of great constancy. After all, Launcelot's riddle of identity is hardly a momentary whim: his father has just surprised him while rehearsing his proposed transformation from being 'Launcelot the Jew's man', a problematic move, since his conscience strongly advises him against it.

Leaving his position as the Jew's man, we learn, is not a mere change of employment: it signifies, it would appear, such a radical shift in his being that a traditional morality play, involving the personified characters of Conscience and the Fiend, is mobilised to discuss its moral grounds. The issue here is the age-old controversy regarding the ethos of unified identity: does integrity necessarily imply a unified subject? In Launcelot Gobbo's little morality play, Conscience obviously advocates a positive answer, but it is the Fiend who has his way: 'the Jew's man' adds a Christian motley to his title, without abandoning, however, his 'Jewish portfolio', at least as regarding Jessica (*The Merchant of Venice*, II.iv.; II.v.; III.v; V.i.). Conceiving oneself as committed to multiple personhoods is hardly a recent phenomenon, not even in an early modern context: 'the capacity to use "I" in shifting contexts, characteristic of every known culture, is the most elemental feature of reflexive conceptions of personhoods.'[2] Here, with Launcelot, the division of identity becomes a central dramatic issue, and its ontological implications within the world of comedy may sustain Old Gobbo's paradoxical query as to 'whether one Launcelot that dwells with [the Jew], dwell with him or no' (II.ii.43–4). Launcelot's cruel game of identity 'confusions' on his way to transform his own identity is not a far cry from the similar game Katherina is coerced by Petruchio to perform when travelling to Padua in variously evaluating the gender identity of Vincentio (*The Taming of the Shrew*, IV.v.27–52), a similar token of her own transformation under way: take out the element of sex wars from Petruchio's motives for initiating the game, and what we have here is the exact replica of Shylock's and Tubal's routine practice of evaluating dangers (I.iii.15–24) and damages (III.i.76–115) in representing them as economic contingencies. This is the only measure by which Shylock will grant one the property of goodness: 'Ho no, no, no, no: my meaning in saying he is a good man, is to have you understand me that he is sufficient' (I.iii.13–15) or express his grief:

> Why there, there, there, there! a diamond gone cost me two thousand ducats in Frankfort, – the curse never fell upon our nation till now, I never felt it till now, – two thousand ducats in that, and other precious, precious jewels; I would my daughter were dead at my foot, and the jewels in her ear: would she were hears'd at my foot, and the ducats in her coffin. (III.i.76–82)

Iago's beguiling manoeuvre whereby Cassio's identity is transformed for the eyes of the hidden Othello from the lover of Bianca to that of Desdemona (*Othello*, IV.i.103ff) is yet another, vicious elaboration of the same 'confusions' game. But the transgression of the common notion of unified subjectivity is not complete before reaching what may be called an early modern stage of reification. The evaluation made by Shylock of Antonio's goodness, his daughter's life or (by the end of the trial scene) of his own existence in terms of property ('you take my life / When you do take the means whereby I live', IV.i.372–3) is continued here by Othello, who invests his entire identity in a piece of property, a handkerchief, which for him is a metonymy of his owning Desdemona. Similarly, Petruchio strives to own Katherina's identity and will by imposing on her his choice of food, clothes ('the gown is made / Just as my master had direction', cries the perplexed tailor, IV.iii.116–17) and timetable for rest and travel. Old Gobbo, who would measure Launcelot's hair by that of Dobbin, employs a metonymy whereby his two major properties, his horse and his son, are matched to partake in a measurable division of identity. All these games of measuring identities by economic values converge, in this chapter, in two major cases: Shylock's attempt to own Antonio through appropriating his pound of flesh, which relies on a solid case and fails just for the lack of an ultimate means of division (blood from flesh) and measurement (an equal pound); and Othello's attempt to own Desdemona's desire which fails when measured by a piece of property, the handkerchief, which makes a poor evidence. It will be our concern here to explore the intricate meaning of such violent power games between individual or public exponents of dominant ideologies and the transgressors of the same, in which identity is invested in, and qualified by, property relations within the context of Shakespeare's Italian plays. And we shall dwell particularly on the two Venetian plays, accommodating these two major cases, as a test case in which such games of power involve brothers and others, perhaps the most conspicuous common trait of the two plays.[3]

In a volume devoted to Shakespeare's Italy this chapter may be an exception in regarding Italy mainly as an absence, rather than a presence, in the poet's mind. It will argue that the major value of Italy in the canon lies less in what it is (or what Shakespeare and his audience knew it to be), but rather in its ontology of negation. It will attempt to demonstrate how the major import of Italy for Shakespeare's theatre lies in its effective representation of the other as constituting a torn communal subjectivity rather than an ideological allegory of the unified subject. The strategy of extending the boundaries of immediate experience as practised by Shakespeare in this context comprises time and space, ranging from history to geography. When the Tudor myth of killing the king is finally consumed in the restrictive framework of the English chronicle play, Shakespeare turns to address the most dangerous facets of the issue from within the alterity of republican Rome. Significantly, even in this ancient context, the theme of brothers and others figures out in relation to the communal identity: both helpers of Brutus and Cassius in their acts of death, Strato and Pindarus, are to mark the hierarchical difference between their masters' respective ideological standings by the end of the play. Cassius, who covers his face while dying, is to immerse into his bondsman's interpretation of liberty as fleeing 'where never Roman shall take note of him' (*Julius Caesar*, V.iii.50), namely beyond the discourse of western culture (a diabolic domain into which Cassius had already been banished in Mark Antony's ironic 'honourable men'), into which Cassius is to 'sink to night' like the setting sun (V.iii.59–61) and his body sent to Thasos. Brutus, who, on the contrary, instructs his helper to turn away his face but looks death in the eye, delegates his nobility to his bondsman's act. Strato is to merit absorption into the ranks of the dominant culture for rendering his service to 'the noblest Roman of them all' (V.v.68): the same Mark Antony now rescues Brutus's name from his former ironic inversion (though disillusioned Brutus himself had already preceded him in proclaiming that 'dishonour shall be humour' (IV.iii.108).

Similarly, when Shakespeare wants to explore the role of otherness within the subject in a contemporary context, he often turns to the mercantile sphere of northern Italy, where the tension between indigenous and alien subjectivity (be it in terms of Eurocentricity, Christianity or patriarchical gender division) may be dramatically pursued to the point of violent dialectics without any mode of censural intervention, whether personal or institutional. In his acute prophetic insight, Shakespeare anticipates the deficiencies of 'focussing principally on *our own* separateness, our own ethnic identity, culture, and traditions.[4] Already in the early modern context he grasps the sense in which the insularity of self is to be conceived of as 'nowhere'.[5] This insight, produced and fostered by an emphatic sentiment of a displaced universe governed, if at all, by a hidden, ultimately distant God, equally applies to individual and communal aspects of subjectivity. To save its still inevitable postulates of integration, Shakespeare's early modern humanist gaze often cunningly requires a strategic distantiation of experience without losing touch at the same time with its ideological core of identity. Italy, both distant and close in its patterns of cultural existence, becomes in this respect a convenient prototype of nowhereland, so often qualifying the communal subjectivity of England and allowing for self-fashioning through the other in constituting the *locus* of Shakespearean representation of reality.

The emblematic subject that links England and nowhere in Shakespeare is that of the traveller, constantly subverting the ideological postulates of stability, whether immersing in the bourn of an 'undiscover'd country' (*Hamlet*, III.i.79) or returning from having 'seen the world' to 'recount no fables' (*Love's Labour's Lost*, V.i.95, 100). The archetypal traveller is, of course, the poet himself, who often delegates his testimonial commitments to one or several of his dramatic fellow travellers within the play: the only 'witness appointees' available for such a 'delegation, substitution or representation'.[6] Corroborating the dialectics of poetic imagination, dramatic travellers, those '[selling their] own lands to see other men's' (*As You Like It*, IV.i.21–2), never lie, 'though fools at home condemn 'em' (*Tempest*, III.iii.26–7). Even when their words of *jouissance* seem suspicious to some –

> But is this true, or is it else your pleasure,
> Like pleasant travellers, to break a jest
> Upon the company you overtake?
>
> (*The Taming of the Shrew*, IV.v.70–2)

– they are always attested by some measure of reality. What these mobile witnesses have to deliver 'to th'yet unknowing world' always betrays the wondrous fluctuations of permanent becoming: learning constantly to absent them from the felicity of belonging, they draw their breath in *this* harsh world (our own, where we, together with their listeners on stage, brace our readiness to give them audience) to tell the story of their own displacement, and how it constitutes a subversive attitude towards the master narrative of unified subjectivity. It is their 'travel's history' (*Othello*, I.iii.139) which has taught them to forgo any excessive insistence on essentialism, when the latter clashes with their inherent mobility:

> Forward, I pray, since we have come so far,
> And be it moon, or sun, or what you please.

> And if you please to call it a rush-candle,
> Henceforth I vow it shall be so for me.
>
> *(The Taming of the Shrew,* IV.v.12–15)

This practice provides more than a hint as to the ways in which human experience is transformed to become animated with emblems of violence, such as

> antres vast, and deserts idle,
> Rough quarries, rocks and hills, whose heads touch heaven [...]
> And [...] Cannibals, that each other eat;
> The Anthropophagi, and men whose heads
> Do grow beneath their shoulders.
>
> *(Othello,* I.iii.140–1; 143–5)

Unrooted in any definite *locus*, neither an antique Roman nor fully a Dane (or Italian, for that matter), the traveller, even when seemingly settled down, becomes the protagonist of otherness. It is a position literally out of place in plays located in England, where the unifying ideological spirit of national solidarity, that 'philosophy of identity made into a collectively organized passion',[7] dictates one's major patterns of empathy: to this, the comic butts of otherness, such as Fluellen, Macmorris and Jamy, those illusory compatriots of Henry V, may attest. The uncanny refuge granted the sufferers of an English tragedy by the homy warmth of Dover is never available for a Shylock or an Othello in Venice, or at most is accorded to Prospero or the Duke Senior at their promised haven of concord, the actual materialisation of which remains much of a riddle, doubtful and ambiguous. Locating the entire action in nowhereland (incorporating subjective desire and the gaze of the other) provides the playwright, his audience and the dramatic constructs inhabiting the play with the opportunity of grounding the argument within a foreign discourse, informed by insoluble ambiguity and torn subjectivities, shunning the false protection of precarious ideological unities. It introduces a different gaze transforming immediate reality into its reflection in a dream of otherness, 'in which the subject is lost for a moment, blown up [...] decomposes, fades away, dissociates into its various egos'.[8] No decisive concord is offered here, and the plurality of experience translates into generic multivocality. It is not fortuitous that the use of foreign localities fostered a growing dependence in Shakespeare on mixed genres of questionable harmony, at the time when such genres gained momentum in the Italian theatre.[9]

The inversion of objective foreignness to alienated subjectivity leads to a different grasp of identity, exposing the issue of the unity of the subject to the dichotomy of self and other ingrained in the core of theatrical epistemology. This manifestly applies to Italy, which, among the host of nowheres inhabiting the canon, holds, as has been noted, a special standing in the poet's imagination. On the one hand, as the site of alterity comprising time (the glorious heritage of ancient Rome) and space (a rival naval and mercantile nation), Italy provides for the English playwright and his audience an appropriate refuge from the pressures of immediacy. A torn and divided state, the Tudor English historian of Italy, William Thomas, chose it 'to show to what dangers the equilibrium of the Tudor state might be exposed'.[10] Italy's political fragmentation may be extended, as it is in Shakespeare, to reflect the personal level in representing the division of identity. On the other hand, it serves as a convenient *alter ego* or a double on which the English gaze may project the immediate pressures of reality. The fashions and manners of 'proud Italy', which (in the wake of Roger Ascham or William Harrison) arouse the choler of Shakespeare's John of Gaunt in seeing his 'tardy-apish nation' limping after them 'in base imitation' (*Richard II*, II.i.21–3) are far from meeting such harsh criticism in Shakespeare's Italian plays.[11] As has been frequently noted, Shakespeare's imagined Italy is far from that Italianate nest of wickedness promoted by Webster, Ford or Ben Jonson. The Venice of *The Merchant of Venice* and *Othello* significantly differs from *Volpone*'s abode of malice and deceit: rather, it is that Venice which merits the uncompromising praises of the traveller (*Love's Labour's Lost*, IV.ii.92): 'To approach the English historians of Italy at this time is to be dazzled by the lustre of Venice [...] Italy was seen in terms of Venice, and her greatest century was thought to be the sixteenth, when Titian, Veronese and Tintoretto were painting and her political reputation was at its height.'[12] Since both Shakespeare and Jonson may have learnt about Venice mostly from Florio, his dictionary and his library, such difference in attitude has to do hardly with knowledge but with dramatic strategy.[13] The elimination of malice and deceit does not rule out power and violence, but their representation is inherent in the inevitable dialectic of brothers and others, in a city of which a contemporary witness says that 'most of their people are foreigners', and where a gaze over one of its places may reveal a crowd of 'Slavs, Greeks, Turks, Moors, Spaniards, Frenchmen, Germans and Italians'.[14] William Thomas in *The Historie of Italie* describes the 'infinite resorte of all nacions that continually is seen there. And I thinke verilie, that in one region of all the worlde againe, are not halfe so many straungers as in Italie'.[15] Venice, a haven of foreigners, enjoys a special standing among other northern Italian cities inhabiting Shakespeare's plots also in the varied, sometimes contradictory levels of its representation. Amidst a host of seemingly well-researched local particularities, such as financial and political realities, the Rialto and the gondolas, one is struck by some notable anomalies. Though Venice was the first Christian city to enforce a closed area of living on its Jews, instituting the first ghetto in 1516, there is no mention of the ghetto throughout the play: Shylock's house is placed among those of his Christian neighbours. This provides for both alienation and familiarity: there were no Shylocks proper in Elizabethan London, but those constituents of the English subject represented by Shylock of Venice were not confined by any form of segregation. Another anomaly, which may be similarly accountable, provides an English palate for bacon-defender Launcelot Gobbo and, as we have noted already, an English name for Dobbin, his father's horse. Not accidentally, those breaches of consistency where England figures out beyond the detailed Italian setting relate mostly to members of underprivileged social groups, such as foreigners (*The Merchant of Venice, Othello*), servants (*The Two Gentlemen of Verona*), or women (*The Taming of the Shrew*). England may be occasionally introduced in lowly or frivolous situations, like the wild drinking party in which Iago tells Cassio that he learnt his drinking song 'in England, where indeed they are most potent in potting' (*Othello*, II.iii.70–2). For Shakespeare, Italy provided a securely remote, yet conveniently close, dramatic *locus* whose token reality, between realism and fable, suited his art of theatrical parable as demonstrated particularly in both his Venetian plays.

A hectic mercantile and travelling centre, constantly on the move, Venice is largely inhabited by actual travellers, such as students, who 'went by boat from Padua to Venice to invest themselves in the cosmopolitan atmosphere of freedom of that city', as well as potential ones, especially of mercantile, maritime or military concerns.[16] The frictions present in any society between brothers and others are particularly enhanced in a community of travellers: 'hence the warnings against Circes by even those authors most loud in praise of travel' (Howard, p. 55). The wider the range of their concerns, the more intricate is the task of administering and regulating the life of the city by a detailed, accurate and complex book of laws: 'already by 1517 [Venice] was famed for political stability [...] the bulk of writing about Venice was to be in praise of her constitution; to understand it, by the end of the sixteenth century, was one of the motives for going to Italy.'[17] Much of the contents of the Venetian book of laws derives from the city's being a site of otherness. The threat to its economy in the absence of foreign commerce enforces Venice to legislate regulations which contradict the conservative ideological common sense. 'The palace of the normal' reflected by the Venetian constitution, to apply a phrase of Stephen Greenblatt, 'is constructed on the shifting sands of the aberrant.'[18] It is not fortuitous that both Shakespeare's most conspicuous protagonists of otherness, Shylock and Othello, find their way to the court of Venice to tackle charges which have to do with their aberrant position within the community. And though, while Shylock fails to terrorise the Venetian legal system by appropriating its word to the detriment of its apparent spirit, Othello seems at first to get the better of his vulnerability, both wind up leaving their impression on Venice in shaking its alleged unity and integrity.

A review of fifteenth- and sixteenth-century Venetian law regarding foreigners reveals an ambivalent attitude: privileges were meant to promote trade, while penalties attempted to eliminate competition. In a legal system liberally promoting 'equality' but in the long run succumbing to the claims of 'authority',[19] the proposed official solution to that ambiguity was promoting a conversion of identity by commitment to the city through avowed citizenship. The definition of the latter had much to do with notions of stability versus reproachable aspects of mobility, a distinction made already in the early sixteenth century by Donato Gianotti and other contemporary writers:

> Citizenship, in sixteenth-century Venice, was a legal status conferring specific social and economic rights. In theory at least, it was granted to persons who, though they might be of non-Venetian origin, had chosen to throw in their lot with Venice and to identify themselves completely with the Venetians [...] The *popolari*, as distinct from citizens, included immigrants who did not choose to identify with the Venetians, but who [...] eventually departed to enjoy elsewhere the riches they had amassed through trade in Venice.[20]

A decree of the Great Council of Venice from 21 August 1552 stipulates the grant of Venetian citizenship by living in Venice and paying its taxes for a certain period, with a marked distinction between those living in town and those wishing to become citizens abroad. The latter must also 'present themselves as Venetian citizens in every part of the world', and 'be obliged to swear [...] a solemn oath that they will observe this decree'.[21] When it comes to commercial transactions involving the import and export of goods, the duty of swearing an oath is extended to 'all Venetians, be they nobles or commoners'.[22] Investing its trust in the power of oath, Venetian authority binds itself to its sworn citizens, including the Shylocks and Othellos. Thus Shylock's insistence on the the oath he has in heaven (IV.i.224) must be tolerated, if begrudgingly, by the Venetian court. Bassanio's plea to the judge to 'wrest once the law to your authority' will not be acceptable. Shylock's privilege becomes his main asset in the violent master game of identity converted into property that he plays against Venetian liberal republican ideology. It is for him an instrument for terrorising Venice, using its own book of law and transforming its spirit according to his will.

Shylock's legal terrorism is a complex and problematic issue, which I have discussed at greater length elsewhere.[23] 'Political terrorism', namely the use of violence to press individuals or society to meet political demands, may betray a peculiar sense of moral (if not legal) legitimation. It is always directed against a guilty party: even though the hegemonic power against which terrorism acts is often officially in the right, it is always tainted by some moral blemish. The latter has to do with some form of absence: a denial of freedom, autonomy or right claimed by the perpetrator of the terrorist act. This is an absence which cannot be acknowledged by the hegemonic power without yielding its power to the claiming party, which is why it does not accord any legitimation to the distinction between violence and terrorism in the system of values it upholds. Rather, it tends to relate the terrorist act to some kind of pathological motive. As Uri Eisenzweig argues, the physical reality of terrorism 'appears to be dramatically unquestionable', whereas its actual legal content is missing from most judicial systems.[24] While terrorism must emanate from a logical procedure which stands outside the normative order, it draws for its validity on a different, meta-normative order, which recognises the dominant ideology as only one of several orders competing in the socio-political consciousness. Such an extra-official validity has no place in any legitimate code of values, and thus it may exist exclusively as an argument or a proposition in the realm of text. Whereas mere violence is often accounted for as 'something that does not speak, or speaks but a little',[25] or 'essentialy wordless and [...] can begin only where thought and rational communication have broken down',[26] it is only the textual argument that relates an act of violence to a political context which acquires a terroristic position for this act. The performative nature of the terrorist text thus becomes indispensable in this process. In this respect any name, word or phrasing constituting the terrorist text may become of great significance, as does, in *The Merchant of Venice*, the exact phrasing of Shylock's bond and, later, that of Portia's ruling in court.

It is the word of Shylock's bond which becomes the symbolic, hence the essential, meaning of the terrorist act he performs. His threat to cut Antonio's pound of flesh presents the Christian society of Venice with a moral riddle to which it must respond by subscribing ideologically to its textual premises. The riddle is transported from its initial logical homogeneity to the multivocal domain of the prophetic, where no simple solutions are available to the terrorist challenge and our moral bearings are less than solid. It invests our consciousness with the coercive presence of the other in me, which no ideological manoeuvre may discard without a denial of mystery that leads to 'a kind of corruption of the intelligence'.[27] In most cases of terrorism 'proper' the primary position of the terrorist text gets its prominence at the expense of the position of the act itself and, indeed, of the identity of the author/performator of the text. The consummation of the act of terrorism is not the actual deed (such as the cutting of the pound of flesh), nor is its author's real identity (as a Jew, a moneylender or a pantaloon) of necessary significance at the crucial moment. This may explain one of the major difficulties which has troubled many critics of *The Merchant of Venice*, namely the discrepancy between Shylock's prominence in the play and his relatively brief presence on the scene, as well as his much-debated absence from the play after the trial scene.

The legal content of terrorism, missing from most judicial systems, clearly resides in Shakespeare's Venetian book of laws: if not nominally, then at least by implication. It is a major token of the tension between England and the Venetian nowhere. No play composed during the reign of Elizabeth could ignore the constant danger of contrivance by strangers.[28] Declared a bastard in Pius V's bull in 1570, Elizabeth was constantly vulnerable to terrorist designs inspired by the Catholic powers of Europe. If native subjects of the Queen (such as member of parliament Dr William Parry) were arrested for an alleged attempt on the Queen's life, foreigners were obviously prone to such suspicions even more. The names of the Italian Roberto Ridolfi (who escaped the gallows) and the Portuguese Jew Dr Roderigo Lopez (who did not manage to do so) are but two of the foreign names (dubiously) associated with such conspiracies during the reign of Elizabeth, which will serve to explain the peculiarly anti-alien nature of the Venetian legislation, as viewed by an Elizabethan writer. After the tables have been turned upon him by Portia in the trial scene, Shylock has to answer the charges made against him in the name of what may be taken as a special anti-terrorist act, implying both private and political offences:

> It is enacted in the laws of Venice,
> If it be proved against an alien,
> That by direct, or indirect attempts
> He seeks the life of any citizen,
> The party 'gainst the which he doth contrive,
> Shall seize one half his goods, the other half
> Comes to the privy coffer of the state,
> And the offender's life lies in the mercy
> Of the Duke only, 'gainst all other voice.
>
> (IV.i.344–52)

The constitution of Shakespeare's Venice pretends to be liberal and egalitarian both on judicial grounds ('the justice of the state') and economic ones ('the trade and profit of the city') (III.iii.29–30). In this respect there is no sense in which the private assault contrived by one individual against another referred to by this law of Venice should be distinguished ethnically or nationally. This latter distinction between alien and citizen thus clearly implies an act of political subversion, or, in other words, political terrorism, even though the term itself is not explicitly employed.

Shylock does not belong to those notorious precursors of modern terrorism, such as Jack Cade and his 'infinite numbers' of rebels, nor Brutus and the rest, who use violence against tyranny. Nowhere in the play does Shylock manifestly proclaim his act to be politically charged. However, it may still be argued that the case of Shylock shares some important features with more obvious representations of political terrorism, and if Shylock does not take hostages illegally, his act of appropriating the law itself is not entirely devoid of ideological grounds.

Hardly an Iago-like 'motive-hunter', Shylock provides some solid reasons for his stubborn insistence on his bond. On the face of it, his reasons have nothing to do with ideology but with 'ancient grudge' (I.iii.42), 'revenge' (III.i.48) or vagaries of will (IV.i.43–62), with the reiterated feeding imagery that lends them a ritualistic or pathological shade. More obvious personal reasons are not hard to find, from material gain to personal revenge, especially since the elopement of Jessica with her Christian lover. On the face of it, the case of Shylock does not manifestly involve plain national offences of the kind Marlowe's Barabas may complain of:

> *Barabas*: Are strangers with your tribute to be tax'd?
> *2 Knight*: Have strangers leave with us to get their wealth?
>   Then let them with us contribute.
> *Barabas*: How, equally?
> *Ferneze*:   No, Jew, like infidels;
>   For through our sufferance of your hateful lives
>   Who stand accursed in the sight of heaven
>   These taxes and afflictions are befall'n.
>
> (*The Jew of Malta*, I.ii.59–65)[29]

No major religious dispute informs the plot of *The Merchant of Venice* in the way the action of Marlowe's play is dependent on the repressive measures taken provocatively at the outset by the governor of Malta against his Jewish subjects. Indeed, Antonio 'rates' Shylock fiercely in the Rialto, but, as the latter is first to admit, it is mainly for his economic practice, namely 'About my moneys and my usances [...] And all for use of that which is mine own' (I.iii.104, 108). The differences in custom and behaviour between Jews and Christians, such as in eating habits, may serve in Shakespeare's play for Launcelot's jesting or provide Shylock with an excuse to avoid social consortship with Antonio and Bassanio (which he will not refuse under different circumstances). They will never be presented, as by Barabas in Marlowe's play, as a defiant tribal self-assertion:

>   'Tis a custom held with us,
> That when we speak with Gentiles like to you,
> We turn into the air to purge ourselves:
> For unto us the promise doth belong.
>
> (II.iii.45–8)

or as a major motivation for action:

> In spite of these swine-eating Christians
> (Unchosen nation, never circumcis'd,
> Such as, poor villains, were ne'er thought upon
> Till Titus and Vespasian conquer'd us)
> Am I become as wealthy as I was.
>
> (II.iii.7–11)

Shylock's subdued, almost routine admission that he hates Antonio 'for he is a Christian' (I.iii.37) is immediately qualified by what he himself rates as more important on his scale of motives:

> But more, for that in low simplicity
> He lends out money gratis, and brings down
> The rate of usance here with us in Venice.
>
> (I.iii. 38–40)

Trying to remain pragmatic and logical even at the peak of his rage, he is not likely to indulge like Barabas in fits of pure religious hatred. We do not know to what extent it is his daughter's flight that induces Shylock to exact his bond upon Antonio, but at least when talking about it with the Christians he stresses the personal aspect of her 'rebellion' (III.i.31) rather than proclaiming it a cause for religious revenge, as Barabas's sharp irony makes clear in similar circumstances: 'Why, brother, you converted Abigail; / And I am bound in charity to requite it' (*The Jew of Malta*, IV.i.106–7). And yet some tokens of ideological motivation are still betrayed in Shylock's behavior. To cite but one example, whether or not we are to believe Jessica's evidence concerning her father's initial intentions to harm Antonio, her reference to Tubal and Chus as Shylock's 'countrymen' (III.ii.284) is significant in this respect. As in the case of Barabas, a self-confessed traveller, who addresses his fellow Jews in a similar way (*The Jew of Malta*, I.i.141), we do not know which is their common 'country' of origin; Shylock's only reference to his travels refers to his business concerns in Frankfort. But this expression, together with Shylock's repeated references to his 'nation' and 'tribe', cast an ideological shade on his attitude throughout the play.

Beside the particular case of his Jewishness, then, Shylock represents a more generally subversive element within the dominant Christian, capitalist order in Venice. Together with Othello he belongs in the company of 'aliens', whose danger to the ideological integrity of the Venetian ruling class (in spite of their probably taken oath of citizenship) is so menacing that special legislation had to be issued to curb their rights and activities within the liberal State of Venice. Shylock is no self-styled machiavel like Barabas, who (cunningly, but decisively) defies the law entirely (unless he can turn it cynically into a vehicle of his anti-Christian vengeance). Barabas's selfish attitude (*'Ego mihimet sum semper proximus'*) is shown not only as subversive towards the State, but indifferent also to his 'tribal' or 'national' solidarity. Shylock's case is made in terms of his 'tribe', while insisting on its legal resolution. Thus his complaint cannot find any institutional outlet until his specific function within the trade-capitalist process which moves Venetian economy is directly addressed. Significantly enough, this opportunity occurs when emotion is mixed with business: the financial implications of courting Portia belong to the subversive parts of 'pure' love in the same way that Shylock the alien is a necessary constituent of the Venetian economic system. It is here that we see power at work, as Foucault has described it, namely as 'force relations [...] forming a chain or a system, or on the contrary, the disjunctions and contradictions which isolate them from one another; and [...] the strategies in which they take effect, whose general design or institutional crystallization is embodied in the state apparatus, in the formulation of the law, in the various social hegemonies'.[30] Once Shylock is allowed to interfere with the financial operations of Venice's prince of merchants, the subversive process of rebellion is set in motion.

Throughout the play Shylock is consistently urged to adopt a 'gentle' attitude ('We all expect a gentle answer, Jew'). This is but another way of demanding of him to embrace a 'gentile' ideology,[31] a demand which is finally imposed on him legally with the verdict of the trial which suddenly turns out to be his own. Shylock's perception of the law of Venice is indeed 'alien', since the use he makes of the Venetian constitution rests on the word of the law but contradicts its spirit. It is, in fact, the very essence of Shylock's terrorism: for he consciously subverts the soul of Venetian order, namely its book of laws, and turns it upon itself. The only counter-measure Venice could take against Shylock's act of legal terrorism is to subvert the spirit of language on which the law rests in order to re-establish the normal procedures of justice and social order by which Venice's mainstream ideology abides. Not, however, that this peculiar counter-measure does not leave much room for ambiguity. Official order is reinstated, but Shylock's moral riddle is far from being solved. Rather than transport our consciousness into an Apollonian dream beyond phenomenal contradictions, it leaves us in a world in which culture is arranged by a multiplicity of discourses and identities, subject and other, desire and bonds. And it is significant that this reinstatement through subversion is brought about by an 'alien' of a different order: a woman disguised as a man; a country feudal who comes from afar in order and in time. An alienating riddle is cracked by a strategy of alienation.

There is hardly an 'alien' better provided for responding to a riddle put to society as a whole than the perfect other of the patriarchal world: woman, whose nature, Freud tells us, is the subject of one of the primary riddles humanity has tackled through the ages.[32] Portia, we may note, makes more of a male identity than all the other heroines in disguise in Shakespearean comedy: in exerting the (ideologically masculine) power of her wealth 'she is quite at home in male disguise' and 'not only begins the jokes about cuckoldry but also intrudes into male competition with Antonio for Bassanio's loyalty'.[33] Interpreting freely the Freudian text, we may deduce from its premises that in becoming a male judge exerting Venetian justice and controlling the game of material power in the play, the riddle of Portia may be construed as materialising a secret desire in effacing the otherness of femininity. This is not exactly the Freudian solution of the riddle of Portia's otherness. Addressing directly the case of the casket contest elsewhere, Freud suggests that in its silence the lead casket, like Cordelia's reticence, offers the male chooser a sublimated option to embrace death in beauty and freedom rather than as a repulsive necessity.[34] Neither of these 'solutions', however, leads one to embrace the full meaning of the cracking of Shylock's terrorist riddle by Portia. This blindness is shared by both the Venetians, who think Shylock's moral riddle to be diametrically opposed to any sense of justice and to Shylock who identifies his bond univocally with the Law of Venice. However, by leaving room for ambiguity in responding to the prophetic riddle, one stands a better chance to withstand the constraining challenge imposed by the world on the individual or society.[35] Official ideology is sometimes protected or saved from the riddling challenge of 'alien' terrorism by a special strategy depending on alienated modes of response best available to 'genuine aliens' or obliging the agents of compromise to adopt an alien identity. That degree of alienation required for the creative interpretation of prophetic riddles transcends class, gender or ethno-religious barriers to form a common brand of socio-political subversion. In the case of The Merchant of Venice the agent of this strategy is Portia, who counters Shylock's Law with 'The quality of mercy' which 'is not strain'd' or bound by any 'compulsion' (IV.i.179–80). In radicalising and homogenising Shylock's discourse, Portia brings him to neglect his symbolic claim to Antonio's body and concentrate on a pragmatic, self-defeating solution of his moral riddle; and in causing him to deny the multivocal premises of mercy, Portia makes him contradict the Law, whereby she may defeat him: for 'to be against the Law is to be outside the Law. But to be against a body is a more ambiguous, unsettling position'.[36]

Unlike the case of his modern counterparts, Shylock's Law is not designed to institute a new order, where the ruling authorities will emanate from below, equally representing all the town's residents. It is too early as yet for such a dream. Shylock's dreams (which inhabit money-bags) are remote even from Gonzalo's utopia which nobody takes too seriously. His imaginary example of abolishing slavery (*The Tempest*, IV.i.90–8) remains a parable, without anybody knowing his own opinion on the matter, except for the fact that the issue seems to him apt to serve as an analogy to his claim on Antonio's pound of flesh (a point to which we shall come back in the following pages). We even do not know for sure whether he would have pursued his murderous act to the very end, had not Portia's 'tarry' stopped him at the last moment. Nor is it crucial for us, or even for Shakespeare to know, since, as we have noted before, the terrorist act performed by Shylock is consummated on the textual, or symbolic, level. We do not need to know any more than the text of the play tells us in order to determine our moral bearings towards his act. Nor do we need any more information to define his act as a terrorist one, for, as Grant Wardlaw is not alone in arguing, 'terrorism is primarily theatre';[37] and it can be conceived in terms of Victor Turner's notion of 'social drama', that 'primordial and perennial agonistic mode' inherent in social life.[38] The gist of such notions is nothing but an extension of the textual identity of the terrorist act, as it is often expressed by a note or a telephone call which brings it to the public attention, into the performative ritual of the theatrical gesture. 'The protagonists of the "social drama" respond to and clothe in their culture's stock of sedimented symbols, archetypal characters, and rhetorical appeals.'[39] Shylock need not act further than lifting his knife on Antonio's breast, since, as the play as a whole shows us, his function in the plot is nothing but that of a catalyst. It is, in other words, the reaction of normative society to an extraterritorial act that the play is about.

Without resorting to the critical fallacies of traditional histori-cism, *The Merchant of Venice* may still show us the ways in which, by temporarily taking hostage the Venetian law, and while the entire audience of the theatre of terrorism hold their breath, Shylock manages to bring forth the very target of political terrorism, namely to expose the moral fragility of the dominant ideology. His act succeeds in undermining the notion of reality as integrated and rational, as appropriated by the dominant ideology. Walter Benjamin tells us that only from the stance of the victors is history viewed as a unitary, homogenous process.[40] In this respect Shylock is a loser. But as a political terrorist he celebrates the losers' victory in naming the name of the game. In this he disappears as a Jew, or a Pantaloon, or even as an 'alien' in the general sense. As the author and perpetrator of the 'terrorist' text of his bond he coerces the legal system, informed by the dominant ideology, to produce a counter-terrorist text of a similar nature, whereby it exposes itself, at least for one cathartic moment of insight, to its own ideological limitations.

Shylock is mainly driven by the desire of a subversive dramatic power for a 'legitimate', self-fashioned identity through gaining an equal legal standing and economic position within the indigenous Christian society. The rivalling ideologies are represented in the play by Eurocentrist unions and the aliens' feeding. Feeding is unifying by way of swallowing, as opposed to ideological unions of identity. Such fine distinctions of meaning are not to be found in the folkloric sources of the play. But in them mostly lies the original contribution of Shakespeare in the play. In translating the language games of folk literature into dramatically charged prophetic riddles Shakespeare relates the fairy-tale plot of the play to acute questions of power struggles and human identity. In this, the play indicates the only two routes for the attainment of the redeeming word, which will defeat Shylock by perpetuating his alienated otherness. The one is the endorsement of official knowledge, namely the 'conscientious' solution of the riddle inscribed on Portia's caskets and converting one's identity accordingly. The other is transcending Shylock's divisive egotism by the power of love, which brings the lovers together in a union of identities. If there is a final recuperation at the end of the play, it lies in Portia's 'egall yoke of love' (III.iv.13), which may serve as the antidote to Shylock's threat on 'an equal pound of [...] fair flesh' (I.iii.145–6). It is the same word which signifies singularity and identity, reification and human solidarity, subversion and redeeming harmony.

If the trial scene of *The Merchant of Venice* brings Shylock's power game with Venice's dominant ideology to its unharmonious close, Othello's hearing at the Duke's court marks the beginning of a parallel game. Like the Jew, the Moor of Venice stands out among his fellow citizens. More crudely than the indirect suggestion of Old Gobbo matching Launcelot and Dobbin, Othello had already been identified by Iago as 'a Barbary horse' (I.i.111), no less violently than Shylock's having been called a cur by Antonio. But whereas Shylock's position allows Antonio to single him out as a beast or the Devil without any pangs of conscience, Othello is considered noble to the point of almost colour-blind tolerance: 'If virtue no delighted beauty lack, / Your son-in-law is far more fair than black' (I.iii.289–90).[41] Even Brabantio, who, denying his former love for him, has just identified the noble Moor with 'Bond-slaves, and pagans' pretending to be statesmen of Venice (I.ii.99), now retracts his 'bad blame' (I.iii.177). Othello's judicial hearing may be placed at the outset since he comes out unanimously acquitted, without any moral blemish, to start his symbolic travel leading the play to its catastrophe, which coincides with Othello's 'journey's end [...] And very sea-mark of [his] utmost sail', when he has nowhere else to go and his power and command 'is taken off' (V.ii.268–9, 272, 332). His otherness, represented by his blackness, cannot assimilate in concord within the world where the utmost visual horror is 'the beauteous scarf / Veiling an Indian beauty' (*The Merchant of Venice*, III.ii.98–99). It will eventually assert itself as Venice's ideological enemy, as does the otherness of Shylock: both their cases are significantly to converge when Emilia will identify Othello as a devil (V.ii.132, 134), an identification commonly made in Venice as regarding Shylock. However, the clash between Othello and Venice, unlike the case of Shylock, will be brought about by way of raging emotional violence rather than by a rational, calculated act of terrorism.

Othello has won the love of Brabantio, his daughter, and indeed the entire Venetian aristocracy, by his testimonial 'travel's history'. His standing as a fellow traveller of the Venetian community is regarded as positive and well integrated, not the least owing to his position as a military protector and redeemer of the city, 'a worthy governor' who 'commands like a full soldier' (II.i.30, 35), whose tranquillity and content lie with 'the plumed troop, and the big wars / That makes ambition virtue' (III.iii.355–6). Unlike Shylock, whose position as a dissenting traveller is just begrudgingly tolerated,

Othello is fully accepted as a benefactor of the commonwealth. It is his voluntary disavowal of his occupation as a military traveller in its dynamic and tumultous multivocality:

> Farewell the neighing steed, and the shrill trump,
> The spirit-stirring drum, the ear-piercing fife;
> The royal banner, and the quality,
> Pride, pomp, and circumstance of glorious war!
> And, O ye mortal engines, whose wide throats
> The immortal Jove's great clamour counterfeit.
>
> (III.iii.357–62)

It is his conversion to a regular citizenship that will start a new phase in his power game with Venice, a phase which brings about his downfall. This conversion of identity is the the major lesson that Iago, Othello's appointed teacher (V.i.33), whose art of teaching does not consist in 'gentle means, and easy tasks' (IV.ii.114), has to teach his most devoted student. It is the most essential contribution of Iago, who proclaims himself from the very outset 'I am not what I am' (I.i.65), a great believer in the multiple personality of all men and women:

> Come on, come on, you are pictures out o' doors,
> Bells in your parlours; wild-cats in your kitchens;
> Saints in your injuries; devils being offended;
> Players in your housewifery; and housewives in your beds.
>
> (II.i.109–12)

This lesson, which Iago has already made Cassio learn the hard way ('to be now a sensible man, by and by a fool, and presently a beast!' II.iii.296–7), he is now to pass to Othello, whom he knows himself to be 'of a constant, noble, loving nature' (II.iii.284). If that is the way his self-confessed enemy describes him, it certainly sums up the way Othello had always identified himself, self-identity being 'not a distinctive trait, or even a collection of traits, possessed by the individual' but rather 'the self as reflexively understood by the person in terms of her or his biography'.[42] Having so far conceived his identity, in terms of his biography which won him the love of Desdemona (from the distressed strokes that his youth suffered (I.iii.157–8) to the present haste which requires of him to travel even before his commission is known) as constant in its permanent mobility,

Othello was always provided to discern mobility from mutability, his 'travel's history' from 'follow[ing] still the changes of the moon' (III.iii.182). Now, however, he is to learn a new lesson of mutability from the same teacher who has instructed Roderigo that 'our bodies are gardens, to which our wills are gardeners' (I.iii.320–1). Iago's Socratic method of instruction has not changed since he made Cassio reach his own conclusions. His manipulation of Othello follows a similar pattern:

> *Iago*:   Men should be what they seem,
>   Or those that be not, would they might seem none!
> *Othello*: Certain, men should be what they seem.
>
> (III.iii.130–32)

This leads him to suspect Desdemona 'that so young could give out such a seeming' (III.iii.213). The Moor, indeed, 'already changes with [his] poison' (III.iii.330). However, when Iago's lesson about the art of shifting identities at will is directed at Othello, a crucial omission occurs, namely the information that 'we have reason to cool our raging motions' (I.iii.330–1). This would serve his purpose with Roderigo (who must be deterred from drowning himself prematurely), but not with Othello, in whom he induces the belief of having been converted from a born traveller, a genuinely subversive other, to an autonomous agent of Venetian ideology, who (unlike Shylock) may appoint himself to execute its justice (which, like Shylock, he reads as devoid of mercy – V.ii.59) without depending on its formal institutions. To achieve this with Othello, Iago must keep his 'raging motions' constantly on fire, luring him to abandon for ever 'the tranquil mind' to see in Desdemona 'that cunning whore of Venice, / That married with Othello' (IV.ii.91–2), or else cool reason will read the multiple identity of Iago, rather than grasping him univocally as 'full of love and honesty' (III.iii.122). Keeping Othello in the dark as for the function of reason in the game of fashioning and shifting identities, Iago may bring the Moor into enacting his former lesson concerning the mutability of women with the terrified Desdemona, to whom Iago directed this very lesson in the first place. When Iago was reasoning his lesson with words, Desdemona could immediately reject them as slanders (II.i.113). Now, however, when Othello's 'raging motions' animate the very act of fashioning with his will serving a gardener to their bodies, words, devoid of reason, lose their meaning to the action:

> *Desdemona*: Upon my knees, what does your speech import?
> I understand a fury in your words,
> But not the words.
> *Othello*: Why, what art thou?
> *Desdemona*: Your wife, my lord, your true and loyal wife.
>
> (IV.ii.31–5)

Unlike Shylock, whose words become performative by virtue of their meaning, Othello's ritual use of words ('swear it, damn yourself') as well as actions ('come hither [...] look in my face') may conjure up identities, as written letters denoting the 'fair paper' or 'goodly book' of the body (IV.ii.73) but in the absence of meaning his action loses the name of conscience. And it is significant that from the moment in which Othello's thoughtless use of words and actions had reached its peak in killing Desdemona, Iago 'never will speak word' (V.ii.305), whereas Othello, coming back to his senses, will conclude his life in 'a word or two' reviewing his identity again in terms of his biography to the very act of kissing which marks his death (V.ii.340–60).

There is, significantly, a change of currency between the two versions of Iago's lesson, as given to Roderigo and Othello. Whereas Roderigo's road from feudal stability to bourgeois mobility should be paved by money, the property Iago chooses for Othello with which to qualify his shift of identity is a handkerchief: no less a reified representation of his person, and yet prone to the illusory mystery of 'the magic in the web' (III.iv.67), as befits Othello's will not marshalled by his reason. Unlike Shylock, who immerses his identity in that of the rational litigator, provided by a bond signed by the person he would own, Othello counts on his 'raging motions' alone when allying his ownership of the handkerchief and the ownership of Desdemona (which, when converted into the status of hiring a strumpet, should be secured with money – IV.ii.95). He is not provided with the law as a means by which to terrorise Venice, nor is he facing Venetian dominant ideology in the shape of a reasoning judge who will defeat him on his own verbal (and hence rational) grounds. Rather, he is measured against a radical interpreter of Venetian bourgeois ideology, the villain of rising individualism, who would carry the new ethos to its bestial extreme, as his bestial vocabulary, conjured into the ritual speech of converted Othello, will attest: 'I had rather be a toad' (III.iii.274); 'a horned man's a monster and a beast' (IV.i.62); 'a crocodile' (IV.i.241); 'goats and monkeys' (IV.ii.259); 'foul toads'

(IV.ii.62). And yet the vocabulary flow is by no means one-directional: both Venetian others, the Jew and the black, use the concept of 'tribe' as the framework of communal subjectivity (*The Merchant of Venice*, I.iii.46, 105; *Othello*, V.ii.349); and it is as significant to find Iago using the same terminology ('Good God, the souls of all my tribe defend / From jealousy' – III.iii.179–80) as it is to hear Shylock using 'countrymen'. Like Shylock, Othello leaves his mark on Venice, as well as on Shakespeare's English audience, who will have to live from now on with the permanent prophetic riddle of brothers and others, whose phrasing echoes in Shylock's intriguing speeches, never fully answered, and the partial harmony towards which it may lead is solely reserved for him 'Who dotes, yet doubts, suspects, yet strongly loves'.

Notes

1 Quotations from Shakespeare are from the New Arden editions, unless otherwise specified.
2 Anthony Giddens, *Modernity and Self-Identity: Self and Society in the Late Modern Age*, Cambridge, 1991, p. 53.
3 The phrase is of course Auden's, in his discussion of *The Merchant of Venice*; see W. H. Auden, *The Dyer's Hand and Other Essays*, London, 1964.
4 Edward Said, 'Identity, authority and freedom: the potentate and the traveller', a lecture delivered at the University of Cape Town, 1991, p. 17.
5 See Georges Bataille, *Visions of Excess: Selected Writings, 1927–1939*, ed. Allan Stoekl, trans. Allan Stoekl with Carl R. Lovitt and Donald M. Leslie, Jr, Minneapolis and Manchester, 1988, pp. 82ff.
6 The phrases relating to the testimonial nature of the poet are appropriated here from Shoshanna Felman and Dori Laub, *Testimony: Crises of Witnessing in Literature, Psychoanalysis, and History*, New York and London, 1992, p. 3.
7 See Said, 'Identity, authority and freedom', p. 17.
8 Jacques Lacan, *The Seminar, Book II*, ed. Jacques-Allain Miller, trans. Sylvana Tomaselli, Cambridge, 1988, p. 176.
9 See Louise George Clubb, 'Shakespeare's comedy and late Cinquecento mixed genres', in *Shakespearean Comedy*, ed. Maurice Charney, New York, 1980, pp. 129ff. David Orr, *Italian Renaissance Drama in England before 1625*, Chapel Hill, 1970.
10 In his *The Historie of Italie*, 1549; see John R. Hale, *England and the Italian Renaissance*, rev. ed., London, 1963, p. 16.
11 Both Ascham, in *The Scholemaster* and Harrison in *A Description of England* stress particularly the Italianate Englishmen's atheism and pretence for self-sufficiency: 'I care not,' he said, 'what you talk to me of God, so as I may have the prince and the laws of the realm on my side' (Harrison, ed. Withington, p. 8); and cf. 'The *Inglese Italianato* mocked God in foreign-bought ribbon that led straight from the tailor to the bawdy house and the pit' (Hale, *England and the Italian Renaissance*, p. 22).

12 *Ibid.*, p. 31.

13 See, e.g., R. B. Parker, 'Jonson's Venice', in *Theatre of the English and Italian Renaissance*, eds J. R. Mulryne and Margaret Shewring, London, 1991, pp. 95–112.

14 The first description is by Philippe de Commynes, a fifteenth-century French envoy; see *Venice: a Documentary History, 1450–1630*, eds David Chambers and Brian Pullan with Jennifer Fletcher, Oxford and Cambridge, Mass., 1992, p. 325. The second comes from a letter (possibly fictitious) from Anton Francesco Doni to Girolamo Fava, 1 March 1550; *ibid.*, p. 181.

15 William Thomas, *The Historie of Italie*, 1549, p. 2; see Clare Howard, *English Travellers in the Renaissance*, London and New York, 1914, p. 51.

16 *English Travellers*, Howard, p. 51.

17 Hale, *England and the Italian Renaissance*, p. 31.

18 Stephen Greenblatt, *Shakespearean Negotiations: the Circulation of Social Energy in Renaissance England*, Oxford, 1988, p. 86.

19 See Gaetano Cozzi, 'Authority and the law in Renaissance Venice', in *Renaissance Venice*, ed. John Hale, London, 1973, p. 317ff.

20 *Rich and Poor in Renaissance Venice: the Social Institutions of a Catholic State, to 1620*, ed. Brian Pullan, Cambridge, Mass., 1971, p. 100.

21 *Venice*, eds Chambers and Pullan, p. 277.

22 *Ibid.*, p. 278.

23 See Avraham Oz, *The Yoke of Love: Prophetic Riddles in 'The Merchant of Venice'*, Newark, 1993.

24 See Uri Eisenzweig, 'Terrorism in life and in real literature', *Diacritics*, fall 1988, p. 32.

25 Gilles Deleuze, *Sacher-Masoch*, trans. Jean McNeil, London, 1971, p. 16.

26 Thomas Merton, in his Introduction to Gandhi's *Non-Violence in Peace and War*; cited in Stephen Segaller, *Invisible Armies: Terrorism into the 1990s*, London, 1986, p. 1.

27 Gabriel Marcel, *Etre et avoir*, 1968; Marcel distinguishes between what we may call here a non-prophetic and prophetic riddles in terms of problem and mystery.

28 See, for instance, Francis Edwards, *The Dangerous Queen*, London, 1964.

29 All quotations from Marlowe are cited from the Everyman edition: see Christopher Marlowe, *Complete Plays and Poems*, ed. Eric D. Pendry, London, 1976.

30 Michel Foucault, *The History of Sexuality: an Introduction*, trans. Robert Hurley, London, 1979, p. 92–3.

31 See Frank Kermode, 'The mature comedies', in *Shakespeare, Spenser, Donne: Renaissance Essays*, London, 1971, pp. 211–15.

32 Freud, 'Femininity', in *New Lectures on Psycho-Analysis, SE*, gen. ed. James Strachey, London, 1953–74, pp. 22, 113.

33 Marilyn L. Williamson, *The Patriarchy of Shakespeare's Comedies*, Detroit, 1986, p. 30.

34 Freud, 'The theme of the three caskets', *The Standard Edition of the Complete Psychological Work of Sigmund Freud, SE*, gen. ed. James Strachey, London, 1953–74, 7.

35 The significance of prophetic riddle in Shakespeare is largely discussed in

Oz, *The Yoke of Love*. The phenomenon of traditional prophecy in Renaissance Italy is studied in Ottavia Niccoli, *Prophecy and People in Renaissance Italy*, trans. Lydia G. Cochrane, Princeton, 1990.

36 Jane Gallop, *The Daughter's Seduction: Feminism and Psychoanalysis*, Ithaca N.Y., 1982, p. 62.

37 Grant Wardlaw, *Political Terrorism*, Cambridge, 1982, p. 38.

38 Victor Turner, *From Ritual to Theatre: the Human Seriousness of Play*, New York, 1982, p. 11.

39 Robin Erica Wagner-Pacifici, *The Moro Morality Play: Terrorism as Social Drama*, Chicago and London, 1986, p. 7; in this book, Wagner-Pacifici analyses the case of Aldo Moro as a social drama, demonstrating the 'theatrical self-consciousness animating the protagonist's procedure'.

40 See Walter Benjamin, 'Theses on the philosophy of history', *Illuminations*, ed. Hannah Arendt, trans. Harry Zohn, London, 1973, p. 258.

41 This may have induced Leslie Fiedler to go so far as to see him as turning 'colorless: a provincial gentleman-warrior, a downright English soldier fallen among foreigners; which means that he no longer functions archetypally even as a stranger, much less a black' (see Leslie A. Fiedler, *The Stranger in Shakespeare*, London, 1973, p. 191). Although the dialectically 'English' constituent in *Othello* might partly sustain the present argument, nothing could be so far removed from any judicious reading of *Othello* than the obliteration of his blackness; cf. Ania Loomba's criticism of Fiedler: Ania Loomba, *Gender, Race, Renaissance Drama*, Manchester and New York, 1989, p. 41.

42 Giddens, *Modernity and Self-Identity*, p. 53.

PART IV

Language and ideology

13

'Of that fatal country': Sicily and the rhetoric of topography in *The Winter's Tale*

Michele Marrapodi

1

The two-plot structure of *The Winter's Tale* has received extensive attention in recent criticism.[1] The echoing and iteration of language and the parallels and contrasts of action between the two halves have long been noted, but the dramatic function of the Sicilian setting in this play does not – as far as I know – seem to have been fully explored. What I wish to do here is to discuss the current critical debate on the matter and suggest a possible explanation of the changes Shakespeare brought about in the conventional image of Sicily.

It may not be superfluous to recall that the dramatist makes two important variations in following his narrative source: the switching round of Greene's two countries and their kings; and a more dramatic use of the time-break in the action which divides the two plots. The importance of this has been succinctly captured by Ernest Schanzer:

> Shakespeare has divided the play into a predominantly destructive half and a predominantly creative and restorative half; into a winter half, concentrating on the desolation that Leontes spreads at his court, and a spring and summer half, concentrating on the values represented by the mutual love of Florizel and Perdita and the reunions at the finale.[2]

The introduction of Time as Chorus in IV.i not only produces the magic effect of attenuating 'that wide gap' between the plots, but, according to Schanzer, 'also creates in us a feeling of repetition. Both parts of the hour-glass look alike, and it may not be fanciful to think that this fact enhances our sense of the similarity of the shape and structure of the two halves of *The Winter's Tale*.'[3] Yet, the emblematic shape of the hour-glass suggests rather a sense of specularity, of juxtaposition, of similarity by contrasts:

> Your patience this allowing,
> I turn my glass, and give my scene such growing
> As you had slept between.

(IV.i.15–17)

Father Time loses here the traditional meaning of circularity to assume a didactic value of transformation, and to become a moral observer of the action, by its gradual regenerative power 'That makes and unfolds error' (IV.i.2). This quality is also adumbrated in the title of Greene's narrative and is allegorically represented in most of the age's emblem collections.[4] The real dramatic efficacy of the structure of *The Winter's Tale* depends on yet another fundamental variation: the reversal of the two settings of the play. Changing the cold Bohemia into Sicilia, Shakespeare rejects the convention of the latter as only an Arcadian country, the stereotyped and monothematic island which Greene inherited from the pastoral tradition. The allegorical nature and the fairy-like quality of romance, however, make it essential that the appropriate setting of Leontes's unexpected jealousy, of his sudden metamorphosis into a bloody tyrant, should become a land overloaded with ambiguous, contrasting and polysemous connotations.[5] For this reason, the dramatist can rely on the complex metaphor of a violent, hellish and wintry country, in which the king's self-destructive madness is symbolised by the sterility of winter, and, at the same time, he can draw the audience's attention to Sicilian classical mythology. What Shakespeare exploits here is the special complexity of a mythical country, whose rich cultural tradition is expressed in a cluster of pluralistic connotations.

Jerry H. Bryant and, more recently, Louise Clubb have pointed out the play's debt to the Italian pastoral drama and its derivative forms on the English stage,[6] but other influential, if indirect, cultural references should be taken into account. A primary role was played by the convention of the island derived from Theocritus, the creator of bucolic poetry, whose idylls equated Sicily with the legendary *locus classicus* of Arcadia. Second, there was the mythological country of classical literature depicted as the favourite territory of monsters, giants and cyclops where tyrannous kings and malignant gods imposed their will and pleasures on a subservient and

terrified population. Third, the lore of classical myths was emphasised by the recurrent image of an insidious and ambiguous isle,
surrounded by strong winds and threatening currents and often
shaken by earthquakes and volcanic eruptions. Fourth, the imaginative vision of Etna, as the ambivalent mountain of contrastive
powers, was confirmed by contemporary travellers' reports, which
characterised the antithetical qualities of the volcano as a producer
of fertility and destruction. George Sandys's *Relation of a Iourney
begun An. Dom. 1610* ... was an influential source for many Stuart
plays set in Sicily.[7] In his work he gives, among other things, an
evocative description of Etna:

> The lower parts are luxuriously fruitfull, the middle wooddy, the
> vpper rocky, steepe, and almost couered with snow: yet smoking in
> the midst like many conioyning chimnies, & vomiting intermitted
> flames, though not but by night to be discerned; as if heate and cold
> had left their contentions, and imbraced one another.[8]

The image of Etna as an oxymoron is extensively employed as a
main rhetorical device in Phineas Fletcher's *Sicelides: a Piscatory*
(1615). This comedy is a parody of the kind of Sicilian mythology and
pastoral romance successfully brought to the stage in those years by
Beaumont and Fletcher:

> I know not what this old man's like, unlesse
> Our hill of *Sicely* the flaming *Ætna*
> Whose parche[d] bowells still in fire consuming
> Fils all the val[e] with flame and pitchy fuming.
> Yet on his top congealed snow doth lye
> As if there were not fire nor *Phoebus* nie.
> Why should we count this strange? when even so
> This old mans heart's all fire, his head all snow?
>
> (III.iii)[9]

In addition, the Sicilians were commonly described as a naturally
jealous, revengeful, cunning and ambitious people, with great skill in
the use of language. William Lithgow is only one of the many visitors
to give a stereotyped account of the Sicilians in his relation *The Totall
Discourse of the Rare Aduentures and painefull Peregrinations ...*:

> The Sycilians for the most part are bred Orators, which made the
> Apulians tearme them, men of three tongues: Besides they are full of

witty sentences, and pleasant in their rancounters, yet among themselves, they are full of envy [...], suspicious and dangerous in conversation, being lightly given to anger and offences, and ready to take revenge of any injury committed.[10]

Lithgow's comment on the death of the Sicilian tyrants is also very revealing. He writes:

> The tyrannies which were used in Sicilia were in times past so famous, that they grew unto this Proverbe, Invidia Siculi non invenire tyranni, tormentum majus. The elder and younger Dionisius, were such odious tyrants, and the third Dionisius worst of all, that when the people powred out continuall execrations on the last, wishing his death; onely one old woman prayed for his life: This reason she gave, since from the grandfather, his father, and he, each succeeding worser and worser, and least (said she) he dying, the divell should come in his place, (for a worser never lived) I wish him to continue still.[11]

Lithgow's account has immediate relevance to *The Winter's Tale*. Paulina's hints at Leontes's 'tyrannous passion' (II.iii.28) anticipate the oracle's accusation of the Sicilian king as a 'jealous tyrant' (III.ii.133), and this, with its theological overtones, focuses our attention on the idea of tyranny in a royal figure, so that the hideous condition of tyranny in kingship sounds both antithetical and blasphemous. Just as Sicily, the isle of sun and pastorals, is described as a wintry country, so Leontes, the tyrant king, is made to embody the two-faced quality of his state in a rhetorical game of ambiguous oppositions which reverberates throughout the play. What in Leontes's case is tragic would become comic in Phineas Fletcher's use of Sicily and Etna as an oxymoron.

This strategy of contrasts is used in a positive way in the second part. Here a well-known Bohemia[12] is transformed into Arcadia, an imaginary bucolic country, where a shipwreck and the death of a man, devoured by a bear, are events represented with such deliberately unnaturalistic detachment that they become suitable material for the clown's comic language.[13] In pastoral Bohemia, washed by the sea, the 'old tale' of the play begins where human life ends: on the fanciful sea-coast where the infant Perdita is abandoned:

> Come, poor babe:
> I have heard, but not believ'd, the spirits o'th'dead

May walk again: if such thing be, thy mother
Appear'd to me last night; for ne'er was dream
So like a waking.

(III.iii.15–19)

The appearance of the bear on stage, as confirmed by the famous stage direction, has the magical power of changing a nightmare into a dream: a passage from the destructive island of death to the fertile country of life ('now bless thyself: thou met'st with things dying, I with things new-born', III.iii.112–13). The bear itself in fact stands for imagination, the very symbol of poetry and art on which the entire play is built. The juxtaposition of the two parts of the play suggests, therefore, an extraordinarily structural link between setting and dramatic action; the affinities and contrasts of the different localities and of their respective worlds (operating both on the internal and external axis) tend to reflect on their inhabitants.

2

The antithesis between a hellish Sicilia and a fantastical Eden-like Bohemia recurs throughout the play, well beyond oneiric symbolism. The Sicilia–Bohemia ratio permeates the opening scenes in a complex language game of binary oppositions which, from the outset, indicates a strong metalinguistic basis ('you shall see, as I have said, great difference betwixt our Bohemia and your Sicilia', I.i.3–4). The allusive nature of this dialectic is stressed by the frequent metonymic substitution of the two countries for their kings ('Sicilia cannot show himself over-kind to Bohemia', I.i.21, etc.). Leontes's unexpected jealousy deeply disturbs the friendly and joyful atmosphere of the opening, revealing the inner contradictions of that seeming harmony. Thus, the switching round of the two countries brings about a general strategy of ironical anticipations, echoes, parallels and contrasts, affecting, in varying degrees, the whole play's verbal and rhetorical structure. The dramatic irony in the opening scene in each of the first three acts anticipates the shift in the play's climate through an ironical reversal of the succeeding action. Archidamus's firm conviction of the two kings' friendship will be soon deluded; Mamillius's innocent tale 'of sprites and goblins' (II.i.25–6), while recalling the title and argument of the play, aptly introduces Leontes's insane outburst; and, in the opening lines of Act III, we are made to realise a similar ironical induction to the main story in the contrast between 'the air most sweet' of Delphos and the corrupted climate of Leontes's court.

Greene depicts Pandosto's jealousy with psychological traits, partly justifying it with reference to his wife's open and liberal behaviour, and showing the mental conflict of the character:

> he called to mind the beauty of his wife *Bellaria*, the comeliness and brauerie of his friend *Egistus*, thinking that Loue was aboue all Lawes and therefore to be staied with no Law; that it was hard to put fire and flaxe together without burning; that their open pleasures might breede his secrete displeasures.[14]

In Shakespeare's Sicilia, unlike the more realistic and sophisticated Venetian society portrayed in *Othello*, this 'infection' breaks out suddenly, without hesitation or rational justification, as if to establish the intrinsic 'old tale' type of romance and to convey the tyrant's spiritual blindness through an indexical imagery of disease.[15] Leontes's sickness is first of all a 'diseas'd opinion', a mental illness which affects the imagination, differing from the physical, metamorphic quality of Othello's.[16] As a consequence, the hero's mind is darkened by erotic visions, evoked by himself, through a crooked process of false deductions and counter-deductions not unlike the reaction – based on a perverse game of falsehood and seeming – of Claudio to Hero in *Much Ado about Nothing*. Perhaps the clearest hint at this perverse eroticism comes from Camillo's observation to Polixenes:

> There is a sickness
> Which puts some of us in distemper, but
> I cannot name the disease, and it is caught
> Of you, that yet are well.

(I.ii.384–7)

The Winter's Tale has no evil tempter like Iago. Here the 'monster' of jealousy is hidden in the mind of the tyrant who embodies the antithetical natures of the Moor and his Ancient. Once Leontes is convinced of his wife's guilt, he feels, like Othello, a greater torment from that very 'proof' which he considers a confirmation of his suspicions. A tragic confusion between appearance and reality is again – as in *Othello* and *King Lear*, or in the other romances – at the basis of a disrupted moral order which, in order to be recovered, necessitates a period of endurance and genuine suffering. But as distinct from the major tragedies, here endurance is not characterised by stoicism; it becomes a means of expiation and a Christian virtue to be rewarded. Leontes's dictum that 'All's true that is mistrusted' (II.i.48) and his infected 'lesser knowledge' are opposed to Hermione's 'clearer knowledge' (II.i.97); the calumnious 'foundations' of the tyrant king are disproved by Hermione's 'better grace' (II.i.122) which will triumph in the conclusion. The Sicilian setting is transformed into a waste land of corrupted morality by Leontes's sexual obsessions, the effects of which produce the death of the king's heir and the dispersion of the royal family. Hermione's 'You speak a language that I understand not' (III.ii.80) confirms the tyrant's self-isolation and brings to a climax the moral separation between the royal couple.

The change of location to Bohemia gives the dramatist further occasions to emphasise the difference between the two countries, and stress the regenerative powers of Time which have awakened Leontes's remorse and repentance: 'Of that fatal country, Sicilia, prithee speak no more; whose very naming punishes me with the remembrance of that penitent (as thou call'st him) and reconciled king, my brother' (IV.ii.20–4). But the new stage-world opens with the same climate of suspicion, intrigue and spying of Leontes's court. The real space-shift takes place out of court, in the country kingdom of romance, where tyrannous passions and patriarchal authority are mitigated by the promptings of nature.[17] The sheep-shearing feast is set in the pastoral world of Arcadia where Perdita, presented as 'Mistress o'th' Feast', becomes 'no shepherdess, but Flora / Peering in April's front' (IV.iv.2–3). Florizel's respectful, if joyful, reference to mythology in lines 25–35, as opposed to Leontes's disobedience to the oracle of Apollo, underlines the consent and participation of the gods in his sincere love for Perdita who symbolises the rebirth of nature over the sterility of winter. At the same time, his courteous language anticipates the theme of metamorphosis in the finale, adding to the concluding episode a further touch of sacred consensus and religious rite.

In *The Winter's Tale*, Perdita's role, like that of the girls in Shakespeare's other romances, reveals the daughter's redemptive powers: those restorative, godlike qualities which seem to redeem the father figure after long suffering, and to recover, in one way or another, what has been lost.[18] The encounter with Polixenes and Camillo in disguise is, in this respect, paradigmatic, since it establishes a symbolic link between the daughter's role and the cyclical renewal of nature. To welcome them, Perdita offers flowers of winter ('rosemary, and rue'), representing grace and remembrance, suited to their age, not those 'carnations and streak'd gillyvors', produced by the artifice of grafting, which challenge the natural order of 'great creating nature.' The king's answer, as Kenneth Muir has put it, 'in arguing the case for grafting is, by a stroke of irony, unconsciously justifying the marriage of his son to the country maiden':[19]

> You see, sweet maid, we marry
> A gentler scion to the wildest stock,
> And make conceive a bark of baser kind
> By bud of nobler race. This is an art
> Which does mend nature – change it rather – but
> The art itself is nature.

> (IV.iv.92–7)

Perdita endorses Polixenes's opinion, but rejects whatever sounds like unnatural sophistication. Her firm belief discloses an uncontaminated moral order which introduces the theme of clothing and disguise in this scene, while it also contrasts with Leontes's easy acceptance of the deceitful world of falsehood and seeming. Florizel, inspired by her 'grace', will answer Polixenes's tantalising invitation to buy her 'knacks', with a testimony of pure love:

> Old sir, I know
> She prizes not such trifles as these are:
> The gifts she looks from me are pack'd and lock'd
> Up in my heart, which I have given already,
> But not deliver'd.

> (IV.iv.357–61)

Thus, the young lovers' mutual confidence is opposed to Leontes's as well as to Polixenes's misleading world of appearance and lack of faith, suggesting the restorative role entrusted to the new generation, and confirming that the moral values of the country outlook, and of its inhabitants, are juxtaposed to the patriarchal ideologies and wicked politics of intrigue, suspicion, surveillance and mistrust located in the court.[20] Autolycus's protean playacting as rogue, trickster and courtier counterpoints the theme of disguise and transformation, while his former service to Prince Florizel makes him appear as a sort of *trait d'union* between court and country. His character serves also as a comical reversal of Leontes's perverted nature, parodying with his ballads the tyrant's visionary fantasies.[21]

Guided by her innate sense of perfection, Perdita, by contrast, prefers to extol the harmony of nature, offering again 'flowers / Of middle summer, [...] / To men of middle age' (IV.iv.106–8) and, addressing Florizel, she compares her own role to that of Proserpine: 'O Proserpina, / For the flowers now that, frighted, thou let'st fall / From Dis's waggon!' (IV.iv.116–18).

In a well-known analysis of the myth of Proserpine in the dramatic texture of the play, E. A. J. Honigmann established the popularity of and the compliance with the use of the Proserpine myth in early seventeenth-century English poetry and drama through the influence of Claudian, Ovid and Bacon.[22] In Shakespeare, Perdita represents, like Proserpine, the arrival of spring and the fertility of the earth, and Hermione is associated with Ceres, the Queen of Sicily and Proserpine's mother. Hence Honigmann's suggestion that 'Shakespeare decided to switch round Greene's two countries and their kings [...] to reinforce the Proserpine–Perdita parallel with Ceres–Hermione a Queen of Sicily as in the myth'.[23] This theory is taken up by Geoffrey Bullough, for whom 'the restoration of Perdita to her mother after long absence during which Hermione has been "dead" may well have reminded Shakespeare of Proserpina and Ceres'.[24] More recently, Stevie Davies has rightly maintained that winter in Sicily, the home of Theocritus and the birthplace of pastoral poetry, 'would imply a pastoralism already stained with an emotion more terrible than pathos',[25] and has argued, convincingly, that the name of Hermione was associated with Demeter/Ceres, whose most frequent function, well recognised by the mythographers, was as Demeter the Law-Giver.[26] However, it is not only the metaphorical use of classical mythology which links *The Winter's Tale* to Sicily. If in Milton's *Paradise Lost* classical mythology serves the epic's proleptic structure, anticipating and emphasising Eve's tragedy in the association with the rape of Proserpine[27] ('Not that faire field / Of *Enna*, where *Proserpin* gathering flours / Her self a fairer Floure by gloomie *Dis* / Was gathered, which cost *Ceres* all that pain / To seek her through the world', *Paradise Lost*, IV. 268–72),[28] Shakespeare re-creates the myth, introduces thematic changes of his own, and enriches an already over-abundant iconology with new connotations.

3

The two young lovers' elopement to Sicilia brings about the return of spring and the renewal of life. This shift takes place offstage, and is reported in the conversation of the three gentlemen which enhances the distinctive, peculiar fable-like quality of the episode as an 'old tale':[29]

> there was speech in their dumbness, language in their very gesture; they looked as they had heard of a world ransomed, or one destroyed: a notable passion of wonder appeared in them; but the wisest beholder, that knew no more but seeing, could not say if th'importance were joy or sorrow; but in the extremity of the one it must needs be. (V.ii.13–19)

However, so that what has been lost may be fully restored and the oracle completely fulfilled, another event, entirely invented by Shakespeare, has to take place: the resurrection of Hermione. The metamorphosis of the statue of Hermione recalls the metaphor of art as nature in Polixenes's speech. For, if art identifies itself with nature in Bohemia through evocative recollection of the imaginary myths and places of Arcadia, the miracle of Hermione's resurrection comes about in a redeemed Sicily, a country restored to life 'As is the spring to th'earth' (V.i.151) by Perdita and Florizel, after the king's long process of expiation. It is worth noting that Leontes's invocation to the gods to purge 'all infection from our air whilst you / Do climate here' (V.i.168–9) employs the same imagery which has been used to suggest the sterility of his reign, showing how the play's language echoes itself, to give a didactic sense of repetition. In the same scene, when Leontes, despite his courtiers' advice, entrusts his life and reign to Paulina, Florizel and Perdita's arrival marks the immediate reward for his faith, and brings back to our mind the parallel episode, in the trial scene, when the king's offence to the deity caused Mamillius's death as heaven's retribution.

The two antagonistic stage-worlds, with their settings inverted in relation to the original story and separated by a consistent time-break, also present linguistic and thematic affinities which contribute to the narrative's dramatic unity. In both localities Camillo plays the important role of counsellor and guide and, directing the lovers' elopement to Sicilia, reminds us of Gower and Prospero and, at the same time, serves as a link between the two halves. As a consequence, Perdita, the lost daughter, and Florizel, the rebel son, with the experience of their respective fathers mirrored and juxtaposed in the two plots, bring about a reconciliation when they arrive in that 'fatal country' where the tale began and which now concludes with the happiest of family reunions.[30]

The extraordinary happening seems all the more magical and miraculous since it is so completely unexpected. For the first time in the canon, Shakespeare infringes his dramatic rule of always informing the audience, by means of asides or soliloquies, about an important change in the action.[31] In *The Winter's Tale*, he uses an effective strategy to make the audience believe in the fiction of Hermione's death:[32] Paulina swears and witnesses to it before the court ('I say she's dead: I'll swear't. If a word nor oath / Prevail not, go and see', III.ii.203–4); Antigonus is led, in his dream–like vision, to believe in either the guilt or the death of his queen:

> I do believe
> Hermione hath suffer'd death; and that
> Apollo would, this being indeed the issue
> Of King Polixenes, it should here be laid,
> Either for life or death, upon the earth
> Of its right father.
>
> (III.iii.41–6)

This deliberate manipulation of information for the audience reveals the dramatic necessity of arousing in the spectator the same surprise and emotion as in Leontes himself.[33] The transfiguration of art into nature is frequently emphasised in the last scenes. In V.ii, we are informed that Leontes, Polixenes and the royal lovers will visit Paulina to admire Hermione's statue,[34] recently 'performed' by

> that rare Italian master, Julio Romano, who, had he himself eternity and could put breath into his work, would beguile Nature of her custom, so perfectly he is her ape: he so near to Hermione hath done Hermione, that they say one would speak to her and stand in hope of answer. (V.ii.96–101)

In the final scene, Paulina's words prepare Leontes to accept the idea of his queen's restoration to life: 'But here it is: prepare / To see the life as lively mock'd as ever / Still sleep mock'd death' (V.iii.18–20). And, to Leontes's objection that Hermione 'was not so much wrinkled', Paulina aptly replies: 'So much the more our carver's excellence, / Which lets go by some sixteen years and makes her / As she liv'd now' (V.iii.30–2).

The gradual process of transformation operates through the

invocation of the lost daughter who kneels before her mother and names her, as does Marina in *Pericles*, 'Dear queen, that ended when I but began' (V.iii.45). Here begins the metamorphosis: Leontes discerns in the statue the first pulsing of life ('Would you not deem it breath'd? and that those veins / Did verily bear blood?' V.iii.64–5) and, to Polixenes's answer of wonder, he admits with amazement, 'we are mock'd with art' (V.iii.68). The sequence is now ready for the final revelation. But there is still the dramatic necessity that Leontes should acknowledge the restorative power of Time, demonstrating how the long period of expiation has endowed him with faith to comprehend the miracle of resurrection.[35] This is, in fact, Paulina's last request:

> Either forbear,
> Quit presently the chapel, or resolve you
> For more amazement. If you can behold it,
> I'll make the statue move indeed; descend,
> And take you by the hand.
>
> (V.iii.85–9)

Then, accompanied with the therapeutic sound of soft music ('Music, awake her; strike!' V.iii.98), the restoration of Hermione takes place by means of a telling process of transcendence, through a moral and didactic transfiguration into art, that constitutes the great metaphor with which the play concludes; a metaphor which also suggests, as Richard Proudfoot has made clear, 'the whole play's emphasis on artifice as the means to the end of art, and of its final creation, in the statue scene, of a living emblem of the Renaissance view of poetry as a "speaking picture"'.[36] And it is a picture that possesses the magic touch of 'an art / Lawful as eating' (V.iii.110–11) which gives Leontes back his lost relatives – a daughter, a son-in-law, a 'dead' queen – and to Paulina, the 'old turtle', a new husband. Appropriately enough, throughout most of the final scene, the pattern of regeneration operates through imagery of breeding, substituting the feminine myths of gender and fertility for the oppressive patriarchal ideologies of the first part.[37] It is no coincidence that this expression of the dramatist's mature genius finds its suitable location in a Sicily which has now become the birthplace of poetry and art, identified with the play itself, and characterising its entire dramatic and moral structure. Thus *The Winter's Tale* is not only a chronological but also a natural

induction to the great allegory of art and theatre as a mimesis of
reality implied in Prospero's island. Anticipating some themes of the
last romance on another island, Shakespeare supplies his contemporaries with a new, extraordinary example of the pliable, polyvalent
iconology of Sicily – a Promised Land, where courtly and country
values, once opposed and 'dis-placed', are again recomposed in the
families' re-creation.

Notes

1 All references to the play are to the Arden Edition, ed. J. H. P. Pafford,
London, 1963.
2 Ernest Schanzer, 'The structural pattern of *The Winter's Tale*', *Review of
English Literature*, 5, 2, 1964, p. 75.
3 *Ibid.*, p. 79.
4 'Pandosto. The Triumph of Time. Wherein is discovered by a pleasant
History, that although by the means of sinister fortune Truth may be
concealed, yet by Time, in spite of fortune, it is most manifestly revealed.
Pleasant for age to avoid drowsy thoughts, profitable for youth to eschew
other wanton pastimes, and bringing both to a desired content. *Temporis
filia veritas.*' Cited from Pafford's edition of *The Winter's Tale*, p. xxvii. See,
in this regard, I.-S. Ewbank, 'The triumph of time in *The Winter's Tale*',
Review of English Literature, 5, 2, 1964, pp. 83–100; R. A. Foakes,
Shakespeare: the Dark Comedies to the Last Plays: From Satire to Celebration,
London, 1971, p. 131; S. Iwasaki, *The Sword and the Word: Shakespeare's
Tragic Sense of Time*, Tokyo, 1973; J. E. Siemon, '"But it appears she lives":
iteration in *The Winter's Tale*', *PMLA*, 89, 1, 1974, pp. 10–16. A fine
discussion of the allegorical figure of 'Father Time' in emblem literature is
to be found in S. Iwasaki's *'Veritas Filia Temporis* and Shakespeare', *English
Literary Renaissance*, 3, 1973, pp. 249–63; and in *The Renaissance Imagination:
Essays and Lectures by D. J. Gordon*, ed. S. Orgel, Berkeley and Los Angeles,
1970, particularly pp. 227–32.
5 Cf. Marcello Cappuzzo, 'Shakespeare e la Sicilia: appunti per una ricerca', in
Viaggio nel Sud, eds Emanuele Kanceff and Roberta Rampone, Biblioteca del
Viaggio in Italia 36, Geneva, 1991, p. 289.
6 J. H. Bryant, *'The Winter's Tale* and the pastoral tradition', *Shakespeare
Quarterly*, 14, 1963, pp. 387–98. More comprehensive than Bryant's is
Louise George Clubb's thorough study *Italian Drama in Shakespeare's Time*,
New Haven and London, 1989, chap. V, pp. 125–52.
7 George Sandys, *A Relation of a Iourney begun An. Dom. 1610. Fovre Bookes.
Containing a description of the Turkish Empire, of Ægypt, of the Holy Land, of
the Remote parts of Italy, and Ilands adioyning*, London, 1615.
8 Cited from *Milton e la Sicilia*, ed. Marcello Cappuzzo, Palermo, 1987, pp. 61–
2. In the same work, see also the evocative reports of Thomas Hoby,
William Lithgow and Peter Heylyn (pp. 32–7, 51–5, and 73–9).
9 *The Poetical Works of Giles Fletcher and Phineas Fletcher*, ed. F. S. Boas, I,

Cambridge, 1908; rpt 1970, pp. 219–20. Cf. M. Marrapodi, *La Sicilia nella drammaturgia giacomiana e carolina*, Rome, 1989, pp. 54–63.

10 William Lithgow, *The Totall Discourse of the Rare Aduentures and painefull Peregrinations of long nineteene Yeares Trauayles, from Scotland, to the most Famous Kingdomes in Europe, Asia, and Affrica*, etc. London, 1632. Two shorter versions appeared in 1614 and in 1616. Cited from the 1906 edition, published by J. MacLehose and Sons, Glasgow, p. 339.

11 *Ibid.*, pp. 345–6.

12 F. A. Yates in *Shakespeare's Last Plays: a New Approach*, London, 1975, claims to establish a number of topical allusions which demonstrate how Bohemia was popular at the time, because of Princess Elizabeth's betrothal. I do not think such alleged topical references influenced the change from Sicily.

13 Cf. R. A. Foakes, *Shakespeare: the Dark Comedies*, pp. 96–8. According to Foakes, 'If these events have meaning, it is not in relation to the characters as such, but rather in relation to a patterning of human affairs by an agency which remains inscrutable to them. In accordance with this, the characters are not typically figures burdened by the anguish of motive, choice and responsibility; they tend to be given, not explained, and they can surprise us by their changes and adaptations to circumstance, just as the world they inhabit is full of accidents and coincidences' (p. 97).

14 *The Life and Complete Works in Prose and Verse of Robert Greene*, ed. A. B. Grosart, IV, New York, 1964, pp. 237–8. On Shakespeare's shift from Greene's narrative, see I.-S. Ewbank, 'From narrative to dramatic language: *The Winter's Tale* and its source', in *Shakespeare and the Sense of Performance*, eds Marvin and Ruth Thompson, Newark, 1989, pp. 29–47.

15 For the concept of 'indexical' imagery, see Keir Elam, *The Semiotics of Theatre and Drama*, London, 1980, pp. 21–2.

16 Cf. Michele Marrapodi, '"A horned man's a monster, and a beast": notes on Shakespeare's treatment of jealousy as metamorphosis in *Othello*', *The Blue Guitar*, 3–4, 1977–78, pp. 151–71.

17 Cf. Graham Holderness, '*The Winter's Tale*: country into court', in Graham Holderness, Nicholas Potter and John Turner, *Shakespeare: Out of Court. Dramatizations of Court Society*, London, 1990, pp. 195–235.

18 Cf. Cyrus Hoy, 'Fathers and daughters in Shakespeare's romances', in *Shakespeare's Romances Reconsidered*, eds C. Mcginnis Kay and H. E. Jacobs, Lincoln, Neb. and London, 1978, pp. 77–90; M. Marrapodi, 'L'odissea di Pericles', *The Blue Guitar*, n.s. 7–8, 1984–87, pp. 117–57.

19 Kenneth Muir, *Last Periods of Shakespeare, Racine, and Ibsen*, Liverpool, 1961, p. 48.

20 Cf. Graham Holderness, '*The Winter's Tale*: country into court', pp. 224–6.

21 Cf. Howard Felperin, '"Tongue-tied our queen?": the deconstruction of presence in *The Winter's Tale*', in *Shakespeare and the Question of Theory*, eds Patricia Parker and George Hartman, New York and London, 1990, pp. 3–18. See also *Northrop Frye on Shakespeare*, ed. R. Sandler, New Haven and London, 1986, pp. 154–70.

22 E. A. J. Honigmann, 'Secondary sources of *The Winter's Tale*', *Philological Quarterly*, 34, 1, 1955, pp. 27–38.

23 *Ibid.*, pp. 37–8. On the origin of the myth, see also Kenneth Muir 'The future of Shakespeare', *Penguin New Writing*, summer 1946. According to Muir, 'The story is, of course, one of the oldest of the myths of the seasons. Proserpine is the Spring Goddess. The Whitsun Pastorals, which Perdita mentions later on, were apparently May Games, celebrating the rebirth of the year; and Flora, whom she is now representing, is the Roman equivalent of the Queen of the May' (p. 119); and J. Armstrong, *The Paradise Myth*, London, 1969, pp. 69–71. Cf. also F. Laroque's 'Feasts and festivity in *The Winter's Tale*: a study of the "sheep-shearing" scenes', *Cahiers Elisabéthains*, 6, 1974, pp. 8–14.

24 Geoffrey Bullough, *Narrative and Dramatic Sources of Shakespeare*, 8, London, 1968, p. 135.

25 Stevie Davis, *The Idea of Woman in Renaissance Literature*, Brighton, 1986, p. 152.

26 According to Davies, 'this association of the goddess with civil law is germane to Shakespeare's treatment of Hermione as the foundation of "civil conversing," sociability and the rule of law in *The Winter's Tale*, and also of the political blight on Sicilia once that law of gods and men is broken' (pp. 153–4). Quoting Ovid's *Metamorphoses*, Davies points out that the special curse of the corn-goddess's corrosive hate and the convention of Sicily as a centre of political corruption and tyranny might explain why 'Grace, reason and nurture are ritually expelled from Sicilia', though Hermione, 'more humanely than Ceres/Demeter [...] forbears to curse Sicily' (pp. 154–5).

27 Cf. J. H. Collett, 'Milton's use of classical mythology in *Paradise Lost*', *PMLA*, 85, 1, pp. 88–96.

28 *The Works of John Milton*, ed. F. Allen Patterson *et al.*, 2, New York, 1931–38.

29 Cf. Stanley Wells, 'Shakespeare and romance', in *Later Shakespeare*, eds J. Russell Brown and Bernard Harris, Stratford-upon-Avon Studies 8, London, 1966, pp. 49–79: 'It appears not only that Shakespeare was fully aware of the unrealities of the story, but that he deliberately played upon the audience's awareness too, inviting them to recall similar situations – even perhaps their memories of the source story itself, and also the centuries of tradition that lie behind it' (p. 65).

30 It must be remembered that Paulina is invited by the penitent King to accept Camillo as 'An honourable husband' (V.iii.143), and that Prince Florizel – introduced to the restored Queen as 'This your son-in-law, / And son unto the king' (V.iii.149–50) – becomes a substitute for the dead Mamillius.

31 Except, perhaps, the mother-recognition scene at the end of *The Comedy of Errors*.

32 The real death of Mamillius has, among other things, the dramatic effect of preparing the audience to accept as true the successive death of her mother.

33 Cf. Kenneth Muir, 'The conclusion of *The Winter's Tale*', in *The Morality of Art: Essays Presented to G. Wilson Knight by His Colleagues and Friends*, ed. D. W. Jefferson, London, 1969, pp. 87–101.

34 On the art-theme in the play, see T. Spencer, 'The statue of Hermione', in *Essays and Studies*, 1977, pp. 39–48: 'The emphasis on the Italian workman-

ship of the supposed statue in Paulina's chapel and praise of its sculptor's art of extreme realism may be due to Shakespeare's having heard tell that, in the early seventeenth century, intensely naturalistic life-size statuary flourished in towns in Lombardy and Piedmont, when they were likely to be seen by travellers and to give them their first impressions of the wonders of contemporary Italian artistry' (p. 48). See also L. Barkan, 'Living sculptures: Ovid, Michelangelo, and *The Winter's Tale*', *ELH*, 48, 4, 1981, pp. 639–67; Andrew Gurr, 'The bear, the statue, and hysteria in *The Winter's Tale*', *Shakespeare Quarterly*, 34, 4, 1983, pp. 420–5.

35 Howard Felperin, in *Shakespearean Romance*, Princeton, 1972, has significantly pointed out: 'That art, as Paulina makes clear, requires that "You do awake your faith" (V.iii.94–5); the faith which now revives Hermione as its absence had previously "killed" her, but also the imaginative faith by which the entire scene works on the stage [...] by which we "credit [this] relation", in Pericles' phrase, "to points that seem impossible" even as we realize that there is no statue, that the art itself is nature, and that all can be rationally explained' (p. 242).

36 'Verbal reminiscence and the two-part structure of *The Winter's Tale*', *Shakespeare Survey*, 29, 1976, p. 78. On the metadramatic quality of the last scene and of the whole play see Agostino Lombardo's '*Il racconto d'inverno*', in *Scritti in onore di Giovanni Macchia*, II, Milan, 1983, pp. 321–43; and J. Hasler's 'Romance in the theater: the stagecraft of the "Statue Scene" in *The Winter's Tale*', in *Shakespeare, Man of the Theater: Proceedings of the Second Congress of the International Shakespeare Association*, eds Kenneth Muir, J. L. Halio and D. J. Palmer, Newark, 1983, pp. 203–11.

37 Cf. Stanley Cavel, *Disowning Knowledge in Six Plays of Shakespeare*, Cambridge, 1987, pp. 218–21.

14

The rhetoric of poison in John Webster's Italianate plays

Mariangela Tempera

'Italian sallet'

An accomplished craftsman on the Jacobean stage, John Webster commands critical attention for a very limited corpus of plays ascribable entirely to his hand: two tragedies and a tragicomedy, all set in Italy and written according to the same highly effective, though perhaps objectionable, formula.[1] Even for an age that took a liberal view of plagiarism, Webster appears, in fact, to be unique in his extensive use of other people's materials. The identification of specific sources for the vast majority of his dazzling lines[2] has left critics in some doubt as to how the literary quality of his work should be evaluated.[3] No such doubt, however, detracts from the appreciation that theatre audiences have repeatedly shown for *The White Devil* (1612) and *The Duchess of Malfi* (1614). No matter how infuriatingly derivative some professional readers may find his plays, or how puzzling some theatre historians may find his mixture of realism and allegory, it would take a very dull production indeed to alienate the favour of Webster's audience.

Although ambition urged him to write with the praise of a sophisticated élite in mind, he had the talent of the professional for giving any audience what it wanted, in terms of plot, language and setting. At a time when Italian settings were fashionable, Webster promptly obliged, with a gusto that set his efforts apart from those of his contemporaries.

While it would be unwarranted to read into his settings a more than superficial familiarity with the Italian Renaissance, it would be equally unfair to judge his choice of location as purely instrumental, and to dismiss his forays into the dark deeds of the Italian aristocracy as nothing but a ploy to comment on the contemporary London scene without running foul of censorship.[4] After all, he introduced an aristocracy whose control over its possessions and whose relative freedom from central authority were much greater than those of their English counterparts. Brachiano and the Duchess of Malfi, hardly the highest ranking among Italian aristocrats, ruled their microcosms with a degree of autonomy that, in England, could only be compared to the king's. The higher authority that finally brought them down was dispersed among degrees of secular and religious power that were not necessarily embodied in a single person. The absence of central authority 'further increases the malleability of the image, for it was only in a cultural sense that Italy was a "country" at all.'[5]

The correspondence between Renaissance Italy and Jacobean England suddenly became relevant when a different class of characters entered the picture: the 'aspiring gentry', vying for office and status.[6] Their plight was familiar to an English audience, and Webster turned them into the new protagonists of his stage: 'In a context of aristocratic hierarchy, he demands the deepest attention be given to those most out of place in this hierarchy, and least definable in terms of it.'[7] Flamineo's Italianate ways turned what could have been a risky exposure of the values of Jacobean society into a harmless variation on an easily identifiable stock-character of the London stage – the machiavel. The extensive bibliography devoted to the misapprehension of Machiavelli's thought in England fully accounts for Webster's corrupt and equivocal courtiers.[8] Stage representations of Italian moral decadence were rooted in historical fact: 'The annals of the Italian age of despots describe tyrannies and atrocities, plots and revolts, which make the inventions of the Jacobeans rather pedestrian.'[9] They fed on an extensive body of travel literature relating the experience of English travellers on the Continent. Whether widely circulated or destined for a small circle of friends, such accounts tended to confirm and reinforce the opinion of Italy that the English had formed from historical and literary sources. The playwrights offered them a redefinition of 'revenge' that allowed them to revamp a tired cliché:

> But the Italyans being still as impatient as euer to bear the least iniurye, and hauing gotten this fayre pretence to avoyde equall Combatts [...] from that tyme haue exercised all revenges vpon all advantages, of nombers, of weapons, and of places, with many

followers and most deadly weapons assayling their enemyes, though vnarmed and alone yea naked in bed and perhapps sleeping.[10]

Revenge for futile reasons, revenge delayed and often delegated to accomplices, became a standard feature of theatrical plots that endlessly combined fragments from sources where fact mixed with fiction:

> For poysons the Italians skill in making and putting them to vse hath beene long since tryed, to the perishing of kings and Emperours by those deadly potions giuen to them in the very Chalice mingled with the very precious blood of our Redeemer. [...]
> In our tyme, it seemes the Art of Poysoning is reputed in Italy worthy of Princes practice.[11]

The traveller lent the credibility of experience to the sort of tale that would constitute the subject-matter of *novelle* and that would combine two basic ingredients of the Italian plot: poison and religion.

Jacobean censorship, carefully picking its way among religious factions, and required to assist the king on improving relationships with Continental powers, would not have welcomed an open indictment of Catholicism as such, but it had no objection to the exposure of the worst excesses of the Roman clergy. The popular drama, therefore, was 'antipapal without being militantly anticatholic'.[12] In Webster's plays, the fragmented aristocracy and the aspiring gentry competed with a degraded political hierarchy in plotting and acting out deeds of ruthless violence with all the devious ingenuity that the Jacobean considered typically Italian. It was as if the Elizabethan infatuation with the Italian Renaissance had infected the nation with a 'lingering poison', whose effect was finally becoming apparent under King James. This dismal picture of Italian mores distinctly failed to impress at least one viewer:

> Another time they represented the pomp of a Cardinal in his identical robes of state, very handsome and costly, and accompanied by his attendants, with an altar raised on the stage, where he pretended to perform service, ordering a procession. He then reappeared familiarly with a concubine in public. He played the part of administering poison to his sister upon a point of honour, and moreover, of going into battle, having first gravely deposited his Cardinal's robes on the altar through the agency of his chaplains. Last of all, he had himself girded with a sword and put on his scarf with the best imaginable grace. All this they do in derision of ecclesiastical pomp which in this kingdom is scorned and hated mortally.[13]

Horatio Busino was in London at the service of the Venetian ambassador Piero Contarini. In this report, his heightened sensitivity to religious slurs combines with the alienating effect of watching another people's view of one's culture to produce a rather partial and distorted summary of *The Duchess of Malfi*. The focus of his note is the staging, in a derogatory context, of the pomp and circumstance of Catholic ritual, the accurate reproduction of vestments and gestures, the altar turned into a stage prop, the disrobing that reveals the soldier beneath the churchman, and the elegance in movement that reveals the courtier beneath the soldier.

Like most people confronted with a play in a foreign language, Busino focused his attention on the visual aspects of the production. This allowed him to take an interesting shortcut through the wealth of contradictory textual information that has bewildered the critics for centuries: the Duchess, he claimed, was killed by her brothers 'upon a point of honour' – a very Italian and straightforward explanation for Ferdinand's tortured jealousy and the Cardinal's unemotional ruthlessness. Of all the violence that left the stage littered with corpses, he singled out only the one instance which most openly combined religion and poison: the Cardinal's poisoning of Julia (misidentified as the Duchess).

Hereward T. Price observed that 'Webster uses poison to express the relation between fair show and foul truth. Poison kills all the more certainly because it is not seen or even suspected.'[14] The Italian setting enhanced the rhetorical effect of Webster's poison imagery and enriched it with unexpected nuances.

The connection between Italy and poison was so firmly established in Jacobean London that when Flamineo momentarily slips into the language of his audience and expresses his fear of being poisoned with a wary expectation of 'an Italian sallet' (*White Devil*, IV.ii.61), he could be sure that his meaning would be generally understood. But the two elements of setting and poison interplay at deeper levels as well: the sophisticated plans of Webster's avengers owed more to popular misreadings of Machiavelli's writings than to the Elizabethan stage tradition. While ostensibly identified as the true *being* of the Whore of Babylon, the inner corruption that poison laid bare hinted at a rotten core hidden under the *seeming* of Jacobean society. The deviousness of the poisoned minds of Webster's characters and their exhalted eloquence are exactly what the public expected of plays which stage 'the whole harlequinade of events and emotions the early seventeenth century thought peculiarly Italian'.[15]

Poisoned kisses and poisoned fantasies

Cariola's promise to conceal the Duchess's secret 'As warily as those that trade in poison / Keep poison from their children' (*Duchess of Malfi*, I.i.353–4) opens up a perspective of awareness of the danger of poison and care in its handling that is belied by the three plots. Quite a few characters have ready access to poison, are familiar with its ingredients and effects, and put it, or at least fantasise about putting it, to rather extravagant uses. Webster alerts his audience not only to the danger of being unwittingly poisoned but even to the disquieting possibility of being unwitting poisoners: when the Duchess is violently sick after eating Bosola's apricots, he himself wonders whether they may not have been poisoned.

Death by poison is staged three times in Webster's tragedies, in ways that confirm the playwright's skill in including the audience's reaction into the overall effect of a scene. Isabella's and Brachiano's deaths are more than announced: the poisoned picture and the poisoned beaver are left on stage as a focus for the attention of an audience that is led to share the poisoners' thrill in watching, from a safe distance, the victims' fatal progress towards their deathtraps. It is a staging that plays on the element which, in England, made death by poison especially repulsive to the commonly accepted code of revenge and compelled public opinion to dismiss it as yet another damnable Italian practice: the surreptitiousness of the action and the comparative safety of a murderer who need never confront his target.

The audience which, in *The White Devil*, enjoys the vicarious thrill of sharing the murderer's knowledge of things to come is made to experience, in *The Duchess of Malfi*, the victim's point of view: the swiftness of the Cardinal's reaction to his lover's importunate questioning catches Julia and the audience completely unawares, and creates a context where suspense is forgone in favour of sudden shock. The indifference of the characters to violent death and their appreciation for the successful murderer are well conveyed by Bosola's comment to Julia's dying words: 'O *foolish* woman / Couldst not thou have poison'd him?' (*Duchess of Malfi*, V.ii.286–7, emphasis mine), a particularly callous reaction that made F. L. Lucas see in the epithet 'not merely the soul of Bosola himself, but all the ruthlessness of Renaissance Italy'.[16]

Isabella's death is presented by means of a Jacobean dumb-show, not re-enacted in the dialogue.[17] The presence of the conjurer brackets the whole episode in a context of black magic well attuned to the ritual performed by Isabella.[18] In a world that leaves no room for complete innocence, even Isabella, the long-suffering wife, is tainted with sin. While carefully mapping her approach to the fatal picture, the stage directions leave no doubt as to the questionable character of her nightly ritual. After leading a procession to a pagan altar, she worships the painted image of her husband as if it were a holy relic. She dies while committing the sin of idolatry, yet another much-deplored practice of Italian Catholicism.

The uncertainty which at the time surrounded the properties of poison is exploited by Webster, who plays upon a very real fear of his audience's in order to achieve the maximum effect on stage: all it takes to 'catch' death by poison, he seems to imply, is a kiss.[19] In the corrupt world of his plays, even the most commonly staged token of love, reverence and trust can prove to be a fatal weakness. Julia dies of the kiss that should seal her holy oath, Isabella dies of her homage to Brachiano's 'dead shadow', Vittoria may be spared the same fate only because Brachiano prevents her from kissing his poisoned lips. Even Giovanni's regret at not being allowed to kiss his dead mother contributes to the overall impression that the slightest lip contact is enough to spread contagion.

Around these three poisonings and the unnerving dramatisation of the hazardous quality of kisses Webster weaves a complex web of references to the various aspects of the art of poisoning, as it was presented in his Italian sources, and then proceeds to colour the language of his plays further by drawing extensively upon a store of folk beliefs and classical reminiscences, from the 'poison'd darts' which Caesar avoided (*Devil's Law-Case*, III.ii.93) to the 'poisoned herbs of Thessaly' (*White Devil*, I.ii.275) evoked by Cornelia.

Poisoning a religious object which will then attract the lips of the victim is not the most ingenious, nor indeed the most original, practice suggested in Webster's plays (after all, a poisoned crucifix had already been featured in the all-English domesticity of *Arden of Feversham*). It is, however, the starting point for more daring flights into a nightmare world, where even more fantastical hypotheses are formed (although not actually tested on stage). As Flaminio puts it: 'he will poison a kiss, and was once minded, for his master-piece, because Ireland breeds no poison, to have prepared a deadly vapour in a Spaniard's fart that should have poison'd all Dublin' (*White Devil*, II.i.300–4). Doctor Julio's extraordinary skill makes receiving a kiss just as risky as giving it, thus further undermining the basis of trust in Webster's portrayal of interpersonal relationships, and contributing to validate a view of the world as a place where human beings should live in fearful dread of all contacts. Refraining from contact is not, however, enough to ensure safety: the bathos of the carnivalesque combines with topicality to inject this sinister tale with the harsh laughter of the grotesque, while, at the same time, establishing a link with London life.[20]

The extravagance of Doctor Julio's reputation is easily topped by Romelio's fantasy of what his disguise as an 'Italianate Jew' will let him achieve:

> To have as many several change of faces
> As I have seen carved upon one cherrystone;
> To wind about a man like rotten ivy,
> Eat into him like quicksilver, poison a friend
> With pulling but a loose hair from's beard, or give a drench,
> He should linger of 't nine years, and ne'er complain,
> But in the spring and fall, and so the cause
> Imputed to the disease natural.
>
> (*Devil's Law-Case*, III.i.4–11)

The tragicomic mode ensures that Romelio's list of horrors will not have any consequence for the plot, and leaves his Marlovian Jew without anybody to kill. His speech, however, 'compose le portrait du parfait machiavel pour un Jacobéen, c'est-à-dire un Juif italianisé'.[21] As such, Romelio can indulge in a fantasy of mischief that distils the very essence of duplicity and deviousness: the poisoning of a friend, rather than the dispatching of an estranged partner or an enemy. Webster then plays again to the expectations of his audience by having his character introduce another trait of the Italian stereotype: the delayed revenge that betrays an unforgiving nature. Colourful tales of 'lingering poison' were frequent in literature and chronicles, but the possibility that a deadly substance might either progressively waste the body or lie dormant in the blood for years, and then be the cause of sudden death, resisted effective staging. To overcome this difficulty, Webster creates a lull in the action which offers Romelio the opportunity to sketch his little scenario for murder.

The notion of a 'lingering poison' is so well suited to enhancing the atmosphere of calculating perversion of the Roman Church that the language of the Cardinal goes back to it with relish in the course of his final confrontation with Julia: she is the 'lingering consumption' of which he is about to be cured and, at the same time, the cause of her own ruin, since she chooses to ignore the sinister warning of his words:

> Be well advis'd, and think what danger 'tis
> To receive a prince's secrets: [...] 'tis a secret
> That, like a ling'ring poison, may chance lie
> Spread in thy veins, and kill thee seven year hence.
>
> (*Duchess of Malfi*, V.ii.259–66)

Webster perfects here his portrait of the Cardinal as a Renaissance prince who wields absolute power and who is ultimately as dangerous to his friends as he is to his enemies.

Romelio's Italianate Jew has unveiled the darkest side of treacherous murder performed with ugly cruelty, but it has also elaborated on the motif of 'ingenious poisoning', which the avengers in *The White Devil* had eagerly explored. Flamineo praises the subtlety of the 'Machivillian' (*White Devil*, V.iii.193) who kills without leaving any trace – 'As if you had swallow'd down a pound of saffron' (V.iii.197): elegance of execution is a worthy objective for the refined courtier, and breaking new ground in all fields appears to be the dream of the Renaissance man. It is a notion that Lodovico stretches to include murder:

> T'have poison'd his prayer book, or a pair of beads,
> The pommel of his saddle, his looking-glass,
> Or th'handle of his racket, – O that, that! [...]
> I would have our plot be ingenious,
> And have it hereafter recorded for example
> Rather than borrow example.
>
> (*White Devil*, V.i.69–77)

Lodovico's speech singles out the detail of a hand that is contaminated by poison simply by touching the most common objects: all acts of everyday life are fraught with danger in a world peopled with machiavels. The presence of the theatre audience allows Lodovico to sacrifice his yearning for acknowledgment without defeating the secrecy which should characterise the *modus operandi* of the poisoner. By the end of the play, 'he can die a happy man, having committed a series of exquisite murders; or rather, having created them. His pleasure is that of the artist revelling in his imaginative power'.[22] As with the listing of Dr Julio's exploits, an available link with Webster's London[23] is the starting point for a flight into fantasy, made possible by the freedom his countrymen associate with visions of Italy, a country whose 'richer life, with its promise of adventure and blood-shed, gave free vein to their thoughts'.[24]

At one level, Webster encourages the escapism of his audience by letting them glimpse some loose pages from a sort of Italian manual devoted not to courtly manners but to the fine art of poisoning; this experience has the excitement of voyeurism without the discomfort of self-recognition, since it is firmly grounded in a foreign culture, and only very loosely connected with the reality of the audience. At another level, however, he forces the spectators to confront their own reality, by bringing the imagery of poison to bear upon the far more disturbing issue of the frailty and inner corruption of the human body.

Poisoned remedies and poisoned bodies

'Physicians, that cure poisons, still work / With counterpoisons' (*White Devil*, III.iii.64–5): with these words Flamineo aptly brings the doctor's trade into the same shadowy aura as the poisoner's. Doctors are stock figures of abuse on the Jacobean stage, and Webster is no more original in his treatment of secondary characters than in his choice of quotations. In his plays, doctors are either introduced to proclaim the venom 'most deadly' (*White Devil*, V.iii.19), and their skills, therefore, quite useless, or to suggest the most far-fetched counterpoisons:

> *First surgeon:* But let's take heed he do not poison us.
> *Second surgeon:* Oh, I will never eat nor drink with him,
>   Without unicorn's horn in a hollow tooth.
>   (*Devil's Law-Case*, III.ii.142–4)

Unicorn's horn is the same all-powerful antidote that Isabella selected as the only term of comparison fit to describe the force of her love for Brachiano (*White Devil*, II.i.14–18), but it was already so thoroughly disqualified at the time[25] as to justify its use in the context of a play where 'the comically inverted health-giving functions of medicine and law reflect a deep-seated social malaise'.[26] Inversion of the function of medicine is not, however, restricted to comic uses: Delio's suggestion that the Duchess may secure some privacy by pretending to use 'some prepar'd antidote of her own, / Lest the physicians should repoison her' (*Duchess of Malfi*, II.i.171–2) is offered in all seriousness and does not strike Antonio as particularly far-fetched.

The ingredients of medicine are 'counterpoisons' which are more likely to kill than to cure, and can satisfy the Jacobean taste for the grotesque. The apothecary who, allegedly, 'makes alum of his wife's urine' (*Duchess of Malfi*, IV.ii.83–4) is akin to Doctor Julio, the 'quack-salving knave' who specialises in outrageous ways of procuring death. Only the Duchess, in this respect as in many others, is singled out as living proof of the potential existence of a more humane world. In her final recommendations to Cariola – 'I pray thee, Look thou givest my little boy / Some syrup for his cold' (*Duchess of Malfi*, IV.ii.203–4) – she lifts medicine above the disreputable space it occupies in Webster's plays, and turns it into a healing symbol of motherly affection.

Even the effectiveness of the love-potion, a traditional device of romance, is questioned, and ultimately denied: while Julia attributes her sudden passion for Bosola to a 'love-powder' in her drink, Jolenta firmly states that only drug-induced insanity could make her accept Ercole as a husband:

> Give me some potion to make me mad,
> And happily, not knowing what I speak,
> I may then consent to't.
>
> (*Devil's Law-Case*, I.ii.84–6)

Julia implies that potions can have the positive effect of inducing welcome feelings, but Jolenta exposes the dark side of forced consent, the loss of self that the potions cause while they work their magic. And the very notion of 'magic' as part of the effectiveness of potions, the value of some esoteric knowledge that presides over the mixing of the drugs and is ultimately responsible for their action is challenged by Ferdinand:

> do you think that herbs or charmes
> Can force the will? Some trials have been made
> In this foolish practice; but the ingredients
> Were lenative poisons, such as are of force
> To make the patient mad; and straight the witch
> Swears, by equivocation, they are in love.
>
> (*Duchess of Malfi*, III.i.72–7)

Ferdinand's 'scientific' approach to the causes of love breaks down the magic potions into ingredients, which are then classified under the heading 'lenative poisons' – substances used to alter the personality, and potentially lethal. It is a definition well suited to Jolenta's plea: a radical change of mind could be brought about only by the action of chemicals on her body. It also makes Julia's mocking inquiry particularly poignant, in the light of her imminent death.

Webster does not stop at introducing poison into his plays: he breaks it down into ingredients, taking pleasure in sounding out their mysterious names, 'mummia', 'alum', 'stibium', 'mercury', 'copperas', 'quicksilver', 'mandragora', 'hemlock', 'catharide' and the like: it is a litany of evil that finds its way into the text as a counterpoint to the deranged behaviour of characters whose evil actions are often rooted in a cluster of natural elements that induce madness and death.

After evoking the deadly ingredients of potions, Webster follows their devastating progress inside the human body, and borrows terms from the scientific observation of the effects of poisons and counterpoisons to introduce imagery that gives full scope to the speaker's revulsion. Thus, in informing Lodovico of his sudden loss of favour among his followers, Gasparo introduces, at the very beginning of *The White Devil*, a brutal image:

> Your followers
> Have swallowed you like mummia, and being sick
> With such unnatural and horrid physic
> Vomit you up i' th' kennel.
>
> (*White Devil*, I.i.15–18)

But it is in Victoria's defence of her right to be tried in plain English rather than Latin that the image acquires its most pregnant sense:

> Surely my lords this lawyer here hath swallowed
> Some pothecary's bills, or proclamations.
> And now the hard and undigestible words
> Come up like stones we use give hawks for physic.
>
> (*White Devil*, III.ii.35–8)

Lawyers and apothecaries share the ability to confuse people with technicalities; it is only appropriate that their words should materialise as something that cannot be digested.

Vomiting betrays the secret action of poison. It signals to the onlooker that something is rotting under the smooth surface of the body. Therefore, in verbal confrontation, it provides the speaker with a powerful image to reduce the *being* of the opponent to a receptacle of falsehood, which all the props of the *seeming* fail to hide. Only when witnessed in the Duchess does vomiting acquire a totally different meaning, which Bosola is quick to guess and turn to his advantage. It signals that her body alone protects a fertile womb, an inner soundness that is at the opposite extreme from the rotten core which is being exposed in other characters.

There is no mention of a lifegiving womb in Monticelso's verbal autopsy of Vittoria, who loses all claim to individuality in the all-encompassing identity of whore:

> [Whores] are first,
> Sweetmeats which rot the eater: in man's nostril
> Poison'd perfumes. They are coz'ning alchemy [...]
> Worse than dead bodies, which are begg'd at gallows [...]
> Take from all beasts, and from all minerals
> Their deadly poison [...]
> I'll find in thee a pothecary's shop
> To sample them all.
>
> (*White Devil*, III.ii.78–106)

The boy actor that stands to receive the full brunt of Monticelso's words is a neutral dividing line between two excesses: the artifice that makes the whore's appearance 'better than' living bodies, and the inner essence of corruption that makes them 'worse than' dead bodies: 'if Vittoria comes across as "less" (or indeed more) than "a natural woman", it is because as a literary construction she distils English fantasies of Italianate excesses into an unstable personification of Venetian vice and allure.'[27]

When his language lingers on the surface of Vittoria's beautiful body, Monticelso draws upon the submotif of 'artistic poisoning' for his choice of insulting words, with the 'poisoned perfume' to evoke the poisoned kisses, and to combine with 'sweetmeats' in isolating yet again the orifices as danger points of access to the body. The Cardinal's eloquence is briefly deflected from the whore to her victim, whose contaminated body begins to rot internally. Finally he focuses on the corruption of the whore: her body is dissected as public property and found to be the source of all the ingredients of death that pollute the text. When Brachiano, in his final ravings, refuses 'quails' (or prostitutes) because 'they feed on poison' (*White Devil*, V.iii.92), the circle is completed: the whore is completely inscribed within the field of poison, she produces deadly substances and is nourished by them.

This degraded view of the female body is not confined to *The White Devil*, where it would be in keeping with both the title and the unresolvable ambiguity of the heroine (fascinating in her beauty and resilience, but, without a doubt, accessory to the crimes committed around her). It is reiterated by Romelio in his exposure of his mother's duplicity:

> Oh the violences of women!
> Why, they are creatures made up and compounded
> Of all monsters, poisoned minerals,
> And sorcerous herbs that grows.
>
> (*Devil's Law-Case*, IV.ii.289–92)

While the whore is compared to 'alchemy' that appears to turn base metals into precious ones, women in general are said to be made of 'sorcerous herbs', which connect them with the despised art of witchcraft, so often evoked in the classic portrait of the evil woman.[28]

This is a cliché that provides Bosola's satirical vein with ample material, in his conventional handling of the theme of the 'lady's closet':

> One would suspect it for a shop of witchcraft to find in it the fat of serpents, spawn of snakes, Jews' spittle, and their young children's ordure – and all these for the face [...]
>
> Though we are eaten up of lice and worms,
> And though continually we bear about us
> A rotten and dead body, we delight
> To hide it in rich tissue.
>
> (*Duchess of Malfi*, II.i.35–58)

While inner corruption is here extended to all humankind, women are singled out for their redoubtable practice of covering the body with yet more corruption. Once again, we have the sordid ingredients of medicine and witchcraft, combined, for maximum effect, with the Jewish religion, as it is reinvented in the horror stories whispered by people far less cultivated and more impressionable than the disappointed serviceman who voices them in this passage. Webster attributes to Bosola words that are, in content, beneath his intellectual

241

level, but he formally elevates them by closely following an Italian literary source, Ariosto's satire, thus deploying them for the general Italianate flavour of the play.

This barren vision of the body as a receptacle for poison is ultimately reaffirmed by Bosola in his reply to the 'all inclusive question which in one form or another is regularly posed in late Elizabethan and Jacobean drama':[29]

> *Duchess:* Who am I?
>
> *Bosola:* Thou art a box of worm-seed, at best but a salvatory of green mummy: what's this flesh? a little crudded milk, fantastical puff-paste; our bodies are weaker than those paper prisons boys use to keep flies in; more contemptible, since ours is to preserve earth-worms. (*Duchess of Malfi*, IV.ii.123–8)

Bosola finds no trace of the lifegiving quality of the Duchess's body, at the moment when the murderer's hands are about to invade it. The phrase 'Thou art ...' destroys any lustre that might still be attached to the Duchess's social position, but 'our bodies' brings together audience, playwright and characters in a common acknowledgment of mortality. He momentarily defeats the Duchess's quest for individual identity, by drowning her personal tragedy in the banality of a universal one, just as effectively as when Monticelso forced Vittoria back into the nameless crowd of the whores.

Such reworkings of the *memento mori*, strongly reminiscent of the morality play tradition in their form and yet fully baroque in their perverse taste for gory details, might make us feel that 'the basic setting of these plays is not a country but the world, with heaven and hell rather than the Alps and the Mediterranean as its boundaries'.[30] One should not, however, take them as reflecting the general mood of the plays. After all, 'a petty Italian court is a poor mirror of the world'.[31] Rather, these scenes shift the whole perspective of their religious models, by focusing on the dissolution of the body while clouding with uncertainty the destiny of the soul. The spectators watch the solid, and indeed sullied, flesh of the characters melt away, corroded by poison while they still inhabit it, or reduced to a 'box of worm-seed' after their lives have been violently and abruptly terminated. As for divine retribution, 'the spectators – even when the stage is strewn with corpses – are not provided the easy assurance that virtue has prevailed on this or on the other side of the grave'.[32] It is a pessimistic, and still potentially controversial, view of life, 'signifying nothing', made less risky by relegating it to another country, where, notoriously, a different world picture prevails.

Poisoned minds and poisoned words

Words can be constructed to kill just as irrevocably and subtly as deadly substances. In *The Devil's Law-Case*, the 'poisoned violence' (IV.ii.239) that Leonora intends to use against her son is entirely verbal, but the presence of poison on Webster's stage is so pervasive that it invites equivocation:

> *Winifred*: Have you poisoned him?
> *Leonora*: No, the poison is yet but brewing.
> *Winifred*: You must minister it to him with all privacy.
> *Leonora*: Privacy? It shall be given him
>   In open court; I'll make him swallow it
>   Before the judge's face.
>   (*Devil's Law-Case*, III.ii.382–6)

The exchange transfers the process of administering poison to the evil rhetoric of slander, and identifies both the common element (the slow, careful preparation of the deadly mixture) and the difference (verbal poisoning must involve an audience, a third party who is willing to be convinced by the words of the slanderer).

In plays where 'evil is consistently located in the antithesis of appearance and reality',[33] language offers itself as a battlefield where rhetoric and truth fight for control over the characters.[34] Verbal poison can be identified as such by the words of the victim, who divests its rhetoric of subtlety, and reduces it to the raw brutality of evil. The 'gilded pills' of rhetoric make language particularly dangerous. In her spirited self-defence, Vittoria was quick to identify them: 'I discern poison / Under your gilded pills' (*White Devil*, III.ii.190–1); but the Duchess did not acquire such clarity of vision until after she had lost her power: 'Pray thee, why dost thou wrap thy poison'd pills / In gold and sugar?' (*Duchess of Malfi*, IV.i.19–20). The awareness of the pervasive presence of poison can mislead a character into taking the parallel too far and thinking that wickedness can be isolated and purged, as in the case of Antonio: 'It may be that the sudden apprehension / Of danger [...] / May draw the poison out of him' (*Duchess of Malfi*, V.ii.68–71). The Cardinal's behaviour betrays a sickness of the mind that Antonio mistakenly connects to deadly potions that alter the will. It is, rather, an inborn malevolence that will resist treatment.

'Poison' is such common currency in the verbal exchanges of Webster's characters that it can be handed out by the guilty as freely as by the innocent. With a foreboding of his own agony, Brachiano fends off Francisco's well-grounded accusations of mistreating Isabella as if they were generated in a section of Francisco's brain that has been polluted and needs purging: 'Spit thy poison' (*Duchess of Malfi*, II.i.69). The same notion, condensed in one of those unforgettable lines that punctuate Webster's writings, is expressed by Brachiano when Francisco exposes his relationship with Vittoria:

> *Francisco*: She is your strumpet, –
> *Bracciano*: Uncivil sir there's hemlock in thy breath.
>
> (*White Devil*, II.i.58–9)

The same compulsion to draw his verbal weapons from the semantic field of poison resurfaces in his final rejection of Isabella:

> *Isabella*: I do not come to chide; my jealousy?
>   I have to learn what that Italian means [...]
> *Bracciano*: O your breath!
>   Out upon sweet meats, and continued physic!
>   The plague is in them.
> *Isabella*: You have oft for these two lips
>   Neglected cassia or the natural sweets
>   Of the spring violet.
>
> (*White Devil*, II.i.160–7)

The exchange signals the subtle connections that can be traced in Webster's apparently loose texts. Like the 'Italian sallet', jealousy is rejected as foreign to the inner truth of characters, who repeatedly distance themselves from their Italian personae. Isabella's lips are isolated as the orifice through which she releases her poison into the air, and will eventually absorb poison from Brachiano's image. The language of love had imposed on Isabella's body an idealised beauty made of 'natural sweets'; the language of hatred destroys that beauty with the sinister artificiality of 'physic' and 'sweet meats' which echo Monticelso's description of the whore and reduce Isabella to the same common denominator of dark corruption as her rival.

A more devious approach to verbal mischief is selected by those who aim at achieving that dreaded result of slander – the poisoning of a person's good name, Jolenta's for example:

Have you not made me yet wretched enough,
But after all this frosty age in youth,
Which you have witched upon me, you will seek
To poison my fame.

(*Devil's Law-Case*, III.iii.76–9)

Jolenta's complaint and her rejection of Romelio's plans reaffirm that the safeguard of one's reputation is a general concern at all levels of society. In the tragedies, the machiavels – Francisco, for example – know very well how effective the attack on a ruler is if conducted via the poisoning of his reputation:

Thy fame, fond duke,
I first have poison'd; directed thee the way
To marry a whore; what can be worse?

(*White Devil*, IV.iii.54–6)

The whole force of Francisco's eloquence has been employed to dress Vittoria in verbal finery capable of creating the illusion of a lady to cover the reality of a whore.

The fame of the Duchess is particularly vulnerable to verbal poisoning. She is herself, as Ferdinand's convoluted threats imply, guilty of hypocrisy:

You live in a rank pasture here, i'th' court –
There is a kind of honey-dew that's deadly:
'Twill poison your fame; look to't: be not cunning:
For they whose faces do belie their hearts
Are witches ere they arrive at twenty years –
Ay: and give the devil suck.

(*Duchess of Malfi*, I.i.306–11)

The irony of the accusation is quite striking. Unlike Vittoria who, along with the vast majority of the characters in Webster, uses manners as protective colouring to hide the natural corruption of her *being*, the Duchess hides her true nature under a mask of conformity to the rules of behaviour that obtain for the aristocracy. But the outward flamboyance of her Italianate *seeming* is at odds with the inner domesticity of her English *being*, all spontaneity and yearning for the simple values of family life. Because it is so unusual, the Duchess's sentimentality proves far more threatening for the prevailing ethos of her society than the outright depravity of the Aragonese brothers.

The innuendos of the courtiers will deface the Duchess's reputation with words that ooze poison:

> *Duchess*: [...] a scandalous report, is spread
>   Touching mine honour.
> *Ferdinand*: Let me be ever deaf to't:
>   One of Pasquil's paper bullets, court-calumny,
>   A pestilent air which princes' palaces
>   Are seldom purg'd of.
>
> (*Duchess of Malfi*, III.i.47–51)

While employing a jaded cliché, Webster tilts it on its axis, to give it a new connotation and to defeat, once again, any attempt at neatly interpreting his texts in terms of binary oppositions: court life is, indeed, rife with slanderous remarks, but in this case the accusations, like 'Pasquil's bullets', are quite accurate.

Thanks to his choice of an Italian setting, Webster is free to reiterate clichés of courtly corruption that might have been objectionable if aimed too near home. The ruler's responsibility for the well-being of the commonweal is an ongoing concern. In Antonio's words:

> a prince's court
> Is like a common fountain, whence should flow
> Pure silver drops in general: but if 't chance
> Some curs'd example poison 't near the head,
> *Death, and diseases through the whole land spread.*
>
> (*Duchess of Malfi*, I.i.11–15)

Antonio's famous speech, which is given special prominence at the opening of the play, introduces the notion of poison issuing from the fountainhead that corrupts the whole land, while reaffirming, at the same time, that the accusation of corruption relates only to countries whose irresponsible leaders do not apply themselves to purging the 'pestilent air', and clearing away the 'rank pasture' – a negligence of which the Duchess could conceivably be accused, since throughout the play she seems to be blissfully oblivious to the political consequences of her behaviour.[35]

Brachiano's court, even more than the Duchess's, is poisoned 'near the head'. We see very little of its life, but the words of the avengers recreate a bowdlerised version of Borgia-like depravity:

Lodovico: You that were held the famous politician;
  Whose art was poison.
Gasparo: And whose conscience murder.
Lodovico: That would have broke your wife's neck down the stairs
  Ere she was poison'd.
Gasparo: That had your villainous sallets –
Lodovico: And fine embroidered bottles, and perfumes
  Equally mortal with a winter plague –
Gasparo: Now there's mercury –
Lodovico: And copperas –
Gasparo: And quicksilver –
Lodovico: With other devilish pothecary stuff
  A-melting in your politic brains.

(White Devil, V.iii.155–63)

All the paraphernalia of Italian villainy is once again paraded before us, from the 'sallets' to the fashionable items hiding death under the cover of beauty. Against this exotic backdrop, Webster stages a very Jacobean agony, which strips to the core both the body and the soul of the dying man. The metaphoric poison on which the machiavel's mind once fed is destroyed by the actual poison that is consuming his brains. The process is monitored by the avengers, who rejoice in wording and rewording the ingredients that are at work inside Brachiano's body, ultimately reducing them to a mesmerising string of sounds: it is indeed 'disturbing to our moral sensibilities that the revengers of the piece are indistinguishable from the guilty ones in their Italianate methods'.[36]

The moral status of the avengers is too ambiguous to ensure a truly cathartic ending, which would clear the pestilent air of the court and neutralise the effects of all poisons. Rather, Webster seems to include the audience in a dismal vision of a world governed by poisonous reactions to all attempts at transcending the prevailing ethos. No matter how good a new play may be, 'the breath that comes from the uncapable multitude is able to poison it' (*White Devil,* 'To the reader', 21–2): in Webster's London, even the works of the best artists could die an ignominious death – by poison, of course.

Notes

1 The claim of collaboration with Thomas Heywood puts *Appius and Virginia* in a different category. All quotations from Webster's works are taken from the following editions: *The White Devil*, ed. John Russell Brown, The Revels Plays, London, 1960; *The Duchess of Malfi*, ed. John Russell Brown, The Revels Plays, London, 1974; *The Devil's Law-Case*, ed. Elizabeth M. Brennan, New Mermaids, London, 1975.

2 See R. W. Dent, *John Webster's Borrowing*, Berkeley, 1960.

3 Three anthologies provide a valuable cross-section of opinions: *John Webster*, eds G. K. and S. K. Hunter, Harmondsworth, 1969; *John Webster*, ed. Brian Morris, London, 1970; *Webster's 'The White Devil' and 'The Duchess of Malfi': a Casebook*, ed. R. V. Holdsworth, London, 1975.

4 Webster's use of Italian settings is examined in depth in Ferdinand Lagarde, *John Webster*, Toulouse, 1968.

5 G. K. Hunter, 'Elizabethans and foreigners', in *Dramatic Identities and Cultural Traditions*, Liverpool, 1978, p. 21.

6 See Giorgio Melchiori, 'John Webster', in Nemi D'Agostino, Giorgio Melchiori and Agostino Lombardo, *Marlowe – Webster – Ford*, Vicenza, 1975, p. 37.

7 Frederick O. Waage, *'The White Devil' Discover'd: Backgrounds and Foregrounds to Webster's Tragedy*, New York, 1984, p. 148.

8 See Felix Raab, *The English Face of Machiavelli*, London, 1965.

9 J. W. Lever, *The Tragedy of State: a Study of Jacobean Drama*, London, 1971, p. 19.

10 Fynes Moryson, *Itinerary*, unpublished chapters printed as *Shakespeare's Europe*, ed. Charles Hughes, London, 1903, p. 403. The chapters of Moryson's *Itinerary* edited by Hughes had been prepared for publication by 1617.

11 Moryson, p. 406. 'The ordinary Englishman did not abjure revenge as such, especially when the duel was the means of action. It was only when the more treacherous and Italianate features were added [...] or when accomplices were hired to revenge [...] that he considered revenge despicable' (Fredson Bowers, *Elizabethan Revenge Tragedy 1587–1642*, Princeton, 1949, p. 37). See also Charles A. Hallett and Elaine S. Hallett, *The Revenger's Madness*, Lincoln, Nebr., 1980.

12 Alfred Harbage, *Shakespeare and the Rival Traditions*, Bloomington, 1952, p. 143.

13 Horatio Busino, *Anglipotrida*, 7 February 1618, *Calendar of State Papers – Venetian Series*, 1617–19, p. 134.

14 Hereward T. Price, 'The function of imagery in Webster', *PMLA*, 70, 1955. Rpt in *John Webster*, eds G. K. and S. K. Hunter, p. 179. In this article, he counts thirty references to poison in *The White Devil* alone. On poison imagery in Webster's plays see also James T. Henke, 'John Webster's motif of "Consuming"', *Neuphilologische Mitteilungen*, 76, 1975, pp. 625–41.

15 J. R. Mulryne, '"What is truth? said jesting Pilate." The truth of illusion in Shakespeare and Webster', in *Vérité et illusion dans le théâtre au temps de la Renaissance*, ed. M. T. Jones-Davies, Paris, 1983, p. 69.

16 John Webster, *The Complete Works of John Webster*, ed. F. L. Lucas, vol. 1, London, 1927, p. 23.

17 'The absence of dialogue in the murder scenes makes them seem like cynical demonstrations of two particularly interesting and ingenious methods of getting unwanted people out of the way, an impression supported by Brachiano's approving remark: '"Twas quaintly done"' (Dieter Mehl, *The Elizabethan Dumb Show: the History of a Dramatic Convention*, London, 1964, p. 141).

18 'Brachiano's curtained picture is positioned as an icon above an altar, and Julio and Christophero, burning perfumes and anointing the picture's lips, are perversions of the priests at the altar, preparing it for the celebration of communion' (Frederick O. Waage. *'The White Devil' Discover'd: Backgrounds and Foregrounds to Webster's Tragedy*, New York, 1984, pp. 47–8.

19 See Fredson Thayer Bowers, ';The audience and the poisoners of Elizabethan Tragedy', JEGP, 36 (1937), pp. 491–504.

20 The editors see here an allusion to the offensive behaviour of a Spaniard in St Paul's.

21 Isabel M. Damisch, *Les Images chez John Webster*, Salzburg, p. 287.

22 T. F. Wharton, *Moral Experiment in Jacobean Drama*, London, 1988, p. 72.

23 In this case, a presumed attempt on the queen's life involving the poisoning of the pommel of her saddle.

24 Lewis Einstein, *The Italian Renaissance in England*, New York, 1902, p. 5.

25 See Herbert Silvette, *The Doctor on the Stage: Medicine and Medical Men in Seventeenth-Century England*, Knoxville, 1967, pp. 116–18.

26 Lee Bliss, 'Destructive will and social chaos in *The Devil's Law-Case*', MLR, 72 (1977), p. 517.

27 Ann Rosalind Jones, 'Italians and others: Venice and the Irish in *Coryat's Crudities* and *The White Devil*', Renaissance Drama, n.s. 18 (1987), pp. 112–13.

28 See Margaret Hallissy, *Venomous Women: Fear of the Female in Literature*, New York, 1987.

29 Alvin Kernan, *The Cankered Muse*, New Haven, 1959, p. 245.

30 Robert C. Jones, 'Italian settings and the "world" of Elizabethan tragedy', *Studies in English Literature 1500–1900*, 10, 2, 1970, p. 265.

31 Gunnar Boklund, *The Sources of 'The White Devil'*, Cambridge, Mass., 1957, p. 185.

32 Larry S. Champion, *Tragic Patterns in Jacobean and Caroline Drama*, Knoxville, 1977, pp. 13–14.

33 Ralph Berry, *The Art of John Webster*, Oxford, 1972, pp. 89–90.

34 'Webster's fascination with double meanings, with the property of ambiguous words to endanger, threaten, corrupt, or destroy relationships, persists throughout his work' (Charles R. Forker, *The Skull beneath the Skin*, Carbondale, 1986, p. 429). On Webster's use of language, see also Alessandro Serpieri, *John Webster*, Bari, 1986.

35 For a view of the Duchess as guilty of overlooking her responsibility to the commonweal in favour of her private happiness, see Joyce E. Peterson, *Curs'd Example: 'The Duchess of Malfi' and Commonweal Tragedy*, Columbia, 1978. However, the Duchess, like most of Webster's characters, defies clear-

cut judgement, by oscillating between extremes of behaviour: 'while it might be far-fetched to associate the Duchess, rather than Ferdinand, with the "curs'd example" [...], it seems mere romantic infatuation with her acknowledged charms to free her of substantial responsibility for what happens, or to claim her as a model of "goodness"' (Robert F. Whitman, 'The moral paradox of Webster's tragedy', *PMLA*, 90, 1970, p. 827.

36 Richard Bodtke, *Tragedy and the Jacobean Temper: the Major Plays of John Webster*, Salzburg, 1972, p. 164.

15

'The soil alters; Y'are in another country': multiple perspectives and political resonances in Middleton's

Women Beware Women

Zara Bruzzi and A. A. Bromham

Thomas Middleton uses very varied locales for his plays: contemporary London, ancient Greece, early Britain, Spain, and even a chess board. Throughout his career he also set a number of plays in Italy, of which the last and most psychologically powerful is *Women Beware Women* (1621). Middleton rarely evoked a place or period in history without a specific purpose, and, towards the end of his career, tended to use locale as a way of commenting covertly on contemporary political and religious concerns in England. His way with names has been examined but a full examination of his choice and use of settings has yet to be made.[1] Despite detailed analysis of the political and religious subtext of other Middleton plays, the potential significance of the Italian setting in *Women Beware Women* has not been fully considered, for two possible reasons: the play is surprisingly domestic, not traditionally Italianate in language or overall dramatic style. Also, Middleton's method of concealed political commentary is not obviously allegorical (apart from *A Game at Chess*). His plays do not lend themselves to a single and sustained political reading, for he creates characters and situations which only at specific moments suggest connections with the world outside the theatre.

The generally accepted date for *Women Beware Women* is 1621. It was an important year nationally: Parliament had been summoned and had revived the practice of impeachment in order to attack leading figures concerned in scandals of bribery and abuse of monopolies; King James's son-in-law, the Elector Palatine, had been driven out of his elective kingdom of Bohemia, and his hereditary territories were under attack; the proposed marriage of the heir to the throne, Prince Charles, to the Spanish Infanta seemed a distinct possibility, and Calvinists were increasingly concerned at the growth of Arminianism within the

Anglican Church as well as the spread of Catholicism. Censorship already limited discussion of public affairs in the theatre; but restrictions on freedom of expression had been increased by King James's proclamations of 1620 and 1621 prohibiting the discussion of affairs of State.[2] Within this context, *Women Beware Women* operates on three levels: on an individual level as a cautionary tale of personal sin and damnation, for which the Italianate setting offers spectacular metaphors. On another level, the play evokes social tensions, the crisis in the conduct of James's servants and courtiers. Here, the Italianate setting offers both mask and mirror. On yet another level, the setting provides opportunity for oblique political comment which could not be openly expressed in the prevailing political climate.

Women Beware Women, set in sixteenth-century Florence, is based on events in the lives of historical characters: Francesco de' Medici, his mistress Bianca Cappello and his brother Ferdinando. Francesco de' Medici, regent of Tuscany from 1564, and Grand Duke from 1574 to 1587, was an unpopular and allegedly incompetent ruler.[3] He seems to have been noted for the scandal that surrounded his private life; for his mysticism; for his patronage of the arts; for his inaccessibility; for his simultaneous neglect of government and tyrannous attitude to power; and for his unwavering support of Spain in foreign affairs. Bianca was born in Venice of patrician parents and, at the age of fifteen, she eloped with a Florentine. She had already become Francesco's mistress by the following year, 1564. In 1566 he married Joanna of Austria, but maintained his liaison with Bianca, whom he married secretly within two months of his wife's death in childbirth, in 1578. He married her officially the following year, and the couple died within a day of each other in 1587, amid rumours of foul play.

As J. B. Batchelor observes, there were conflicting accounts of these events; the suggestion is an interesting one which warrants fuller investigation.[4] Venetian sources (including Middleton's presumed source, Malespini) tended to reflect the change in Venice's attitude to Bianca and her husband from initial punitive severity to recognition of her as Daughter of the Republic when she became Grand Duchess of Tuscany.[5] This more sympathetic attitude came to permeate accounts of her earlier years in Florence as well, to a certain extent condoning her adultery. The Florentine version was a very different one. Bianca was regarded by the populace as a whore, a poisoner and a witch, controlling Francesco's affections by magic.[6]

Hostile contemporary accounts depict Francesco as God's punishment for Florence's sins: the magistrates corrupt, the patriciate weakened, citizens forced to prostitute their wives, the country famished.[7] Francesco's misrule was blamed on Bianca (although defenders of Bianca assert that she was blamed for his failings), and the extensive popular rejoicing on Francesco's death indicates a widespread disaffection.

The dual picture continues into accounts of the couple's deaths: the hostility of Cardinal Ferdinando towards Bianca led to rumours that he had poisoned them, which autopsies did nothing to dispel. Other versions, including non-Venetian sources possibly used by Middleton, ascribed the crime to Bianca, who attempted to murder the Cardinal with a poisoned tart, which was accidentally tasted by Francesco, and then deliberately consumed by Bianca so that she could share the Duke's fate.[8] Batchelor suggests that the first three acts of *Women Beware Women* draw on the Venetian tradition of this story, but that with the entry of the Cardinal in the fourth act a critical Florentine view is introduced. The audience is lulled into a false sense of security and sympathy only to be surprised by the Cardinal's vehement denunciation, and the multiple deaths of the final scene. Batchelor also notes that the play is punctuated by five scenes of spectacle, one in each act: the State procession (I.iii), the chess scene (II.ii), the banquet (III.iii), the wedding procession (IV.iii) and the masque (V.ii). Although he does not make the observation, it is in these scenes that the audience is made particularly aware of the Florentine setting and of Italianate qualities, as opposed to the more familiar domesticity of other scenes.

There is much in the early domestic scenes to evoke sympathetic responses towards Bianca and Isabella. Bianca stands silently, alone, awaiting a welcome and acceptance into the household while mother and son discuss her. She is regarded by her husband as a possession to be locked up, while Isabella is forced against her will into a marriage with the coarse, immature Ward. The audience's first experience of Livia, from whose later actions the play's multiple disasters derive, is also favourable. She is critical of the marital business arrangements of Fabritio and Guardiano, and speaks up for women in more general terms, criticising their subjection in a strongly patriarchal society. The dramatist encourages the audience to endorse her views as he ruthlessly delineates the unfeeling nature of Isabella's father and the unsuitability of her prospective husband. As the play progresses this initial view has to be revised. Nevertheless, there is likely to be an ambivalent response towards Livia even when she is quite obviously vicious and destructive. She is a witty contriver, solving problems of desire. In a city comedy such a character would be applauded, but in *Women Beware Women* this female trickster figure is not the healthy exposer of human folly or the punisher of avarice, but the deeply corrupt encourager of vice. Yet even in the chess scene, when she is engaged in her insidious betrayal of Bianca's innocence, audience response to her is likely to be ambivalent. The theatrical verve of the scene, paralleling chess game with sexual assault, lower with upper stage, humour and *double entendre* with horror and anguish, makes the audience conscious of the dramatist, aware not only of the story but of how it is being told. The scene is a witty contrivance by Middleton, but it is also a scene written by Livia. If we applaud the dramatist we are also applauding her.

Response to the powerless Bianca seems altogether less problematic. As the betrayed and ruined girl she draws the common sympathy accorded to victims. Yet, in a scene of great clarity and detail, Middleton leaves an important point unclarified. Is Bianca raped, or is she seduced? Does her lack of response to the Duke's offer of material comforts and protection indicate that she is tempted and that she succumbs, or does it indicate that she is exhausted by her protests and struggle, and has no more strength to resist? The first part of the play seems to lay heavy emphasis upon the subjection of women to male power, and in doing so generates sympathy for them. But there is a counterview established through the sequence of the Italian scenes of spectacle, which present a strong counterpoint of strict morality to human sympathy. The chess scene represents the events it portrays as the eruption and penetration of sin in a way that is, for its immediacy of assault, reminiscent of the attack of Maleger on the House of Alma in *The Faerie Queene*.[9] The language of the chess game evokes the struggle between good and evil in terms of colour symbolism, battle, and earthly pilgrimage. The Duke is identified with the black king, the Devil, as well as with the black rook. Emphasis on lascivious paintings suggests an assault on the senses, and the Duke's final speech to Bianca identifies him with the serpent addressing Eve. As the shocked Bianca descends after her ordeal, she describes the Duke in diabolic terms:

> Infectious mists and mildews hang at's eyes,
> The weather of a doomsday dwells upon him ...

I thank thy treachery, sin and I'm acquainted,
No couple greater.

(II.ii.420–1 and 439–40)

Bianca perceives the horror of her experience, but nevertheless succumbs to the temptation she has confronted. But if she forgets this moment, Middleton does not allow the audience to do so. The allusions to the Fall and to doomsday within the same scene provide a temporal perspective of human history, of sin leading to judgement, which the structural sequence of scenes of spectacle visually demonstrates.

Calvinist writers and preachers on the regeneration of the sinner indicate that an essential condition for repentance is the acknowledgement of sin.[10] A determined refusal to confront it, a wilful blindness, is demonstrated in the banquet scene at the play's centre. Bianca seems to have accepted her new life with no moral qualms, and indeed to have developed a cynical hardness that is disturbing. At this point the two plots meet, and lack of moral awareness is particularly stressed through Isabella's deception and her acceptance of adultery. In the scene depicting the wedding procession, the morally blind are confronted by the Cardinal, who speaks the language of Puritan sermons.[11] Bianca accuses him of a lack of charity, but there is a clear sense of her insincerity: neither she nor the Duke is a converted sinner, and there is an evident refusal to confront their sins. Bianca's words about grace suggest a Catholic or Arminian view, that grace can be won by good works. The Cardinal adopts an opposing Calvinist stance, that God's grace is necessary to enable the sinner to see her or his sins and then to repent; grace precedes rather than succeeds repentance. By associating the moral spokesman of the play with Calvinist theology, Middleton by implication associates Catholic or Arminian views with moral laxity which undermines society. Finally, the masque scene presents the doomsday of a society that refuses to acknowledge its sins in a vision of apocalyptic destruction and judgement. Human beings have made gods of themselves and their appetites, and have revelled in their power to control and manipulate the lives of others. Here the gods fall from the sky, and human beings create their own hell into which they subsequently fall.

If the play on one level presents a tale of individual sin and damnation in which a strict and unalterable system of moral law is set against human sympathy for young women, on another level *Women*

255

Beware Women provides an analysis of social divisions, and dramatises tensions between city and court which were evident in the Jacobean period. The 1620s were a time when these tensions were increasing, and Middleton's perspective seems to be that of the city.[12] He presents in *Women Beware Women* a society sharply divided between those who have to work hard to survive and the powerful who lead idle and corrupt lives. The play's social concerns are emphasised by transitions in the location of the action from the house of a citizen to that of a courtier, and finally to the court itself. This movement up the social scale demonstrates how citizens are affected by the corruption at the top, drawn to embrace court values and their own destruction. Nevertheless, Middleton carefully encourages the audience to establish connections with Jacobean society. Although he sets the play in Italy, he provides no clear mention of the Florentine location until the end of the first scene. The citizen's house and the familiar mundane details of life, combined with the lack of hint of any foreign colour or custom, must encourage an audience, for want of any signs to the contrary, to assume that the action takes place in London. Indeed, opening the play in a citizen's house might set up generic expectations of a city comedy rather than a tragedy.[13] Furthermore, although the second plot deals with the sensational Italianate subject of incest, the figure of the Ward situates the play, for a contemporary audience, within debates about the lucrative but controversial system of wardship.

Thus the Italian setting of *Women Beware Women* may at first suggest an exaggeratedly foreign corruption, but the play encourages comparisons with contemporary England, in which, as Thomas Gataker observes, 'all the Vices of former times be gathered together'.[14] The hostility of the city towards the court sprang partly from indignities suffered at the hands of courtiers. John Chamberlain records one such occasion when Knights of the Bath were entertained by the Lord Mayor and disgraced themselves by their treatment of citizens' wives, putting them 'to the squeake, so far foorth that one of the sheriffes brake open a door upon Sir Edward Sackvile'.[15] The debauching of the citizen Leantio's wife in *Women Beware Women* in this context may be taken to reflect citizen anxieties about the misconduct of courtiers, which the king seemed to be doing little to discourage or prevent. G. P. V. Akrigg records that the 'most unsavoury side of Jacobean court life was that of pimps and procuresses': Livia would obviously have been a recognisable figure.[16]

In the eyes of the Puritan city, the court was a source of corruption, a place of conspicuous consumption and waste: clothes, house furnishings and entertainments all provided opportunities for displays of wealth to enhance a courtier's standing. Court banquets were often as lavish as the entertainment in *Timon of Athens,* and gluttony was accompanied by drunkenness and disorderly behaviour. Thus frequent references to food in *Women Beware Women* and the presentation of a banquet in its central scene evoke contemporary criticisms of court life.

In addition to the general loucheness associated with the court, there were also gross scandals. Prominent among these was Frances Howard's divorce from the Earl of Essex on grounds of failure to consummate the marriage (which she maintained was the result of witchcraft), to enable her to marry the king's favourite, Robert Carr, created Earl of Somerset for the occasion. The match caused religious and political concern, as Frances was a member of the pro-Spanish Howard family. Popular hatred was vindicated when it later emerged that she had succeeded, after several attempts including a gift of poisoned tarts, in murdering her husband's former confidant, Sir Thomas Overbury, to silence his opposition to the match.[17] The Somersets were tried and convicted of murder in 1616, but as punishment were merely detained in the Tower. These events still rankled in 1621, but it was the official face of court corruption that was scrutinised by the 1621 Parliament. Its programme of enquiry into judicial and fiscal corruption resulted in the impeachment and dismissal from office of the Lord Chancellor, Francis Bacon, for accepting bribes, the flight of Sir Giles Mompesson faced with charges of extortion and abuse of the monopolies system, and an (abortive) attack on relatives of the Marquis of Buckingham. Thus accusations of corruption were getting uncomfortably close to the crown.[18]

Although a generalised criticism of misconduct at the Jacobean court could be inferred from the depiction of the Duke's court in *Women Beware Women,* it is not until the final scene that Middleton inserts typically cryptic allusions to public events which would confirm the play as identifiably concerned with matters in England. This effect is achieved by means of a subtle intertextuality, insertion into the play of iconographic and thematic details from English court masques which recall actual occurrencies. As did the Medici, the Stuarts celebrated themselves as celestial beings in elaborate and expensive entertainments, praising such ideals as majesty, honour and the institution of marriage, but performed by courtiers whose very lives seemed to outsiders to be the negation of those ideals. It would, therefore, seem a device elegantly appropriate to Middleton's satiric purpose that it is in the masque that allusions to court figures and corruption are made much more explicit. Critics have commented on the rather discordant juxtaposition in the play of psychological realism with the satirical extravagance of the masque, with its combination of the lurid and the comic which recalls the 'horrid laughter' associated with Italianate tragedy earlier in the century. Mulryne notes M. C. Bradbrook's view that the whole masque seems 'an old-fashioned affair'.[19] Indeed, the text tells us that this is precisely what it is. Livia tells Hippolito that she and Guardiano had planned to honour the Duke's first marriage 'with an invention of his own'; the production was ready, the expenses paid, but the death of Isabella's mother had caused it to be cancelled: ''Tis a device would fit these times so well too' (IV.ii.202–8). Middleton's style is very spare in his mature tragedies, so we may assume that the information is significant. How significant becomes immediately apparent as the courtiers make up the cast for their masque (and plot mutual murder):

> *Guard*: Your pages, madam, will make shift for Cupids.
> *Liv*: That will they, sir.
> *Guard*: You'll play your old part still?
> *Liv*: What is't? good troth, I have ev'n forgot it!
> *Guard*: Why, Juno Pronuba, the marriage goddess.
> *Liv*: 'Tis right, indeed.
> *Guard*: [To Isabella] And you shall play the nymph
> That offers sacrifice to appease her wrath.
>
> (IV.ii.214–19)

The purpose of this exchange seems to be the witty display of malicious puns, 'sacrificed' and, later, 'incensed'; but Middleton also seems to be preparing the audience for the masque by signalling what to look out for, and by revealing its provenance. Emphasis is given to Cupids and Juno Pronuba. As the Revels edition points out, Juno Pronuba is the title given to Juno in Virgil's *Aeneid* and cited by Ben Jonson in the notes to his masque *Hymenaei*, a text where Jonson frequently repeats the word 'sacrifice' in association with marriage:

> *Hymen*: Sit now propitious aides
> To rites so duly prized,

And view two noble maids
Of different sex to Union sacrificed.[20]

Hymenaei was performed at court in 1606 to celebrate Frances
Howard's (first) marriage to the Earl of Essex. The Revels edition
suggests convincingly that the motif of the descent of Juno in *Women
Beware Women* derives from a similar spectacle in *Hymenaei*, where the
elaborate and magnificent descent of nuptial Juno is the centrepiece of
the occasion.[21] The initial moments of the play masque confirm that
the dialogue between Livia and Guardiano is calling attention to
Jonson's text. *Hymenaei* opens to reveal an altar. The stage directions
indicate an altar is on stage in *Women Beware Women*. Jonson then
brings on pages bearing tapers, escorting the bridegroom; Middleton
brings on Nymphs bearing tapers. Jonson then introduces Hymen,
escorting the bride, whose head is dressed with a garland of roses like
a turret. Middleton has already introduced Hymen in Bianca's independent interlude, but he then brings on Isabella dressed with flowers
and garlands. Both masques then proceed with a song to Juno. There
seem to be too many echoes to be coincidental; and it is possible that
members of an audience who had seen *Hymenaei* would have realised
that they were watching a close imitation of its opening, and might
have been reminded of Frances Howard.

There could have been few in an audience with such an exclusive
experience (although many masques were published in Quarto editions, as was *Hymenaei*). Nevertheless, the impression that the audience is
being deliberately reminded of Frances Howard is strengthened by
further allusion to entertainments written for her in Middleton's text.
There are, by implication, two Cupids in the play masque, and their
specific iconographic significance is explained by Juno:

He of those twain which we determine for you
Love's arrows shall wound twice; the later wound
Betokens love in age, for so are all
Whose love continues firmly all their life-time
Twice wounded at their marriage; else affection
Dies when youth ends.

(V.ii.109–14)

The differentiation between youthful attraction and lasting matrimo-
nial affection is reminiscent of Ben Jonson's *A Challenge at Tilt* written
for the festivities for Frances Howard's (second) marriage to Robert

Carr in 1613. The entertainment shows two identical Cupids accusing each other of imposture. The argument is a childishly petulant one between the superior claims of men and women and the rival attractions of bride and groom. The dispute culminates in a tilt of champions, and Hymen enters to end the discord. He explains that the Cupids are both true children of Mars and Venus: one is Eros, who bestows sexual attraction, the other Anteros, reciprocal affection, created to rectify the deficiences of the first Cupid by bestowing a lasting love in marriage. The sentiment would seem an appropriate one for a second marriage after a divorce, and Hymen's address is distinctly homiletic. The reference to *A Challenge at Tilt* is also ironically appropriate to the sexual conduct of the masquers in *Women Beware Women*. Middleton's Cupids would have been recognised as Jonson's Eros and Anteros by any member of an audience conversant with *A Challenge at Tilt*. There seems little doubt that the allusions to the two Jonsonian masques within the text of *Women Beware Women* are intended to invoke Frances Howard.[22]

Middleton would have been particularly interested in masques written for Frances Howard, as one of his first commissions as writer of official shows and entertainments for the City had been his *Masque of Cupid* to celebrate her marriage to Robert Carr. He experimented with different ways of writing about her. In *The Witch* (1614) he distributes various accusations made against her, adultery, witchcraft, murder, among different female characters. We have argued elsewhere that Beatrice-Joanna, in *The Changeling* (1622), could on one level be read as a sustained portrait of her, a sombre and pitiless psychological study of the transformation of a shallow aristocratic girl into a woman erotically and spiritually corrupted by her complicity with murder and adultery.[23] The method in *Women Beware Women* is very different in that the allusion does not appear to be exclusively to her: all of the women who are sexually active take lovers and commit murder. There seems to be no suggestion that any one character should be identified with her, and the specific link that might have been made between Bianca and Frances Howard, the detail of the poisoned tarts, is altered from the source material into poisoned wine. Thus Middleton may be essaying a complex interaction between Italy and England in the final scene. On the one hand he shows a celebrated case of Florentine scandal in Bianca's attempted poisoning of the Cardinal, her accidental murder of the Duke, and her own suicide. Within the masque, concealed behind Italian court figures and Italianate detail of spectacle, he makes obvious reference to the Stuart scandal of Frances Howard, adulteress, witch and poisoner, as representative of a class destroying itself, and implicitly the nation, through its own lust and greed. The Florentine events were history (or Middleton's version of it). The implicit English parallel seems to be proleptic irony. Frances Howard, and the class she represents, had not yet been punished by divine justice. Yet, the play suggests, their time would come.

The ruler is not exempt from blame in the final debacle. The Duke is bewildered by events, unaware that his own secret murder – for the duel imposed on the plebeian Leantio must be interpreted as murder – has precipitated the catastrophe occurring before his eyes. But his own tolerance of creatures he despises as members of his court co-involves him in their disintegration. Thus Middleton may have had a further motive in evoking *Hymenaei*. David Norbrook has observed that when *Hymenaei* was staged, radical Puritans had been agitating for a relaxation of the prohibition against divorce. Part of the masque's solemn emphasis on the sanctity of marriage could, therefore, have been in support of James's and the bishops' opposition to divorce.[24] With regard to Frances Howard, the king's attitude could be interpreted as inconsistent. On the one hand, he had promoted the Essex marriage when the couple were very young. In a sense, the match could be said to have been a sacrifice to national unity, for it attempted a dynastic solution to the factional enmity between the powerful Essex and Howard families. On the other hand, James had facilitated Frances Howard's divorce and subsequent marriage to his current favourite, Robert Carr. These were actions that had promoted scandal and national division. The inclusion within *Women Beware Women* of citations from both of Frances Howard's marriage masques may imply fierce comment on James's inconsistency and lack of moral leadership, particularly in a play which places such emphasis on marriage as 'that immaculate robe of honour'. Indeed, if Cope's suggestion is accepted that Guardiano's and Isabella's reiteration of 'sacrifice' is an allusion to *Hymenaei*, then this is one of the few indications of compassion for Frances Howard's predicament in Middleton's writing, and the possibility gives added point to Isabella's and Bianca's meditations on their upbringing and marriage arrangements: 'Oh the heartbreakings / Of miserable maids, where love's enforced!' (I.ii.166–7). For *Women Beware Women* echoes one of the central themes of *Hymenaei*, the debate between the pleasures and pains of matrimony. The theme is central to *Women Beware Women*, and the courtly values of arranged marriages and adultery contrast sharply with radical Protestant (and citizen) ideas of the importance of affective bonds within marriage.[25]

However, *Hymenaei* is concerned with more than the marriage of individuals. The text is dominated by a pun on Juno's name, Juno Pronuba as Iuno, union. The word 'union' is repeated throughout the text in this double sense. The masque is thus a political event, celebrating the union of England and Scotland under one sovereign as well as the matrimony of two of his courtiers. The heavily Roman ceremonies are as much a tribute to James as an imperial Augustus Caesar, bringer of peace and founder of a fruitful dynasty, as to the bridal pair. Behind the individual marriage celebrations lie suggestions of the monarch's marriage of and to his peoples. The Neoplatonic philosophy underpinning the masque relates macrocosm to microcosm, arching from God to nation to the individual subject:

> And as in circle you depart
> Linked hand in hand, so heart in heart
> May all those bodies still remain
> Whom he, with so much sacred pain,
> No less hath bound within his realms
> Than they are with the ocean's streams.
> Long may his union find increase
> As he to ours hath deigned his peace.[26]

Hymenaei is a text that functions on two levels, the private and the public, concerned with both the relationship between man and woman, husband and wife and that between prince and subject. It combines these levels into a single discourse of national union, just as James's State discourse, spoken and written, had, from the inception of his reign, applied metaphors of family relationships, father, husband, to the figure of the ruler. It was precisely this union between king and people which critics of the court regarded as jeopardised by James's policies and the conduct of the aristocracy by 1621. Allusions to *Hymenaei* in *Women Beware Women*, therefore, invite retrospective reflection on the connections between the play's open concern with sexual relations and marriage, and the more discrete concern with relations between prince and subject. The dilemmas of the women in the play become, on a national level, those of the subject under the rule of an unjust or misguided prince. The women in the play take an improper course, grotesque rebellion against moral law, for which they are ultimately punished. Yet, in the confusions and temptations they face, they are also victims, prey to disorderly conduct that might have been avoided in a different kind of social order. In this sense, even the corruption of courtiers is to be laid at the door of the ruler. On the level of political commentary, James's ultimate responsibility for the corruption of his officials and aristocracy is implied. The citation and imitation of Frances Howard's two marriage masques serve as a reminder, an illustration almost, of James's decline in prestige and popularity since 1606 and some of its causes. Thus the masque in *Women Beware Women* might be seen as showing national unity in a state of collapse for lack of a virtuous princely authority. Indeed, this is the accusation made by the Cardinal:

> great man,
> Ev'ry sin thou commit'st shows like a flame
> Upon a mountain, 'tis seen far about,
> And with a big wind made of popular breath
> The sparkles fly through cities – here one takes,
> Another catches there, and in short time
> Waste all to cinders. But remember still
> What burnt the valleys first came from the hill.
>
> (IV.i.207–14)

The phrase 'popular breath' is interestingly ambiguous: it seems to signify rumour, or popular reputation. The reference could be taken, in 1621, to 'the generall Torrent of Discontent that raigns with such a seditious Noyse over [the] whole Kingdome' which illicit pamphlets claimed had arisen over the Spanish marriage and the conduct of the aristocracy.[27] Although the social focus of the play seems to be upon the conduct of the upper classes, perhaps there is a hint here that lesser subjects are also being led astray by the conduct of their prince. This reading would ultimately depend upon the extent to which the Italian setting of the play could be applied in some way to King James.

Recent work on censorship and political comment in Jacobean drama has shown that it was a widely adopted formula to find a plot which had suggestive analogies with the forbidden material to be treated, frequently one based on a different historical period. The technique was one of intermittent implication of comparability rather than the continuous narrative parallel of allegory. This method was, of necessity, less exact than that of allegory, because reliant for contemporary political relevance upon an audience's ability to supply the analogy. Nevertheless, as Annabel Patterson suggests, greater specificity could be achieved by what she terms an 'entry code', or an occasional encoded reference to contemporary events.[28] Such an invitation to speculation about, or entry code into, a comparison between Francesco and James is possibly provided in Leantio's reference to the 'good king that keeps all in peace' (I.iii.48), followed by the information later in the same scene that the Duke is fifty-five (James's fifty-fifth birthday was on 19 June 1621). James's personal motto was *Beati Pacifici*, and allusions to him are often encoded in references to peace. This impression is strengthened by the continuous references to peace throughout the play, which strongly suggest a subtext concerned with James's aims in the conduct of foreign policy.[29]

Thus the choice of the Italian setting of *Women Beware Women* may have been made very carefully, for the purpose of encouraging comparison between the two rulers. We are not suggesting that this would be a reading open to an entire audience. It would, of necessity, be for a restricted or coterie group which could supply the comparisons demanded by such a reading. Nor are we suggesting that James is to be totally identified with the Duke in the play, for he was neither a rapist nor a murderer. Critics of James, however, might have perceived illuminating parallels between his personality and rule, and that of Francesco. Both men, though in very different ways, were scholars: Francesco had taken Solomon as a central myth of his rule, and comparisons to Solomon constituted an important aspect of the iconography associated with James.[30] James was, like Francesco, frequently absent from his capital. Both Francesco and James ruled when their countries were experiencing economic recession. The heavy taxes imposed by Francesco were blamed for the collapse of agricultural colonies and the high price of grain. Margot Heinemann has written of the hard times endured by the people of England during the last years of James's rule, with the collapse of the wool trade and the widespread famine caused by disastrous harvests.[31] Both men's predecessors had built up navies which Francesco and James were accused of neglecting. Rightly or wrongly, James's opponents were accusing him of being a tyrant for his absolutist views and his attitude to the privileges parliamentarians regarded as theirs by inherited precedent. Like Francesco, James was accused of allowing judicial and financial corruption among his ministers. Like Francesco, James had adopted a pro-Spanish policy (though he had no intention of subsidising Spain as Francesco had done). Many of these discontents had surfaced in England in the parliament of 1621, and the specific Italian setting provides an opportunity for drawing attention to grievances which could not be openly stated.

The figure of the Cardinal is of significance within this context; for Francesco's brother Ferdinando was a cardinal before he became Francesco's successor, and his policies as Grand Duke were very different from Francesco's.[32] He gained lasting popularity through his personal distribution of grain in Florence after the floods in 1589. He also instituted a policy of land drainage to enhance grain supplies and supported trade by reviving the local silk industry and creating a large international trading port at Livorno. Moreover, he strengthened the navy. Sir Robert Dallington reported on the weakness of the Tuscan navy on visiting Florence in 1596. By 1608, however, Tuscany had won two resounding sea victories over the Turks.[33] His government relaxed central control, returning to the republican magistrates, and consequently to the patriciate, some of the powers which Cosimo I had in effect, if not nominally, removed. He reversed Francesco's pro-Spanish policy by marrying Christine of Lorraine in 1589, and he strongly supported Henry of Navarre, subsidising his fight for the French crown. He strengthened ties with France by arranging the marriage of Francesco's surviving daughter, Maria, to Henry IV in 1600 (though, to maintain good relations with the Habsburgs, he later arranged the marriage of his heir Cosimo to the Archduchess Maria Maddalena of Austria). Many of the policies pursued by Ferdinando are comparable to those which a number of James's critics in Parliament were advocating, and the dialogue between Francesco and Ferdinando in *Women Beware Women* could thus be read, by a restricted group, as an encoded reproach to the sovereign, with the Cardinal's oppositional stance supplying an analogy to parliamentarian opposition to James's current political stance. Significantly, however, the implied criticism is expressed by one royal personage to another.

Ferdinando's voice would not have been interpreted as totally hostile. His relations with England were good. He is already on record as receiving English aristocrats cordially in the 1590s, but his relationship with James, who was a kinsman of Christine of Lorraine, was particularly friendly. Ferdinando supported James's claim to the English throne, and was in correspondence with him in the late 1590s. There was even some discussion of the betrothal of Prince Henry to one of his daughters in 1601.[34] There were very strong cultural links between Florence and Prince Henry before his death. Indeed, the architect that Ferdinando sent to Henry, Constantino de' Servi, had previously been in the service of Francesco. The influence of Medicean on Stuart culture in the first decade of the seventeenth century was the dominant one, and correspondence between the courts and personal visits by members of the group of cognoscenti surrounding the Prince (which included the young third Earl of Pembroke) could well have been a source of information about Francesco and Ferdinando.[35]

It is, therefore, of interest that the Cardinal in Middleton's play speaks with esteem and affection as well as asperity:

> What a grief 'tis to a religious feeling
> To think a man should have a friend so goodly,
> So wise, so noble, nay, a duke, a brother,
> And all this certainly damned?
>
> (IV.i.185–9)

The harsh words which follow are set within a context of concern and grief. The two facets of the Cardinal's attitude, concern for and appreciation of the person on the one hand, and the strict application of inescapable moral law on the other, may be linked to the ambivalences of response, choice and character portrayal which run through the play, especially to the strangely double nature of the Duke, both 'goodly gentleman' and diabolic Italian. By expressing the play's ambivalence through its moral spokesman, Middleton expresses conflicting feelings about writing drama which was, or could be perceived as, critical of the monarch. The dilemma of the dramatist goes to the heart of what it means to be a good subject. Should he show respect for the ruler by unquestioning, passive obedience, or are there occasions when his concern for his master demands that he act and speak out, and, in doing so, risk punishment? It is a question that Middleton had treated in *The Old Law* (1618), and seems to have used the Italian historical background to *Women Beware Women* to resolve. The Cardinal would seem to present the proper course: to speak out, but also to love and, ultimately, to obey the prince.

Here again, the Cardinal speaks and acts as a Calvinist. The Cardinal is no more a full portrait of Ferdinando de' Medici than the Duke is of King James. An important area where Ferdinando's policy was not in accord with that advocated by James's critics was that of foreign policy. In a sense, Ferdinando's position on European politics was not so different from that of James. There was always a pro-Spanish faction, but until the later shift in official policy towards an alliance with Spain, there were two principal factions in the Privy Council: one argued for vigilant and armed peace, whilst the strongly Protestant group believed in war with Spain, and political alliance with and support for the Dutch and European Protestantism.[36] To this latter group belonged the Archbishop of Canterbury, George Abbot, and Middleton's aristocratic patron, the third Earl of Pembroke. James, of course, was for peace and a balance between enemies to be maintained by dynastic marriages. His desire, however, to restore his daughter and son-in-law to their hereditary Palatine lands by means of a marriage alliance with Spain, without embroiling the nation in the European war, was perceived by militant Protestants as foolish and wrong.[37] To them the Protestant cause in Europe lay bleeding, and marriage to a Spanish, Catholic princess augured disaster for the nation's political and religious autonomy. None of this could be said openly in a public performance, yet the Italian setting of *Women Beware Women* seems to afford an opportunity for oblique comment. The concentration in the play on grotesque disharmony in marriage, and the play's emphasis on adulterous relationships, does not at first suggest any political context, but the entry of the Cardinal alters the discourse as well as events. He denounces the Duke for his marriage to a whore:

> Vowed you then never to keep strumpet more,
> And are you now so swift in your desires,
> To knit your honours and your life fast to her?
> Is not sin sure enough to wretched man,
> But he must bind himself in chains to 't. Worse!
> Must marriage, that immaculate robe of honour,
> That renders virtue glorious, fair and fruitful
> To her great master, now be made the garment
> Of leprosy and foulness?
>
> (IV.iii.9–17)

This is the language of Calvinism, with its metaphors of the purity of the true Church opposed to the adultery of Catholicism. The Protestant exegetic and iconographic tradition of depicting Catholicism as the Whore of Babylon would make an audience very aware of the possibility of giving a political gloss to these words as an attack on the Spanish marriage (and such an interpretation might account for Middleton's alteration of his sources by depicting the Duke's marriage as fatal to him); but the fact that it is a Cardinal, a Catholic, reproving the Duke seems to deny this interpretation as it is made.[38]

The Italian setting of *Women Beware Women* offers a dramatic experience on different levels: as a thriller, as a moral tale, and as criticism of court corruption. But there also seems evidence, particularly in the deft intertextual allusions, that the play spoke for a particular group at a particular time: militant Protestant parliamentarians, and their patrons and supporters, profoundly concerned for the state of the country's administration, and for the nation's future. Margot Heinemann has observed that 'there was far less serious dramatisation of the relations between king and counsellors, court and people from 1615 onwards' and that the great Jacobean tragedies of state written by Webster, Chapman and Jonson belonged to an earlier decade.[39] We believe that Middleton did not abandon political commentary in his great tragedies of the 1620s, but that in the current political climate he had to be more circumspect. Nevertheless, we suggest that, once the political significance of the Italian setting is appreciated, *Women Beware Women* becomes a very powerful play, incorporating both an older style of satiric ridicule, and sombre denunciation.

Notes

1 William Power, 'Middleton's way with names', *Notes and Queries*, n.s. 7, 1960, pp. 26–9, 95–8, 136–40, 175–9.

2 See Samuel Rawson Gardiner, *Prince Charles and the Spanish Marriage 1617–1623: a Chapter of English History*, 2 vols, London, 1869, and *Stuart Royal Proclamations*, eds F. Larkin and P. Hughes, Oxford, 1973, 1, pp. 496, 519–20.

3 Luciano Berti, *Il principe dello studiolo: Francesco de' Medici e la fine del Rinascimento fiorentino*, Florence, 1976, and J. R. Hale, *Florence and the Medici: the Pattern of Control*, London, 1977. Reference has also been made to Marcello Vannucci, *I Medici: una famiglia al potere*, Rome, 1987, and to Eric Cochrane, *Florence in the Forgotten Centuries*, London and Chicago, 1973, and his 'A case in point: the end of the Renaissance in Florence' in *The Late Italian Renaissance 1523–1630*, ed. E. Cochrane, London, 1970; also G. F. Young, *The Medici*, 2 vols, London, 1926, and Riguccio Galluzzi, *Istoria del granducato di Toscana sotto il governo della casa Medici*, 5 vols, Florence, 1781.

4 J. B. Batchelor, 'The pattern of *Women Beware Women*', *Yearbook of English Studies*, 2, 1972, pp. 76–88.

5 See Raffaello Gualterotti, *Feste nelle nozze del Serenissimo Don Francesco Gran Duca di Toscana et della Sereniss. Sua Consorte la Sig. Bianca Cappello*, Florence, 1579.

6 For the Venetian side of the story, see excerpts from Celio Malespini's *Ducento Novelle*, Venice, 1609, translated by J. R. Mulryne and printed in

Appendix 1 to his edition of *Women Beware Women*, The Revels Plays, London, 1975, pp. 168–79, henceforth referred to as Mulryne. All quotations from the play are from this edition.

7 Diary of Bastiano Arditi, cited in Berti, *Il principe dello studiolo*, p. 182.

8 For a full discussion of Middleton's sources, see Mulryne, pp. xxxviii–li.

9 Edmund Spenser, *The Faerie Queene*, ed. A. C. Hamilton, London and New York, 1977, book II, canto XI, pp. 272–81.

10 Herschel Baker in *The Wars of Truth*, Cambridge, Mass., 1952, provides a detailed summary of the stages of spiritual regeneration as outlined by Puritan writers.

11 Arthur Dent's *A Sermon of Repentance* was very popular and went through twelve editions between 1582 and 1643.

12 Margot Heinemann argues that this is Middleton's consistent perspective in *Puritanism and Theatre: Thomas Middleton and Opposition Drama under the Early Stuarts*, London, 1980.

13 Connections between city comedy and *Women Beware Women* are examined by R. B. Parker in 'Middleton's experiments with comedy and judgement', in *Jacobean Theatre*, eds John Russell Brown and Bernard Harris, London, 1960, pp. 178–99.

14 *A Sparke Towards the Kindling of Sorrow for Sion*, 1621, sig. A2r.

15 *The Letters of John Chamberlain*, ed. N. E. McClure, Philadelphia, 1932, 2, p. 315.

16 G. P. V. Akrigg, *Jacobean Pageant, or the Court of James I*, Cambridge, Mass., 1963, p. 241.

17 'One batch of poisoned tarts was sent over to the Tower by a certain Simon Merston who, unaware of their lethal content, helped himself to some of the syrup overflowing from them. He was lucky to escape with nothing worse than the loss of his nails and hair' (Akrigg, pp. 194–5). For detailed accounts of the scandals, see William McElwee, *The Murder of Sir Thomas Overbury*, London, 1952, and Beatrice White, *Cast of Ravens: the Strange Case of Sir Thomas Overbury*, London, 1965.

18 For detailed discussion of the 1621 Parliament, see Conrad Russell, *Parliaments and English Politics 1621–1629*, Oxford, 1979, and Robert Zaller, *The Parliament of 1621: a Study in Constitutional Conflict*, Berkeley, 1971. Gardiner gives a very full discussion of the fall of Bacon.

19 Mulryne, p. 159. Nicholas Brooke discusses the mixed tone of Italianate tragedy in *Horrid Laughter in Jacobean Tragedy*, London, 1979.

20 *Ben Jonson: the Complete Masques*, ed. Stephen Orgel, New Haven and London, 1969, p. 79, ll. 92–5, referred to henceforth as *Complete Masques*. Visual and verbal echoes, including 'sacrifice', have been noted by Jackson. I. Cope, 'The date of Middleton's *Women Beware Women*', *Modern Language Notes*, 76 (1961), pp. 295–300.

21 Mulryne, pp. 145 and 159–62.

22 Further attention would have been drawn to *Hymenaei* and *A Challenge at Tilt* by their publication in the 1616 Folio. Jonson was so disgusted by the revelations of witchcraft and murder which emerged at that time that he expunged all reference to the occasions for which they were written and the notes to *Hymenaei* in the Folio edition.

23 A. A. Bromham and Zara Bruzzi, *The 'Changeling' and the Years of Crisis 1619–1624: a Hieroglyph of Britain*, London, 1990, chapter 1.

24 David Norbrook, *Poetry and Politics in the English Renaissance*, London, 1984, p. 206.

25 For conflicting attitudes to marriage at this time, see Lawrence Stone, *The Family, Sex and Marriage in England 1500–1800*, Harmondsworth, 1977, especially chapter 5.

26 *Complete Masques*, p. 89, ll. 381–8. For a full commentary on the philosophy and politics of *Hymenaei* see *The Renaissance Imagination: Essays and Lectures by D. J. Gordon*, collected and edited by Stephen Orgel, Berkeley, 1975, pp. 157–84.

27 *Tom Tell-Troath* in *A Fourth Collection of Tracts on All Subjects*, ed. John Somers, London, 1809, p. 116. For a discussion of the circulation of oppositional views at this time, see Thomas Cogswell, *The Blessed Revolution: English Politics and the Coming of War 1621–1624*, Cambridge, 1989, pp. 5–53; for an examination of Middleton's negotiation between censorship and suppressed Protestant protest, see Bromham and Bruzzi, *'The Changeling' and the Years of Crisis*.

28 Annabel Patterson, *Censorship and Interpretation: the Conditions of Writing and Reading in Early Modern England*, London, 1984, especially chapter 2.

29 For discussion of references to peace in the play, see A. A. Bromham, 'The tragedy of peace: political meaning in *Women Beware Women*', *Studies in English Literature*, 26, spring 1986, pp. 309–29.

30 For a discussion of Francesco as Solomon, see Berti, *Il principe dello studiolo*, chapter 6, and for iconography associated with James, see Graham Parry, *The Golden Age Restor'd: the Culture of the Stuart Court, 1603–42*, Manchester, 1981.

31 Heinemann, *Puritanism and Theatre*, p. 134.

32 The principal sources for Ferdinando are those cited for Francesco, especially J. R. Hale.

33 Sir Robert Dallington, *A Survey of the great Dukes State of Tuscany, in the yeare of our Lord 1596*, London, 1605, p. 43. Dallington (and Fynes Moryson) stress Ferdinando's sponsorship of the silk industry, a detail likely to be of interest to someone like Middleton's patron, Sir Thomas Myddleton, a parliamentarian who was strongly opposed the Cokayne monopoly granted by James for the exporting of finished cloth, which had helped to damage the wool industry.

34 J. D. Mackie, *Negotiations Between King James VI and I and Ferdinand I Grand Duke of Tuscany*, London, 1927.

35 Roy Strong, in *Henry Prince of Wales and England's Lost Renaissance*, London, 1986, makes out an impressive case for cultural links with the court of Ferdinando, from earlier visits in the 1590s when Florence opened up again to foreigners, such as Edward and William Cecil, Francis Manners, Inigo Jones, Robert Dallington, to visits in the early seventeenth century of grandees like the Earl of Shrewsbury and the Earl of Arundel. He shows how greatly Henry was influenced by Medici taste and patronage.

36 Simon Adams, 'Spain or the Netherlands? The dilemmas of early Stuart foreign policy', in *Before the Civil War*, ed. H. Tomlinson, London, 1983, pp.

79–101.

37 An interesting interpretation of why James's stance had become outmoded through a shift in the European balance of power is offered by Maurice Lee Jr., *James I and Henri IV: an Essay in English Foreign Policy 1603–1610*, London, 1970, in the concluding chapter. Perhaps the most cogent (and certainly one of the most amusing) tracts against the Spanish marriage is S. R. N. I. [John Reynolds], *Vox Coeli, or Newes from Heaven*, printed in 1624 but written, as we argue in *The 'Changeling' and the Years of Crisis*, in 1621.

38 For discussion of Puritan discourse and iconography, see Bromham and Bruzzi, *'The Changeling' and the Years of Crisis*, chapters 2, 4, and Postcript.

39 Heinemann, *Puritanism and Theatre*, p. 135.

16

'Under the dent of the English pen': the language of Italy in English Renaissance drama

A. J. Hoenselaars

In studying the language of Italian-based drama of Shakespeare and his contemporaries, one broad observation may be made at the outset. The plays were written by English dramatists for English audiences and since 'intelligibility is the *sine qua non* of any stage dialect', the characters frequenting the Italian scene mainly speak English.[1] In the world beyond the stage, the .thought that Italians at home should communicate in English inevitably conflicts with our sense of realism. In the play-world, audiences confronted with this phenomenon have always been willing to suspend their disbelief. English, however, is not the only language spoken in the Italian settings. The predominant tongue is frequently set off with a variety of foreign language devices, not excluding Italian. This raises the issue to what extent these foreign variants either challenged or supported the illusion of the English language as the natural tongue of the stage Italians. The interaction between these types of native and foreign speech is heightened by the fact that on a number of occasions European vernaculars are explicitly mentioned. It is my contention that the Italian setting popular during the early modern period served as a main foreign locus to rehearse concerns about the English language which was still 'currency with no international value'.[2] Consequent on the as yet poor status of English, the Englishman was forced to study foreign languages. This issue is prominent in the plays with native English settings frequented by gibberish-babbling strangers. It also manifests itself in the foreign Italian setting, though in a different manner. Studies of the foreign language device have ignored this difference in a failure to recognise location as a determinant.[3] Following a comparison, therefore, between the language concerns in the English and Italian settings, I hope to demonstrate that the Italian setting enabled playwrights to transcend existing preoccupations with the low reputation of the English language as well as the need of foreign-language learning. On stage the Englishman's native tongue paradoxically gained the international status which the Italian language instructor Florio considered it lacked when he stated in *His Firste Fruites* that English 'is a language that wyl do you good in England, but passe Douer, it is woorth nothing'.[4]

In a number of ways, the juxtaposition of English and other language varieties in Italian settings is comparable to that in the English location. The most popular and practical use of the foreign language device in London is that of distinguishing native characters and foreigners. The mechanism is prominent in plays like Haughton's *Englishmen for My Money*, Marston's *Jack Drum's Entertainment* and *The Dutch Courtesan*, as well as Dekker's *The Shoemaker's Holiday*. Shakespeare made extensive use of the foreign language variety in *The Merry Wives of Windsor* where Parson Evans speaks with a Welsh accent and Doctor Caius both French and broken English. It has been suggested that such foreign language usage was more likely to emerge in an English setting because it was 'easier to manage [...] than in a play set in France or Italy, and peopled with "native" characters'.[5] This view seems confirmed by the fact that Shakespeare largely eschewed it in his Italian comedies. Nevertheless, in the Italian settings of the other dramatists various recognisable European languages are frequently used to limn the scene more clearly. They serve that purpose in Middleton's *Blurt Master Constable* and Marston's *What You Will*, in Dekker's *The Honest Whore, Patient Grisill* and *The Wonder of a Kingdom*, as well as in the anonymous *The Telltale*, Brome's *The Novella*, and Shirley's *The Humorous Courtier*.

The foreign language device in the largely metropolitan London location appealed to the audience's patriotic sense of national and, by extension, linguistic identity. The English language in the English-based drama tends to set a standard, and on occasion functions as a shibboleth. In *The Life and Death of Jack Straw* the inability to speak correct English is presented as a matter of life and death. As the English rebel puts it to the predictably unfortunate Fleming: 'as many of you as cannot say bread and cheese, in good and perfect English [...] die for it.'[6] In *Englishmen for My Money*, the vernacular is advanced as the only language to court London maidens in: 'If needes you marry with an *English* Lasse, / Woe her in *English*, or sheele call you Asse.'[7]

Predictably, no such extreme uses of the shibboleth device may be found in the Italian settings, nor are instances of linguistic friction accompanied by such explicit utterances about the English language as in Haughton's comedy. It may be argued that any such overt references to English would have conflicted even with the Renaissance dramatists' flexible sense of realism. This would also explain why the number of characters in the Italian location speaking gibberish – here defined as broken English – is small. Those instances are intriguing where British accents or dialects are spoken other than 'standard' English. Traces of rural dialect may be heard in *Blurt Master Constable*, where it serves to mark Lazarillo de Tormes's foreignness in the Venetian setting. Also in the Italian plot of Yarington's *Two Lamentable Tragedies* a country dialect is used for disguise purposes when Falleria reverts to the garb of a shepherd.[8] In Dekker's *Patient Grisill*, Sir Owen Ap Rice and widow Gwenthian treat the audience to a fair share of Welsh, and Jamy in *The Honest Whore* speaks an Irish brogue. In Middleton's *The Witch*, set in and around Ravenna, the Italian Gentleman who brings Antonio news from his mother speaks with a Scottish accent.[9] Possibly the illusion in *The Witch* was upheld by the assumption that a language variety spoken in the north of the British Isles might equally well be employed in 'the northern parts' of Italy from which the Gentleman derives.[10] In all these instances, it concerned language varieties that the Englishman – following Puttenham and his theory of a 60-mile-radius around the court or London – had conveniently marginalised at home, and which could, as a consequence, have been appreciated as foreign tongues in the Italian location.[11]

Correctly spoken European languages are also used frequently: a proficiency in foreign languages is considered a merit in both the Italian and the English setting when it concerns characters who adopt a disguise, and whose stratagems prove successful thanks to their foreign language skills. The success of English disguise characters in Dekker's *The Shoemaker's Holiday*, the anonymous comedy *The London Prodigal*, Middleton's *Anything for a Quiet Life*, Brome's *The Damoiselle* and *The New Academy*, Marston's *The Dutch Courtesan*, and even in Ben Jonson's *The Alchemist*, is inseparable from their proficiency in the foreign language adopted by the disguise characters. The number of foreign language disguises in the Italian setting, however, is smaller than in the English setting.[12] In the latter, they are generally reserved for comic tricksters. This may be related to the different status granted to foreign-language learning in Italy and England. Unlike England,

Italy is the nation that characters like Mulleasses in Mason's *The Turk*, and even Jonson's Would-Bes, visit to learn the language. Truepenny in *Blurt Master Constable* manifests a degree of pride in knowing foreign tongues when interrogated about the Frenchman Fontinelle:

> *Hippolyto*: Sirra Mephostophiles, did not you bring letters from my Sister to the Frenchman?
> *Truepenny*: *Signior* no.
> *Camillo*: Did not you fetch him out of the Tennis Court?
> *Truepenny*: No, point, *per ma foy*, you see I haue many tongues speake for me.[13]

One may note the difference with Firk in *The Shoemaker's Holiday*. This London apprentice wants to have Hans Meulter (alias Lacy) hired so he can 'learn some gibble-gabble'.[14] The divergent attitudes rehearsed in the English and the Italian settings are best demonstrated by means of a comparison between Haughton's *Englishmen for My Money* and *Blurt Master Constable*. In Haughton's London-based comedy, Pisaro's daughters refuse to learn foreign languages. Mathea, who is to be wedded off to the Frenchman Delio, expresses her aversion as follows:

> Thinke you Ile learne to speake this gibberidge,
> Or the Pigges language? Why, if I fall sicke,
> Theyle say, the *French* (*et-cetera*) infected me. (sig. D2r)

In the Venetian setting of *Blurt Master Constable*, however, Violetta considers the same foreign language a valuable asset:

> I loue a life to heare a man speake French,
> Of his complection: I would vnder-goe
> The instruction of that language rather far,
> Than be two weekes vnmarried (by my life)
> Because Ile speake true French, Ile be his wife.[15]

Violetta eventually wins the Frenchman for herself, whereas Pisaro's daughters deem themselves fortunate that their father should have hired a French language instructor who is in reality the monolingual Englishman Anthony in disguise; they ultimately have their will, and all marry Englishmen.

The image of the monolingual Englishman brings into focus the phenomenon that the English characters peopling the Italian scene invariably speak English as the stage language of the nation they visit. No comic concessions of a linguistic kind were deemed appropriate for stage Englishmen in Italy, and none of the English characters in *Thomas Lord Cromwell*, Day's *The Travailes of the Three English Brothers*, Webster's *Duchess of Malfi* and *The White Devil*, Heywood's *The Fair Maid of the West*, Shirley's *The Gentleman of Venice*, or even in Jonson's *Volpone*, is made to look ridiculously helpless on account of a poor proficiency in the language of Italy. Such a state of affairs could be considered a flattering type of self-representation, fortuitously sanctioned by dramatic expediency. Portia's characterisation of Faulconbridge as a 'dumb-show' suggests that the truly monolingual Englishman could be granted no stage dialogue.[16] However, Portia's description may too easily be granted stereotypical status.[17] Indeed, it is echoed in Beaumont and Fletcher's *The Double Marriage*, where the oppressed and tongue-tied Neapolitans are addressed by the Duke with the question: 'Your tongues seal'd up; Are ye of several Countries, You understand not one another?' A Gunner, intent on apologising for his countrymen, replies: 'That's an *Englishman*, He looks as though he had lost his dog.'[18] Also, Portia's image corresponds to John Florio's view of the nation, on which it may well have been modelled.[19] No doubt in an attempt to propagate the learning of Italian in England, the language instructor noted: 'What a shame is it, that you shal see an Englishman come in company of straungers, who can neyther speake, nor vnderstand with them, but standes as one mute, & so is he mocked of them, and despised of al, and none wyl make accou[n]t of hym?' (*Firste Fruites*, p. 63). Such views cannot be ignored, but greater emphasis on voices such as Richard Carew's in *The Excellencie of the English Tongue* may serve to redress the balance. Carew, a native Englishman, adopts a stance which is diametrically opposed to the Italian's: 'turne an Englishman at any time of his age into what countrie soever allowing him due respite, and you shall see him profit so well that the imitation of his utterance, will nothing differ from the patterne of that native language.'[20] And Carew echoes William Harrison who in *The Description of Britaine* remarked about the English, to which he counted himself, that 'we may with much facilitie learne any other language, beside Hebrue, Gréeke & Latine, and speake it naturallie, as if we were home-borne in those countries'.[21] Given such contrasting views, it seems worth exploring the ways in which these concerns also determined the language usage in the Italian-based drama.

As Lievsay has put it, 'Almost every cultivated Elizabethan had at least a smattering of Italian'.[22] If an increasing proficiency in foreign languages may be demonstrated on the part of the higher-educated, it should be noted that the average Englishman, too, was equipped with a range of foreign words and phrases which the dramatists drew on generously to establish local colour.[23] Thus, a degree of place realism was provided by means of the forms of address observed by the characters. Italian men of rank are generally referred to as *signior*, and the representatives of other nations visiting Italy are addressed in accordance with the forms appropriate to their respective nationalities. The Spaniard is referred to as a *don*, the Frenchman as *monsieur*, and the Englishman as *sir*.[24] Dekker observes the device strictly in *Patient Grisill*. Suggesting that the Welshman and the Italian engage in a duel, Urcenze, in a single breath, asks: 'will not thy master Sir *Owen* and *Signior Emulo* fight?'[25] In Beaumont and Fletcher's *The Chances* – with its two Spaniards Don John and Don Fredrick caught up in the Bolognian intrigue – the form of address is inseparable from the action. This is initiated when Don John is erroneously taken for 'signieur *Fabritio*' (I.iii.18), and a baby left in his care. This very misconception then informs most of the Cervantes plot of two 'Don-ships' abroad.[26] As is the case with most phenomena in English Renaissance drama, the plays present the critic with a series of discontinuities rather than a hermetic theory. The form of address is not used consistently and exceptions abound, as in the anonymous *Wit of a Woman* where the English form of address is used throughout. Also in Jonson's *Volpone*, the English and Italian terms are used indiscriminately, and only on paper do editors of the play succeed in distinguishing the form of address for Volpone from that for the impolitic Englishman, whose title is (appropriately) printed with a capital 'S'.

Other instances of blending the native English language with speech appertaining to the Italian location, thus presuming audience understanding, are the characters' names. Either these may be derived from Italian sources or they are Italian-sounding names. The most intriguing names in the latter category are charactonyms like Amoroso, Malevole, Benvolio, Sordido, Prospero, Biancha, Puttota, or Nymphadoro, and one is fortunate to have the two versions of Jonson's *Every Man in His Humour* to study the substitution from Italian to anglicised names in action. Charactonyms are used prominently in *The Revenger's Tragedy*. With its notoriously slight attention to Italian topography – a single reference early in the play has to suffice[27] – the names of Vindice, Lussurioso and Spurio in the play establish standard Italian personalities and, by extension, the Italian location, so forcefully that a reading of the many revenge plots which stresses universal values may well venture beyond Tourneur's original objective.[28] The names in *Volpone* serve as a similar mode of semantic reference that would have stood contemporary audiences in good stead. Yet, it is surprising that in the critical debate around *Volpone* those critics versed in onomastics and skilled at analysing the symbolic nature of Jonson's charactonyms have not noted as quaint the counterpoint which the names inevitably provide to what other critics praise as the hyper-realistic Venetian setting in Jonson's comedy. Conversely, topographical critics have not allowed their allegations regarding place realism to be modified by the determinant of nomenclature.

Beyond forms of address, names and charactonyms, Italian words, expressions, or even longer stretches of the language are frequent. Generally, they serve a meticulously controlled dramatic purpose. In *The Chances*, Beaumont and Fletcher effectively employ a single word of Italian, namely *Basta* (II.ii.37). It is spoken by the Spaniard Don John. His use of intelligible Italian marks that he is, on this occasion, in Italian disguise, wearing the Duke of Ferrara's hat. A measure of the dramatists' control even of such a brief utterance as *Basta* is that Don John's reversion to his Spanish identity, is again marked by code-switching. In the following scene, Don John doffs his disguise hat and in an aside exclaims the phrase '*O de dios*' (II.iii.17). In Ford's *'Tis Pity She's a Whore* Vasques's '*Troppo sperar, inganna*' (IV.i.76) may be shortlived, but underpins the objective, throughout the tragedy, of the Spaniard intent on excelling the Italians at revenge. The character temporarily merges with the nation he means to imitate. Touching is the instance of code-switching in *Blurt Master Constable*, when Blurt asks Lazarillo if he has indeed been visiting a prostitute. Still reeking of the urine that was emptied on his head outside her residence, the humiliated Spaniard confesses in the language of the place: '*Signior see*' (sig. G1v). A subtle use of Italian, with an appeal to the audience's foreign language proficiency may also be found in Yarington's *Two Lamentable Tragedies*. In the northern Italian setting, Falleria orders two ruffians to kill Pertillo. One of the bandits – aware that after this hazardous enterprise the danger will remain – asks Falleria to delete the letter 't' from Pertillo's name and to reconsider his request:

2 Ruffian: Call you him *Pertillo*, faith, leaue out the *T.*
Fallerio: Why so?
1 Ruffian: Because *Perillo* will remaine. (sig. D2r).

The Italian word thus produced would have been close enough to English *peril* to ensure communication. Most importantly, however, given the second ruffian's cryptic question that Fallerio fails to understand, the audience would have been placed in a position to produce its own Italian. Apart from flattering the audience, it would have furthered the prime objective of limning the Italian against its parallel English setting. However, in most instances, the foreign language inserts serve little or no part of any extended dialogue, and the regular transaction of information by these means is rare. They are perhaps best appreciated in semiotic terms, as abstract aural signs. This is confirmed by Annabella's use of her native tongue in *'Tis Pity She's a Whore.* The lines from an Italian song she sings – *'Che morte più dolce che morirei per amore'* and *'Morendo in gratia a lui, morirei senza dolore'* – are meaningful to anyone versed in the language, but in performance mere otherness suffices in order to mark Annabella's refusal to enter into the dialogue, which, on this occasion, is Soranzo's interrogation.[29]

On the whole, foreign tongues were considered a communication barrier, and the dramatists developed ample means to have their audience, not considered fluent in foreign tongues, share in the linguistic richness of the Italian setting by various means. In Beaumont and Fletcher's Genoa-based *The Nice Valour*, intelligibility is guaranteed by means of translation. In order to focus the persona of the Frenchman Lapet, the audience is informed that *'Lapet* [...] is *La Fart*, after the English letter'.[30] A more subtle form of audience-oriented translation takes place in Marston's *The Malcontent* when Genovese Malevole tells Duke Pietro that he is a cuckold:

Malevole: Duke, thou art a becco, a cornuto.
Pietro: How!
Malevole: Thou art a cuckold.[31]

Marston both provides linguistic local colour and ensures understanding for any member of the audience still unfamiliar with the meaning of his stage Italian. Marston's subtly hides any extradramatic need for translation behind the veil of dramatic necessity. As part of his satirical role – 'I may speak foolishly, ay, knavishly' (I.iv.159) – Malevole misinterprets Pietro's exclamation of surprise as a request to have translated the Italian terms used. Equally covert is the translation exercise in *Women Pleased*. Penurio has arranged a meeting between Claudio and Isabella, and now the knavish servant wishes to know if he has done well: 'Are ye pleas'd now? have I not wrought this wonder. *Non è ben fatto Signieur?*'[32] Dexterity at scheming and foreign language skills are merged, as the solicitation for approval of the clever deed is translated into another tongue, and bilingual understanding guaranteed.

Shakespeare, too, meets the audience's needs halfway in *The Taming of the Shrew*. In the second scene of the comedy proper, Petruchio's good-natured quarrel with Grumio is interrupted by the arrival of Hortensio, and the following dialogue ensues:

> *Petruchio*: Signior Hortensio, come you to part the fray?
> *Con tutto il cuore ben trovato*, may I say.
> *Hortensio*: *Alla nostra casa ben venuto, molto honorato signior mio Petrucio.*[33]

It has been noted that the use of Italian serves to establish the locale shortly following the transition from the Cotswolds of the Induction to the Padua location of the inset comedy.[34] The dialogue, however, cannot be dissociated from the lines that follow. Hortensio turns to Grumio with the promise to end the quarrel, to which the servant replies: 'Nay, 'tis no matter, sir, what he 'leges in Latin' (I.ii.28). Any local colour that may have been established by means of the dialogue in Italian is undermined by the fact that an Italian character should prove unable to draw a distinction between Latin and his native tongue. On these grounds, Hibbard, rehearsing Portia's remark as a stereotype, has observed that 'Grumio, despite his name, is a good solid English character who does not know the difference between Latin and Italian.'[35] More cautious, though equally unconvincing, is Morris's interpretation that Grumio is 'Italian only in his name' (note to I.ii.28). A more plausible reading is that Grumio's is in part an extradramatic remark, drawing attention to himself as the English actor playing Grumio who has just stepped out of the native Cotswold Induction into the Italian play. Given the fact that the English language is an obvious necessity for an audience unversed in Italian, it is worth noting that Shakespeare refrains from referring to the audience's poor proficiency. Instead, Grumio is the opportune scape-goat for monolinguists. The audience was made to feel superior to the servant since it could, unlike him, distinguish between Latin and Italian, and, given the popular speech act performed by Petruchio and Hortensio, would even have been capable of intuiting the meaning of the exchange in Italian about which Grumio claims total ignorance.

However, not on all occasions did the dramatists subtly cater to the audience's limited knowledge of Italian, or suggest foreign language skills. A case in point is *Antonio and Mellida*, where the eponymous characters, meeting after a period of separation, switch from English to Italian. T. S. Eliot had problems accounting for this procedure, and noted that 'it is difficult to explain, by any natural action of mediocrity, the absurd dialogue in Italian in which Antonio and Mellida suddenly express themselves in Act IV, Sc. 1'.[36] It is indeed surprising that as macaronic a poet as Eliot should have found fault with Marston's device, especially since the Page's comment on the dialogue provides the key to an understanding: 'I think confusion of Babel is fallen upon these lovers, that they change their language.'[37] With these lines Marston connects the fate of his two lovers with the Babel theme introduced in the opening scene of the play around Mellida's father. There, the vain Duke Pierro Sforza scoffs at his courtier Felice's caveat that 'Confusion's train blows up [...] Babel pride' (I.i.58). In accordance with this opening, Sforza's composure gives way to chaos as soon as he hears of Mellida's projected elopement with Antonio:

> Antonio! His head, his head! Keep you the court; the rest stand still, or run, or go, or shout, or search, or scud, or call, or hang, or do - do - do - do so-so-so-something. I know not wh-wh-wh-what I do - do - do, nor wh-wh-wh-where I am.
>   *O trista traditrice, rea, ribalda fortuna,*
>   *Negandomi vendetta mi causa fera morte*
>
> (III.ii.197–204).

The pride of Marston's Duke results in linguistic confusion of a biblical kind familiar with theatre audiences. The star-crossed lovers, though, establish a mode of understanding that mystifies their Italian compatriots as much as the theatre audience. The Italian language in which Antonio and Mellida communicate – representing a 'discontinuous variousness of experience' – is elevated to a type of language alien to their countrymen for psychological reasons.[38] This linguistic alienation effected within the plot context operates as an apt correlative to the alienation of an audience largely unversed in the Italian language.[39]

To the degree that the average Tudor or Stuart Englishman was a monolinguist, the dramatists therefore took great pains either to make intelligible what might be misunderstood, implying foreign language skills nevertheless, or, as in *Antonio and Mellida*, by creating dramatic situations in which non-intelligibility was the effect aimed at and conveniently shared by stage characters.

For all the dramatists' attempts to sustain the illusion of Italy by means of foreign tongues both within the context of the plot and in the interaction with London theatre audiences, the plays contain many instances that curiously alert the English audience to language in general, and its own. This furthers credibility instead of undermining it, as when a play more or less openly acknowledges its derivation from an Italian source as in Heywood's *A Maiden-head Well Lost.*[40] Matters are more complex in *The Wit of a Woman* where the pedant priest indulges in Latin and is criticised by Ferio with the words: 'I pray thee leaue thy latine, and in plaine mother-tongue, do that I will entreat thee to.'[41] The situation resembles that in *The Wonder of a Kingdom* where Angelo symbolically disguises as a French-speaking doctor to restore the speech of Fiametta, his beloved whom he is not to meet owing to parental control. Even in a context where language and speech are the main themes, Dekker does not hazard credibility when Angelo's disguise is in jeopardy. Hearing Fiametta speak, her father enters. She wants him to forgive Angelo and is ready to spoil the latter's disguise: 'Leave off thy gibberishe, and I prethee speake / Thy Native language.'[42] The illusion seems barely upheld when Angelo insists 'Par-ma-foy all French' (III.ii.64). Also in Brome's *The Novella*, Swatzenburgh speaks German and is asked by Fabritio to 'speake in the proper language of / The Nation [they] are in'.[43] It is another version of the dialogue spoken during the arraignment of Vittoria in *The White Devil.* Instead of Latin, the heroine asks the Lawyer to 'speak his usual tongue'.[44] As Dena Goldberg has convincingly argued, the request involves not a potential breach of illusion, but a subtle means of involving the theatre audience, which is addressed in Vittoria's two-edged explanation for her request: 'amongst this auditory / Which come to hear my cause, the half or more / May be ignorant in't'.[45] Nevertheless, the illusion would seem to become particularly strained, when the language of the stage nation is no longer referred to as the 'mother-tongue', 'native tongue', or 'usual tongue', but explicitly named, as in Ford's *Love's Sacrifice*, where the disguised Roseilli speaks a nonsense language and Mauruccio comments: 'Oh Sir, had you heard him as I did, deliuer whole histories in the *Tangay tongue*, you would sweare there were not such a linguist breath'd againe; and did I but perfectly vnderstand his langnage (*sic*), I would be confident in lesse than two houres, to distinguish the meaning of Bird, Beast, or Fish, naturally, as I my selfe speake Italian.'[46] An extreme is reached when the language spoken in Italy is referred to as English. This happens in Chapman's *May Day* when Innocentio tries to test the tailor's son's Latin:

> *Innocentio*: How make you this in Latin, boy. 'My father is an honest tailor'?
> *Boy*: That will hardly be done in true Latin, sir.
> *Innocentio*: No? Why so, sir?
> *Boy*: Because it is false English, sir.
> *Quintiliano*: An excellent boy!
> *Innocentio*: Why is it false English?
> *Boy*: Marry, sir, as *bona mulier* is said to be false Latin, because, though *bona* be good, *mulier* is naught; so to say my father is an honest tailor, is false English; for though my father be honest, yet the tailor is a thief.[47]

The frequency of such instances may be interpreted as a measure of the spell of Italy created by other dramatic means. Yet, it would be wrong to explain such incidents as mere slips of the dramatists' careless pen, moments unobtrusive to audiences due to an arguably naive sense of realism. Such occasions established a dual focus to rehearse, briefly, some essentially early modern concerns about the English language which, unlike Latin, Italian, Spanish and Turkish, had no international status, and which lead Mulcaster in 1582 to note about the English language that 'our state is no Empire to hope to enlarge it by commanding ouer cuntries. What tho? tho it be neither large in possession, nor in present hope of great encrease, yet where it rules, it can make good lawes, and as fit for our state, as the biggest can for theirs.'[48] Samuel Daniel's famous lines from *Musophilis* indicate that the expansionist idea at least had not yet faded by the end of the 1590s:

And who in time knows whither we may vent

> The treasure of our tongue, to what strange shores
> This gain of our best glorie shal be sent,
> T'inrich vnknowing Nations with our stores?
> Which world in th'yet vnformed Occident
> May come refin'd with th'accents that are ours.[49]

If Bailey terms Daniel's speculations 'pure patriotic pipe dream' at least their dream status is not challenged (p. 97), and it may be demonstrated that mainly in the popular Italian stage setting – though also, for example, in the Troyes setting of *Henry V* – the English language could be rehearsed in the commanding role it had been assigned in Ireland and Wales following the Henrician acts of 1535 and 1537, and which it was effectively to obtain in the course of the seventeenth century once extra-European colonisation got under way. Thus, on occasion, in the plays under consideration, the validity of the Italian language that creeps into the dialogue is with sardonic frankness dismissed, and the characters cheerfully continue in English. In *A Knack to Know an Honest Man*, Franco offers himself as a servant with the words '*Eta serua vostra fettisima seruidore siniore*', to which Fortunio's reply runs 'Speakes in parables'.[50] Italian is blandly reduced to the status of a riddle and the speaker silenced. The dialogue then continues in English at a pace suggestive of delight in the self-sufficiency of the chosen stage tongue, in a manner that recalls the attitude of Englishmen abroad of whom Camden fully approved: 'not long since for the honour of our native tongue, *Henry Fitz-Allan* Earle of Arundel, in his travaile into Italie, and the Lord *William Howard* of *Effingham*, in his government of Calice, albeit they were not ignorant of other forraine tongues, would answer no strangers by word or writing but onely in English' (Dunn, p. 30). In *The Gentleman Usher*, the same Chapman who stressed the use of English in *May Day* uses Italian to ridicule the pedant Sarpego who asks Bassiolo to demonstrate the front and back of his nightcap in the following terms:

> Good Master Usher, will you dictate to me
> Which is the part precedent of this night-cap,
> And which posterior? I do *ignorare*
> How I should wear it.[51]

Chapman deftly relegates Sarpego's use of Italian to the rhetorical variant known to English audiences as bombast, thus voicing an implicit claim for the purity of the English language.

A related procedure may be witnessed in *Fedele and Fortunio*, the English translation of Luigi Pasqualigo's *Il Fedele*. Here Fedele receives a letter from Victoria with the shocking news that she wishes him to cease his advances to her. Asked about the tenor of the letter by Crackstone – disguised as a pedant – Fedele replies with exasperation: 'Read it thyself and see.'[52] The letter which Crackstone continues to read out loud for the audience is entirely in Italian. Then, after a brief comment on the letter's contents as well as its language – 'This is strange upon strange' – he translates the letter into English (II.i.53). This is a remarkable proceeding for several reasons. The Italian text of the letter is derived nearly verbatim from the original play. There, however, it is spoken by Fedele himself without, of course, inviting a translation from Crackstone. On one level, the adaptation seems motivated by the translator's wish by comic means to draw attention to the Italian source text. On another level, the translator creates a situation via Crackstone to display his own language skills in action, thus focusing attention to the comedy as an English language construct. He establishes with the audience a dual language focus before reasserting his native English. The emotions thus rehearsed in *Fedele and Fortunio* do not seem at a far remove from those expressed by Philemon Holland in the preface to the 1601 edition of his translation of Livy. To translate, he states in belligerent and expansionist terms that recall Mulcaster and Daniel, is: 'to triumph now over the Romans in subduing their literature under the dent of the English pen, in requitall of the conquest sometime over this Island, atchieved by the edge of their sword'.[53] That for Holland translation into English involved an explicit nation-change is equally demonstrated by the dedication to Queen Elizabeth. Holland asks her: *'reach forth your gracious hand to* T. Livius: *who having arrived long since & conversed as a meere stranger in this your famous Iland, & now for love therof learned in some sort the language, humbly craveth your Majesties favour, to be ranged with other free-denizens of that kind.'*[54] The metaphor suggested in *Fedele and Fortunio* and elaborately developed by Holland was not incidental. It recurs in Thomas Dekker's lines of praise for the translator of *Il Fedele*. In his short poem to the volume that marked the completion of Munday's *Palmerin of England* project, Dekker stated about the original:

For tho in courtly French he sweetly spake,
In fluent Thuscane, grave Castillian

A harder labor thou doest undertake
Thus to create him a fine Englishman,
Whose language now dare more than any can,
Nor thou, nor Palmerin in choice doe err:
Thou of thy scholler, he his schoolmaster.[55]

Given the context of the occasions on which the dramatists challenged the undoubtedly flexible realism of their Italian stage settings, one may turn to *The Merchant of Venice* and Portia's description of Faulconbridge as a 'dumb-show' (I.ii.70). If Shakespeare may be said to draw on the image of the monolingual Englishman – explicitly referred to in *The Double Marriage* and carefully catered for by the careful use of the foreign language device in the drama as a whole – he also joins his fellow-dramatists in their defence of English. It is rarely noted that Portia's reference to Faulconbridge is in part an apology for her own *English* language skills. As the somewhat irritated Lady of Belmont puts it to her servant Nerissa: 'you will come into the court and swear that I have a poor pennyworth in the English' (I.ii.67–9). In one sense, Shakespeare counters the allegations about the monolingual Faulconbridge with those, perhaps equally stereotyped, voiced by the same authors who wrote in defence of the English language. Carew, prefacing his praise of the Englishman's foreign language proficiency, noted that the stranger 'carrieth evermore a watch-word upon his tong to descrie him by' (Dunn, p. 40). Following his praise of the Englishman, Harrison added, in comparable terms, that 'yet on the other side it falleth out, I wot not by what other meanes, that few forren nations can rightlie pronounce ours, without some and that great note of imperfection' (Bolton, p. 19). In an extended sense, Portia's words also foreshadow sentiments like those formulated a decade later by Heywood, when he noted that thanks to the stage the English language had 'growne to a most perfect and composed language' and that 'many Nations grow inamored of our tongue (before despised)'.[56] More significantly, however, for a brief moment, Shakespeare's deft instance of dramatic irony arouses sympathy for the unwitting speaker, not merely because she appeals to the language of the audience, but also because she speaks it better than she herself has been led to believe. And if Shakespeare only briefly alludes to the fact that his Italian heroine speaks English – thus suggesting to the audience that she belonged, as Edmund Spenser put it, to 'the kingdom of our own language'[57] – Lewis Machin took the device to its extreme in *The Dumb Knight*. As if subscribing to Richard Carew's view that Shakespeare's English rendering of Ovid was superior reading to the original (Dunn, p. 43), Machin has his Sicilian clerk, symbolically named 'President' (or, Precedent), praise *Venus and Adonis* as the 'best booke in the world' and as a text 'that neuer an Orators clark in this kingdome but is beholden vnto'.[58] His praise is, not surprisingly perhaps, interlarded with generous quotations from the English original (sigs. F1r–F2r). It is difficult indeed to find a clearer example of the dual consciousness which informs the theatre audience's contemporary response to the language of the Italian plays, and, given the frequency of the self-conscious references to the English language in the Italian based drama, one is tempted to rephrase Mulcaster's remark about the limited geographical range of the English language. If Mulcaster argued that it was 'fit for our state', the dramatists made it 'fit for our stage'.

Recording the impressions of his stay in England – which included a performance of *Julius Caesar* – Thomas Platter noted that 'the English pass their time, learning from the plays what is happening in other lands; indeed, men and women visit such places without scruple, since the English do not travel much, but prefer to learn of strange things [...] and take their pleasures at home'.[59] Steven Mullaney has interpreted the phrase 'strange things' as foreign languages, and developed the brilliant theory that the Englishman's study of languages other than his own was a theatrical capacity 'with which boundaries between nations, tongues and classes [could] be crossed with liberty' (Mullaney, p. 79). This, he demonstrates with reference to Shakespeare's second tetralogy, where, following a temporary rehearsal of foreign tongues, the voice of the other is silenced as a foregone conclusion before re-establishing the English language as standard. In linguistic terms, the Italian-based drama acts as a correlative to the English history plays. The audience is both invited and aided to appreciate the voice of the other, but it is not made to forget that the foreign voice could be silenced once the English language travelled and triumphed, in the imagination still, abroad.

Notes

1 Helge Kökeritz, *Shakespeare's Pronunciation*, New Haven, 1953, p. 36.
2 Richard W. Bailey, *Images of English: a Cultural History of the Language*, Cambridge, 1992, p. 98.

3 See Eduard Eckhardt *Die Dialekt- und Ausländertypen des älteren Englischen Dramas*, Louvain, 1910–11; W. O. Clough, 'The broken English of foreign characters of the Elizabethan stage', *Philological Quarterly*, 12, 1933, pp. 255–68; Annegret Staufer, *Fremdsprachen bei Shakespeare: das Vokabular und seine dramatischen Funktionen*, Frankfurt am Main, 1974; Marlene Soares dos Santos, 'Theatre for Tudor England: an investigation of the ideas of Englishness and foreignness in English drama, c. 1485–1592, with particular reference to the interludes', Ph.D. diss., The Shakespeare Institute, Birmingham, 1980; N. F. Blake, *Non-Standard Language in English Literature*, London, 1981, pp. 63–92; and Vanna Gentili, 'Lingua nazionale/lingue altre: note sull'ambivalenza elisabettiana con esempi da Shakespeare', *Rivista di letterature moderne e comparate*, 39, 2, 1986, pp. 107–25.

4 John Florio, *His Firste Fruites* (London, 1578), The English Experience, 95, Amsterdam, 1965, p. 50.

5 Jeanne Addison Roberts, *Shakespeare's English Comedy: 'The Merry Wives of Windsor' in Context*, Lincoln, Nebr., 1979, p. 54.

6 *The Life and Death of Iacke Strawe, a notable Rebell in England: Who was kild in Smithfield by the Lord Maior of London*, London, 1593, STC 23356, sig. C4v.

7 *Englishmen for My Money, or A Woman Will Have Her Will, by William Haughton, 1616*, The Tudor Facsimile Texts [1911], New York, 1970, sig. E2r.

8 *Two Lamentable Tragedies ... By Rob. Yarington*, London, 1601, STC 26076, sigs H3v–I1r.

9 *Three Jacobean Witchcraft Plays: 'The Tragedy of Sophonisba', 'The Witch' and 'The Witch of Edmonton'*, ed. Peter Corbin and Douglas Sedge, The Revels Plays Companion Library, Manchester, 1986, II.i.163–72.

10 *The Witch*, II.i.168. The play is notorious for its Scottish connections. For Middleton's songs in the Hecate scenes of *Macbeth*, see *Macbeth*, ed. by Kenneth Muir, The Arden Edition, London, 1972, pp. xxx–xxxiii. Of interest in this context is also Middleton's indebtedness to Reginald Scot's *The Discovery of Witchcraft*. See *The Witch*, ed. Frank Sullivan, unpublished thesis, Yale University, New Haven, 1940, pp. 183–91; and Corbin and Sedge, *Three Jacobean Witchcraft Plays*, pp. 13–18.

11 A historical survey of the Englishman's attitude towards Irish, Welsh, Scottish and Cornish is provided in Richard W. Bailey, *Images of English*, pp. 17–30.

12 Picentio disguises as a French doctor in the Italian setting of the *Telltale*, Angelo in *The Wonder of a Kingdom* gives himself out as a French-speaking doctor, and Don John in Beaumont and Fletcher's *The Chances* briefly disguises as the Duke of Ferrara. Only Fabritio in Brome's *The Novella* is unsuccessful. His disguise flounders on linguistic grounds when he is confronted with the same German Swatzenburgh whom he himself tries to impersonate.

13 *Blvrt Master-Constable: or The Spaniards Night-Walke*, London, 1602, STC 17876, sigs. C1v–C2r. Given the fact that Truepenny is addressed as 'Mephostophiles', his answer may also allude to the devil's proficiency in languages.

14 Thomas Dekker, *The Shoemaker's Holiday*, ed. R. L. Smallwood and Stanley Wells, The Revels Plays, Manchester, 1979, scene 4, line 91.

15 *Blvrt Master-Constable*, sig. E2r. Compare the discussion between Eulalia and the second countryman in Richard Brome's *The Queen and Concubine*. Here, French is a language granted certain merits as a matter of course. See *The Dramatic Works of Richard Brome Containing Fifteen Comedies Now First Collected in Three Volumes*, 3 vols, London, 1873, 2, IV.iii, p. 87. At Davenant's Sicilian court in *The Platonic Lovers*, French is referred to as a 'the smoothest and most prosperous' language for courtship. The status of the French language is not challenged; the only problem is that as a man of war Gridonell only knows the soldier's terms in that tongue. See *The Platonic Lovers* in *The Dramatic Works of Sir William D'Avenant*, eds James Maidment and W. H. Logan, Edinburgh, 1872–74, vol. 2, III.i, p. 54.

16 *The Merchant of Venice*, ed. John Russell Brown, The Arden Edition, London, 1959, I.ii.65–70.

17 See among others R. V. Lindabury, *A Study of the Patriotism in the Elizabethan Drama*, Princeton, 1931, pp. 112–13.

18 *The Double Marriage*, in *The Works of Francis Beaumont and John Fletcher*, ed. Arnold Glover, 10 vols, Cambridge, 1905–12, 6 (1908), III.i, p. 360.

19 R. C. Simonini, Jr, *Italian Scholarship in Renaissance England*, University of North Carolina Studies in Comparative Literature 3, Chapel Hill, N.C., 1952, p. 94.

20 William Camden, *Remains Concerning Britain*, ed. R. D. Dunn, Toronto, 1984, p. 40, lines 10–14.

21 William Harrison, 'Of the languages spoken in this Iland', in *The English Language: Essays by English and American Men of Letters, 1490–1839*, ed. W. F. Bolton, Cambridge, 1966, p. 19.

22 John L. Lievsay, *The Elizabethan Image of Italy*, Ithaca, N.Y., 1964, p. 9.

23 See Mario Praz, 'The Italian element in English', *Essays and Studies*, 15, 1929, pp. 20–66; and Inna Koskenniemi, *Studies in the Vocabulary of English Drama, 1550–1600 (Excluding Shakespeare and Jonson)*, Turku, 1962, pp. 47–58.

24 As Praz has noted, the Italian form of address is poor Italian when used before a family name ('The Italian element', p. 24, n.1). The semantic function, however, remains uncontested.

25 *The Dramatic Works of Thomas Dekker*, ed. Fredson Bowers, 4 vols, Cambridge, 1953–61, 1 (1953), II.i.6–7.

26 *The Chances*, ed. George Walton Williams, in *The Dramatic Works in the Beaumont and Fletcher Canon*, 4 (1979), V.iii.129. In Heywood's *A Maidenhead Well Lost*, the French nationality of the tutor to the Prince of Florence is established solely by means of the form of address *Monsieur*. Ghost characters pervade Balurdo's dream in *Antonio's Revenge*. Their nationalities, too, are established by the form of address. The English page 'Master Even-as' and the French page 'Mounser Even-so' flank the native Italian 'Signior Simile [who] stalked most prodigiously in the midst'. See John Marston, *Antonio's Revenge*, ed. W. Reavley Gair, The Revels Plays, Manchester, 1978, I.iii.65–7.

27 Cyril Tourneur, *The Revenger's Tragedy*, ed. R. A. Foakes, The Revels Plays,

London, 1966, I.ii.57.

28 See, for example, Maurice Abiteboul, 'L'Italie dans l'imaginaire de trois
    dramaturges jacobéens: Tourneur, Webster et Middleton', in L'Angleterre et
    le monde méditerranéen, Centre Aixois de Recherches Anglaises 7, Aix–en–
    Provence, 1989, pp. 1–10.

29 The Selected Plays of John Ford: 'The Broken Heart', "Tis Pity She's a Whore',
    'Perkin Warbeck', ed. Colin Gibson, Cambridge, 1986, IV.iii.59 and IV.iii.63.
    Song proved an opportune non-dialogic occasion to employ Italian without
    the need for a translation. In Chapman's The Gentleman Usher, Bassiolo
    sings a song with an Italian refrain. See The Plays of George Chapman: the
    Comedies, 2, pp. 289–90. In case of need, a translation was provided for
    longer stretches of Italian, as with the challenger's motto in The Partial
    Law. See The Partial Law, a Tragi-Comedy, ed. Bertram Dobell, London,
    1908, p. 19.

30 The Nice Valour, ed. George Walton Williams, in The Dramatic Works in the
    Beaumont and Fletcher Canon, 7 (1989), IV.i.272–3. Also in The Lady's Trial
    Ford bridges an assumed language barrier by providing a running
    translation of Guzman's utterances. See 'A critical, modern-spelling edition
    of John Ford's "The Lady's Trial"', ed. Katsuhiko Nogami, unpublished
    Ph.D. dissertation, The Shakespeare Institute, Birmingham, 1989,
    IV.ii.125–45.

31 John Marston, The Malcontent, ed. Bernard Harris, The New Mermaids,
    London, 1967, I.iii.71–3.

32 Women Pleased, ed. Hans Walter Gabler, in The Dramatic Works in the
    Beaumont and Fletcher Canon, 5 (1982), II.vi.2.

33 The Taming of the Shrew, ed. Brian Morris, The Arden Shakespeare,
    London, 1981, I.ii.23–6.

34 Annegret Staufer, Fremdsprachen bei Shakespeare, pp. 78–9.

35 The Taming of the Shrew, ed. G. R. Hibbard, New Penguin Shakespeare,
    Harmondsworth, 1968, p. 189.

36 T. S. Eliot, 'John Marston', in Elizabethan Dramatists, London, 1963, p. 156.

37 The Selected Plays of John Marston: 'Antonio and Mellida', 'Antonio's Revenge',
    'The Malcontent', 'The Dutch Courtesan', 'Sophonisba', eds Macdonald P.
    Jackson and Michael Neill, Cambridge, 1986, IV.i.209–11.

38 John Marston, Antonio and Mellida: the First Part, ed. G. K. Hunter, London,
    1965, p. xx.

39 Philip J. Finkelpearl accounts for the couple's Italian on the grounds of
    decorum, arguing that 'English is apparently too gross a language to
    indicate the depth of their emotion' (John Marston of the Middle Temple: an
    Elizabethan Dramatist in his Social Setting, Cambridge, Mass., 1969, pp. 143–
    4). This fails to account for Piero's distracted reversion to Italian. See also
    Michael Scott, John Marston's Plays: Theme, Structure and Performance,
    London, 1978, pp. 77–81. On the use of the Babel theme underlying such
    language usage in the play, see my 'Reconstructing Babel in English
    Renaissance drama: William Haughton's Englishmen for My Money and John
    Marston's Antonio and Mellida', Neophilologus, 76, 1992 , pp. 464–79.

40 A Pleasant Comedy, called A Mayden-Head Well Lost, London, 1634, STC
    13357, sig. G1v.

41 *The Wit of a Woman, 1604*, ed. W. W. Greg, Malone Society Reprints, Oxford, 1913, lines 1547–8.

42 *The Wonder of a Kingdom*, in *The Dramatic Works of Thomas Dekker*, 3 (1958), III.ii.62–3.

43 *The Novella*, in *The Dramatic Works of Richard Brome*, 1, p. 169.

44 John Webster, *The White Devil*, ed. John Russell Brown, The Revels Plays, London, 1960, III.ii.13.

45 *The White Devil*, III.ii.15–17. See also Dena Goldberg, "'By report': the spectator as voyeur in Webster's *The White Devil*', *English Literary Renaissance*, 17, 1987 , p. 71.

46 *Loues Sacrifice: a Tragedie*, London, 1633, *STC* 11164, sig. G2v. Comparable examples may be found in Shirley's *The Traitor* where Sciarrha advises his sister Amidea to develop an affection for Lorenzo with the words: 'in plain Italian, Love him' (*The Dramatic Works and Poems of James Shirley*, 2, II.i, p. 118).

47 *The Plays of George Chapman: the Comedies*, 2, II.i.567–79.

48 Richard Mulcaster, *The First Part of the Elementarie VVhich Entreateth Chefelie of the Right Writing of Our English Tung*, English Linguistics, 1500–1900, 219, Menston, 1970, p. 256.

49 Samuel Daniel, *Poems and a Defence of Ryme*, ed. A. C. Sprague, London, 1950, p. 96. A stimulating reading of the language concerns in *The Tempest* seen partly in the light of Daniel's verse continues to be Terence Hawkes, '*The Tempest*: speaking your language', in *Shakespeare's Talking Animals: Language and Drama in Society*, London, 1973, pp. 194–212.

50 *A Knack to Know an Honest Man*, Malone Society Reprints, Oxford, 1910, lines 393–4.

51 *The Gentleman Usher*, in *The Plays of George Chapman: the Comedies*, 2, II.i.126–8.

52 Richard Hosley, *A Critical Edition of Anthony Munday's 'Fedele and Fortunio'*, New York, 1981, II.i.46.

53 *Sixteenth-Century English Prose*, ed. Karl J. Holzknecht, New York, 1954, p. 36.

54 *The Romane Historie Written by T. Livivs of Padva.* [...] *Translated out of Latine into English, by Philemon Holland, Doctor in Physicke*, London, 1600, *STC* 16613, sig. A2r.

55 Quoted in M. T. Jones-Davies, *Un Peintre de la vie londonienne: Thomas Dekker (circa 1572–1632)*, 2 vols, Collection des Études Anglaises 6, Paris, 1958, 2, p. 213. For further examples, see R. F. Jones, *The Triumph of the English Language: a Survey of Opinions Concerning the Vernacular from the Introduction of Printing to the Restoration*, Stanford, Calif., 1952, pp. 168–213.

56 Thomas Heywood, *An Apology for Actors*, ed. Richard H. Perkinson, New York, 1941, fol. 3.

57 See Richard Helgerson, 'The kingdom of our own language', in *Forms of Nationhood: the Elizabethan Writing of England*, Chicago, 1992, pp. 1–18.

58 Lewis Machin, *The dumbe Knight: a historicall Comedy*, London, 1608, *STC* 17398, sig. F1r.

59 Quoted in Steven Mullaney, *The Place of the Stage: License, Play and Power in Renaissance England*, Chicago, 1988, p. 75.

Afterword

17

Shakespeare and Italy, or, the law of diminishing returns

Manfred Pfister

There is a genre of books and articles about Shakespeare that could be identified as the 'Shakespeare and ...' variety. Shakespeare and Montaigne, Shakespeare and music, Shakespeare and melancholy, Shakespeare and medicine. What tends to be problematic about this conjunctive genre is that in such studies one often learns much about the second term and very little about the first, that is about Shakespeare and his work. The 'Shakespeare and Italy' sub-variety so popular with German, American and Italian scholars for more than a century bears this out, as do the two most recent book-length studies, both written by American scholars, Murray J. Levith's *Shakespeare's Italian Settings and Plays*, and David C. McPherson's *Shakespeare, Jonson, and the Myth of Venice.*[1]

These works sift and compile what is to be known about the Elizabethans' knowledge of Italy, its sources and modes of transmission, the established facts and the fantasies, and no one but the few specialists in the field will not learn a good deal from them. For all the wealth of interesting material such studies present, the problem begins when they turn to the plays. Levith, arranging the relevant plays geographically – from the Veneto to the inland localities – does not manage to provide more than a variety of main stream readings of the plays. The wealth of historical information is not brought to fruition in these interpretations. The heuristic potential is not turned into a hermeneutic *Mehrwert* that would create new perceptions of the plays. It remains arrested in the historical limbo of 'background' and 'context' material, good enough to proffer the occasional gloss or improve upon extant annotations, but incapable of generating new interpretations.

Something similar applies to McPherson's monograph. His

account of Shakespeare's and Jonson's sources for the *matière vénitienne* and of the myth of Venice – Venice the Rich, Venice the Wise, Venice the Just, *Venetia città galante* – is more substantial than any given so far, and yet his interpretations of *The Merchant of Venice, Othello* and *Volpone* derive their most revealing and pertinent insights not from this material but from other considerations. The attempt to read the plot of *The Merchant of Venice* in terms of a 'Turn Landward' (pp. 56–61) in Venetian social economy, a turn from sea-trade to landowning, remains mainly guesswork and adds less to our understanding of Portia and Bassanio than the author claims. However, to read *Volpone* in the light of Jonson's dictum in the *Discoveries* – namely that 'our whole life is like a *Play*: wherein every man, forgetfull of himselfe, is in travaile with expression of another' and where 'wee so insist in imitating others, as wee cannot (when it is necessary) returne to our selves' (p. 92) – puts Volpone's late Roman histrionics into an incisively original perspective, which is only marginally indebted to the myth of Venice. Part of this myth, to be sure, was the idea of a *translatio imperii* from ancient Rome to Renaissance Venice (p. 94f.), but what contemporary Italian and British writers saw as being transferred from Rome to Venice were values such as wisdom, fortitude and justice as opposed to a sophisticated hedonism and its attendant theatricality.

The Shakespeare-and-Italy line of research appears to be a case of the law of diminishing returns. The more information scholars gather together concerning Renaissance Italy and the Elizabethan awareness of Italy, the less this knowledge increase yields new insights into the plays of Shakespeare and his contemporaries. How has this come about? What, if anything, has gone wrong? To answer these questions, I shall first try to reconstruct the history of the research into Shakespeare's Italian connection, consider what kinds of interest have directed it, and which problems it has tried to solve.

The first paradigm of research was strictly positivistic. It was part of the nineteenth-century attempt to explain Shakespeare's work in terms of the sources it drew upon, and to establish a factual basis for the biography of its author. Typical examples of this kind are the 'Italienische Skizzen zu Shakespeare' drawn by Theodore Elze during an extended stay in Venice.[2] These sketches, a series of scattered observations and annotations rather than a coherent argument, compare Shakespeare's Italian plays with their Italian sources, Italian geography and cultural history. The main thrust of his observations is to find correspondences between Italian fact and English fiction. For example he identifies Portia's Belmont as a villa near Dolo on the Brenta and Dr Bellario as the famous Paduan professor of law, Ottonello Discalzio.[3] Also, he proves, at least to his own satisfaction, that Desdemona is blond like Portia, their blondness reflecting the new ideal of beauty set up by Venetian painters of the sixteenth century such as Titian, Giorgione or Veronese, and that Prospero's island can be none other than Pantelleria. Where fact and fiction do not seem to tally, he goes out of his way to prove that Shakespeare did not blunder. One of the Italian 'coasts of Bohemia' is, for instance, that of Padua in fruitful Lombardy rather than the Veneto. Elze tries to account for this in terms of a wider definition of Lombardy current in the sixteenth century.[4] Aesthetic considerations of the theatrical medium or of genre are rigorously shunned in this kind of research and even the distinction between fact and fiction is disregarded. What is at stake, rather, is the extent of Shakespeare's knowledge of Italy and how he came by it. With questions such as these it becomes evident that a narrow positivistic framework, short-circuiting fact and fiction and disregarding conventions of fictionality, theatrical presentation and genre, cannot provide satisfactory answers. The problem with this approach is not only that it has not led to any conclusive results but that it has long prevented the pursuit of more incisive lines of inquiry.

Geistesgeschichte, or the history of ideas, has contributed a good deal towards placing Shakespeare's theatrical representations of Italy within the wider context of the Elizabethan reception of Italian Renaissance culture. Within the paradigms of 'influence' and 'reception' it has studied the one-way traffic in ideas and cultural informations between Italy and England, focusing on intercultural transactions such as travel writing,[5] the mediating work of Italians in England,[6] and translations and adaptations of historiographical, philosophical and literary texts.[7] Within the field of literature a number of traditions and a few individual authors have received particular attention: Petrarch and the sonnets, the epic of chivalry and the *novella*, the *commedia dell'arte* and *commedia erudita*, pastoral and tragicomedy, historiography and poetics, courtesy books and the art of *conversazione*, the political ideas of Machiavelli, and the satire and eroticism of Aretino.

Owing to this kind of historical scholarship we have a fairly clear and detailed picture of what was variously called 'Shakespeare's Italy' or the 'Elizabethan image of Italy'.[8] Or, to be more precise, one should speak of – at least – two Elizabethan images of Italy co-existing and confronting one another. One image is that of the humanists, an image of Italy as the original home of classical antiquity and the cradle of a rich and sophisticated Renaissance culture; an Italy of ancient monuments and of libraries and art collections, of academies and universities, in which a new discourse about the dignity and the infinite possibilities of man is evolved from ancient philosophy and literature; an Italy of villas and courts, where social life and self-fashioning are refined into the elaborate rituals of *cortesia* and *sprezzatura*. The other image is that of militant Protestantism, in which Italy appears as the seat of the Papal Whore of Babylon, whose poisonous influence breeds idolatry and atheism, a decadence of the senses and the most sophisticated vices, Machiavellian policy and devilish crimes. Often these two images co-exist within the work of one and the same author, even within one and the same text. Roger Ascham and Thomas Nashe are examples of this. Ascham, though deeply indebted to Italian Renaissance humanism and in particular to Castiglione's *Cortegiano*, yet warns young Englishmen in the most forceful terms against exposing themselves to the 'Siren songs of Italy'.[9] And Nashe's unfortunate traveller experiences Italy in similarly ambivalent terms as both a place of pilgrimage for Petrarchan lovers and a school for 'the art of atheism, the art of epicurising, the art of whoring, the art of poisoning, the art of sodomitry'.[10]

The study of literary and cultural influences and of *Geistesgeschichte* has thus been transformed over the last few decades into a kind of historical 'imagology', applied to the hetero-stereotypes controlling the perception and representation of Italy in early modern England. Its heuristic value for the study of Elizabethan and Jacobean drama has been considerable: individual playwrights and individual plays can now be compared and contrasted in terms of their selection from the range of images available, and in terms of their fulfilling or defeating the concomitant stereotyped expectations. Thus, it has been rightly emphasised by Mario Praz to what unusual degree Shakespeare's plays with Italian settings are free from the Italianate horrors and the moral monstrosities which characterise the Italian plays of Marston, Webster, Tourneur, Massinger, Ford, and others. Where his analysis falls short is, however, in acknowledging the existence of the opposite stereotype of a courtly, pastoral and humanist Italy, operative particularly in non-tragic genres. And Shakespeare's Italian plays are in fact all comedies, with the sole exceptions of *Romeo and Juliet* and *Othello*. In this sense, the representation of Italy in Shakespeare's plays is not disruptive of the stereotyped image: it follows a different stereotype.[11]

But where does one go from here? How can one go beyond describing these stereotypes in ever more detail, and studying them in ever more plays of the period – again with gradually diminishing returns? One way might be to analyse more closely the status and functions of these stereotypes and images. The paradigms of influence and reception suggest too one-directional a model and do not sufficiently take into account the *constructedness* of the stereotypes. What is at stake is not simply images of Italy, reflecting Italian reality, but constructions of Italy reflecting at least as much the interests, needs and anxieties of the English themselves. Walter Cohen, arguing from a Marxist perspective, has gone a long way towards elucidating this dialectic with reference to *The Merchant of Venice*: 'in *The Merchant of Venice* English history evokes fears of capitalism, and Italian history allays these fears. One is the problem, the other the solution, the act of incorporation, of transcendence, toward which the play strives.'[12] The dialectic at work here is one of auto- and hetero-stereotypes: the construction of the Other is always at one and the same time a construction of oneself, and vice versa. And Elizabethan culture was as much created by its contacts with Italian culture as it, in turn, created its own Italy, or rather its own Italies.

Preoccupied with the sources and the factual correctness or incorrectness of Shakespeare's Italian topography and with the Italian literary and intellectual influences upon him, Shakespeare criticism has dedicated little time to studying the dramaturgy and the dramatic functions of the Italian locations in his plays and in those of his contemporaries. If the positivistic scholars of the nineteenth and the early twentieth centuries considered the theatrical dimension in this context at all, their concern was with costume and sets rather than dramatic structure and the dramatic functions of space. A key term in this context was 'local colour', and Shakespeare came to be celebrated as an early master of local colour to be surpassed only by Ben Jonson.[13] The pictorial metaphor in itself, on which this concept is based, makes it sufficiently clear that it does not address itself to the dramatic structures and functions of localisation, but to a very narrow aspect of verbal and visual suggestiveness. To create the illusion of an Italian setting through a few carefully chosen details and particularities was seen very much as an art for art's sake, detached from the wider thematic concerns of the play and contributing only to the persuasiveness of the theatrical illusion. Any local references that are factually incorrect or do not fit into the Italian picture came to be regarded as signs of Shakespeare's ignorance or carelessness, and his Italian plays in general were described as showing 'a strange mixture of ignorance and knowledge – perhaps the natural consequence of an education largely self-acquired'.[14] The 'local colour' critics tended to read these plays as if they proclaimed one thing only: 'Our scene is Italy.' Actually, however, their scene is England almost as much as Italy, as they carefully mingle English and Italian local colour. Or, to put it less metaphorically, they superimpose the spatial context of the performance – the theatre and the London and England of performers and audience – with that of the fictional Italian setting. This, however, was either disregarded or frowned upon as an inconsistency, rather than appreciated and explored in its creative potential of negotiating the values of the self and the other.

Such an exploration would have to go beyond the frequent attempts to read Shakespeare's Italy as a mirror of Elizabethan policy, to construe allegorical equations between fictional plots and current politics, or to regard the Italy of these plays 'as metaphor for Shakespeare's England'.[15] Starting perhaps from Robert Weimann's analysis of the spatial dialectic of *locus* and *platea* in Shakespeare and the popular theatre of his time,[16] one would have to study how the construction of the fictional other, the other place, is foregrounded in the theatrical representation itself and what purposes this serves.

The underlying opposition of England and Italy, in Shakespeare's plays inscribed into the disruptive heterogeneity of the theatrical space and in Jonson's *Volpone* made explicit in the English travellers' sub-plot, provides a spatialised model for basic and culture-specific value oppositions constructed across (border) lines such as northern *versus* Mediterranean, Protestant versus Catholic, nature versus artifice, authenticity versus sophistication, plebeian versus middle class versus aristocratic, land versus trade, country versus city, male versus female, etc. etc.[17] And the underlying cross-cultural oppositions between England and Italy, between the site of performance and the sights arranged in the fiction, are modulated and varied in the smaller-scale spatial oppositions set up within the plays.

The important question, therefore, is not how Shakespeare's Venice and Shakespeare's Belmont relate to the topographical reality of the sixteenth century, but how they relate to each other as two different English constructions of Italy.[18] What would also have to be taken into account in such an analysis is genre, the genre-specific constructions of Italy that often criss-cross each other in a single play. There are comic, tragic, pastoral, romance, satirical or heroic constructions of Italy, and there are, moreover, the Italies of political, religious, philosophical and topographical discourses, each drawing upon its own traditions, each with its own commonplaces available for the constructions of this other place. And finally, Italy was not the only projection screen for Elizabethan fantasies of otherness. There were, most notably, the New Worlds beyond the Atlantic, and the Mediterranean and the Transatlantic were conflated in many ways that further need to be traced. The Americas, bearing an Italian name, intuited by Florentine cartographers and first 'discovered' by an Italian in Spanish services, were to English adventurers and colonists not only a place of encounter with savage aborigines, but also with Mediterranean Catholicism. And, on the other hand, turning from history – or faction – to fictions, Prospero's island is at one and the same time Mediterranean and Transatlantic, an island between Naples and Tripolis and one of the far Bermudas.[19]

Clearly, the New Historicism has not yet visited Shakespeare's and the Elizabethans' Italy. It might, in many different ways, along with the proposals of the present volume, contribute towards breaking the law of diminishing returns.

Notes

1 Murray J. Levith, *Shakespeare's Italian Settings and Plays*, London, 1989; David C. McPherson, *Shakespeare, Jonson, and the Myth of Venice*, Newark, 1990.

2 Theodore Elze, *Shakespeare Jahrbuch*, 13, 1878, pp. 137–57; 14, 1879, pp. 156–79; 15, 1880, pp. 230–65; these articles were later included in his *Venezianische Skizzen zu Shakespeare*, Munich, 1899.

3 *Shakespeare Jahrbuch*, 13, 1878, pp. 142–5, and pp. 149–52.

4 *Shakespeare Jahrbuch*, 15, 1880, 231f. Other notorious Italian 'coasts of Bohemia', which continue to be pointed out as geographical blunders or, respectively, to be explained away with the help of historical information, are Valentine's voyage by boat from Verona to Milan in *The Two Gentlemen of Verona* and Milan's location at or near the sea in *The Tempest*. Cf. John W. Draper, 'Shakespeare and the Lombard cities', *Rivista di Letteratura Moderne*

e Comparate, 4, 1953, pp. 54–8, arguing for Shakespeare's ignorance in these matters, and Edward Sullivan, 'Shakespeare and the waterways of northern Italy', *The Nineteenth Century*, 64, 1908, trying to prove that these alleged blunders are not blunders at all but demonstrate Shakespeare's intimate familiarity with all things northern Italian.

5   Cf., for instance, John Stoye, *English Travellers Abroad*, 1604–1667, London, 1952; revised ed. New Haven, and London 1989, chap. 2; George B. Parks, *The English Traveler to Italy*, Rome, 1954; Kenneth R. Bartlett, 'The strangeness of strangers: English impressions of Italy in the sixteenth century', *Quaderni d'italianistica*, 1, 1980, 46–63; Attilio Brilli, *Il viaggio in Italia*, Milan, 1987; Manfred Pfister, '"The fatal gift of beauty:" das Italien britischer Reisender', in *Reisen in den Mittelmeerraum*, ed. Hermann H. Wetzel, Passau, 1991, pp. 55–101, pp. 67–76).

6   Cf. Frances Yates, *John Florio*, Cambridge, 1934.

7   Cf. the recent reassessment in G. H. McWilliam, *Shakespeare's Italy Revisited*, Leicester, 1974. The title harps back to Mario Praz's 'Shakespeare's Italy' in *The Flaming Heart*, New York, 1958, pp. 146–67; and in M. Praz, 'Italy', in *A Shakespeare Encyclopaedia*, eds O. J. Campbell and E. G. Quinn, London, 1966, pp. 388–93.

8   John Lievsay, *The Elizabethan Image of Italy*, Folger Shakespeare Library Publications, Ithaca, N.Y., 1964.

9   *The Whole Works of Roger Ascham*, ed. D. Giles, 3 vols, London, 18664, 3, p. 152.

10 *The Unfortunate Traveller and Other Works*, ed. J. B. Steane, Harmondsworth, 1972, p. 289.

11 Mario Praz, 'Shakespeare's Italy', pp. 147f. Following this generic line of argument, one could regard Italian proper names in Elizabethan drama as markers of genre, indicating either romantic comedy or revenge tragedy. The half score of Italian names in *Hamlet*, strangely out of place in Denmark, could thus be seen as a way of foregrounding the play's generic status as a revenge tragedy, traditionally set in Mediterranean countries.

12 Walter Cohen, '*The Merchant of Venice* and the possibilities of historical criticism', ELH, 49, 1982, 765–89 (p. 772).

13 Cf., for instance, John W. Draper, 'Some details of Italian local colour in *Othello*', *Shakespeare Jahrbuch*, 68, 1932, pp. 125–7.

14 John W. Draper, *ibid.*, p. 127.

15 See Murray J. Levith, *Shakespeare's Italian Settings and Plays*, p. 11. How arbitrary such equations can be is demonstrated in Levith's interpretation of *The Tempest*, where, within one and the same paragraph, both the island and the Italian mainland are seen 'as a convenient metaphor for England' (p. 86).

16 Robert Weimann, *Shakespeare und die Tradition des Volkstheaters. Soziologie, Dramaturgie, Gestaltung*, Berlin, 1967.

17 My suggestion is, of course, based on the semiotic model of Juri M. Lotman, *Die Struktur literarischer Texte*, transl. by R.-D. Keil, Munich, 1972, p. 330.

18 Catherine Belsey in 'Love in Venice', *Shakespeare Survey*, 44, 1991, pp. 41–53, has gone some way towards putting such questions in a historical perspective far-ranging enough to include our present-day problematic.

19 A first step in this direction, correlating a variety of Elizabethan experiences of otherness or foreignness, can be found in George K. Hunter, 'Elizabethans and foreigners', *Shakespeare Survey*, 17, 1964, reprinted in George K. Hunter, *Dramatic Identities and Cultural Tradition: Studies in Shakespeare and his Contemporaries*, Liverpool, 1978, pp. 3–30.

Bibliography

compiled by Michele Marrapodi
and A. J. Hoenselaars

We would like to point out that the following is a bibliography of secondary sources. We have chosen to make no reference at all to any of the plays, nor to the various pamphlets, diaries, and travellers' reports concerning the subject-matter. The same applies to the numberless treatises, journals, dictionaries, sayings and proverbs of the age which directly or indirectly refer to Italy and its inhabitants. Most of these works are frequently listed in any critical approach to this topic. But the real reason for not having taken into account these entries, apart from the limited space available, lies in the fact that we are not reconstructing the Renaissance image of Italy in the Elizabethans' imagination but are concerned with location, with its idea and function in the construction and general design of Renaissance drama. Our major emphasis is therefore on those critical works which treat the problem at issue, or some aspects of it, and particularly on those which privilege the Italian setting and/or discuss its presence as a structural element of the text. A few seminal works regarding issues of influence, cultural tradition, intertextuality, and dramatic genres are however listed.

The reader interested in all the plays will find a useful guide in E. H. Sugden's *A Topographical Dictionary to the Works of Shakespeare and his Fellow Dramatists*, Manchester, 1925, and in T. L. Berger and W. C. Bradford's *An Index of Characters in English Printed Drama to the Restoration*, Englewood, Colorado, 1975. E. K. Chambers's *The Elizabethan Stage*, 4 vols, Oxford, 1923, G. E. Bentley's *The Jacobean and Caroline Stage*, 7 vols, Oxford, 1941–68, as well as W. W. Greg's *Bibliography of the English Printed Drama to the Restoration*, 4 vols, London, 1951, contain the greatest amount of information for any historically-minded reader. For this same reason, other relevant items such as John Florio's works and the huge number of Elizabethan translations of Italian *novelle*, poetry and drama are not listed in our bibliography. Whenever modern editions of Renaissance plays or works are mentioned they are listed in view of the relevance of their editor's introduction.

Abiteboul, M. 'L'Italie et l'Angleterre des Tudors: voyageurs et traducteurs', *Helios*, University of Avignon, 2, 1976, pp. 1–12.

— 'Les Rapports de l'éthique et de l'esthétique chez Cyril Tourneur, John Webster et Thomas Middleton: Trois moments de la sensibilité jacobéenne', diss. Montpellier, 1984.

— 'L'Italie dans l'imaginaire de trois dramaturges jacobéens: Tourneur, Webster et Middleton', in *L'Angleterre et le monde méditerranéen*, ed. N.-J. Rigaud, Centre Aixois de Recherches Anglaises 7, Aix-en-Provence, 1987, pp. 1–10.

Andrews, John F., ed. *William Shakespeare: His World, His Work, His Influence*, 3 vols, New York, 1985.

Andrews, Richard. *Scripts and Scenarios: the Performance of Comedy in Renaissance Italy*, Cambridge, 1993.

Ascoli, A. R. and Kahn, V., eds. *Machiavelli and the Discourse of Literature*, Ithaca, N.Y., 1993.

Auden, W. H. 'The alienated city: reflections on *Othello*', *Encounter*, August 1961, pp. 3–14.

Barish, Jonas A. 'The double plot of *Volpone*', *Modern Philology*, 51, 1953, pp. 83–92.

Bartlett, Kenneth R. 'The strangeness of strangers: English impressions of Italy in the sixteenth century', *Quaderni d'italianistica*, 1, 1980, pp. 46–63.

Barton, Anne. *Essays Mainly Shakespearean*, Cambridge, 1994.

Barton, C. A. *The Sorrows of Ancient Romans: the Gladiators and the Monster*, Princeton, 1993.

Bate, Jonathan. 'The Elizabethans in Italy', in *Travel and Drama in Shakespeare's Time*, eds J.-P. Maquerlot and M. Willems, Cambridge, 1996.

Bates, C. 'Weaving and writing in *Othello*', *Shakespeare Survey*, 46, 1994, pp. 51-60.

Bawcutt, N. W. '*The Revenger's Tragedy* and the Medici family', *Notes and Queries*, 202, 1957, pp. 192–3.

Belsey, Catherine. 'Love in Venice', *Shakespeare Survey*, 44, 1992, pp. 41–53.

Bennett, K. C. 'Reconstructing *The Winter's Tale*', *Shakespeare Survey*, 46, 1994, pp. 81-90.

Berek, Peter. 'The two Italies of *Romeo and Juliet*', *The Shakespeare Newsletter*, 35, 4, 1985, p. 42.

Berner, Samuel. 'Florentine society in the late sixteenth and early seventeenth centuries', *Studies in the Renaissance*, 18, 1971, pp. 203–46.

Berveiller, M. 'Influencias italianas en las comedias de Ben Jonson', *Filosofia y letras*, 3, 1942, pp. 51–71.

Bond, R. Warwick, ed. *Early Plays from the Italian*, Oxford, 1911.

Boughner, Daniel C. 'Lewkenor and Venice', *Notes and Queries*, 207, 1962, pp. 124–30.

Bowers, Fredson T. 'The audience and the revenger of Elizabethan tragedy', *Studies in Philology*, 21, 1934, pp. 160–75.

— 'The audience and the poisoner of Elizabethan tragedy', *Journal of English and Germanic Philology*, 36, 1937, pp. 491–504.

— *Elizabethan Revenge Tragedy 1587–1642*, Princeton, 1940.

Bradbrook, Muriel C. 'Love and courtesy in *Two Gentlemen of Verona*', in *Shakespeare a Verona e nel Veneto*, ed. Agostino Lombardo, Accademia di Agricoltura Scienze e Lettere di Verona, Verona, 1987, pp. 25–40.

— 'Courtier and courtesy: Castiglione, Lyly and Shakespeare's *Two Gentlemen of*

Verona', in *Theatre of the English and Italian Renaissance*, eds J. R. Mulryne and M. Shewring, London, 1991, pp. 161–78.

Breslow, M. A. *A Mirror of England: English Puritan Views of Foreign Nations, 1618–1640*, Harvard Historical Studies 84, Cambridge, Mass., 1970.

Bridgewater, H. '"Shakespeare" and Italy', *Baconiana*, 23, 1938, pp. 157–66.

Brockbank, Philip. *Urban Mysteries of the Renaissance: Shakespeare and Carpaccio*, International Shakespeare Association, Occasional Paper 4, Hertford, 1989.

Brustein, Robert S. 'Italianate court satire and the plays of John Marston', Ph.D. diss., Columbia University, 1957.

Bryant, J. A., Jr. 'Jonson's revision of *Every Man in His Humour*', *Studies in Philology*, 59, 1962, pp. 641–50.

Bullough, Geoffrey, ed. *Narrative and Dramatic Sources of Shakespeare*, 8 vols, London, 1957–73.

Bulman, J. C., ed. *Shakespeare, Theory, and Performance*, London, 1966.

Burke, P. *The Fortunes of the Courtier. The European Reception of Castiglione's Cortegiano*, Cambridge, 1995.

Butler, Martin. *Theatre and Crisis, 1632–1642*, Cambridge, 1984.

Caliumi, Grazia, ed. *Shakespeare e la sua eredità*, Parma, 1993.

Cantor, Paul A. *Shakespeare's Rome: Republic and Empire*, Ithaca, N.Y., 1976.

Capocci, Valentina. *Genio e mestiere: Shakespeare e la commedia dell'arte*, Bari, 1950.

Cappuzzo, Marcello. *Milton e la Sicilia*, Palermo, 1987.

— 'Shakespeare e la Sicilia: appunti per una ricerca', in *Viaggio nel Sud*, eds Emanuele Kanceff and Roberta Rampone, Biblioteca del Viaggio in Italia 36, Geneva, 1991, pp. 283–90.

Caputi, Anthony. *John Marston, Satirist*, Ithaca, N.Y., 1961.

Cawley, R. R. *Unpathed Waters: Studies in the Influence of the Voyagers on Elizabethan Literature*, Princeton, 1940.

Chojnacki, Stanley. 'Patrician women in early Renaissance Venice', *Studies in the Renaissance*, 21, 1974, pp. 176–203.

Clark, Cumberland. *Shakespeare and National Character: a Study of Shakespeare's Knowledge and Dramatic and Literary Use of the Distinctive Racial Characteristics of the Different Peoples of the World*, London, 1932.

Clubb, Louise George. *Italian Drama in Shakespeare's Time*, New Haven and London, 1989.

— 'Il teatro manieristico italiano e Shakespeare', in *Cultura e Società nel rinascimento fra riforme e manierismi*, eds Vittore Branca and Carlo Ossola, Florence, 1984, pp. 427–48.

Cohen, Ralph. 'The setting of *Volpone'*, *Renaissance Papers*, spring 1978, pp. 65–75.

Cohen, Walter. '*The Merchant of Venice* and the possibilities of historical criticism', *ELH*, 49, 1982, pp. 765–89.

Colafelice, Franco L. 'Shakespeare in Italia', *Insegnare*, 8, 1953, pp. 25–30.

Colognesi, S. and Tosi, F. 'Shakespeare e la Puglia', *Studi Inglesi*, 1, 1974.

Colombo, Rosa Maria. 'Venezia nel *Volpone* e nell'*Othello'*, in *Shakespeare e Jonson: il teatro elisabettiano oggi*, ed. Agostino Lombardo, Collana del teatro di Roma 8, Rome, 1979, pp. 95–111.

Corti, Claudia. 'Shakespeare e i luoghi storici: spazio della drammatizzazione/ drammatizzazione dello spazio', *Anglistica: Annali Istituto Universitario Orientale*, 30, 1–2, 1987, pp. 1–28.

Cox, V. *The Renaissance Dialogue: Literary Dialogue in its Social and Political Context*, Cambridge, 1992.

Creaser, John W., ed. *Volpone, or The Fox*, The London Mediaeval and Renaissance Series, London, 1978.

Crewe, J. V. 'Death in Venice: a study of *Othello* and *Volpone*', University of Capetown Studies in English, 4, 1973, pp. 17–29.

Cross, G. 'The retrograde genius of John Marston', *Review of English Literature*, II, 1961, pp. 19–27.

Cunliffe, J. W., 'The influence of Italian on Elizabethan drama', *Modern Philology*, IV, 1904, pp. 597–604.

Dasenbrock, Reed W. *Imitating the Italians: Wyatt, Spenser, Synge, Pound, Joyce*, Baltimore and London, 1991.

Davidson, Clifford. 'Doctor Faustus at Rome', *Studies in English Literature*, 9, 1969, pp. 231–9.

Dessen, Alan C. 'The logic of "place" and locale', in *Elizabethan Stage Conventions and Modern Interpreters*, Cambridge, 1984, pp. 84–104.

Donaldson, Ian. 'Jonson's Italy: *Volpone* and Fr. Thomas Wright', *Notes and Queries*, n.s. 19, 1972, pp. 450–2.

Draper, John W. 'Some details of local colour in *Othello*', *Shakespeare Jahrbuch*, 68, 1932, pp. 125–7.

— 'Shakespeare and Florence and the Florentines', *Italica*, 23, 1946, pp. 287–93.

— 'Shakespeare and the doge of Venice', *Journal of English and Germanic Philology*, 46, 1947, pp. 75–81.

— 'Shakespeare and the Lombard cities', *Rivista di Letterature Moderne e Comparate*, n.s. 4, 1953, pp. 54–8.

— *The 'Othello' of Shakespeare's Audience*, Paris, 1952; rpt New York, 1966.

Ducharte, Pierre Louis. *The Italian Comedy*, trans. Randolph T. Weaver, New York, 1966.

Eckhardt, Edouard. *Die Dialekt- und Ausländertypen des älteren Englischen Dramas*, Materialien zur Kunde des älteren Englischen Dramas nos. 27 and 32, Louvain, 1910–11.

Einstein, Lewis. *The Italian Renaissance in England*, New York, 1903.

Elze, Karl. *Essays on Shakespeare*, trans. L. D. Schmitz, London, 1874.

Elze, Theodore. *Venezianische Skizzen zu Shakespeare*, Munich, 1899.

Farinelle, Arturo. 'La vision de Italia en la obra de Shakespeare', *La Nación*, Buenos Aires, 9 and 16 July 1939.

— 'Shakespeares Italien: eine Festrede', *Shakespeare Jahrbuch*, 75 [= n.s. 16], 1939, pp. 16–35.

Fellheimer, Jeannette. 'The Englishman's conception of the Italian in the age of Shakespeare', thesis, London University, 1935.

— 'The section on Italy in the Elizabethan translations of Giovanni Botero's *Relationi universali*', *English Miscellany: a Symposium of History, Literature and the Arts*, 8, 1957, pp. 289–306.

— 'The "subtlety" of the Italians', *English Miscellany: a Symposium of History, Literature and the Arts*, 12, 1961, pp. 21–31.

Ferber, Michael. 'The ideology of *The Merchant of Venice*', *English Literary Renaissance*, 20, 3, 1990, pp. 431–64.

Fiedler, Leslie. 'The Jew as stranger: or, "These be the Christian husbands"', in

The Stranger in Shakespeare, New York, 1972, pp. 85–136.

Foster, Verna. "'Tis Pity She's a Whore as city tragedy', in *John Ford: Critical Re-Visions*, ed. Michael Neill, Cambridge, 1988, pp. 181–200.

Frank, Thomas. 'Elizabethan travellers in Rome', *English Miscellany: a Symposium of History, Literature and the Arts*, 4, 1953, pp. 95–132.

Gaeta, Franco. 'Alcune considerazioni sul mito di Venezia', *Bibliothèque d'humanisme et Renaissance*, 23, 1961, pp. 58–75.

Gardette, R. 'Les Amants de Venise, ou le second retour des argonautes: du mythe à sa représentation', in *'Le Merchand de Venise' et 'Le Juif de Malte': Texte et représentations*, eds Michèle Willems, Jean Pierre Maquerlot and Raymond Willems, Publications de l'Université de Rouen 100, Rouen, 1985, pp. 99–110.

Gaunglett, M. 'Playing on the margins: theatrical space in Othello', *Essays in Theatre*, 10, 1991-92, pp. 17–29.

Gentili, Vanna. *La Roma antica degli elisabettiani*, Bologna, 1991.

Gianakaras, G. J. 'Jonson's use of "Avocatori" in *Volpone*', *English Language Notes*, 12, 1974, pp. 8–14.

Gigliucci, R. *Lo spettacolo della morte*, Anzio, 1994.

Gilbert, Felix. *Machiavelli and Guicciardini: Politics and History in Sixteenth-Century Florence*, Princeton, 1965.

Gillies, John. *Shakespeare and the Geography of Difference*, Cambridge, 1994.

Greenblatt, Stephen J. 'The false ending in *Volpone*', *Journal of English and Germanic Philology*, 75, 1976, pp. 90–104.

Greg, W. W. *Pastoral Poetry and Pastoral Drama: a Literary Inquiry, with Special Reference to the Pre-Restoration Stage in England*, London, 1906.

Grillo, Ernesto. *Shakespeare and Italy*, Glasgow, 1949.

Gurr, Andrew. 'Shakespeare's localities', in *Shakespeare a Verona e nel Veneto*, ed. Agostino Lombardo, Accademia di Agricoltura Scienze e Lettere di Verona, Verona, 1987, pp. 55–66.

Hale, J. R. *England and the Italian Renaissance: the Growth of Interest in Its History and Art*, London, 1954.

— *Machiavelli and Renaissance Italy*, London, 1961.

— ed. *Renaissance Venice*, London, 1973.

Hamlin, W. M. *The Image of America in Montaigne, Spenser, and Shakespeare*, London, 1995.

Hattaway, M., Sokolova, B. and Roper, D., eds. *Shakespeare in the New Europe*, Sheffield, 1995.

Hendricks, Margo. '"The Moor of Venice", or the Italian on the Renaissance English stage', in *Shakespearean Tragedy and Gender*, eds S. N. Garner and M. Sprengnether, Bloomington,1996.

Hodge, Nancy Elizabeth. 'Shakespeare's merchant and his Venice: setting Antonio to scale in his proper world', diss., Vanderbilt University, 1984.

Hoenselaars, A. J. 'Broken images of Englishmen and foreigners in English Renaissance drama', *Germanisch-Romanische Monatsschrift*, n.s. 41, 2, 1991, pp. 153–73.

— *Images of Englishmen and Foreigners in the Drama of Shakespeare and his Contemporaries: a Study of Stage Characters and National Identity in English Renaissance Drama, 1558–1642*, Rutherford, N.J., 1992.

— Europe staged in English Renaissance Drama', *Yearbook of European Studies*, 6, 1993, pp. 85-112.

— ed. *Reclamations of Shakespeare*, Amsterdam and Atlanta, 1994.

Howard, Clare. *English Travellers of the Renaissance*, London, 1914.

Hunter, G. K. 'Elizabethans and foreigners', in *Dramatic Identities and Cultural Tradition: Studies in Shakespeare and his Contemporaries*, English Texts and Studies, Liverpool, 1978, pp. 3–30.

— 'English folly and Italian vice: the moral landscape of John Marston', in *Dramatic Identities and Cultural Tradition: Studies in Shakespeare and his Contemporaries*, English Texts and Studies, Liverpool, 1978, pp. 103–21; originally published in Jacobean Theatre, eds J. R. Brown and B. Harris, Stratford-upon-Avon Studies 1, London, 1960, pp. 85–111.

— 'Italian tragicomedy on the English stage', *Renaissance Drama*, n.s. 6, 1973, pp. 123–48.

Jeffery, Violet M. 'Shakespeare's Venice', *Modern Language Review*, 27, 1932, pp. 24–35.

Johnson, D. *Shakespeare and South Africa*, Oxford, 1996.

Jones, Ann Rosalind. 'Italians and others: Venice and the Irish in *Coryat's Crudities* and *The White Devil*', *Renaissance Drama*, n.s. 18, 1987, pp. 101–19.

— 'Italian and others', in *Staging the Renaissance: Reinterpretations of Elizabethan and Jacobean Drama*, 'eds D. Kastan and P. Stallybrass, New York and London, 1991.

Jones, Robert C. 'Italian settings and the "world" of Elizabethan tragedy', *Studies in English Literature, 1500–1900*, 10, 2, 1970, pp. 251–68.

Jones-Davies, M.-T., ed. *L'Image de Venise au temps de la Renaissance*, *SIRIR*, 14, Paris, 1989.

Joughin, J. J. *Shakespeare and National Culture*, Manchester, 1993.

Kahn, V. *Machiavellian Rhetoric: from the Counter-Reformation to Milton*, Princeton, 1994.

Kawachi, Y. *Shakespeare and Cultural Exchange*, Seibido, 1995.

Keates, Jonathan. *Italian Journeys*, London, 1991.

Kirkpatrick, Robin. *English and Italian Literature from Dante to Shakespeare: a Study of Source, Analogue and Divergence*, London, 1995.

Kishi, T., Pringle, R. and Wells, S., eds. *Shakespeare and Cultural Traditions. The Selected Proceedings of the International Shakespeare Associaton World Congress, Tokyo, 1991*, Newark, 1994.

Knopp, L. 'Sexuality and urban space: a framework for analysis', in *Mapping Desire: Geographies of Sexuality*, eds D. Bell and G. Valentine, London, 1995.

Koeppel, E. 'War Shakespeare in Italien?', *Shakespeare Jahrbuch*, 35, 1899, pp. 122–6.

Lagarde, Fernand. *John Webster*, Publications de la Faculté des Lettres et Sciences Humaines de Toulouse, vol. 7, Toulouse, n.d [= 1968].

Lambin, Georges. *Voyages de Shakespeare en France et en Italie*, Geneva, 1962.

Lea, K. M. *Italian Popular Comedy: a Study in the Commedia dell'Arte, 1560–1620, with Special Reference to the English Stage*, 2 vols, Oxford, 1934; rpt New York, 1962.

Lee, Vernon [= Violet Paget]. 'The Italy of the Elizabethan dramatists', in *Euphorion: Being Studies of the Antique and the Medieval in the Renaissance*, second and revised edn, London, 1884, pp. 57–108.

Leech, Clifford. 'Ephesus, Troy, Athens: Shakespeare's use of locality', in *Stratford Papers on Shakespeare*, ed. B. W. Jackson, Toronto, 1964, pp. 151–69.

— 'The function of locality in the plays of Shakespeare and his contemporaries', in *The Elizabethan Theatre. Papers Given at the International Conference on Elizabethan Theatre held at the University of Waterloo, Ontario in July 1968*, ed. and with an Intro. by David Galloway, London, 1969, pp. 103–16.

— ed. *The Two Gentlemen of Verona*, London, 1969.

Lever, J. W. *The Tragedy of State: a Study of Jacobean Drama*, London and New York, 1971.

Levin, Harry. 'Shakespeare's Italians', *Harvard Library Bulletin*, n.s. 1, 4, 1990–91, pp. 1–9.

Levith, Murray J. *Shakespeare's Italian Settings and Plays*, Houndmills and London, 1989.

Lewis, Wyndham. *The Lion and the Fox: the Role of the Hero in the Plays of Shakespeare*, London, 1966 (1927).

Lievsay, John. *The Elizabethan Image of Italy*, Folger Shakespeare Library Publications, Ithaca, N.Y., 1964.

Lindabury, R. V. *A Study of the Patriotism in the Elizabethan Drama*, Princeton, 1931.

Lombardo, Agostino. 'Il metateatro, il Veneto e Shakespeare', in *Shakespeare a Verona e nel Veneto*, ed. Agostino Lombardo, Accademia di Agricoltura Scienze e Lettere di Verona, Verona, 1987, pp. 81–99.

— 'La Roma di Shakespeare', *Studi Romani*, 42, 1994, pp. 5–15.

Long, Michael. 'The Moor of Venice', in *The Unnatural Scene: a Study in Shakespearean Tragedy*, London, 1976, pp. 37–58.

Loomba, Ania. 'Shakespeare and cultural difference', in *Alternmive Shakespeares*, 2, ed. T. Hawkes, London and New York, 1996.

Lutwack, Leonard. *The Role of Place in Literature*, Syracuse, N.Y., 1984.

Lyons, Charles R. 'Character and theatrical space', in *The Theatrical Space*, ed. James Redmond, Themes in Drama 9, Cambridge, 1987, pp. 27–44.

McPherson, David C. *Shakespeare, Jonson, and the Myth of Venice*, Newark, London and Toronto, 1990.

McWilliam, George H. *Shakespeare's Italy Revisited*, Leicester, 1974.

Magnus, Laurie. *English Literature in Its Foreign Relations: 1300 to 1800*, London, 1927.

Mahler, Andreas. 'Referenzpunkt oder semantischer Raum? – Zur Funktion der italienischen Stadt im englischen Drama am Beispiel Venedigs', in *Die italienische Stadt als Paradigma der Urbanität*, ed. Klaus Dirscherl, Passauer Mittelmeerstudien 1, Passau, 1989, pp. 85–103.

Maquerlot, J.-P. and Willems, M., eds. *Travel and Drama in Shakespeare's Time*, Cambridge, 1996.

Marrapodi, Michele. *La Sicilia nella drammaturgia giacomiana e carolina*, Rome, 1989.

— ed. *Il mondo italiano del teatro inglese del Rinascimento: relazioni culturali e intertestualità*, Palermo, 1995.

Masello, S. J. 'Thomas Hoby: a Protestant traveler to Circe's court', *Cahiers Elisabéthains*, 27, 1985, pp. 67–81.

Matchett, William. 'Shylock, Iago, and Sir Thomas More: with further discussion on Shakespeare's imagination', *PMLA*, 92, 1977, pp. 217–30.

311

Maurer, Margaret. 'Figure, place, and the end of *The Two Gentlemen of Verona*', *Style*, 23, 1989, pp. 405–29.

Melchiori, Giorgio. 'Da Verona a Windsor', in *Shakespeare a Verona e nel Veneto*, ed. Agostino Lombardo, Accademia di Agricoltura Scienze e Lettere di Verona, Verona, 1987, pp. 41–53.

— *Shakespeare's Garter Plays. Edward III to Merry Wives of Windsor*, Newark, 1994.

Miola, Robert S. *Shakespeare's Rome*, Cambridge, 1983.

— *Shakespeare and Classical Tragedy: the Influence of Seneca*, Oxford, 1992.

— *Shakespeare and Classical Comedy: the Influence of Plautus and Terence*, Oxford, 1994.

Mitchell, R. J. 'Italian "nobilità" and the English idea of the gentleman in the XV century', *English Miscellany: a Symposium of History, Literature and the Arts*, 9, 1958, pp. 23–37.

Montgomery, Robert M. 'A study of setting in Christopher Marlowe's plays', M.A. thesis, University of Pittsburgh, 1931.

Mooney, Michael E. 'Location and idiom in *Othello*', in *'Othello': New Perspectives*, eds Virginia Mason Vaughan and Kent Cartwright, Rutherford, 1991, pp. 115–34.

Muir, Kenneth. *The Sources of Shakespeare's Plays*, London, 1977.

Mulryne, J. R. 'History and myth in *The Merchant of Venice*', in *Mélanges offerts à Marie-Thérèse Jones-Davies: L'Europe de la Renaissance. Cultures et Civilisations*, eds Jean-Claude Margolin and Marie-Madeleine Martinet, Paris, 1988, pp. 325–41.

Mulryne, J. R. and Shewring, M., eds. *Theatre of the English and Italian Renaissance*, London, 1991.

Mumford, I. L. 'Relationships between Italian Renaissance literature and Elizabethan literature 1557–1603', *Italian Studies*, 9, 1954, pp. 69–75.

Murray, R. J. *The Influence of Italian upon English Literature during the XVI and XVII Centuries*, London, 1986; rpt New York, 1971.

Neill, Michael. 'Changing places in *Othello*', *Shakespeare Survey*, 37, 1984, pp. 115–31.

Nicoll, Allardyce. *The World of Harlequin: a Critical Study of the Commedia dell'Arte*, Cambridge, 1963.

Orkin, Martin. 'Othello and the "plain face" of racism', *Shakespeare Quarterly*, 38, 1987, pp. 166–88.

Orsini, Napoleone. *Studii sul Rinascimento italiano in Inghilterra*, Florence, 1937.

Palermo Concolato, Maria. 'Inglesi in Sicilia nel cinquecento', in *Viaggio nel Sud*, Biblioteca del Viaggio in Italia 36, eds Emanuele Kanceff and Roberta Rampone, Geneva, 1991, pp. 269–82.

Parker, R. B., ed. *Volpone*, Manchester, 1985.

— 'An English view of Venice: Ben Jonson's *Volpone*', in *Italy and the English Renaissance*, eds Sergio Rossi and Dianella Savoia, Milan, 1989, pp. 187–201.

— 'Jonson's Venice', in *Theatre of the English and Italian Renaissance*, eds J. R. Mulryne and M. Shewring, London, 1991, pp. 95–112.

Parks, George B. *The English Traveler to Italy*, 2 vols, Rome, 1954.

— 'Travel as education', in Richard Forster Jones, *The Seventeenth Century: Studies in the History of English Thought and Literature from Bacon to Pope by Richard*

Forster Jones and Others Writing in His Honor, Stanford, Calif., 1951, pp. 264–90.

— 'The decline and fall of the Renaissance admiration of Italy', *Huntington Library Quarterly*, 31, 1968, pp. 341–57.

Partridge, A. C. 'Shakespeare and Italy', *English Studies in Africa*, 4, 1961, pp. 117–27.

Paster, Gail Kern. T*he Idea of the City in the Age of Shakespeare*, Athens, Ga, 1985.

Pellegrini, Giuliano. *Barocco inglese*, Messina, 1953.

— 'The Roman plays of Shakespearean Italy', *Italica*, 34, 1957, pp. 228–33.

Peltrault, Claude. '"An extravagant and wheeling stranger": Les voix et les voies de l'altérité dans O*thello*', in *Différence et identité*, ed. CARA, Aix, 1992.

Perkinson, Richard. '*Volpone* and the reputation of Venetian justice', *Modern Language Review*, 35, 1940, pp. 11–18.

Perosa, Sergio. 'Impressioni sul Veneto di Shakespeare', in *Shakespeare a Verona e nel Veneto*, ed. Agostino Lombardo, Accademia di Agricoltura Scienze e Lettere di Verona, Verona, 1987, pp. 7–24.

Pfister, Manfred. 'News from new worlds: Elizabethan poetry and the voyagers', *The Blue Guitar*, 7–8, 1984–87, pp. 91–116.

— 'Elizabethan atheism: discourse without subject', *Shakespeare Jahrbuch*, 1991, pp. 59–81.

— '"The fatal gift of beauty": das Italien britischer Reisender', *Reisen in den Mittelmeerraum*, ed. Hermann H. Wetzel, Passauer Mittelmeerstudien 3, Passau, 1991, pp. 55–101.

Pietropaolo, Domenico, ed. *The Science of Buffoonery: Theory and History of the Commedia dell'Arte*, University of Toronto Italian Series 3, Ottawa, 1989.

Pinciss, G. M. *Literary Creations: Conventional Characters in the Drama of Shakespeare and his Contemporaries*, Wolfeboro, N.H., 1988.

Potter, Nick. '*The Merchant of Venice*', in *Shakespeare: the Play of History*, eds G. Holderness, N. Potter and J. Turner, London, 1987, pp. 160–79.

— '*Othello*', in *Shakespeare: the Play of History*, eds G. Holderness, N. Potter, and J. Turner, London, 1987, pp. 180–203.

Praz, Mario. 'The Italian element in English', *Essays and Studies*, 15, 1929, pp. 20–66.

— *Machiavelli in Inghilterra ed altri saggi*, Rome, 1942.

— ed. *Volpone*, Florence, 1943.

— *Ricerche anglo-italiane*, Rome, 1944.

— 'Shakespeare's Italy'. *Shakespeare Survey*, 7, 1954, pp. 95–106.

— *The Flaming Heart: Essays on Crashaw, Machiavelli, and Other Studies in the Relations between Italian and English Literature from Chaucer to T. S. Eliot*, Garden City, N.Y., 1958; rpt Gloucester, Mass., 1966; New York, 1973.

— 'The politic brain: Machiavelli and the Elizabethans', in *The Flaming Heart: Essays on Crashaw, Machiavelli, and Other Studies in the Relations between Italian and English Literature from Chaucer to T. S. Eliot*, pp. 90–145.

— 'Ben Jonson's Italy', in *The Flaming Heart: Essays on Crashaw, Machiavelli, and Other Studies in the Relations between Italian and English Literature from Chaucer to T. S. Eliot*, pp. 168–85.

— 'Italy', in *A Shakespeare Encyclopedia*, eds Oscar James Campbell and Edward G. Quinn, New York, 1966, pp. 388–93.

— 'Shakespeare e l'Italia', in *Caleidoscopio Shakespeariano*, Biblioteca di Studi Inglesi 15, Bari, 1969, pp. 75–107.

Pullan, Brian. 'Shakespeare's Venice', *Listener*, 18, 1, 1973, pp. 79–82.

Raab, Felix. *The English Face of Machiavelli: a Changing Interpretation, 1500–1700*, London, 1964.

Rebora, Piero. *L'Italia nel dramma inglese (1558–1642)*, Milan, 1925.

— *Civiltà italiana e civiltà inglese: studi e ricerche*, Florence, 1936.

— 'Un eccentrico viaggiatore inglese del primo Seicento', *English Miscellany: a Symposium of History, Literature and the Arts*, 2, 1951, pp. 85–93.

Redmond, James, ed. *The Theatrical Space*, Themes in Drama 9, Cambridge, 1987.

Rigaud, N. J., ed. *L'Angleterre et le monde méditerranéen*, Centre Aixois de Recherches Anglaises 7, Aix-en-Provence, 1987.

Riposio, D. 'Fra novella e tragedia: Giraldi Cinthio e Shakespeare', in *Metamorfosi della novella*, ed. G. Bàrberi Squarotti, Foggia, 1985.

Rodriguez, C. A. 'The tragedy of Shakespeare's Venice: cosmopolitanism and internal collapse', *Dissertation Abstracts International*, 53, 1992-93.

Rossi, Sergio. *Ricerche sull'Umanesimo e sul Rinascimento in Inghilterra*, Milan, 1969.

— ed. *Saggi sul Rinascimento*, 1, Milan, 1984.

— *I documenti della cultura italiana in Inghilterra: Il Rinascimento*, 1, Milan, 1986.

Rossi, Sergio and Dianella Savoia, eds. *Italy and the English Renaissance*, Milan, 1989.

Salingar, Leo. *Shakespeare and the Traditions of Comedy*, Cambridge, 1974.

— Postscript: Elizabethan dramatists and Italy', in *Theatre of the English and Italian Renaissance*, eds J. R. Mulryne and M. Shrewing, London, 1991, pp. 221–37.

Santos, Marlene Soares dos. 'Theatre for Tudor England: an investigation of the ideas of Englishness and foreignness in English drama, c. 1485–1592, with particular reference to the interludes', Ph.D. diss., The Shakespeare Institute, University of Birmingham, Birmingham, 1980.

Schell, Edgar. 'Volpone in the land of unlikeness', in *Strangers and Pilgrims: from 'The Castle of Perseverance' to 'King Lear'*, Chicago, 1983.

Schelling, F. E. *Foreign Influences in Elizabethan Plays*, New York, 1923.

Scolnicov, H. 'Theatre space, theatrical space, and the theatrical space without', in *The Theatrical Space*, ed. James Redmond, Themes in Drama 9, Cambridge, 1987, pp. 11–26.

Scott, Margaret. 'Machiavelli and the machiavel', *Renaissance Drama*, n.s. 15, 1984, pp. 147–74.

Scott, Mary A. *Elizabethan Translations from the Italian*, Boston and New York, 1916.

Scragg, Leah. *Shakespeare's 'Mouldy Tales': Recurrent Plot Motifs in Shakespearean Drama*, London, 1992.

Segré, Carlo. *Relazioni letterarie fra Italia e Inghilterra*, Florence, 1911.

Sells, Lytton A. 'Englishmen in Padua', *Durham University Journal*, n.s. 9, 1947.

— *The Italian Influence in English Poetry: from Chaucer to Southwell*, London, 1955.

— *The Paradise of Travellers: the Italian Influence on Englishmen in the Seventeenth Century*, London, 1964.

Serpieri, Alessandro. 'Contratti d'amore e di morte nel *Mercante di Venezia*', in *Shakespeare a Verona e nel Veneto*, ed. Agostino Lombardo, Accademia di Agricoltura Scienze e Lettere di Verona, Verona, 1987, pp. 67–79.

Simpson, Lucy. 'Shakespeare and Italy', in *The Secondary Heroes of Shakespeare and Other Essays*, London, 1950.

Smith, Winifred. *The Commedia dell'Arte*, Columbia University Studies in English and Comparative Literature 43, New York, 1912; rpt New York and London, 1964.

Sorelius, G. *Shakespeare's Early Comedies: Myth, Metamorphosis, Mannerism*, Studia Anglistica Upsliensia 83, Uppsala, 1993.

Sorelius, G. and Srigley M., eds. *Cultural Exchange between European Nations during the Renaissance*, Uppsala, 1994.

Spriet, Pierre. '*The Winter's Tale* or the staging of an absence', in *The Show Within: Dramatic and Other Insets, English Renaissance Drama (1550-1642)*, ed. François Laroque, Montpellier, 1992.

Steer, Barbara D. G. 'Shakespeare and Italy', *Notes and Queries*, 198, 1953, p. 23.

Stoye, John Walter. *English Travellers Abroad, 1604-1667: their Influence in English Society and Politics*, London, 1952; revised ed. New Haven and London, 1989.

Sullivan, Edward. 'Shakespeare and the waterways of northern Italy', *The Nineteenth Century*, 64, 1908.

Suvin, Darko. 'Verso una topoanalisi ed una paradigmatica dello spazio drammaturgico', *Intersezioni*, 6, 3, 1986, pp. 503–27.

Tessari, Roberto. *La Commedia dell'Arte nel Seicento: 'Industria' e 'Arte Giocosa' della Civiltà barocca*, Florence, 1969.

Thomas, William. *The History of Italy* (1549), ed. G. B. Parks, Ithaca and New York, 1963.

Tulip, J. 'The intertextualities of Ben Jonson's *Volpone*', *Sydney Studies in Literature*, 20, 1994-95, pp. 20-35.

Turner J. G. *Sexuality and Gender in Early Modern Europe: Institutions, Texts, Images*, Cambridge, 1993.

Vaughan, Virginia M. *Othello: a Contextual History*, Cambridge, 1994.

Wells, Stanley, ed. *Shakespeare and Cultural Exchange. Shakespeare Survey*, 48, Cambridge, 1995.

Wiggins, Martin. *Journeymen in Murder. the Assassin in English Renaissance Drama*, Oxford, 1991.

Wilson, R. and Dutton, R., eds. *New Historicism and Renaissance Drama*, London, 1992.

Winstanley, Lilian. '*Othello' as the Tragedy of Italy: Showing that Shakespeare's Italian Contemporaries Interpreted the Story of the Moor and the Lady of Venice as Symbolizing the Tragedy of their Country in the Grip of Spain*, London, 1924.

Withington, Robert. 'Shakespeare and race prejudice', in *Elizabethan Studies and Other Essays in Honor of George F. Reynolds*, University of Colorado Studies, Boulder, 1945, pp. 172–84.

Worthen, W. B. 'Disciplines of the text/sites of performance', *The Drama Review*, 39, 1, 1995, pp. 13-44.

Yates, Frances A. *John Florio: the Life of an Italian in Shakespeare's England*, Cambridge, 1934.

Young, S. *Shakespeare Manipulated: the Use of the Dramatic Works of Shakespeare in teatro di figura in Italy*, London, 1996.

Zacharasiewicz, Waldemar. *Die Klimatheorie in der englischen Literatur und Literaturkritik von der Mitte des 16. bis zum frühen 18. Jahrhundert*, Wiener Beiträge zur englischen Philologie 77, Vienna, 1977.

— 'Der Perfekte Rachemord: Bemerkungen zum Italienbild der Engländer im 16. und 17. Jahrhundert', in *Studien zu Dante und zu anderen Themen der romanische Literaturen: Festschrift für Rudolf Palgen zu seinem 75. Geburtstag*, eds Klaus Lichem and Hans Joachim Simon, Graz, 1971, pp. 221–34.

Zimmerman, S., ed. *Erotic Politics. Desire on the English Renaissance Stage*, London, 1992.

Index

List of editors and contributors

Michele Marrapodi is Associate Professor of English Literature at the University of Palermo. He is Associate Editor of *Cahiers Elisabéthains* and Assistant Editor of *Seventeenth-Century News*. His books include *'The Great Image': figure e immagini della regalità nel teatro di Shakespeare*, Rome, 1984, and *La Sicilia nella drammaturgia giacomiana e carolina*, Rome, 1989.

A. J. Hoenselaars is Associate Professor of English Literature at the University of Utrecht. He is the author of *Images of Englishmen and Foreigners in the Drama of Shakespeare and his Contemporaries: A Study of Stage Characters and National Identity in English Renaissance Drama, 1558-1642*, Rutherford, NJ, 1992.

Marcello Cappuzzo is Professor of English Literature at the University of Palermo. His studies of seventeenth- and nineteenth-century literature include books on Shakespeare (*Macbeth*), Milton (*Paradise Lost*), Winstanley and Wordsworth.

Lino Falzon Santucci was Professor of English Literature at the University of Messina. His publications include books and articles on Shakespeare, theatre criticism and methodology, and Harold Pinter.

Harry Levin was Irving Babbitt Professor of Comparative Literature Emeritus at Harvard University. His publications include important books on Marlowe, Shakespeare and Joyce.

Andreas Mahler is Lecturer in English at Munich University. He has written several articles and notes on English Renaissance drama.

Angela Locatelli is Professor of English Literature at the University of Bergamo and Adjunct Professor at the University of Pennsylvania, Philadelphia. Her most recent book is *L'eloquenza e gli incantesimi: Interpretazioni shakespeariane*, Milan, 1988.

J. R. Mulryne is Professor of English at the University of Warwick. He has edited a number of Renaissance plays and published several works on Shakespeare and Elizabethan drama.

Giorgio Melchiori is Professor of English Literature at the University of Rome. He has edited plays by Shakespeare and his fellow dramatists and published books on Shakespeare, Yeats and Joyce.

Sergio Rossi is Professor of English Literature at the University of Milan. He has written books on the English and Italian Renaissance and co-edited *Italy and the English Renaissance*, Milan, 1989.

Viviana Comensoli is Assistant Professor of English at Wilfrid Laurier University, Canada. She has published several articles on Shakespeare and Renaissance drama.

Agostino Lombardo is Professor of English Literature at the University of Rome. He is the author of many works on a wide range of English and American authors, and on medieval and Renaissance English drama.

Roberta Mullini is Professor of English Literature at the University of Messina. Her books include *Corruttore di parole: il fool nel teatro di Shakespeare*, Bologna, 1983, and *La scena della memoria: intertestualità nel dramma Tudor*, Bologna, 1988.

Leo Salingar is Senior Lecturer in English Literature at Trinity College, Cambridge. His books include *Shakespeare and the Traditions of Comedy*, Cambridge, 1974, and *Dramatic Forms in Shakespeare and the Jacobeans*, Cambridge, 1986.

Avraham Oz is Professor of English Literature at the University of Haifa and Tel Aviv. He has published several works on Shakespeare and Renaissance drama.

Mariangela Tempera is Associate Professor of English Literature at the University of Ferrara. She is the editor of the series *Shakespeare: dal testo alla scena*, Bologna, 1984-.

Zara Bruzzi and *A. A. Bromham* are Lecturers in English at the West London Institute of Higher Education. They have recently published *'The Changeling' and the Years of Crisis 1619-1624: a Hieroglyph of Britain*, London, 1990.

Manfred Pfister is Professor of English Literature at the Free University of Berlin and co-editor of *Shakespeare Jahrbuch*. He is the author of *The Theory and Analysis of Drama*, Cambridge, 1988.